Y0-DRX-433

THE YALE EDITION

*of the*

GEORGE ELIOT LETTERS

*In Seven Volumes*

VI

# THE

# George Eliot Letters

EDITED BY Gordon S. Haight

*Professor of English, Yale University*

VOLUME VI
1874 - 1877

*New Haven:* YALE UNIVERSITY PRESS

*London: Geoffrey Cumberlege, Oxford University Press*

1955

PUBLISHED ON THE LOUIS STERN MEMORIAL FUND

*Copyright, 1955, by Yale University Press. Printed in the United States of America by Vail-Ballou Press, Inc., Binghamton, N. Y. All rights reserved. This book may not be reproduced, in whole or in part, in any form (except by reviewers for the public press), without written permission from the publishers. Library of Congress catalog card number: 52-12063*

823.8
El4h
v.6

# CONTENTS OF VOLUME VI

*LETTERS 1874-1877*





48875

# *LETTERS 1874-1877*

# Beginning *Daniel Deronda*

| | |
|---|---|
| *1874 February 3* | GE has first of severe attacks of kidney stone, which recur at intervals till her death. |
| *1874 March 30* | Maud Southwood Lewes born. |
| *1874 May* | *The Legend of Jubal and Other Poems* published. |
| *1874 June 2—September 25* | At Earlswood Common. Househunting. |
| *1874 June 11* | GHL reads opening chapters of *Daniel Deronda.* |
| *1874 August 21–22* | Lord Lytton comes to visit. |
| *1874 September 28* | GE and GHL visit W. H. Hall at Six Mile Bottom. See races at Newmarket. |
| *1874 October 3–19* | Holiday in France and Belgium. |
| *1874 October 20–31* | Two excursions in Wiltshire: Salisbury and Stonehenge; Devizes and Marlborough. |
| *1874 November 20 and 22* | Go to Russian church. |
| *1874 December 31* | Two-thirds of Vol. I of *Daniel Deronda* written. |

## GE JOURNAL, LONDON, 1 JANUARY 1874

*MS:* Yale. *Published:* Cross, III, 221–222.

1874 January 1. The happy old year in which we have had constant enjoyment of life notwithstanding much bodily malaise, is gone from us for ever. More than in any former year of my life, love has been poured forth to me from distant hearts, and in our own home we have had that finish to domestic comfort which only faithful, kind servants can give. Our children are prosperous and happy, Charles evidently growing in mental efficiency; we have abundant wealth for more than our actual needs; and our unspeakable joy in each other has no other alloy than the sense that it must one day end in parting. My dear husband has a store of present and prospective good in the long work which is likely to stretch through the remaining years of his intellectual activity, and there have not been wanting signs that what he has already published is being appreciated rightly by capable persons. He is thinner than ever and is only just getting the better of much dyspeptic discomfort that has beset him since the beginning of November, but still he shows wonderful elasticity and nervous energy.

I have been for a month rendered almost helpless for intellectual work by constant headache and nausea, but am getting a little more freedom. Nothing is wanting to my blessings but the uninterrupted power of work. For as to all my unchangeable imperfections I have resigned myself.

## GE TO CHARLES EDWARD APPLETON, LONDON, 5 JANUARY 1874

*MS:* Mr. J. H. Appleton. *Hitherto unpublished.*

**The Priory, | 21. North Bank, | Regents Park.**
January 5. 74.

Dear Mr. Appleton

I saw Lord Arthur Russell yesterday, and thinking it possible that you might not yet have made a satisfactory and permanent arrangement with a Parisian correspondent I mentioned to him the search that you had been making. He is quite disposed to help you, if he can, and he has allowed me to say to you, that if you still need a <political> correspondent resident in Paris and not only acquainted with affairs but able to write well about them, he will be glad to receive a note from you to that effect, and will take it as a signal for immediately inquiring of the person most likely to know of any available talent such as you want. You are probably aware that Madame Perronet,[5] Lord Arthur's mother-in-law, is one of the very best writers on political and social matters, but it appears that she is not sure of remaining in Paris and that she is no longer inclined to write. However, if you are still seeking, he is ready to do what he can in helping you.

Yours very truly
M. E. Lewes.

## GE TO CHARLES EDWARD APPLETON, LONDON, 7 JANUARY 1874

*MS:* Mr. J. H. Appleton. *Hitherto unpublished.*

**The Priory, | 21. North Bank, | Regents Park.**
January 7. 74.

Dear Mr. Appleton

I must tell you that owing to a mistake of our News Agent who sent us the Architect instead of the Academy, we did not get our ordered copy until Monday, so that I wrote my last letter in ignorance of your excellent first number of which both Mr. Lewes and I think very highly. The Parisian letter [6] is nicely done and escapes a certain offensive jauntiness which is in the usual fate of such correspondence.

We are distributing the 3 extra copies, munificently forwarded to us from the office, among friends in the country, by way of advertisement. Mr. Lewes hopes that this first number is being well made known in this way.

The single paragraph on the pressure of radiation [7] is worth more than the price of the paper to people who care about such subjects, and for tastes of another sort there is work very thoroughly done—

5. Lord Arthur Russell married at Paris, 25 September 1865, Laura, daughter of Count de Peyronnet, and granddaughter of Count de Peyronnet, Minister of Charles X. (Burke, *Peerage,* 1880, p. 100.) Mrs. Gaskell had introduced her to George Smith, who engaged her to write for the *Pall Mall Gazette.* (J. W. Robertson Scott, *The Story of the* Pall Mall Gazette, 1950, p. 59.)

6. *Academy,* 3 January 1874, pp. 11–12, signed Evelyn Jerrold.

7. Report of Crookes's experiments on the radiation of heat presented to the Royal Society 11 December 1873. (p. 15.)

the account of Mr. A. J. Ellis's labours,[8] for example, and Max Müller's article.[9] Then, Miss Cobbe and Mr. Simcox [1] have done their criticisms very gracefully.

The particular Sunday on which Lord A. Russell will come again is incalculable, but I need not say that we shall be happy when any chance or purpose brings you among our friends. I gathered from what he said of Madame Peyronnet that her engagement with the P.M.G. was at an end.

Sincerely yours
M. E. Lewes.

## GE TO JOSEPH MUNT LANGFORD, LONDON, 7 JANUARY 1874

*MS:* Mrs. Dorothy Hicks. *Hitherto unpublished.*

**The Priory, | 21. North Bank, | Regents Park.**
January 7. 74.

Dear Mr. Langford

I am very much obliged to you for the trouble you have kindly taken in getting my little volume [2] bound with this desired but hardly hoped-for speed. The taste shown in the selection of binding is perfect, and seems to cast a charitable mantle over my small productions, giving them grace enough for presentation to a dear friend.

All good wishes for the New Year from

Yours very sincerely
M. E. Lewes.

8. For his *Early English Pronunciation,* appearing in parts. (p. 16.)

9. A review of Isaac Taylor, *The Etruscan Language.* (pp. 13–14.)

1. Frances Power Cobbe reviewed the *Personal Recollections of Mary Somerville,* (pp. 1–2), and G. A. Simcox, Lytton's *The Parisians,* (pp. 6–7.)

2. Bound together in this most interesting little volume, now in the possession of Miss Druce, are separate printings of *How Lisa Loved the King,* Boston, Fields, Osgood and Company, (Successors to Ticknor and Fields), 1869, and *Agatha,* printed by Trübner at GHL's request in 1869 to secure the copyright before its appearance in the *Atlantic Monthly.* In *Agatha,* p. 10, GE has corrected "Eislében" to "Einsiedeln," and at the end (A8 verso) has written "Christmas, 1868." She has also made a few corrections in *How Lisa Loved the King,* pp. 24, 34, and 47, and on the half title has written: "To Mrs. Cross, | In grateful, loving remembrance, | from George Eliot. | Jan. 1874. | 'For they the royal-hearted women are | Who nobly love the noblest, yet have grace | For needy suffering lives in lowliest place, | Carrying a choicer sunlight in their smile, | The heavenliest ray that pitieth the vile.'" (*The Legend of Jubal,* 1874, p. 160.)

## GHL TO ALEXANDER MAIN, LONDON, [8 JANUARY 1874]

*Text:* Main's copy owned by Mr. John R. Sprunt. *Hitherto unpublished.*

**The Priory, | 21. North Bank, | Regents Park.**

Dear Main

You will lay up a store of uneasiness in life if you do not learn to "take much for granted"—and do not get into your head the fact that other people are not so impatient as yourself. Here you have been uneasy because of not hearing from us about the "Sayings," and we have had other things to do than even to look into the book! —Nay if we had looked into it can't you realize what a burden our *necessary* correspondence is and how we shirk all unnecessary writing, so that we should have waited until writing to you on other points to mention anything about the "Sayings."

I heard at Chapman's last week that Johnson would be subscribed this week.

That was a pleasant sentence from Ritter—he is one of the readers worth having.

Ever yours
G. H. L.

## GE TO JOHN WALTER CROSS, LONDON, 12 JANUARY 1874

*MS:* Yale. *Envelope:* John Cross Esq. | Weybridge Heath | Weybridge | S.W. *Postmarks:* LONDON-N.W | E2 | JA 12 | 74; WEYBRIDGE-STATION | C | JA 12 | 74. *Hitherto unpublished.*

**The Priory, | 21. North Bank, | Regents Park.**
January 12. 74.

My dear Nephew

Just after you were gone yesterday, entered Mr. Fred. Myers of whom you may have heard us or others speak with regard and admiration. He is coming to <dine> lunch with us next Sunday (at ½ past 1).[3] When Mr. Lewes asked him whom he would like to meet, he said, "Do you know the Cross's? I should like to meet some of them."

3. GE and GHL also met Myers on Friday, 16 January 1874 at the Erasmus Darwins', where they all attended a spiritualist séance. "The Charles Darwin family, Myers, Mrs. Bowen, Galton, etc. there. But as complete darkness was insisted on we left in disgust." (GHL Diary.) Cf. H. E. Litchfield, *Emma Darwin, Wife of Charles Darwin,* 2 vols., 1915, II, 216. Myers had become deeply interested in spiritualism; in 1882 he was one of the founders of the Society for Psychical Research.

Therefore—will you keep yourself free from other engagements for next Sunday, and will you beg the fair Emily to accompany you *in good time* for lunch? [4]

I was rather miserable yesterday fearing that dear Mary [5] had a very dull visit. My small capacity for looking after my guests is always absorbed by the least interesting persons who happen to be present, and after Mr. and Mrs. Cornish [6] came in, I lost sight of everybody else's fortunes and could only wonder whether they were as little amused as I was. This, in confidence from your venerable aunt. With best love to all

Yours affectionately
M. E. Lewes.

## GE TO ALEXANDER MAIN, LONDON, 14 JANUARY 1874

*MS:* The late Mr. Arthur Pforzheimer. *Hitherto unpublished.*

**The Priory, | 21. North Bank, | Regents Park.**
January 14. 74.

My dear Mr. Main

On looking at the date of your kind inscription in the new edition of the "Sayings," I see December 30th [7]—fully a fortnight ago. But I feel sure that you will revoke any conclusion taxing me with indifference to your sympathetic work when I tell you that I have been more than usually a victim to incapacitating headache and other miserable sensations for the last six weeks, and that my days have glided by leaving me little more than a registry of loss.

I have just been looking through the extracts from Middlemarch which make the 'differentia' of the new edition, and I find your choice marked as usual by a keen sensibility and penetration. The only objection I see possible to urge is, that there are perhaps too many, and that the work is left too nearly in the condition of the gutted house.

4. "Sir H. Maine, Myers, J. and Emily Cross to lunch." (GHL Diary, 18 January 1874.)

5. Mary Finlay Cross (1843–1902).

6. Francis Warre-Cornish (1839–1916), an assistant master at Eton, married in 1866 Blanche, a sister of Annie Thackeray's future husband, Richmond Ritchie. According to the *DNB* Mrs. Cornish "wrote two successful novels and was a brilliant conversationalist." He adopted the surname Warre-Cornish in 1892.

7. *Wise, Witty, and Tender Sayings in Prose and Verse Selected from the Works of George Eliot,* 2nd ed., 1873. The inscription in this copy, which was given to me by Mrs. Ouvry in 1954, reads: "To Mr. and Mrs. G. H. Lewes, with Alexander Main's loving devotion, Dec. 30th 1873."

The book has now so goodly an embonpoint, that it gives at least this amount of cheerfulness to the probability that I shall never write another book worth extracting from, namely, that the "Sayings" will not bear any addition.

If I had not already allowed so much time to pass before thanking you for what you have done in painstaking judgment applied to Middlemarch, I should have waited to write until I could tell you my impression from your work on Johnson. But I cannot bear to delay my little sign of grateful remembrance longer, especially as I fear that you may have felt a wound from the wantonly expressed *animus* of the notice which the Athenæum hurled at you.[8] Yet, you would see that there was no pretence of a judgment determined by examination of your work, and the notice may have been prompted solely by some backstairs influence of a publisher. Happily, Mr. F. Chapman, when Mr. Lewes saw him the other day, laughed at the notice and showed that his publishing withers were unwrung.

I am delighted to tell you that my husband's health is much improved under the guidance of a friendly physician, and he works with much enjoyment. But there is rather an excess of occupation just now, owing to the pleasant fact that his volume already published is going out of print, and he has to revise it for going to press again.[9]

In reading this scanty letter you must allow for the fact that I am writing in the first hour of freedom from a trying attack of dyspepsia, and am very much below par. Still, I make myself happier by writing, instead of bearing you on my mind with a sense that I have omitted the discharge of a debt.

Always yours most faithfully
M. E. Lewes.

8. "Mr. Alexander Main has certainly immortalized himself, for his wondrous attempt to 'rewrite' the most perfect biography in the language will probably be alluded to often enough by our great-grandchildren as a signal example of folly and bad taste. To Mr. G. H. Lewes belongs the honour of conceiving the ingenious project carried out by Mr. Main, and we cannot understand how a man of his experience came to make such a mistake. The fates are cruel, and we suspect that Mr. Main, who has tumbled into the ditch, will be remembered, while it will soon be forgotten who led him there." (*Athenaeum,* 10 January 1874, p. 54.)

9. GHL called on Trübner who told him that only 130 copies of *Problems of Life and Mind* remained and that a new edition must be prepared. (GHL *Diary,* 11 January 1874.)

## JOHN BLACKWOOD TO GHL, EDINBURGH, 17 JANUARY 1874

*Text:* Copy in Blackwood Letter Book. *Hitherto unpublished.*

45 George Street | Edinburgh January 17/74.

My Dear Lewes

I have the pleasure of enclosing a cheque £807.11/- being £785.13/- on account of Middlemarch and £21.18/- on account Spanish Gypsy as per accompanying Memorandum.

Nothing could be more satisfactory than Middlemarch and the continued sale of the 21/- edition is a grand triumph.

I hope the New Year has opened pleasantly to Mrs. Lewes and you and that it will prove one of health and happiness to you both.

We are all well except Willie who, unlucky fellow that he is, still is lame from a hunting accident he met with nearly three months ago. However his general health is excellent and the doctor says that the bruise is mending as well, but also I should say as slowly, as could be expected. A bruised ankle and foot is always a tedious thing.

However I shall write to Mrs. Lewes in a day or two with any news I can think of. In the meantime with best regards to her and you, I am

ever yours truly

(signed) John Blackwood.

G. H. Lewes Esq.

THE SPANISH GYPSY 4th Edition

| | |
|---|---|
| 489 | Copies on hand December 1872 |
| 197 | do. on hand December 1873 |
| 292 | |

Royalty at 1/6 per Copy £21.18/-[1]

1. Commenting on this memorandum in her Journal GE noted that "out of 4470 which have been printed, 4273 have been distributed."

MIDDLEMARCH

in 8 Parts at 5/ and in 4 Volumes at 42/-

| | *Presentation Copies Reviewers etc.* | *Odd Books gratis to Trade* | *Sold* | *On Hand* | *Total* |
|---|---|---|---|---|---|
| Book I | 144 | 262 | 6289 | 5 | 6700 |
| " II | 126 | 231 | 5552 | 4 | 5913 |
| " III | 103 | 223 | 5349 | 0 | 5675 |
| " IV | 107 | 222 | 5334 | 97 | 5760 |
| " V | 102 | 220 | 5286 | 42 | 5650 |
| " VI | 97 | 220 | 5263 | 70 | 5650 |
| " VII | 100 | 220 | 5269 | 61 | 5650 |
| " VIII | 104 | 231 | 5565 | 0 | 5900 |
| | | | 43907 | | |

| | | |
|---|---|---|
| Sales accounted for 8th August 1872 | 19342 | |
| Do. 21st December 1872 | 22431 | |
| Do. January 1874 | 2134 | 43907 |

The Same in 4 Volumes at 21/-

| | | | |
|---|---|---|---|
| Printed | February 1873 | 1045 | Copies |
| | April " | 530 | " |
| | June " | 624 | " |
| | November " | 525 | " |
| | | 2724 | |

| | | |
|---|---|---|
| Delivered to Reviewers etc. | 9 | |
| Odd Books gratis to Trade 25/24 | 95 | |
| Sold | 2291 | |
| On hand December 31. 1873 | 329 | 2724 |

| | |
|---|---|
| Royalty of 2/- each on 2134 Parts at 5/- | £213.8- |
| Do. 5/- each on 2291 Copies at 21/- | 572.5- |
| | £785.13- |
| Royalty on Spanish Gypsy as per accompanying note | 21.18- |
| | £807.11/- |

## GHL TO JOHN BLACKWOOD, LONDON, [17 JANUARY 1874]

*MS:* National Library of Scotland. *Hitherto unpublished.*

**The Priory, | 21. North Bank, | Regents Park.**
Saturday.

My dear Blackwood

Your note with the checque for £807.11 arrived this morning and gave a pleasant filip to our appetites at breakfast. The sale of the Spanish Gypsy is *especially* gratifying. Mrs. Lewes will be glad of your letter of gossip and will no doubt send you a feeble budget in return. In fact *nothing* has occurred since we last wrote except a succession of headaches and malaises on her part—although on mine there has been marked improvement from a new and severe regimen.

I am hard at work and wish she were; but she simmers and simmers, despairs and despairs, believes she can never do anything again worth doing etc. etc. A word from you may give her momentary confidence. Once let her *begin* and on she will go of her own impulse.

The first edition of Problems is just at an end and I am preparing a second. If any of your metaphysical contributors has a mind to write a good *attack* on it, don't you stop him, on my account, for a really sharp discussion would do me and the book good, and as to differences of opinion or unfavorable estimates of my power I am très coriace and can bear equanimously a great deal of refutation.

Sorry to hear of Willie's continued lameness. Cela lui servira de leçon, as the judge said when he condemned a man to death.

Ever yours
G. H. L.

## GE TO MRS. MARK PATTISON, LONDON, 18 JANUARY 1874

*MS:* British Museum. *Hitherto unpublished.*

**The Priory, | 21. North Bank, | Regents Park.**
January 18. 74.

Dear Figliuolina

Welcome to our neighborhood again! But I cannot ask you to come to me before Sunday,[2] for of late—the last six weeks—I have been pitiably out of health, and am under a doctor's care, which is a very rare form of desperation with me. I light up every Sunday to see my friends, but go out smokily, like a lamp out of order, on the Monday.

Come in good time on Sunday before the *monde*.

Yours always affectionately
M. E. Lewes.

## GHL TO ALEXANDER MAIN, LONDON, [20 JANUARY 1874]

*Text:* Main's copy owned by Mr. John R. Sprunt. *Hitherto unpublished.*

**The Priory, | 21. North Bank, | Regents Park.**
Tuesday.

Dear Main

As you seem unhappy about some attack or other I must write a word of advice. Brace yourself to meet all attacks and all complaints by the consideration that no book ever was or will be written up, or written down by critics—it stands or falls by its own vitality: and all the buffets of adverse winds, all the puffs of vanity, leave it just what it is. Consider, there is not a single cell but is opposed by the forces of this whole universe—yet it resists them as long as it has *life*—and succumbs as vitality ebbs. If you reflect on the treatment which some of the greatest works have received, the abuse heaped upon the purest and wisest, you will see that if adverse opinion had the power to obstruct truth the world would be in a sad plight.

Don't look at what is said about your work, but do your work hon-

2. Mr. and Mrs. Pattison are listed among the callers Sunday, 25 January 1874 with the Charles Leweses, Mr. and Miss Simcox, Sanderson, Mr. Bell, Johnnie Cross, and Robert Browning. (GHL Diary.)

estly and carefully. I haven't seen the Saturday [3] and shall probably not see it—certainly should not go out [of] my way two yards either to see or avoid it.

I can't promise to read your book for some time yet, I am so busy in other ways nor do I think Mrs. Lewes will be able to do so. But if we thought it a masterpiece *that* wouldn't alter the fact—and if we thought it rubbish hundreds of others might think it a masterpiece—and *they* are its real public. A beef steak is not food for a cow or a camel, but very good food for us and Christian dogs.

Ever yours
G. H. L.

## GE TO MME EUGÈNE BODICHON, LONDON, [9] FEBRUARY 1874

*MS:* Mr. Philip Leigh-Smith. *Hitherto unpublished.*

**The Priory, | 21. North Bank, | Regents Park.**
Feb. 2.[4] 74.

My dear Barbara

Rejoiced to hear that you are coming home so soon! This note is simply to give the assurance that I am still alive to love you, and that we shall probably be on the old premises when you get home—a moment which will be, I imagine, a little too early for the brief trip to Heidelberg and Tübingen which we contemplate.

I have been a sad invalid lately, and last week had a severe attack of a new sort—neuralgia just above the left hip. I am so far better that I have had no fit of pain for several days, but I am still rather 'done up,' and tired this morning by having received rather a large party of visitors yesterday—the first day for a week that I have been beyond the door-sill.[5]

3. "A Hash of Boswell's Johnson," *Saturday Review,* 17 January 1874, pp. 83–84, expresses astonishment that GHL should have put his name to such a work. Main is attacked for conceit, ignorance, and carelessness; if he "wishes to pose as a pigmy Carlyle, he would do well to choose for his hero some one not quite so big as Johnson."

4. The date is clear. But GE has picked the wrong Monday from her calendar; the illness she describes did not begin till 3 February.

5. "Polly had bad attack of pain in her left side, lasting five or six hours in spite of fomentations etc. Went to see Dr. Clark who prescribed temporary remedy till he could arrive. Sat with her all day and read Times and Dickens [*Life*] vol. III to her." (GHL Diary, 3 February 1874.) The next day Dr. Clark came; "fears concretion in the kidney, but not quite sure yet." Another attack followed 5 February, after which GE grew better. She was up 7 February and able to walk out a little Sunday, 8 Feb-

Mr. Lewes is *un*usually well, so that between us we have nearly the usual share of health. But that doesn't serve me to write letters with, any more than the high average of food-consumption nourishes all the hungry.

Do you mind about the Conservative majority? [6] I don't.

I trust that your health is none the worse, since you seem to write in spirits—and that on the whole I shall hear of your risky journey having been a success. Best love to Nannie.

Always your affectionate
Marian.

## GE TO ALBERT COHN, LONDON, 9 FEBRUARY 1874

*MS:* Huntington Library. *Hitherto unpublished.*

**The Priory, | 21. North Bank, | Regents Park.**
February 9. 74.

Dear Mr. Cohn

Will you kindly let me know whether you have yet printed your edition of the Spanish Gypsy?

If not, I should be glad to send you the numerous corrections which I have made in the Fifth Edition.[7] This wish of mine comes too late, I fear, and I much regret that the right opportunity slipped by me without being used.

Always yours truly
M. E. Lewes.

Albert Cohn Esq.

ruary, when the company included Lady Colville, Mrs. Strachey, Clifford, Mr. and Miss Simcox, Mr. Champneys, Du Maurier, Lyulph Stanley, Mrs. Orr, Dr. Hughlings Jackson, Dr. Payne, Mr. Payne, Ralston, *Ruskin*, Appleton, and Charles Lewes.

6. Gladstone announced that Parliament would be dissolved 26 January 1874. In the ensuing election Disraeli and the Conservatives won a majority of 46 in the first election held under the ballot. The Conservative party had not been in a majority since 1841.

7. The 5th ed. did not appear till January 1875. GE's copy of the 4th with the corrections in her hand was given to Yale by John Walter Cross 3d.

## GE TO SARA SOPHIA HENNELL, LONDON, 10 FEBRUARY 1874

*MS:* Yale. *Hitherto unpublished.*

**The Priory, | 21. North Bank, | Regents Park.**
Tuesday Evening | February 10. 74.

Dear Sara

Oh what a picture that is which you have been so good as to give me of Harriet!—how deeply pathetic, and yet almost happy from the rays of affectionate goodness both in her and in her poor friend Ann! I am quite grateful to you for taking the trouble to write me the narrative, and I quite share your comfort in the sense that Harriet is now in kind keeping and sure to have the needful tendance.

I have read both the newspaper slips. Your letter to the Examiner [8] is much milder than I expected, and hardly makes apparent the severe objections you mentioned to me. But I am not sorry that there should be a little boiling of the peas shot at poor Mr. Spencer just now, for he is running the gauntlet in rather a fatiguing way between Cambridge men who are criticising his physics and psychology, and historians who are criticising the 'Sociological Tables' on which he has already spent £500, in the hope that he is doing the world a service. Perhaps you do not see 'the Academy,' which has been regenerated and has started on its new life with great vigour: it is in this periodical that the 'Tables' have been discussed.[9] Then there is Moulton,[1] a Cambridge mathematician, who is carrying on a venomous as well as harassing attack in the British Quarterly; and there are various bitings and snappings of metaphysicians in other directions. Such are the delights of philosophical celebrity—of a better sort however than those of poor Dickens, as they are painfully revealed in this third and last volume of his Life.[2]

8. "Mr. Spencer and the Women," *Examiner,* 7 February 1874, p. 135, an attack on Spencer's *Study of Sociology,* in which he assumes a "normal limitation" in their capacity for government etc.

9. Alexander Gibson and S. R. Gardiner were Spencer's principal critics in the *Academy,* 10 January—7 February.

1. John Fletcher Moulton (1844–1921), Senior Wrangler in 1868, was a Fellow of Christ's College, Cambridge 1868–75. He wrote an article attacking Spencer, *British Quarterly,* 88 (October 1873), 472–504, which Spencer answered in the *Fortnightly Review* for November. Moulton retorted with a "Note to the Article on Herbert Spencer October 1873," *British Quarterly,* 89 (January 1874), 215–218, questioning his philosophical method, and Spencer defended himself in "a pamphlet which I distributed widely among leading men in the scientific world . . . issued early in 1874." (*Autobiography,* II, 258.)

2. Forster's *Life of Dickens,* Vol. III, published 31 January 1874, covers the years 1852–70.

I have been almost constantly an invalid during the last seven weeks or more, and last week I had quite a new form of an ailment which Dr. Andrew Clarke is inclined to dignify with the name of lumbar neuralgia. The pain was very trying while it lasted, but happily it came on in fits and after a few hours would leave me suddenly like a cast out dæmon. However, I have now been free for several days and am cheerfully hoping that the enemy will not return.

The dirty Christians [3] are very dilatory too, but I suppose we must allow for an immense amount of pressing business in which dear Cara's story seems to lie like one pebble in a heap as seen from the Secretary's point of view, he having painfully to dispose of the heap pebble by pebble. I have been thinking of it almost daily, and have been tempted to the irrationality of writing to ask her whether she had had any news of it.

Your handsome green volume [4] has been duly sent to me—but only the other day. The paper-covered parts are pleasant to hold, but not so good for reference. Thank you for this extra gift.

Do you know that the 'Examiner' is now the property of Mr. Peter Taylor?—who, by the way, is one of the minority of returned Liberals, keeping his old seat for Leicester. Surely the Mr. Jackson you mention must be the son of Peter Jackson? But who is 'old Sam Carter'? [5] However the story you tell of his behaviour is very pretty.

I am not yet quite up to my ordinary pitch of strength, and find my inevitable letter-writing a little too much for me. But I am very glad of the occasion which has made me scribble this to you the last thing before going to bed. I read your account of Harriet to Mr. Lewes, who has entered into it very keenly. Best love to all from

Your ever affectionate
Pollian.

I return the slips, lest you should not have any duplicates. Mrs. William Smith has written a very interesting memoir of her husband (the author of Thorndale) which is appended to his Essays on Knowing and Feeling originally published in the Contemporary.[6]

3. Society for Promoting Christian Knowledge.

4. *Present Religion,* Vol. II, 1873.

5. Samuel Carter (1805–1878), the unsuccessful Liberal candidate for Coventry at the General Election 5 February 1874, represented the city from March to November 1868 in place of another Liberal candidate Henry Mather Jackson, whose election had been declared void. His father Samuel Carter had been an officer of the Corporation of Coventry.

6. *Contemporary Review,* June and October 1870 and February 1871.

## GE TO MRS. WILLIAM SMITH, LONDON, 12 FEBRUARY 1874

*Text:* Cross, III, 223–224.

We have received the volume [7]—your kind and valuable gift—and I have read it aloud with Mr Lewes, all except the later pages, which we both feel too much to bear reading them in common. You have given a deeply interesting and, we think, instructive picture, and Mr Lewes has expressed his wish that it had not been restricted to a private circulation. But I understand your shrinking from indiscriminate publicity, at least in the first instance. Perhaps, if many judges on whom you rely concur with Mr Lewes, you will be induced to extend the possible benefit of the volume.[8] I care so much for the demonstration of an intense joy in life on the basis of "plain living and high thinking," [9] in this time of more and more eager scrambling after wealth and show. And then there are exquisite bits which you have rescued from that darkness to which his self-depreciation condemned them. I think I never read a more exquisite little poem than the one called "Christian Resignation"; [1] and Mr Lewes, when I read it aloud, at once exclaimed, "How very fine. Read it again!" I am also much impressed with the wise mingling of moderation with sympathy in that passage, given in a note, from the article on Greg's 'Political Essays.' [2]

What must have been the effort which the writing cost you I can—not fully but—almost imagine. But believe, dear friend, that in our judgment you have not poured out these recollections in a cry of anguish all in vain. I feel roused and admonished by what you have told, and if I—then others.

7. *Knowing and Feeling: A Contribution to Psychology,* by William Smith. With a Memoir. For Private Circulation. 1874. The later pages give a minute account of his last hours.

8. It was appended to the second edition of *Gravenhurst, or Thoughts on Good and Evil,* 1875.

9. Wordsworth, "O Friend! I Know Not Which Way I Must Look," line 11.

1. A 12-line poem by William Smith printed on p. 170. See 1 July 1874.

2. Pages 226–228. It appeared originally in the *Contemporary Review* for June 1872, having been found too daring for *Blackwood's.*

## GE TO ROBERT BROWNING, LONDON, 16 FEBRUARY 1874

*Text:* Maggs Brothers Catalogue 322 (March–April 1914), item 961.

Regents Park.

Will you kindly let me know the address of your friend, M. Milsand?[3]

I want it for the widow of Mr. William Smith, the author of 'Thorndale,' a work on which M. Milsand wrote a highly appreciative article in the Revue des deux Mondes. Mrs. Smith wishes to send him, in sign of her gratitude, a memoir of her husband (printed for private circulation).

M. E. Lewes.

## GE TO MRS. CHARLES BRAY, LONDON, 17 FEBRUARY 1874

*MS:* Yale. *Hitherto unpublished.*

**The Priory, | 21. North Bank, | Regents Park.**
February 17. 74.

My dear Cara

I am thoroughly disappointed at this result of all your labour and long waiting. If it had been due to the behaviour of a single person or a firm, I should have said that you had been treated abominably, but I suppose that Christian Committees have no conscience, any more than other boards, and what their Secretary had said would have no binding power on them.

However, Mr. Lewes is not yet in despair, and I hope soon to write to you again. Meanwhile, revoke your very false conclusion that you "have no talent for this sort of thing." You have none, certainly, for enforcing such motives as the dread of devils and hell-fire—a talent

3. Joseph Antoine Milsand (1817–86). His notice of William Smith's *Gravenhurst* in the *Revue des deux mondes,* II 40 (15 August 1862), 988–1008, "had a *tenderness* in its appreciation" that made Mrs. Smith want to send him her account of her husband; having seen in the *Contemporary Review,* 22 (June 1873), p. 100, a reference to Milsand as a friend of Browning, she wrote GE 14 February [1874]. (Yale.) She met Milsand at Cambridge in May or June and found him "inexpressibly kind and pitiful." (Letter to GE, 27 June [1874]. Yale.) An extract from his article on *Gravenhurst* is included in the Memoir. (*Knowing and Feeling,* 1874, pp. 189–190.)

which might perhaps find a larger recognition. But the testimony of the Christian Knowledge reader should prove to you that your story seemed good enough to him to be recommended in spite of his objections to it.

That is depressing news about the "Humanity School Books," and is one of the many facts that are constantly turning up to check one's too hasty hopes about the improvement of public opinion. But we will not yet be quite downhearted about "Paul Bradly" at least, and I am sure that the book would interest boys and girls, if we could get it circulated.

Thank Sara for sending me the Coventry election news. I have been discussing it today with Mrs. Congreve, who was also puzzled as to the particular 'Sam Carter' concerned and shared my identification of Mr. Jackson with the son of our old acquaintances. I remember hearing of Miss Jane Carter.

I am better now, and have not had any new attack of pain. With best love to all

Yours always
Marian.

## JOHN BLACKWOOD TO GE, EDINBURGH, 18 FEBRUARY 1874

*MS:* National Library of Scotland. *Hitherto unpublished.*

**45, George Street, | Edinburgh.**
February 18/74.

My Dear Mrs. Lewes

The sudden political convulsion made letter writing difficult to me, not that it is ever very easy. It is a wonderful change and I hope we are now in for a quiet steady government, able to attend to the business of the Country without being forced to count the votes of extreme sections.

I was truly glad to hear that the continued sale of Spanish Gipsy pleased you so much and it continues to move as I see in London there were 31 sold in December and 12 in January. Middlemarch holds on its course, 99 in December and 85 January. The political excitement is succeeded at home by that of a ball which we are going to give in honour of my daughter's first year. It is most amusing to see her opening the notes and registering her numbers in the most methodical way. I call it the Butterfly's Ball.

Our Cook who had been with us for 14 years recently left us and married a Home Missionary. She was a great artist and great favourite and my feelings towards the Missionary were not particularly friendly. There must however be good about him as she writes in great glee that with her husband's warm approval she is coming from Glasgow to help to cook the supper for Missie's Ball.

Mrs. Trollope came down from London last night to pay us a short visit. She is looking well and gave a very amusing account of her experiences of American and Australian travelling. Anthony seems to be flourishing and hunting. What an indefatigable fellow he is.

I hope the new work is taking form in your mind and partly on paper. I long to hear about it.

Do you read the Magazine much? I like greatly to hear what Lewes and you think of anything in it.

Willie is getting better but is still very lame. However his health is good. We are rather in the cripple line as my boy has got his collar bone broken in a foot ball match but is mending all right. After the accident he played on to the end of the match which was not a good thing, but I daresay he did not know what had happened and thought much more of the match than of his own pain.

Hoping to hear that Lewes and you are well, I am always

yours truly

John Blackwood

How do you like Lytton's Fables. If by any chance I have not given the order to send you a copy write and let me know.

## GHL TO ALEXANDER MAIN, LONDON, [19 FEBRUARY 1874]

*Text:* Main's copy owned by Mr. John R. Sprunt. *Hitherto unpublished.*

**The Priory, | 21. North Bank, | Regents Park.**
Thursday.

My dear Main

At last I can give you my opinion of the Johnson, which is very much the opinion of Mrs. Lewes, my son, and a few candid friends who have spoken to me about it. I haven't seen a single newspaper notice, so I can only tell what is thought in our private circle. First then we all agree that the story is very well told and the condensation very well made. But there is a chorus of objection against the excessive *showmanship* of the commentary—the framing and glazing of the pictures, with the obtrusion of superfluous indication as to their merits. One reader said he was in a perpetual state of irritation at your not allowing him to enjoy a good thing but insulting him by pointing out that it was good. Again I think the excessive use of quotation (against which I warned you) gives a patchy and made up look to the book especially as so many of the quotations are threadbare from frequent use. Further your delight in italics and small caps is objectionable—it is like a man raising his voice and thumping on the table to enforce opinions which ought to carry their own force. As a rule italics always give a small appearance unless very specially or carefully employed and small caps is mere *loudness* not force.

These are defects which you will not fall into in future work and I therefore rely on the sterling qualities of the book as evidence that you may do a good book not open to the criticisms which diminish the effect of this one.

Mrs. Lewes has had a bad attack (it is feared of *stone)* since I last wrote; between five and six hours of agony. But she has had no pain now for a fortnight, and seems on the way of getting into condition. I am unusually well and very hard at work. I don't know whether you can see the "Academy" in your town—if so look at Prof. Clifford's review of the "Problems" [3a] in the number for February 7th and you will see a review which has *gratified* me more than anything else written about my book before. Pages of laudation would be trivial compared with such appreciation.

Ever yours
G. H. L.

## GE TO JOHN BLACKWOOD, LONDON, 20 FEBRUARY 1874

*MS:* National Library of Scotland. *Extracts published:* Cross, III, 224–227.

**The Priory, | 21. North Bank, | Regents Park.**
February 20. 74.

My dear Mr. Blackwood

I imagined you absorbed by the political crisis—like the rest of the world, except the Lord Chief-Justice, who must naturally have felt his summing-up [4] deserving of more attention. I who am no believer in

3a. *Academy,* 7 February, pp. 148–150. Main's reply to this letter, 24 February 1874 is in Mrs. Ouvry's collection.

4. Sir Alexander James Edmund Cockburn (1802–80), Lord Chief Justice of the Queen's Bench, 1859–75, was pre-

Salvation by Ballot, am rather tickled that the first experiment with it has turned against its adherents. And I heartily wish that with the outgoing of this ministry there might go out for ever the fashion of indulging an imbecile literary vanity in high places—as if it were not putting on a fool's cap instead of laurels for a man who has the most responsible business in the country to be turning the Shield of Achilles into doggrel of this sort—

"Boötes, hight to boot the Wain." [5]

The Ball is a very pretty occasion which I like to think of you and Mrs. Blackwood witnessing. And the collar bone of the son and heir (who I hope will be publishing the best books forty years hence) can hardly hinder him from dancing, since the breakage did not hinder him from finishing the football match. I wonder whether the cook who accepted the Home Missionary is that cook of Gypsy blood, whose pulse beat irregularly in the neighbourhood of her tribe? You remember telling me that the clergyman had been called in to help in quieting her mind.

Apropos of Gypsies, I have been making what will almost certainly be my last corrections of the Spanish Gypsy, and that causes me to look forward with especial satisfaction to the probable exhaustion of the present edition. The corrections chiefly concern the quantity of the word Zincalo, which ought to be Zíncalo,[6] but there are some other emendations, and altogether they make a difference to more than 70 pages. But it would still be worth while to retain the stereotypes, replacing simply the amended pages, there being about 400 in the whole book. I am sadly vexed that I did not think of having these corrections ready for the German reprint.

I have been compunctious lately about my having sprinkled cold water on the proposal suggested by Mr. Simpson, of bringing out my novels in a cheaper way—on thinner paper and without illustrations. The compunction was roused by my happening, in looking at old records, to alight on some letters, one especially, written by a working man, a certain E. Hall, more than 10 years ago, begging me to bring out my books in a form cheap enough to let a poor man more easily get "a read of them." [7] Hence if you and Mr. Simpson see good to revive the design in question I am perfectly in accord.

siding in the trial of the Tichborne claimant, whom the jury found guilty of perjury after half an hour's deliberation, 28 February 1874.

5. W. E. Gladstone, "The Shield of Achilles," in *Contemporary Review,* 23 (February 1874), pp. [329]–344. GE quotes from memory "Pleiads, Hyads, strong Orion, | Arctos, hight to boot the Wain." (p. 337.)

6. See GE to Robert Lytton, [1868].

7. Cross, II, 90–91.

You *did* send me a copy of Lord Lytton's Fables—many thanks for doing so. Mr. Lewes had seen several of them in manuscript, and thought well of their merits. I am reading them gradually. They are full of graceful fancies and charming verse. So far as cleverness goes, it seems to me he can do almost anything, and the leanings of his mind are towards the best things. The want I feel is of more definiteness and more weight. The two stanzas to his wife placed before 'Far' and 'Near' are perfect.[8]

I think I have never written to you since I wanted to tell you that I admired very much the just spirit in which the notice of Mill's Autobiography was written in the Magazine. Poor Dickens's latter years wear a melancholy aspect, do they not?—in the feverish pursuit of loud effects and money. But some of the extracts from his letters in this last volume have surprizingly more freshness and naturalness of humour than any of the letters earlier given. Still, something should be done by dispassionate criticism towards the reform of our national habits in the matter of literary biography. Is it not odious that as soon as a man is dead his desk is raked, and every insignificant memorandum which he never meant for the public, is printed for the gossiping amusement of people too idle to re-read his books? "He gave the people of his best. His worst he kept, his best he gave" [9]—but there is a certain set, not a small one, who are titillated by the worst and indifferent to the best. I think this fashion is a disgrace to us all. It is something like the uncovering of the dead Byron's club foot.

Mr. Lewes is in a more flourishing condition than usual, having been helped by Dr. Andrew Clarke, who ministers to all the brain-workers. I have been ill lately, weeks of malaise having found their climax in lumbar neuralgia or something of that sort which gave fits of pain severe enough to deserve even a finer name. My writing has not been stimulated as Scott's was under circumstances of a like sort, and I have nothing to tell you securely. Please give an expression of my well-founded sympathy to Mr. William Blackwood. My experience feelingly convinces me of the hardship there must be in his. I trust I shall hear of the lameness as a departed evil.

Always yours truly
M. E. Lewes.

8. Robert, Lord Lytton's *Fables in Song*, 2 vols., 1874, VII, "The Blue Mountains; or, The Far" and VIII, "A Wheat-Stalk; or, The Near."

9. Tennyson, "You Might Have Won the Poet's Name," line 26.

## GE TO FRANÇOIS D'ALBERT-DURADE, LONDON, 23 FEBRUARY 187[4]

*Text:* Copy by D'Albert-Durade in Tinker Collection, Yale. *Hitherto unpublished.*

The Priory | 21 North Bank | Regent's Park | February 23. 76.

My dear Friend

In reply to your kind letter received on Saturday I can tell you without delay that Mlle. Herzog repaid the £30 only a few days after the sum had been transmitted to her.[1] Your suggestion that her pictures may be part of the property consumed with the Pantechnicon [2] makes me feel a pitying alarm on her account. I trust a little in the various possibilities that may have led her to some other place of deposit. She would indeed be an object of sympathy if her pictures were consigned to the Pantechnicon *uninsured.*

I am made the happier when I think of you by knowing that our mild winter has made life gentler to you by telling favourably on dear Madam D'Albert. Give her my tender love and assure her that Mr. Lewes always counts it a gain to him that our visit to Geneva gave him the true delightful image of her.

He is in great [form] just now from improved health and is writing and studying with much enjoyment. It will perhaps interest you to hear that that incalculable entity, the Public, seems enamoured enough of "Middlemarch" to go on spiritedly buying a guinea edition which came out last summer. But I am correcting the sheets for a new edition.[3]

We enter thoroughly into the repose of mind which you find in the wellbeing of your sons, and the sense that in quitting life you will leave no hardship to press on those who are still at the early point of their journey. Believe me, dear Friend

Yours ever with grateful affection
M. E. Lewes.

1. GHL sent Elise Herzog £30 19 January 1874.

2. In a letter to GE from Manchester, 23 February 1874 Mlle. Herzog, who was then trying to dispose of the patent rights to a Swiss silk-spinning machine, explained that her friends had not sent the paintings to London, wanting to avoid the expense to her. (Yale.) The Pantechnicon, despite the best efforts of Captain Shaw and his firemen, was entirely destroyed by fire 12 February 1874.

3. In 1 vol. at 7/6, printed for the 1st time May 1874 in an ed. of 3150. By April 1876 more than 18,000 copies had been printed.

## GE TO MRS. THEODORE MARTIN, LONDON, [3 MARCH 1865]

*Text:* Sir Theodore Martin, *Helena Faucit* (*Lady Martin*), 2d ed., Edinburgh and London, 1900, pp. 335–336.

The Priory, | [21.] North Bank, | [Regents Park.] | Tuesday Morning.
My Dear Mrs Martin,

Perhaps the finest edge of all the pleasure we get is the delightful feeling of gratitude that it creates towards the giver. That is just the feeling I want to tell you of after my pleasure in seeing you yesterday.[4] Is it not nearly ten years—just ten—since I heard at Glasgow the tones, the rich laughter of Beatrice? I heard them again yesterday from Lady Teazle, and lost no syllable. Some little sadness mingled itself with the charm of her bearing and the music of her movements? It was that the refinement and elevation which they give to comedy, often beyond the vision of the writer, should be felt by us to be unique, and without visible sign of spreading for the general benefit that deep benefit which comes from seeing a high type of womanly grace, to shame away false ideals. . . .

You must be half dead to-day, after giving out all the nervous energy necessary to do what you did in defiance of cold and cough; but you will come to life again the more joyously for looking back on an effort which ended in full achievement. . . .

Always yours most sincerely.
[M. E. Lewes.]

## GE TO JOHN BLACKWOOD, LONDON, 6 MARCH 1874

*MS:* National Library of Scotland. *Mostly published:* Cross, III, 227–228.

**The Priory, | 21. North Bank, | Regents Park.**
March 6. 74.

My dear Mr. Blackwood

I send you by this post a small collection of my poems which Mr. Lewes wishes me to get published in May.[5]

4. In Sheridan's *School for Scandal,* Drury Lane, 2 March 1874, a benefit for Benjamin Nottingham Webster, who had just retired from the stage.

5. *The Legend of Jubal, and Other Poems,* 1874.

Such of them as have been already printed in a fugitive form have been received with many signs of sympathy, and every one of those I now send you represents an idea which I care for strongly and wish to propagate as far as I can. Else I should forbid myself from adding to the mountainous heap of poetical collections.

The form of volume I have in my eye is a delightful duodecimo edition of Keats's poems (without the Endymion) [1] published during his life. It is printed on good paper and contains thirteen poems—about 200 pages of 18 lines: just the volume to slip in the pocket. Mine will be the least bit thicker.

I should like a darkish-green cover, with Roman lettering. But you will consider the physique and price of the book, and kindly let me know your thoughts.

Please thank Mr. William for his letter, enclosing one of those endless requests for an autograph which I have learned to leave unnoticed, and thus giving the otherwise worthless enclosure a pleasant value.

Always yours sincerely
M. E. Lewes.

We have been grieved to see in the 'Times' that Lady Lytton has lost another boy—the one that came to console her after the loss of the fine Little Roland.[2]

## GE TO MRS. ELMA STUART, LONDON, 8 MARCH 1874

*MS:* British Museum. *Published:* Stuart, pp. 18–20.

**The Priory, | 21. North Bank, | Regents Park.**
March 8. 74.

My dear daughter Elma

I must send you a few words, in spite of your considerate prohibition, to say that the pretty little book is arrived with your precious letter, which makes me very grateful—and what feeling is happier than gratitude? since it takes all the good that is given us, as the goodness of others.

1. *Lamia, Isabella, The Eve of St. Agnes, and Other Poems,* 1820. This copy of the 1st ed. with margins and text scored in ink and with an occasional note by GHL, "wanting the half-title, strip cut from margin of title and some leaves stained" was sold at Sotheby's, 27 June 1923, item 539.

2. Henry Meredith Edward Lytton (22 March 1872–1 March 1874).

You will not surprize me by any stories of energy on your part, for you struck me as an incarnation of fun, industry, and lovingness—three best forms of energy. And it is cheering to think that there are blue clocks as well as troubles in the world. There is another spiritual daughter of mine whom I should gladly see eager about some small delight—a china monster or a silver clasp—instead of telling me that nothing delights her. One can never see the condition of the world truly when one is dead to little joys.

I should like to know something else about Mrs. Fitzgerald than that she is rich. But I am uneasy in the sense that at the moment she and her companion appealed to my attention in that pretty way, I was distracted by thoughts of the half-blind lady on my arm, and I fear that I should hardly know Mrs. F. again so as to give the sign of recognition which I owe her.[3]

Mr. Lewes is very well and working briskly. I am better, but (since we sent you any news, I imagine) I have been an invalid with bad attacks of pain, probably neuralgic. I shall always feel sure that I may write you as short a letter as I like, because you enter into the reasons which make letter-writing a burthen to me.

As to my hands, dear pagan, they are ugly—but you have a vision of your own, oh why should I undo it? It is good for you to worship as long as you believe that what you worship is good.

Farewell, dear. Mr. Lewes is always gladdened by what you write to us, and wafts you many remembrances.

Always yours maternally
M. E. Lewes.

## JOHN BLACKWOOD TO GE, EDINBURGH, 9 MARCH 1874

*MS:* National Library of Scotland. *Hitherto unpublished.*

**45, George Street, | Edinburgh.**
March 9/74.

My Dear Mrs. Lewes

Your welcome note with the poems came safely on Saturday and by a mistake between Willie and myself their receipt was not acknowl-

3. I cannot identify Mrs. Fitzgerald. The episode GE alludes to is perhaps the one that occurred after the concert, Saturday, 28 February 1874. "Sat next to Mr. and Mrs. Lewelyn Davies. As we were coming out an elderly lady approached Polly and begged to be allowed *to kiss her hand.* This done, another

edged. It will make a most delightful volume and will I am pretty sure be a success. Before sending the "copy" into the Printing Office I have been looking through the Poems. They are truly good and have their meaning.[4] Mr. Simpson got the edition of Keats you mentioned out of the Advocates Library. The look of it took me back to the days of my youth. Do you think we should have the paper so narrow? The type to be used will enable us to submit it to you in both forms, like Keats and a little broader.

Willie is going up to London tomorrow so hopes to see you very soon. He is still very lame but otherwise well. He will be at the Burlington. Mary's ball came off on Friday and was a tremendous success. The Missionary came to see the supper his wife had so efficiently prepared. Gunter [5] could not have beat it. She is the same of whom I told you the story long ago. The clergyman whom we got in to speak to her was one of our best and luckily came from the same part of Roxburghshire where Gipsy blood is a large element. For the ball the artful Mary had secured more dancing men than ladies so that all were provided with partners. She amused me with her description of one of her partners who "held me at arm's length and kicked me all round the room so that I was afraid my ankles were bleeding, but he was so pleasant that I forgave him." This must be a dangerous fellow.

One feature since she came out tickles me—in the streets I am constantly being saluted by the sort of youngsters whom I remember 30 years ago coming into my room saying "Won't you have a turn, old fellow." Collins has sent me the inclosed photo. of his Lowick Church and Rectory. Isn't it English all over?

I am sincerely grieved about the Lyttons' loss. It will press hard upon them. I hope you will write to him or her. Hoping to get good accounts of you from my nephew, I am always

yours very truly
John Blackwood.

I read Mr. Forster's most outrageous attack upon Lewes' Dickens Article.[6] It looks like an outbreak of bad health and worse temper.

younger lady did the same, declaring herself 'one of the many thousands.' " (GHL Diary.) John Llewellyn Davies (1826–1916), noted preacher, and a friend of F. D. Maurice, was Rector of Christ Church, Marylebone, 1826–89. Mrs. Davies was a sister of Henry Crompton.

4. *The Legend of Jubal, and Other Poems,* 1874. Other readers have been as hard pressed as Blackwood to find something to say about them.

5. The confectioner in Berkeley Square.

6. "Dickens in Relation to Criticism," *Fortnightly Review,* 17 (February 1872), 141–154. GHL pointed out that in Dickens's mind images had the coercive force of realities; "in no other perfectly sane

## GE TO MRS. WILLIAM CROSS, LONDON, 11 MARCH [1874]

*MS:* Yale. *Hitherto unpublished.*

**The Priory, | 21. North Bank, | Regents Park.**
Wednesday March 11.

My dear Mrs. Cross

When my nephew the other day proposed that he should bring you to see us on a Sunday I protested against that because I thought first, that you would not like so well to leave home on that day, and secondly, that I should not have time to say as much to you, or rather hear as much from you of all I omitted to hear last week,[7] as I should like to do. But it has since occurred to me that you might possibly not object to come early and lunch with us on Sunday: we should then have in every sense 'a good time' before other visitors came, and if they came I should be very proud to show them my dear friend Mrs. Cross, while she perhaps might be rather amused by a little variety.

But will you decide at least to come one day or other by ½ past 1 o'clock? That will be to give us warm pleasure, as I hope you already believe—understanding that I never urge you to make such exertion for our sake lest I should be teazing you. It is possible that this treacherous behaviour of the weather may make you afraid of a railway journey, but in any case I wish you to know that we are here ready to receive any pleasant announcement from you.

Conceive that I was out till 1 o'clock this morning hearing Joachim and Piatti! [8] I write like a person who was tipsy overnight.

George has just come up and tells me that he and Johnnie made a positive arrangement on Monday *against* your coming to luncheon on Sunday.

mind (Blake, I believe, was not perfectly sane) have I observed vividness of imagination approaching so closely to hallucination." Forster would brook no criticism of his idol; in Vol. III of the *Life*, pp. 300–307, he made a vitriolic personal attack on GHL: "the trick of studied depreciation was never carried so far or made so odious as in this case, by intolerable assumptions of an indulgent superiority. . . . Since Trinculo and Caliban were under one cloak there has surely been no such delicate monster with two voices." See Gordon S. Haight, "Dickens and Lewes," *PMLA*, 70 (December 1955).

7. "We went for the day to Weybridge." (GHL Diary, 4 March 1874.)

8. *"Dined (Polly also) at the Colvile's:* present Sir John and Lady Grant, George and Mrs. Howard, Browning, and Joachim. In the evening a party: Joachim, Piatti, Strauss, and Agnes Zimmermann played 2 trios of Beethoven's and a sonata for violin and piano by Mozart. Talked with Spencer, Mrs. Strachey, Lady Thompson, Agnes Zimmermann, Miss Ritchie. Home at 1." (GHL Diary, 10 March 1874.)

I have said what *I* should like, but better than anything else I shall like what you prefer. With best love to all

Your affectionate
M. E. Lewes.

## GE TO GEORGE SIMPSON, LONDON, 12 MARCH 1874

*MS:* The late Mr. Oliver R. Barrett. *Hitherto unpublished.*

**The Priory, | 21. North Bank, | Regents Park.**
March 12. 74.

Dear Mr. Simpson

The two specimen pages you have sent me are certainly quite narrow enough for verses of five feet and had better not be reduced in width. I observe that the heading is a trifle wider than in the Keats, which is not an advantage, unless you find it necessary in order to get an agreeable proportion of the different margins. What I chiefly care for is to have the volume such as may be easily carried in the pocket.

The "Bothwell" [9] is a pretty edition. I like plain lettering and some little emblem, or else a repetition of the title, on the upper side. But we must not make my little book too costly.

Yours sincerely
M. E. Lewes.

## GHL TO ALEXANDER MAIN, LONDON, 13 MARCH [1874]

*Text:* Main's copy owned by Mr. John R. Sprunt. *Hitherto unpublished.*

**The Priory, | 21. North Bank, | Regents Park.**
13 March.

My dear Main

You are right in supposing I should be gratified by your sympathy. I have also been interested by your acuteness in respect of Clifford and Hutton.[10] The latter is really too feeble. My disappointment was great.

9. W. E. Aytoun's *Bothwell; a Poem in Six Parts,* published by Blackwood in 1856.

10. *Spectator,* 28 February 1874, pp. 271–273, a careful, unfavorable review of *Problems of Life and Mind.* Hutton says: "but for our very great impression of Mr. Lewes's ability, we should say that he had utterly ignored the chief problem, and not even adequately attacked it."

I was prepared for and *wished* for a strong opposition from him—but I hoped it would be strong. The first edition was so nearly sold out that Trübner asked me to prepare a second when the elections suddenly intervened, and for three weeks not a copy was sold; since then the demand has revived again and we calculate on getting out no. 2 in May.

But what will interest you more is that Mrs. Lewes has at last consented to send a volume of poems to press—including reprints of Jubal, Armgart, Agatha, and Lisa, besides some lovely new things of small length. She does not get strong however, and I look forward to our quiet retirement during the summer to set her up. I continue flourishing—very hard at work getting my second volume recast and getting daily clearer in my laborious effort to determine the homologies of the Brain and Spinal Cord.

The day before yesterday Mrs. Lewes committed the rare excess of dining out—a thing not done twice a year. But Lady Colvile seduced her with Joachim, Piatti, Strauss, and Agnes Zimmermann—such music heard in private was not to be resisted; so we had a delightful dinner and a glorious evening. But headaches had to be the price all next day!

Ever yours
G. H. L.

## GE TO EDWARD AUGUSTUS BOND, LONDON, 19 MARCH 1874

*MS:* Mr. Gordon S. Haight. *Hitherto unpublished.*

**The Priory, | 21. North Bank, | Regents Park.**
March 19. 74.

Dear Mr. Bond

Unless you can let us have the pleasure of seeing you again very soon—which would be quite the most agreeable way for me to learn anything from you—will you kindly let me know whether the plan we talked of has been making progress, and what is the amount already assured? [11]

Sincerely yours
M. E. Lewes.

11. Edward Augustus Bond (1815–98), a librarian in the British Museum, was associated with Octavia Hill in many of her charitable activities. In 1874 "a group of friends raised a fund which freed Miss Hill for the future from the necessity of earning money, and left her at liberty to devote herself to housing reform." (*DNB*.) The accounts in GHL's Diary for 1874 show that he and GE contributed £200.

## GE TO ALICE HELPS, LONDON, 19 MARCH 1874

*MS:* Mr. Arthur Helps. *Hitherto unpublished.*

**The Priory, | 21. North Bank, | Regents Park.**
March 19. 74.

Dear ministering Spirit

I shall be still further grateful if you will order me the cloak lined with squirrel, just like your own. Why it should be dearer now than at the beginning of Winter is one of the mysteries of retail trade, with respect to which I suppose we are to be religiously unenquiring.

If the cloak makes a reason for you to come again soon,[1] I shall be doubly a gainer.

Yours always
M. E. Lewes.

## GE TO MRS. CHARLES BRAY, LONDON, 25 MARCH 1874

*MS:* Yale. *Endorsed:* 1874. *Extracts published:* Cross, III, 228–229.

**The Priory, | 21. North Bank, | Regents Park.**
March 25. 74.

My dear Cara

Tracy has sent Mr. Lewes also a rigmarole to much the same effect as what he sent you. As to the objection that the anecdotes are taken from the Animal World—that is ridiculous. As if boys were running about to select anecdotes for their own improvement!

I fear the fatal fact about your story is the absence of God and Hell. "My dear madam, you have not presented *motives* to the children!" It is really hideous to find that those who sit in the scribes' seats have got no farther than the appeal to selfishness which they call God. The old Talmudists were better teachers. They make Rachel remonstrate with God for his hardness, and remind him that she was kinder to her sister Leah than He to his people—thus correcting the traditional God by human sympathy. However we must put up with our contemporaries since we can neither live with our ancestors nor with posterity.

1. Alice Helps had been among the Sunday visitors 1 and 15 March 1874. For the cloak see 28 March 1874.

Would not the respectable Partridge [2] publish 'Paul Bradly'? I have just been looking again over the 'tiny' Richard Barton, and the charm of the illustrations both in the story and in the pages of advertisement gives me quite an affection for that publisher. I am loth to have the tale cut up into parts until its publication as a whole is proved quite hopeless.

It is cheering to see the programme of your new Society. There certainly is an awakening of conscience about animals in general as our fellow-creatures—even the vogue of Balaam's ass is in that sense a good sign. A lady wrote to me the other day that when she went to church in the island of Sark, the sermon turned on that remonstrant hero or heroine.

Thanks, I have been on the whole better this last week or two, though this morning it happens that I have a nasty headache.

Don't imagine that *we* have had any trouble which should vex you. There is nothing for you to be vexed about except the fact that it is difficult to get good wholesome teaching into print.

Always your loving
Marian.

## GE TO WILLIAM ALLINGHAM, LONDON, 26 MARCH 1874

*MS:* Privately owned. *Published: Letters to William Allingham,* ed. H. Allingham and E. Baumer Williams, 1911, pp. 176–177.

**The Priory, | 21. North Bank, | Regents Park.**
March 26. 74.

Dear Mr. Allingham

Sincere thanks for the gift of "Laurence Bloomfield." [3] I have just finished reading it to the end, and you will not think me impertinent if I indulge my wish to tell you that its wisdom and fine sympathies have cheered me greatly.

In the far off days of my early teens I used to enjoy Crabbe, but if my imperfect memory does him justice, your narrative of homely life is touched with a higher poetry than his.

Always sincerely yours
M. E. Lewes.

W. Allingham Esq.

2. Samuel William Partridge, publisher and bookseller, 9 Paternoster Row.

3. William Allingham (1824–89) was a frequent caller at the Priory after his

## GE TO SARA SOPHIA HENNELL, LONDON, 27 MARCH 1874

*MS:* Yale. *Extracts published:* Cross, III, 229–230.

**The Priory, | 21. North Bank, | Regents Park.**
March 27. 74.

My dear Sara

I can imagine how great an encouragement you feel from the enthusiasm generously expressed in Mr. Cupples' [4] letter. It is always an admirable impulse, to express a deeply felt admiration, but it is also possible that you have some grateful readers who do not write to you. I have heard men whose greatest delight is literature, say that they should never dream of writing to an author on the ground of his books alone.[5] I don't remember that I have ever heard where Mr. Cupples lives or other particulars about him, unless indeed I am right in conjecturing that he is the friend of Stirling, the polemical metaphysician.[6]

Poor Mr. Francis Newman must be aged now and rather weary of the world and explanations of the world. He can hardly be expected to take in much novelty. I have a sort of affectionate sadness in thinking of the interest which in far-off-days I felt in his "Soul" and Phases of Faith, and of the awe I had of him as a lecturer on mathematics at the Ladies' College. How much work he has done in the world, which has left no deep, conspicuous mark, but has probably entered beneficently into many lives!

I think, from your first prompting to ask me to return the copy of Mr. Cupples' letter, that it may probably be of use to you, so I return it, for I habitually think of death as so near that I see all documents

removal to London in 1870 to work on *Fraser's Magazine,* of which he became editor in 1874. *Laurence Bloomfield in Ireland,* 1864, 2d ed. 1869, is his most ambitious work.

4. George Cupples (1822–91), born in Scotland, studied theology, but "recoiled from the stairs of a Free Church pulpit." See Amelia Stirling, *Life of James H. Stirling,* 1912, ch. 19. He was the author of *The Green Hand, Bill Marlin's Tales of the Sea,* etc., in all about 30 books and 250 tales and articles.

5. GE seemed to be growing more inclined to do it as her own correspondence increased. A letter from Turgenev, Paris, 25 February 1874 thanks her for her kind and flattering letter. "To have written something approved of by George Eliot . . . one of the greatest and most sympathetic authors of our time, is gratifying indeed." (Berg Collection, NYPL.) Her letter has not been found.

6. James Hutchison Stirling (1820–1909), Scottish philosopher, author of *The Secret of Hegel, Being the Hegelian System in Origin, Principle, Form, and Matter,* 2 vols., 1865, a book of wide influence. He had attacked Huxley's theory of protoplasm in 1869.

in the light of things left behind for others, rather than kept for myself.

I hope you are well, and not yet exhausted of the refreshment you got from your visit to Ravensbourne.

Your affectionate
Pollian.

## GE TO ALICE HELPS, LONDON, 28 MARCH 1874

*MS:* Mr. Arthur Helps. *Hitherto unpublished.*

**The Priory, | 21. North Bank, | Regents Park.**
March 28. 74.

My dear—may I call you Alice?—as I suppose I should do if we were angels in heaven and had to think of our white raiment there?

I shall gratefully welcome you at ½ past 4 on Monday,[7] but I would arrange to be at liberty any other hour or day that would be easier to you.

Yours always
M. E. Lewes.

## GE TO MRS. ELMA STUART, LONDON, 29 MARCH 1874

*MS:* British Museum. *Published:* Stuart, pp. 20–22.

**The Priory, | 21. North Bank, | Regents Park.**
March 29. 74.

Dear Elma

The looked-for table [8] more than fulfills my expectations: the design and the colour of the wood both delight me. It seems to me out of keeping to say so common a word as 'Thanks'—let me rather say that your sweet love, and the plenteous signs it makes, are among the blessed influences of my life. That, I am sure, is the end your love contemplates.

7. "Alice Helps brought cloak and hood, and talked over costumes with Polly. She stayed dinner." (GHL Diary, Monday, 30 March 1874.)

8. Sold at Sotheby's, 27 June 1923, item 630: "A carved oak table, on tripod spiral legs, the top finely carved with flowers, inscribed: *'Elma Stuart fecit, for George Eliot,* 1874.' 22 *in. diam."* It is now in the possession of Mrs. Ouvry.

Please give my grateful affection to Roly, and tell him that I have tapped my Eau de Cologne with a satisfactory sense of being copiously provided with a relief under the oppression of heated rooms and close railway carriages.

The brush which you have so thoughtfully sent will I hope be used solicitously to hinder any dimming of the beautiful lines chiselled by your skilled hand—lines which seem to float about the fine brown surface like inspired waters bent on imitating their memory of flowers once flung on them. It is so pretty of you to think of little Blanche! She will not be allowed to eat the Bon-bons, but the quaint shoes will enlarge her imagination. As to the cat, it is a piece of magic.

I spoke to Mrs. Fitzgerald [9] the other day, after having been in doubt about her identity, from the hurry of the scene in which she introduced herself to me, but being guided at last by the benevolent expression in a fine face which repeatedly met mine as if expecting a recognition.

Good bye, dear daughter. Do not let us be very long without hearing of your welfare, which will always make a part in that of

Your affectionate
M. E. Lewes.

## JOHN BLACKWOOD TO GE, EDINBURGH, 1 APRIL 1874

*MS:* National Library of Scotland. *Extract published: John Blackwood,* p. 380.

**45, George Street, | Edinburgh.**
April 1/74.

My Dear Mrs. Lewes

Along with this I send the rest of the Revise of your Poems. My idea is to make the Impression 1500. What do Lewes and you think as to price of the little volume? I daresay 5/- is the right thing. We have not said anything about Terms of publication but I propose to offer you either two thirds of profits or a lordship on each copy sold when we have settled the selling price.

I have had a copy of the proofs lying in my dressing room and have been reading and rereading the Poems at night. They are very beautiful. There is a solemn cadence and power, almost a warning voice about them all, which becomes very impressive when thought

9. GHL's Diary has her name immediately after his note of the Saturday concert, 21 March 1874. See 8 March 1874.

over. You must have been thinking if not writing Poetry all your life, and if you have any lighter pieces written before the sense of what a great author should do for mankind came so strongly upon you, I should like much to look at them. Turning over the leaves of the revise I see you have removed the dates which stood originally at the end of each Poem. Something should be said as to previous publications of the Poems. Do you intend a preface or should something be said in contents indicating the facts of previous appearance? Mr. Simpson is very anxious to hear whether he has met your views as to handiness of form etc.

I expect Willie home tomorrow night and hope to get good accounts of you both from him. He has been seeing no end of people and must I fear be rather knocked up. He has been much with the Ashanti Warriors. Indeed during the turmoil of receptions and reviews Brackenbury has half pitched his tent at the Burlington as being more handy than his own home at Shooters Hill. Brackenbury's History of the Expedition [1] promises to be both interesting and very curious. He has Wolseley's consent to publish everything.

We have had such a fine winter that we began to brag over Italy and all the rest of the world, but during the last few days we have winds and rain, which tell that Scotland is Scotland still.

We do not think of going up to London until the middle of May. Will you still be there at that time?

always yours truly
John Blackwood.

## GE TO JOHN BLACKWOOD, LONDON, 2 APRIL 1874

*MS:* National Library of Scotland. *Hitherto unpublished.*

**The Priory, | 21. North Bank, | Regents Park.**
April 2. 74.

My dear Mr. Blackwood

Thanks for your letter and the Revise. I should think that 1500 is a fairly hopeful number for the impression [2]— I don't know whether

1. Henry Brackenbury (1837–1914), Professor of Military History at Woolwich Academy since 1868. Wolseley took him to Ashanti in 1873 as his assistant military secretary. *The Ashanti War. A Narrative Prepared from the Official Documents,* was published by Blackwood, 2 vols., 1874.

2. The Blackwood record shows 1609 in the 1st impression.

you mean to prepare for stereotyping. Five shillings as the price, would have been my notion too, but I am no judge in these matters, and Mr. Lewes urges that 6/ is the regular charge for such volumes—vide, the advertisement sheets. Browning's Ring and the Book is even charged 7/ per volume.

A royalty seems to us the simpler and preferable plan. If you have any grave doubts as to the propriety or wisdom of the 6/ pray mention them.[3]

When I return the Revise I will write to Mr. Simpson about some points important to be attended to. But perhaps I had better say now that I wish to restore the dates of the poems—*not* the months, but simply the years.[4] And I will put the statement about the reprints in the Table of Contents.

I was very glad to see Mr. William Blackwood looking thoroughly healthy, notwithstanding the lingering lameness.[5] But he complained already of some fatigue from the necessity of seeing (and dining with) so many old and new acquaintances, and he must be trebly tired now. It is a very interesting experience for him to see so much of the Ashante Campaigners in the freshness of their memories.

We hope to make our migration into the country at the end of May, but not before, and I am very glad to hear that you will come at a time when you will have no trouble to get to us.

That you should have had any pleasure in my poems gives *me* pleasure. I know you always mean what you say about such things.

Yours always truly
M. E. Lewes.

Mr. Lewes has just come up to say that he has gone through the Revise, since I finished reading it, so that he is going to despatch it by post. I wished to beg Mr. Simpson to attend to certain details, namely, that full stops should not be left where I have marked commas. For some reason or other (probably of a mechanical kind) the printers have constantly made this mistake in printing verse, and in the Spanish

3. The price was set at 6/. Blackwood paid GE 1/6 royalty.

4. In the MS the following dates appear, most of them added in the violet ink of 1874: "The Legend of Jubal," December 1869 (f. 35); "Brother and Sister," July 31. 1869 (f. 90); "Armgart," August 1870 (f. 117); "A Minor Prophet," 1865 (f. 133v); "Two Lovers by a Moss-Grown Spring," Sepr 1866 (f. 142); "Arion," 1873 (f. 146); "The Choir Invisible," August, 1867 (f. 148). At the beginning of the MS GE has written: "To my beloved Husband, George Henry Lewes, | whose cherishing tenderness for twenty years | has alone made my work possible to me. | 'And the last parting now began to send | Diffusive dread through love and wedded bliss, | Thrilling them into finer tenderness.' | May, 1874." (BM.)

5. William Blackwood lunched at the Priory, 14 and 20 March 1874. (GHL Diary.)

823.8
E24h



Gypsy there are numerous cases. Also, I beg him kindly to compare my corrections himself, as there are various important mistakes in the Revise—chiefly left by my own oversight.

The indenting of the final couplets in "Brother and Sister" will make an improvement, and is always done in the Shakspearian sonnet.

## GHL TO ALBERT DRUCE, LONDON, 13 APRIL [1874]

*MS:* Miss Elsie Druce. *Hitherto unpublished.*

**The Priory, | 21. North Bank, | Regents Park.**
13 April.

My dear Druce

Letters such as yours are the best rewards an author can get. I must suppose that my exposition has been faulty in some respect since you misapprehend me about universality and necessity. I certainly did think they were stated in terms of experience, and refer you especially to §§ 167–183 to show that I am not converting a postulate of practice into an axiom of reason. The experience which tells us that a thing is what it is, tells us that it *must* be what it is *universally* so long as the conditions are unaltered. That is the only universality and necessity I recognize and I especially decry the metempirical uniformity of Nature or universality which is *not* the uniformity of uniform conditions, the universality of conditions universalized.

Give our love to your wife and our hopes that the sea breezes are cooperating with Problems in giving vigour to your constitution.

Yours ever
G. H. Lewes.

## GHL TO GEORGE SIMPSON, LONDON, 22 APRIL 1874

*MS:* National Library of Scotland. *Address:* Mr. Simpson | 45 George St. | Edinburgh. *Postmark:* ST JOHNS WOOD | C 5 | AP 22 | 74 | N.W. *Hitherto unpublished.*

Priory Wednesday.

Dear Sir

Time runs on! Any decision as to covers? When will the book be ready for publication?

Yours truly
G. H. L.

48875

## GE TO SARA SOPHIA HENNELL, LONDON, 23 APRIL 1874

*MS:* Yale. *Extract published:* Cross, III, 230.

**The Priory, | 21. North Bank, | Regents Park.**
April 23. 74.

Dear Sara

I am very glad to know that you and Cara have been comforted by finding Harriet in comparatively cheerful circumstances. It is of more importance that she should have her prospective delight in Cremation than that we should settle whether the hope is premature.

Give my love to Cara and tell her I shall long for some news of Paul Bradly—which I am sure she will not fail to give me.

We have fixed on our country house for the summer and shall go to it at latest by the beginning of June. How glorious this opening Spring is! At this moment even London is so beautiful that I come home filled with the Park landscapes and see them as a background to all my thoughts.

Your account of Mr. George Dawson is rather melancholy.[6] I remember him only as a bright vigorous young man—such as perhaps his sons are now. I imagine it is his fortune or rather misfortune to have talked too much and too early about the greatest things.

Miss Beedy's account of the way Mr. Spencer arrived at his present point of view [7] is not quite correct, I think. His opinions, I should say, do not take date from his acquaintance with Mr. Youmans, or with any facts about American women.

We have a second granddaughter—a little Maud [8] to pair with Blanche, and in all respects we are faring as well as mortals can do—who are no better than we are, I mean, organically and morally better.

It would surely be the more satisfactory alternative that the Syden-

6. Dawson had been lecturing in Coventry on the Tichborne Trial. "He is such a wreck of what he used to be—it is quite piteous to see him. . . . He seems almost to have become misanthropic—jaded and spineless and . . . spoke with especial scorn of 'theology and philosophy'" (S.S. Hennell to GE, 21 April 1874, Yale.)

7. Three ladies—Miss Eliza Sturgis, Mrs. Ashford, and Miss Beedy—were visiting Coventry in behalf of Women's Suffrage. Miss Beedy, an American whom Miss Hennell found very congenial, told her that Spencer's defection from their cause was owing to his friend E. L. Youmans, who had frightened him about the American women.

8. Maud Southwood Lewes, Mrs. John Rowland Hopwood (30 March 1874–1942).

ham tenant should stay on, and that Cara should have no trouble of mind or body about a second house.

Always your affectionate
Pollian.

## JOHN BLACKWOOD TO GHL, EDINBURGH, 24 APRIL 1874

*Text:* Copy in Blackwood Letter Book. *Hitherto unpublished.*

45 George St. Edinburgh | April 24/74.

My Dear Lewes

The specimen copies of Jubal will go to you tonight and Mr. Simpson will write with explanation. Business has been so dull that we have not been hurrying anything on. We have as I told you printed 1500 copies and the lordship we propose to pay is 1/6 on each copy sold. The Advertising must be so heavy on the first edition that it will not bear more than that, even selling at 6/- which is a high enough price for a Volume of the size. I think however that the appreciators of Mrs. Lewes' Poetry do not care much whether they pay 5/- or 6/-.

I hope you are both well and enjoying this fine weather. Some of our days are almost finer and warmer than anything we had except for two or three days last summer.

Willie can walk for a moderate distance now without visible lameness and he can get on a horse again which is a great solace to him and seems to act like a "hair of the dog that bit him." . . .

This is the "Preachings" here this week and Willie has gone to the country otherwise he would join me in best remembrances to Mrs. Lewes. Our intention is to be in London on 17th May and I was selfishly glad to hear that you would still be there.

Ever Yours Truly
(Signed) John Blackwood.

G. H. Lewes Esq.

## GE TO GEORGE SIMPSON, LONDON, 25 APRIL 1874

*MS:* Herter Collection, New York Public Library. *Hitherto unpublished.*

**The Priory, | 21. North Bank, | Regents Park.**
April 25. 74.

Dear Mr. Simpson

I am thoroughly satisfied with the red cover which I now return. That sober red, the tone of fine Russia, is a favourite with me, and I should be glad to have all my books put into that colour. I agree with you that it is not desirable to pare off the front edges. You rightly conjecture that my Keats is bound,[9] and I see that a copy in boards pared down to the same size would make a miserable figure when it came to be bound.

Is the paper quite as good as what you generally use for poems? That used in the cheaper edition of the Spanish Gypsy seems to me much nicer, and has a creamy tint which I think specially desirable. But I suppose it is too late to make that remark now. The volume looks poorer than I expected, and in my opinion it would be hideously high-priced at 6/. But I leave that point to be settled by Mr. Lewes and Mr. Blackwood.

The *erratum*[10] is just what it should be. The page is a pretty one, and the printing seems to have been very carefully managed. It is only the dead-white paper that I am rather down-at-heart about. It is the first time I ever thought your choice of paper otherwise than handsome.

Yours sincerely
M. E. Lewes.

## GHL TO JOHN BLACKWOOD, LONDON, [26 APRIL 1874]

*MS:* National Library of Scotland. *Hitherto unpublished.*

**The Priory, | 21. North Bank, | Regents Park.**
Sunday | (Before the guests come)

My dear Blackwood

Your proposal is quite acceptable and accepted; and your intimation of being soon in town makes the beer bottles lively in expecta-

9. See 6 March 1874.

10. The erratum correcting "songs" to "hugs" in the 7th "Brother and Sister" sonnet was inserted after the table of contents.

tion! We have got our country house for the summer; but don't emigrate until June.

We are both flourishing and both writing. This lovely weather would be too enchanting were there not a dark cloud of suspicion behind it in the shape of certain east wind and probably snow. Willie once more on horseback is a "good line in the bills."

Mrs. Lewes is uncomfortable in the belief that the paper which the poems are printed on is that of the specimen volumes sent for the boarding; but I assure her that *they* are proofs and that W. B. and Sons are more inclined to err on the side of too good a paper than too poor a paper. After all, I say to her, it is what is printed on the paper, not what is the paper printed on which she ought most to regard.

You see how the heat diverges my pothooks. When the score or more guests [1] have come and gone I shall probably go to bed!

Ever yours
G. H. L.

## JOHN BLACKWOOD TO GE, EDINBURGH, 1 MAY 1874

*MS:* National Library of Scotland. *Hitherto unpublished.*

**45, George Street, | Edinburgh.**
May 1/74.

My Dear Mrs. Lewes

Mr. Simpson has I doubt sent you an elaborate explanation about the paper, the quality of which is very provoking. Like Lewes I thought at first the copies might not have been fully pressed. It is to be hoped that only experts like ourselves will feel the thing. I send you a list of presentation copies of Jubal that we are sending out, and there are some we have not sent, thinking you might wish to send them yourself. Suggest any others you think of.

I was glad to see from Lewes' note that you were both well and *both* writing. I hope this means writing books not letters. Simpson was so engrossed about the paper catastrophe that he did not observe the expression about both writing and I had a laugh at him.

We are going over to Strathtyrum tomorrow for a week in a sort

1. "Mrs. Pattison and the Rector, Clifford, Barbara, Lord Arthur Russell, Otter, Sanderson, Mrs. Orr, Mrs. Wingfield, Lady Castletown, Mrs. Morrison, Bond, Mr. and Mrs. Crompton, Dr. Payne, Bagehot." (GHL Diary, 26 April 1874.)

of Pic Nic fashion. It will do me good before going to London. There was not a bad one at Randolph Cres[cen]t the other day. A little housemaid grounded an application for a rise of wages on the rise in the price of every thing!! Her mistress said "Why Mary, what have you to provide yourself with? You rather give a reason why I should reduce wages."

always yours truly
John Blackwood.

## GHL TO JOHN BLACKWOOD, LONDON, [MAY 1874]

*MS:* National Library of Scotland. *Hitherto unpublished.*

The Priory, | 21. North Bank, | Regents Park.

My dear Sir

Will you please post a set of sheets of "Jubal etc." to Messrs. Asher and Co. 53 Mohrenstrasse Berlin.[2]

The thick paper copies deepen our regret that all were not printed on a tinted paper, not quite so thick but still thicker than the actual edition.[3]

Yours truly
G. H. L.

## GE TO JOSEPH MUNT LANGFORD, LONDON, 4 MAY 1874

*MS:* Mrs. Dorothy Hicks. *Hitherto unpublished.*

**The Priory, | 21. North Bank, | Regents Park.**
May 4. 74.

Dear Mr. Langford

Mr. Simpson writes me word that some copies of Jubal have been printed on thick paper, and I have requested him to send 4 of them to you in order that you may (if it is not too late) give them to the

2. GHL wrote to Tauchnitz, Cohn, and Osgood about the new volume of poems 11 March 1874. "Mrs. Lewes will publish a volume of poems, a small one, in May," he wrote Cohn; "if you should contemplate including it in your series please send me your proposal without delay." (Maggs Brothers Catalogue, 306 [March–April 1913], item 1174.) Cohn agreed to pay £50 for reprinting it in Asher's Collection of English Authors.

3. A note in George Simpson's hand is added to this letter: "Tinted paper ought never to be used with modern faced type. It suits ancient face only. The paper was chosen thin to meet Mrs. Lewes's wish expressed to have the volume as portable as possible, although

Binder instead of the white-papered copies which distress my eyes.[4]

Thanks for the offer of the Birket Foster proof.[5] I *should* like it.

Yours very sincerely
M. E. Lewes.

## GE TO JOSEPH MUNT LANGFORD, LONDON, 7 MAY 1874

*MS:* Mrs. Dorothy Hicks. *Hitherto unpublished.*

**The Priory, | 21. North Bank, | Regents Park.**
May 7. 1874.

Dear Mr. Langford

I think the 'Birket Foster' charming—not quite the Middle Mercian physiognomy in its grand distance, but perhaps not more than a fair average of characteristic English beauty.

I have another request to make, namely, that you will oblige me by sending a copy (green, if possible) of the last edition of the *'Sayings'* to *Miss Hennell, 3 Barrs Hill Terrace, Coventry.*

I suppose the new 'Middlemarch' is not yet out.

With thanks for your kind attention

Yours sincerely
M. E. Lewes.

## GE TO MRS. WILLIAM GRIFFITHS, LONDON, 9 MAY 1874

*MS:* Mrs. Michael Womersley. *Hitherto unpublished.*

**The Priory, | 21. North Bank, | Regents Park.**
May 9. 74.

My dear Niece[6]

Many thanks for the photographs which I am delighted to have. Dear old Griff still smiles at me with a face which is more like than

its thinness is aggravated by its defective quality."

4. The Berg Collection has two presentation copies on thick paper, one to "Caroline Bray, May 1874, with the author's compliments," the other "To Anthony Trollope with the affectionate admiration and regard of George Eliot. May 1874." The Parrish Collection has one inscribed "To Alexander Main. In memory of his helpful sympathy, from George Eliot, May 1874." A fourth copy inscribed "To Susanna Lewes from her affectionate sister George Eliot" and, on the half-title, "With the author's compliments," was sold at Sotheby's, 5 June 1944, item 925. I have not seen this copy.

5. Of the frontispiece to the 1-vol. *Middlemarch.*

6. Edith Evans, eldest daughter of GE's brother Isaac, called at the Priory 15 April 1874 with her husband, the

unlike its former self, and I seem to feel the air through the window of the attic above the drawing room, from which when a little girl, I often looked towards the distant view of the Coton 'College' [7]—thinking the view rather sublime.

The return of the bitter winds has made me ill and we are longing for our retreat to the country which is not to happen till the end of the month. Town, with its necessity of receiving numerous visitors, soon becomes a weariness to my country-bred nature, and with the first hour of stillness among the fields and lanes and commons I get a delicious sense of repose and refreshment.

I will ask Mr. Lewes about the possibility of sending his carte de visite. I am sure he will send it at your request if he happens to have a copy remaining. With best remembrances to Mr. Griffiths,

Yours always affectionately
M. E. Lewes.

## GE TO MRS. NASSAU JOHN SENIOR, LONDON, [MAY 1874]

*MS:* Parrish Collection, Princeton. *Hitherto unpublished.*

**The Priory, | 21. North Bank, | Regents Park.**

Dear Friend

I think your report [8] is admirable for fullness, clearness, and wisdom of suggestion. But I can understand how the pointing out of evils under a system may be regarded by officials as an "attack," and that as the old professor considered Sir Humphrey Davy "a verra troublesome fellow" in chemistry, so a clear-eyed ardent practical woman may be found very troublesome as an inspector.

I confess that the Report deepens my sad conviction that the whole Poor Law System is an evil to be got rid of as soon as possible rather than developed. And on this ground it would seem to me an unspeakable advantage if you could evoke voluntary work quite independently of the Government organization.

But though I saw a great deal of the Poor in my early youth,

Rev. William Griffiths. Educated at Bishop Hatfield's Hall, Durham, he had been Chaplain of Woodbury Hill Reformatory and Rector of Shelsley Walsh, 1857–63; Vicar of St. Nicholas, Birmingham, 1869–75. (*Crockford's Clerical Directory,* 1881.)

7. The Workhouse, which appears as the "College" at Shepperton in *Scenes of Clerical Life.*

8. "Education of Girls in Pauper Schools," *Parliamentary Reports: Education,* 25 (1874), 22, pp. 311–394, signed Jane Elizabeth Senior.

I have been for so many years aloof from all practical experience in relation to them, that I am conscious of my incompetence to judge how far it would be wise to use existing arrangements rather than to try and supersede them. I have a dreadfully distinct vision of that typical pauper girl whom you describe—"stubborn, apathetic, capable of violence." [9] And I am not sure that she would be a better mother or sister of the race than one who would be usually ranked as more vicious but who would have a more human sort of passion in her.

I enter so heartily into what you say about the superiority of that home education which calls out the emotions in connection with all the common needs of life, and creates that interest in means and results which is the chief part of cleverness. That is a pregnant little paragraph in which you mention "the germs of all valuable qualities."

Do what one will with a pauper system it remains a huge system of vitiation, introducing the principle of communistic provision instead of provision through individual, personal responsibility and activity. But what evil can be got rid of on a sudden? Only it makes a difference when the evil is recognized as an evil, because then the action is adjusted to gradual disappearance instead of contemplated permanence. And you have very firmly and clearly expressed your recognition of the whole Poor Law System as an unhappy heritage which we have to hinder as far as possible from descending to future generations. Perhaps that is part of your "attack"?

I am chatting with you to please myself—not with the notion of saying anything that you don't already know better than I. My chat is just an outflow of the strong interest your Report has excited in me.

M. E. L.

## GE TO MARY FINLAY CROSS, LONDON, 11 MAY 1874

*MS:* Tinker Collection, Yale. *Published:* Cross, III, 230–231.

**The Priory, | 21. North Bank, | Regents Park.**
May 11. 74.

My dear Mary

I could not dwell on your sweet gift [1] yesterday—I should perhaps have begun to cry, which would not have been 'convenable' in a

9. Cf. pp. 329–330; 362.

1. "A vase with paintings from 'Romola' on tiles." (Cross's note.) John and Mary Cross were among the Sunday visitors, 10 May.

hostess. For I have been in a suffering depressed condition lately, with a general sense that I am out of place above ground and ought to have a hiding-place in some Cave of Machpelah.[2] So your good loving deed has come just at the right time—when I need the helpfulness that love brings me—and my heart turns to you with grateful blessing this Monday morning.

I have been looking at the little paintings with a treble delight, because they were done for *me,* because you chose for them subjects of my 'making,' and because they are done with a promising charm of execution (which Mr. Lewes feels as well as I). It gives me special gladness that you have this sort of work before you. Some skill or other with the hands is needful for the completeness of the life, and makes a bridge over times of doubt and despondency.

Perhaps it will please you to know that nineteen years ago, when Mr. Lewes and I were looking at a print of Goethe's statue by Ritzchl,[3] which stands on a pedestal ornamented with bassi relievi of his characters, I said (little believing that my wish would ever be fulfilled)—"How I should like to be surrounded with creatures of my own making!" And yesterday when I was looking at your gift, that little incident recurred to me. Your love seemed to have made me a miniature pedestal.

I was comforted yesterday that you and Johnnie had at least the pleasure of hearing Bice Trollope[4] sing, to make some amends for the long, cold journey. We suspect that you left a cloak behind you, which will make a reason for one of you to come again. Please do not any of you forget that we shall only be three weeks more in this corner of the world, and that we want to see you as often as you care to come.

With best love to all, the Mother being chief among them all,

Your affectionate Aunt,
M. E. Lewes.

2. Abraham's burial place, Genesis 25:9.

3. Ernst Rietschel (1804–61) did the back of this statue and Rauch the front while Goethe posed between them in a frock coat in 1828. Medallions on the base show scenes from *Faust* etc. See Andreas Oppermann, *Ernst Rietschel,* Leipzig, 1863, pp. 97–98.

4. Miss Trollope and her father Thomas Adolphus Trollope lunched at the Priory 10 May. (GHL Diary.)

GE TO ALEXANDER MAIN,

LONDON, 13 MAY 1874

*MS:* Huntington Library. *Extracts published:* Cross, New Edition, pp. 524–525.

**The Priory, | 21. North Bank, | Regents Park.**
May 13. 74.

My dear Mr. Main

Your affectionate letters are very cheering to me. Though your praise[5] is to be measured by your own enthusiasm rather than by my merit—by your own fulness rather than by mine—there is always this satisfaction for me less alarmingly due to my vanity, namely that what you quote and emphasize is almost always what I most felt and believed in when I wrote it.

Thanks for your thought about our health. Mr. Lewes continues to enjoy more than his average amount of bodily comfort and working power. He is far on towards the end of his second volume now. I have lately had a relapse into feebleness and discomfort owing to a cold taken in the change of weather. I have been unusually depressed, but I am recovering and getting my chin above the muddy slough. My malaise has been giving me a sort of perpetual nightmare in which ideas have thronged upon me and made me feel the more miserably unable to grasp and use them.

I am grieved to hear that your Mother's days are passed in suffering—I think you had not mentioned that before.

We shall leave town at the beginning of June, but if you come to London we shall probably be able to arrange that you should come to us in the country, as the house we have taken is not out of reach. You will tell us all about yourself then, will you not?—Give me an account of your studies, and how your activity has hitherto shaped itself, and what you look forward to with the most yearning. I think you have a strong faith, as I have, in the influences of a life apart from authorship, and in that dignity of work which comes from the thoroughness of doing, rather than from the *order* of the work.

Agatha was written after a visit to that St. Märgen described at the beginning of the poem. There was really an aged woman among those green hills who suggested the picture of Agatha. Always

Yours with affectionate interest
M. E. Lewes.

5. In his letter 9 May 1874 Main thanked GE for *The Legend of Jubal.* He wrote again 11 May commenting on "Brother and Sister" and "Agatha" after a 2d reading. "Give me Shakespeare, and George Eliot, and Robert Burns," he wrote. (NLS.)

Mr Lewes is downstairs working at his desk, else he would send his love to you. We laughed at your prediction that he would call your letter "one of Main's screeds." He has really used that word, but you can hardly imagine how pleased he is with a "screed" which has me for its subject. His happy nature assimilates all agreeable things, and especially any tribute to me. I am much gratified, for your sake as well as his, with the signs of your having given real study and appreciation to the 'Problems.' It would make a sad gulf between us if you did not care for Science—'Wissenschaft' in the largest sense.

## JOHN BLACKWOOD TO WILLIAM BLACKWOOD, LONDON, 22 MAY 1874

*MS:* National Library of Scotland. *Hitherto unpublished.*

George Eliot and Lewes are looking wonderfully well. Lewes is positively blooming and does immortal credit to St. Andrew, as he calls his doctor. Her new novel is actually on the stocks and he thinks she is nearing the point when her doubts, which oppress her so dreadfully at starting, will disappear and she will go full swing at it. This is good news.

They were delighted to hear what I had to tell of the sale of Middlemarch and also of the Poems [5a] and that will stimulate the new work.

## GE TO MRS. WILLIAM CROSS, LONDON, [26 MAY 1874]

*MS:* Yale. *Hitherto unpublished.*

**The Priory, | 21. North Bank, | Regents Park.**
Tuesday Evening.

My dear Mrs. Cross

Alas, we have no time for anything this week except leaving undone what we want to do. We can see no part of a day on which we could get to you to have a parting kiss.

But is that pleasure forbidden to us on another arrangement? Would it be too toilsome for you to come and lunch with us on Sunday—you and my nephew Johnnie? [6] That would be a delight to us, but I know that it is a great exertion to ask from you. I have faith

5a. Nearly 3000 of the new ed. of *Middlemarch* had been sold and 800 of *The Legend of Jubal.*

6. They came with the Charles Leweses Sunday, 31 May 1874. (GHL Diary.)

that you will give us this pleasure if you can do so without tasking yourself in any way, which you understand would be a grief to me.

We have an engagement for tomorrow afternoon,[7] on Thursday we expect visitors,[8] on Friday we go to the theatre,[9] and Saturday we must if possible keep open for little preparations towards departure. Thus, you see, we have no choice but necessity to follow in giving up a journey to Weybridge.

Anyhow—whether you can come to us or not—you are with us very effectively in our memory and love. Mr. Lewes is gone to bed, but you believe in his affection without the testimony of a message. Greetings to all my family from

Yours ever affectionately
M. E. Lewes.

## GE TO MRS. DANA ESTES, LONDON, 28 MAY 1874

*MS:* The late Dr. Herman T. Radin. *Envelope:* Mrs. Louise R. Estes | care of Estes and Lauriat | 143 Washington Street | Boston | U.S.A. *Postmarks:* BOSTON | JUN | 9 | PAID; ST JOHNS WOOD N.W | 8 2 | MY 28 | 74. *Hitherto unpublished.*

**The Priory, | 21. North Bank, | Regents Park.**
May 28. 74.

Dear Madam

I value very highly, and I shall bear in mind very gratefully what your letter[1] tells me of the feeling with which you regard my books and, in consequence, the unknown remainder of myself. That my work

7. "Went to Lady Castletown's for afternoon music. Bice Trollope, Signor [Alfonso] Rendano, Mrs. R. Lehmann, and Du Maurier. Introduced to Col. [George Wentworth Alexander] Higginson, who invited us to hear the band tomorrow at the barracks." (27 May.)

8. "Went to the Wellington Barracks to hear the Grenadier Band play from 12 till ¼ to 2. The Blackwoods called and then Edith Simcox." (28 May.)

9. "Went to the French Play: Le Gendre de M. Poirier. *Got* fine. The others detestable. Barbara went with us. Walked home and ate supper with appetite." (29 May.)

1. Louisa S. Reid, who was married in 1867 to Dana Estes (1840–1909), of the publishing firm of Estes and Lauriat, Boston, wrote GE 3 May 1874: "I feel the most intense desire to know you, to actually look at, talk and clasp hands with you. . . . Do you ever receive people *just because they love* you? That is the only excuse for the boldness of this request. . . . I care for you as the embodyment of my highest principles, and after reading your books with me my husband shares my enthusiasm. If we may never see you, we have much true, married happiness to thank you for." (Berg Collection, NYPL.) When she called, Sunday, 6 June 1875 GHL listed her as "an American worshipper." (GHL Diary.)

should have made any happy difference in your life is a joy to me of the kind I most care for, and the modest tone of affection which your letter breathes is very sweet to my inward ear.

We are often out of town for some months together, and the frailty of my health obliges me to limit as narrowly as I can the reception of strangers, but after your letter I will not call you a stranger, and if I am in town when you visit England I shall be much pleased to shake hands with you. But pray remember that the best of an author is, or ought to be, in his books. Believe me, dear Madam,

Yours faithfully
M. E. Lewes.

Mrs. Louise Reid Estes.

## GE TO MRS. CHARLES BRAY, LONDON, 29 MAY 1874

*MS:* Yale. *Hitherto unpublished.*

**The Priory, | 21. North Bank, | Regents Park.**
May 29. 74.

My dear Cara

You must not *please* grieve me by applying any of the £50 which you earned by writing Paul Bradly to what it was never intended for.

The plan of printing it is good, but you must let me pay for it as my contribution towards the good ends of your Society for the Prevention of Cruelty to (or the protection of) Animals.

I have faith in your affection for me, that you will not set up any difficulty in the way of my doing this small quota towards what you are working for.

We start for our country Hermitage—The Cottage, Earlswood Common [2]—on Tuesday next. We take all our servants else I would have asked you whether you could have made use of our house during any part of your stay in town. But the people in charge are not such as would "do for you." With best love to all,

Your faithfully affectionate
Marian.

2. "We went to Red Hill and saw two houses on Earlswood Common." (GHL Diary, 16 April 1874.) 20 May GHL went into town to see the house agent, and Tuesday, 2 June they took possession.

## GE TO JAMES THOMSON, LONDON, 30 MAY 1874

*MS:* Fitzwilliam Museum, Cambridge. *Endorsed:* George Eliot (Mrs. Lewes) (re City of Dreadful Night) 30.5.74. James Thomson 1834–1882. *Published:* Mathilde Blind, *George Eliot,* 1883, pp. 171–172.

**The Priory, | 21. North Bank, | Regents Park.**
May 30. 74.

Dear Poet

I cannot rest satisfied without telling you that my mind responds with admiration to the distinct vision and grand utterance in the poem [3] which you have been so good as to send me.

Also, I trust that an intellect informed by so much passionate energy as yours will soon give us more heroic strains with a wider embrace of human fellowship in them—such as will be to the labourers of the world what the odes of Tyrtæus were to the Spartans, thrilling them with the sublimity of the social order and the courage of resistance to all that would dissolve it. To accept life and write much fine poetry, is to take a very large share in the quantum of human good, and seems to draw with it necessarily some recognition, affectionate and even joyful, of the manifold willing labours which have made such a lot possible.

Yours sincerely,
M. E. Lewes.

## GE TO MRS. JAMES T. FIELDS, EARLSWOOD COMMON, 5 JUNE 1874

*MS:* Harvard. *Hitherto unpublished.*

The Cottage | Earlswood Common | Surrey | June 5. 74.

Dear Mrs. Fields

Your letter [4] is very sweet to me. When I had half read the first page and was not quite sure as to the writer, I turned to the signature and found the sympathetic words all the more precious because they came from one whose brief presence had been enough to give me a strong interest in her. Such proofs of the far-off spiritual contact be-

3. "The City of Dreadful Night," which had been published serially in the *National Reformer,* 22 March—17 May 1874. For his reply see 18 June 1874.

4. Dated 148 Charles Street, Boston, 20 May 1874. (Yale.)

tween us are a great help to me and are often needed to counterbalance depressing influences which arise within from perturbed health and without from the mixed conditions of our social life, in which it often seems that the noise and hurry—the 'too much' of everything—which seems continually on the increase must almost nullify one's small individual efforts.

It is not for want of hope and belief in America as the scene of a great future, nor for want of real delight in the graceful kindliness which I have felt in all the distinguished natures from the United States with whom I have had any intercourse, that I give up the sight of the great New World.[5] And will you, please, tell dear Mrs. Stowe, when you see her, that I am not failing in memory of her and her husband although as a correspondent I am dumb? My nervous energy has been much drawn upon by neuralgic pain, from unavoidable colds which beset me in this climate and I have little margin for any letter writing save such as business or rigorous courtesy demands.

I received the splendid photograph of her "Rabbi," and am proud to possess it.

Pray present my best regards to Mr. Fields. If it were not that I bear in mind how much he suffers from the voyage, I should hope that you would both find reason to come to Europe again. Mr. Lewes is one with me in pleasant recollections of all our intercourse with Mr. Fields and our pretty glimpses of you.

Believe me, dear Mrs. Fields,

Yours with high esteem
M. E. Lewes.

You see we are 'en retraite,' and have escaped the turmoil of London. We came here three days ago. It is extremely difficult to get a permanent house such as we want in Kent or Surrey and we have been searching in vain for the last two years.

5. "Both Mr. Fields and myself were sorry to hear through Mrs. Stowe that you and Mr. Lewes had no intention of coming to America," Mrs. Fields wrote, extolling the potential glories of the New World.

## GE TO MRS. WILLIAM CROSS, EARLSWOOD COMMON, 14 JUNE 1874

*MS:* Tinker Collection, Yale. *Mostly published:* Cross, III, 232–233.

The Cottage | Earlswood Common | June 14. 74.

My dear Mrs. Cross

I have so much trust in your love for us that I feel sure you will like to know of our happiness in the secure peace of the country, and the good we already experience in soul and body from the sweet breezes over hill and common, the delicious silence, and the unbroken spaces of the day. Just now the chill east wind has brought a little check to our pleasure in our long afternoon drives, and I could wish that Canon Kingsley and his fellow-worshippers of that harsh divinity could have it reserved entirely for themselves as a tribal god.[6] But we live in hope that the kindlier air which we revelled in for the first week after our arrival will by and by return. Meanwhile I am wearing winter clothing in this middle of June. Perhaps our wide common, which we delight in, gives us an extra share of breeze.

We think this neighbourhood so lovely that I must beg you to tell my nephew Johnnie we are in danger of settling here unless he makes haste to find us a house in your "country-side." [7] We have actually seen one that would do for us, if it were not for a vile, threatening board set up in an adjoining piece of land—"To be let on building leases." The house is excellent, just spacious enough, the garden and shrubbery charming, the entrance gate taken care of by a convenient little lodge for the gardener, and the situation (but for that fatal board!) altogether agreeable and commodious. How shall we interpret this 'dispensation'? Is the board put there specially to save us from settling so far away from you? And may we therefore rest in faith that Johnnie will find a house with undeniable charms, on high ground in a strictly rural neighbourhood (water and gas laid on nevertheless) to be vacant precisely this autumn?

By the way, Mr. Lewes says that he troubled you or some one of our family, with a book called "Papa's own Girl." I have just had a

6. For example, his "Ode to the North-East Wind."

7. They looked over two when they spent the day at Weybridge, 24 April 1874. (GHL Diary.) The search went on frantically all summer; they looked over houses at Reigate, Dorking, Burstow, Holmwood Common, Croydon, and Penshurst (near Tunbridge), some of them several times. The one mentioned here was probably at Reigate.

long letter from the authoress,[8] desiring my opinion of it, without a suspicion that I could have any reason for not eagerly devouring it immediately on its arrival. Has anyone at Weybridge read enough of it to decide whether it is good for anything? If it happened to be trash I would not occupy myself with answering her letter, which seems to indicate a self-estimate in no need of consolation.

My philosopher is writing away with double *verve* in a projecting window where he can see a beautiful green slope crowned and studded with large trees. I too have an agreeable corner in another room, but without any other view than a conservatory. Our house has the essentials of comfort, and we have reason to be contented with it.

I confess that my chief motive for writing about ourselves is to earn some news of you, which will not be denied me by one or other of the dear pairs of hands always ready to do a kindness. I hear the dishes rattling for luncheon, which will be the sweeter that we have not to receive Sunday visitors after it. Our Sunday is really a Sabbath now—a day of thorough peace. But I shall get hungry for a sight of some of the Sunday visitors before the end of September.

I include all my family in a spiritual embrace and am

Always yours lovingly
M. E. Lewes.

## GE TO JOHN BLACKWOOD, EARLSWOOD COMMON, 16 JUNE 1874

*MS:* National Library of Scotland. *Extracts published:* Cross, III, 233–235.

The Cottage | Earlswood Common | June 16. 74.

My dear Mr. Blackwood

I had imagined you back at Strathtyrum, but I take your stay in London as a pleasant sign that you are finding much enjoyment there,

8. Marie Howland wrote GE from Casa Tonti, Hammonton, New Jersey, 30 May 1874: "It may be that you will find crudities in *Papa's Own Girl,* [New York and Boston, 1874] which your rare and high culture, your knowledge of the world and the good fortune, which I am told you enjoy, of the confidence and affection of such a superb intelligence as that of Herbert Spencer, would have enabled you to avoid. Still, the work is certainly a significant one, and I am proud to lay it at the feet of one to whom I owe much, and whom I so honor and love. It is written from a full heart, inspired by the tenderest love of one of the noblest and finest of men, my husband. It must breathe the spirit of our most fortunate union and our mutual passion for the culture and progress of humanity. You, dear madame, who have loved so grandly a great and good man, will understand what such inspiration means to woman."

if not of a direct at least of a fatherly sympathetic sort. We on the other hand are revelling in the peace of the country and have no drawback to our delight except the cold winds which have forced us to put on winter clothing for the last four or five days. Our wide common is very breezy and the wind makes mournful music round our walls. But I should think it is not possible to find a much healthier region than this round Reigate and Redhill, and it is prettier than half the places one crosses the Channel to see. We have been hunting about for a permanent country home in the neighbourhood, but no house is so difficult to get as one which has at once seclusion and convenience of position, which is neither of the suburban villa style nor of the grand Hall and Castle dimensions.

You never told me the fine story about Henry the waiter before, and it is worth repeating many times as a parallel to the Balzacian view of Paris. Paris—a melancholy word! The restoration of the Empire which is a threatening possibility seems to me a degrading issue. In the restoration of the Monarchy I should have found something to rejoice at, but the traditions of the Empire, both first and second, seem to my sentiment bad. Some form of military despotism must be as you say the only solution where no one political party knows how to behave itself. The American pattern is certainly being accepted as to Senatorial manners. I daresay you have been to Knebworth and talked over French matters with Lord Lytton. We are grieved to hear from him but a poor account of sweet Lady Lytton's health and spirits. She is to me one of the most charming types of womanliness, and I long for her to have all a woman's best blessings.

The good news about the small remainder of 'Jubal' is very welcome, and I will write at once to Mr. Simpson to send him my two or three corrections and my wishes about the new edition. The price of the book will well bear a thicker and a handsomely tinted paper, especially now it has proved moveable, and I felt so much the difference to the eye and touch of the copies on rich tinted paper that I was much vexed with myself for having contributed to the shabby appearance of the current edition by suggesting the thin Keats volume as a model. Since the days when Tennyson's earlier editions made their appearance in an ugly limp physique, people have become used to more luxurious editions, and I confess to the weakness of being affected by paper and type in something of the same subtle way as I am affected by the odour of a room.

Many thanks for Lord Neaves's pleasant little book, which is a capital example of your happily-planned publication—thanks also for the complete series which Mr. Langford has sent down here instead of to the Priory.[1] However, they have the excellent quality of compactness and can be stowed without great difficulty.

I hope you will all carry away not less than your average health as well as amusing memories from London. I came down half-poisoned by the French theatre, but I am flourishing now, and am brewing my future big book [2] with more or less (generally less) belief in the quality of the liquor which will be drawn off. The secured peacefulness and the pure air of the country make our time of double worth.

We have had a Scotch lady [3] (from Brittany) to see us on her way to Scotland, but otherwise our quiet has been uninterrupted, and we mean to give no invitations to London friends desirous of change. We are selfishly bent on dual solitude.

Always yours truly
M. E. Lewes.

## GE TO [GEORGE SIMPSON?]
## EARLSWOOD COMMON, 16 JUNE 1874

*Text:* Anderson Gallery, 25 April 1916, item 322.

I have just been writing to London to Mr. John Blackwood—that the price of the book, especially since it turns out saleable, can well allow a handsome tinted paper, and I rejoiced so much in the sight of the extra copies in which my verses were on a paper which invited and cherished my eye, that I was angry at my own share in the choice of a thin volume—

Have you still a copy (or two) to spare? If you have, I should be much obliged by your sending them to us, as we want them to present to friends. We have had seven I think.

1. Charles Neaves, Lord Neaves (1800–76), *The Greek Anthology,* 1870, in Blackwood's Ancient Classics series.

2. "On the 1st of June we go into the country, to The Cottage, Earlswood Common, for 4 months, and I hope there to get deep shafts sunk in my prose book." (GE Journal, 19 May 1874.)

3. "Mrs. Stuart and her son came down on a flying visit, very pleasant. After lunch we drove her to the station." (GHL Diary, 8 June 1874.) Roland Stuart gives his impression of the visit in an interesting note, Stuart, p. 22.

## GE TO JOHN WALTER CROSS, EARLSWOOD COMMON, 17 JUNE 1874

*MS:* Yale. *Envelope:* J. W. Cross Esq | Weybridge Heath | Weybridge. *Postmarks:* B | REDHILL | JU 17 | 74; WEYBRIDGE STATION | C | JU 17 | 74. *Hitherto unpublished.*

The Cottage | Earlswood Common | Junc 17. 74.

My dearest Nephew

Your letter has pierced me to thc hcart and yet I would rather suffer with you than remain in ignorance of your trouble.[4] What we both of us earnestly beg of your kindness is that you will let us know how all our dear ones, nurses as well as patients, go on. It seems a great deal to ask that you should write often, since we can do nothing but feel with you, but I cannot refrain from asking it, for ignorant thoughts about you all would make us intolerably anxious. We both shall keep you in our heart continually, and the sunshine will not be without sadness until we know that all grave cause for alarm is at an end. The dear child is sure to have a long long time of weakness after such an attack of fever, but that can be made less of an evil for one who is surrounded with tenderness.

Yours all of you, with anxious affection in which you know that your uncle is one with me,

M. E. Lewes.

## GHL TO CHARLES LEE LEWES, EARLSWOOD COMMON, [17 JUNE 1874]

*Text:* Paterson, pp. 165–166, dated 18 June 1874.

The Cottage, | Earlswood Common, | Red Hill.
Thursday, June 18, 1874.[5]

Dearest Charles,

You will be glad to hear what report we have to make of this place after a fortnight's trial. It is worth going through the London racket to realize the bliss of perfect seclusion, and the long days of sunshine (moral and physical). We are both beginning to turn the colour of berries and propose "putting on flesh" before we leave. The cottage is very comfortable but we are out of doors many hours of the day,

4. See 23 June 1874.

5. I suspect this date to be from an endorsement or postmark. Under Wednesday, 17 June GHL says: "Wrote to Charles, Susanna, and Agnes."

either strolling in the garden or on the common, or driving. The long spaces of uninterrupted work are good for the "Foundations" which are being laid with concrete.[6]

"Middlemarch" has to be reprinted and "Jubal" is rapidly approaching that pleasant state.

We have two dogs here—one a dear brown spaniel very like Dash—the other a Skye terrier all hair and irritability, his yapping takes away from his fascinations and I am going to try to get him removed.

The Mutter says she has nothing to send but her love and a wish to hear how Gertrude and the children are.

Ever your loving
Pater.

## JAMES THOMSON TO GE, LONDON, 18 JUNE 1874

*MS:* Alderman Library, University of Virginia. *Hitherto unpublished.*

60 Tachbrook St. | Pimlico, S.W. | 18 June '74.

Dear Madam,

Having been absent for several days, I am only now able to thank you for your very kind letter,[7] for your generous expression of praise, and for your yet more generous trust, though this I fear will prove to be misplaced.

I have no Byronic quarrel with my fellows, whom I find all alike crushed under the iron yoke of Fate; and few of whom I can deem worse than myself, while so many are far better. I certainly have an affectionate and even joyful recognition of the willing labours of those who have striven to alleviate our lot, though I cannot see that all their efforts have availed much against the primeval curse of our existence. Has the world been the better or the worse for the life of even such a man as Jesus? I cannot judge, but on the whole I fear considerably the worse. None the less I can love and revere his memory. A physician saves a life, and does well; yet perchance it were better for the patient himself and for others that he now died. But it is not for me to introduce such thoughts to you.

I ventured to send you a copy of the verses (as I ventured to send another to Mr. Carlyle) because I have always read, whether rightly or

6. The subtitle of GHL's *Problems of Life and Mind* was *The Foundation of a Creed.*

7. 30 May 1874.

wrongly, through all the manifold beauty and delightfulness of your works, a character and an intellectual destiny akin to those of that grand and awful Melancholy of Albrecht Dürer which dominates the City of my poem.

I cannot conclude without expressing to you my gratitude for many hours of exquisite enjoyment. I am, Madam, with profound respect,

Yours sincerely,
James Thomson
(*B.V.*).

## JAMES THOMSON TO GE, LONDON, 20 JUNE 1874

*MS:* Alderman Library, University of Virginia. *Hitherto unpublished.*

60 Tachbrook St., S.W. | 20 June '74.

Dear Madam,

In my note of Thursday I omitted to qualify, as I intended, the general statements by the distinct admission, of what however is in all likelihood quite obvious, that the poem in question was the outcome of much sleepless hypochondria. I am aware that the truth of midnight does not exclude the truth of noonday, though one's nature may lead him to dwell in the former rather than in the latter.

Pray pardon me for troubling you on so small a matter.

Yours very respectfully,
James Thomson
(*B.V.*).

## GHL TO JOHN BLACKWOOD, EARLSWOOD COMMON, 23 JUNE 1874

*MS:* National Library of Scotland. *Hitherto unpublished.*

The Cottage | Earlswood Common | Red Hill | Sunday.

My dear Blackwood

I see you have brought out Flint's Philosophy of History [8]—if the book is yours I should very much like to have a copy.

We are greatly enjoying our sweet monotony of existence—never seeing a soul—but working like negros. Mrs. Lewes is fairly now at her

8. Robert Flint (1838–1910), *The Philosophy of History in France and Germany* was published by Blackwood, 1874.

new novel, and that means 'going on.' She is continually receiving some gratifying testimony about the poems. How are they selling? By the way what strange fancy possesses Langford to advertize Middlemarch separately as if it were a new book and relegate the poems to the list of old ones? Surely this is not the way to 'catch the public eye'?—

The weather has been horrid of late—cold winds and rain—but the country is so lovely here that we have resolved if possible to find a retreat for our old age in this region.

I wish you could get some one of your metaphysical contributors to attack my Problems. A good rattling attack would call the attention of metaphysicians far more than a eulogy, and no one seems disposed to gratify me in that way.

Ever yours truly
G. H. L.

## GE TO MRS. WILLIAM CROSS, EARLSWOOD COMMON, 23 JUNE 1874

*MS:* Yale. *Hitherto unpublished.*

The Cottage | Earlswood Common | June 23. 74.

Dearest Mrs. Cross

I cannot help writing you a scrap to express my gratitude and relief on receiving our dear Johnnie's letter this morning. With my usual tendency to imagine sorrow, I had had a terrible vision of *your* being ill, because he had mentioned that you had taken a chill. But now, although the beloved patient is nearly in the same condition as when I heard before, I have the assurance that there has been no added trouble, and I will not conjure up any evil again, but explain silence as simply the absence of any marked change.

It is tiresome to have troubles insisted on in helpless words, and I need forgiveness for indulging myself in this expression of my relief. Take it only as a weak sign of my love, which always tends to anxiety.

When I next hear, I trust that there will already have been benefit felt from the sea-air. I will wait patiently, remembering how great a patience is demanded of you.

Yours always with deep grateful affection

M. E. Lewes.

## GE TO ROBERT EVANS, EARLSWOOD COMMON, 23 JUNE 1874

*MS:* Miss Dorothy Evans. *Hitherto unpublished.*

Earlswood | June 23. 74.

My dear Nephew

We have been settled in the country for the summer since the beginning of June, and your letter was forwarded to me a few days ago. In the variety of my preoccupations I have omitted to write you a note which would account to you for my not having at once answered your proposal to call on me. You would conclude, however, that I was out of town. I hope you would have been able to tell me that your family was well and happy, and that the subject which you believed would engage my sympathy was not any calamity.

If you feel any desire to write to me what you had not the opportunity of telling me viva voce, please address the letter to our house in town, from which it will be forwarded.[9] Believe me, with best remembrances,

Your affectionate aunt
M. E. Lewes.

Robert Evans Esq.

## EDWARD LIVERMORE BURLINGAME TO GEORGE BANCROFT, NEW YORK, 27 JUNE 1874

*MS:* Berg Collection, New York Public Library. *Hitherto unpublished.*

**Office of the N. A. Cyclopædia, | Appletons' Building, | 551 Broadway, New York,**
June 27, 1874.

My dear Mr. Bancroft:

Mr. Ripley [1] has assigned to me, among my other work, the preparation of Mrs. Lewes' (George Eliot's) biography for the new edition of the cyclopædia; and at a conversation yesterday, in which I spoke of your acquaintance with Mr. and Mrs. Lewes, he suggested that I should take the liberty of asking information from you. —The books are almost entirely wanting in even the most important facts regarding Mrs.

9. An envelope addressed to Robert Evans Esq | The Park | Nottingham, postmarked ST JOHN'S WOOD N. W | C3 | SP 26 | 74, is in Miss Evans's collection, but the letter has not been found.

1. Edward Livermore Burlingame

Lewes; and yet we are especially anxious to devote to her an article so complete as to pay proper tribute to her. Can we rely upon your kindness to let us have from you such details as you may have in mind? —Even the date of her birth it is impossible to give, even approximately; and all information is wanting as to her early residence. In short we can find out accurately little besides the dates of her works. —We are very near to the article in our printing, too; but there is still time for this note to reach England and receive an answer, if we may ask you to take this trouble. It will be one of many kindnesses you have done the cyclopædia. . . .

Pray convey to Mrs. Bancroft most cordial messages from my mother and myself, and believe me

Very Faithfully Yours
Edward L. Burlingame.

## GE TO MRS. WILLIAM SMITH, EARLSWOOD COMMON, 1 JULY 1874

*Text:* Cross, III, 236–238.

Only the day before your letter[2] came to me I had been saying—"I wonder how our dear Mrs William Smith is?"—so that your impulse to write to me satisfied a need of mine. I cannot help rejoicing that you are in the midst of lovely scenery again, for I had had a presentiment that Cambridge was anti-pathetic to you; and indeed I could not have imagined that you would be in the right place there, but for the promised helpfulness of your presence to a young friend.[3]

You tell me much that is interesting. Your picture of Mr and Mrs Stirling,[4] and what you say of the reasons why one may wish even for the anguish of being *left* for the sake of waiting on the beloved one to the end—all that goes to my heart of hearts. It is what I think of almost daily. For death seems to me now a close, real experience, like the approach of autumn or winter, and I am glad to find that advancing life brings this power of imagining the nearness of death I never had till of late years.[5] I remember all you told me of your niece's expected mar-

(1848–1922) had been working for two years under George Ripley revising the *New American Cyclopaedia.*

2. Dated Nursery Garden, Dunkeld, N.B., 27 June [1874]. (Yale.)

3. Fanny Tolmie. "Cambridge was very dreadful. . . . I went you know in the hope of helping on a bright younger mind, not however as it proved to be helped *so*."

4. A frail old couple in Edinburgh with whom Mrs. Smith spent a week.

5. Mrs. Smith discusses the Leweses' views on immortality in a letter to

riage, and your joy in the husband who has chosen her.[6] It is wealth you have—that of several sweet nieces to whom being with you is a happiness. You can feel some sympathy in their cheerfulness, even though sorrow is always your only private good—can you not, dear friend?—and the time is short at the utmost. The blessed reunion, if it may come, must be patiently waited for; and such good as you can do others, by loving looks and words, must seem to you like a closer companionship with the gentleness and benignity which you justly worshipped while it was visibly present, and still more perhaps now it is veiled, and is a memory stronger than vision of outward things. We are revelling in the sweet peace of the country, and shall remain here till the end of September.

Mr Lewes sends his affectionate remembrances with mine. I am scribbling while he holds my bed candle, so pray forgive any incoherency.

## GE TO MRS. PETER ALFRED TAYLOR, EARLSWOOD COMMON, 1 JULY 1874

*Text:* Cross, III, 235–236.

I am so glad to know from your kind letter that you are interesting yourself, with Madame Belloc, in the poor workhouse girls. You see my only social work is to rejoice in the labours of others, while I live in luxurious remoteness from all turmoil. Of course you have seen Mrs Senior's report. I read it, and thought it very wise, very valuable in many ways, and since then she has sent me word how much she has been worried about it by (as I imagine) obstructive officials.

We are revelling in our country peacefulness, in spite of the chills and rain—driving about every day that the weather will allow, and finding in each drive new beauties of this loveliest part of a lovely country. We are looking out for a house in this neighbourhood as a

Noah Porter, President of Yale, 13 August 1874, apropos of William Smith's poem "Christian Resignation." "To them, apart from its melodiousness, the charm probably lay in the renunciation of a future bliss, the acceptance of love and sorrow *here*. You know they are Positivists. Oh, Dr. Porter! You wonder how *I* can have a doubt of immortality! . . . I strive, I pray, I *die* to believe what you do, even more and more. I could not let Mrs. Lewes suppose for a moment I thought as she did. Her gentle hand would not put out any light, however irrational she may hold that intermittent ray which is yet *my all*." (George S. Merriam, *The Story of William and Lucy Smith*, Boston and New York, 1889, pp. 475–476.)

6. Mary Wrench's marriage to Archibald Constable.

permanent retreat—not with the idea of giving up our London house, at least for some years, but simply of having a place to which we may come for about six months of the year, and perhaps finally shrink into altogether.

## GE TO MRS. MARK PATTISON, EARLSWOOD COMMON, 3 JULY 1874

*MS:* British Museum. *Hitherto unpublished.*

The Cottage | Earlswood Common | July 3. 74.

Dear Figliuolina

We retired from the world on the 2d of June and are to remain in strict religious retreat here till the end of September. Our souls and bodies are much the better for it.

I waft you a kiss and a blessing. I received your pretty note, but trusted to your comprehension of silence as that of an aged person to whom the necessity of answering letters is the worst of Grasshoppers.[7] Of course I like to receive them, so please let yourself be numbered among the loving creatures who give me in this kind, asking for nothing again.

We drive about in this enchanting country looking at all the promising houses that are to let, having concluded that we should like to have a fixed summer retreat hereabout.

I hope the Rector is dismissing his proof sheets [8] and is as well as can be expected under these circumstances.

I was ill when I came down, but have not for a long while been so well as I am now. Mr. Lewes is gone to town on business this morning, and I am going to have a windy walk by myself. This Common, I suppose, was considered a bracing place for the idiots [9]—which may account for my being so well here.

Faithfully and affectionately yours
M. E. L.

7. i. e. burdens. See Ecclesiastes, 12:5.

8. For his *Isaac Casaubon, 1559–1614,* 1875.

9. The Earlswood Asylum for Idiots, built in 1856, housed at this time over 500 patients. It was open to visitors every Monday. See [R. J. King], *A Handbook for Travellers in Surrey, Hampshire, and the Isle of Wight,* 3d ed., 1876, pp. 44–45. GHL went there Monday, 24 August 1874; "saw one or two interesting cases but on the whole not much interested." (GHL Diary.)

## GE TO GEORGE BANCROFT, EARLSWOOD COMMON, 15 JULY 1874

*Text:* Typewritten copy in Massachusetts Historical Society. *Hitherto unpublished.*

The Cottage | Earlswood Common | July 15, 74.

My dear Mr. Bancroft,[1]

We have been in strict retreat here since the first of June and the persons in charge of our house have orders not to give our address. If we had been at home we should have been delighted to shake hands once more with you and Mrs. Bancroft. I trust that I may entirely congratulate you both on the prospect of being restored to the United States, notwithstanding the many happy, affectionate associations you have with Berlin. I lose not a minute in answering your letter which has just been brought to our breakfast table.

In the first place I feel much gratified by the delicacy of Mr. Burlingame in asking you to be an intermediary. I have had various applications from America of a somewhat similar kind, from writers unknown to me, who apparently expected me to furnish them with an elaborate account of myself or of the "origin of my works," and who had felt no need of an introduction.

I perceive from the few words—highly considerate words, in which you put Mr. Burlingame's proposal,[2] that I may count on your full understanding and your discreet conveyance of what I say to you on the subject.

I am thoroughly opposed in principle (quite apart from any personal reference to myself) to the system of *contemporary* biography. I think it one of the abuses of print and reading that the mass of the public will read any quantity of trivial details about a writer with whose works they are very imperfectly, if at all, acquainted. Even posthumous biography is, I think, increasingly perverted into an indulgence of this time-wasting tendency: for example, a great poet's

1. Passing through London at the end of his appointment as United States Minister to Berlin, George Bancroft called at the Priory, 12 July 1874. The maid could not give GE's address. The next morning he sent GE the letter just received from Burlingame. Both Bancroft's and Burlingame's letters are in the Berg Collection, NYPL.

2. "If you are willing to send me any little autobiographical hints, they shall rest sacredly in my hands, and I will as of my own intuitive knowledge impart to young Burlingame such notices as I can." (NYPL.)

trash, written when he was a schoolboy, trash which, if he had remembered it, he would have burnt, is brought into quite mortifying publicity at the end of half a century, and poor Dickens's small scraps of memoranda certainly meant for no eyes but his own, are raked from his desk to the amusement of the most contemptible of his readers and (I trust) to the indignation of all who respected him.

I say these things merely to indicate the point of view from which I take my objection to furnishing particulars about myself for any compendium such as our own "Men of the Time." It seems to me that just my works and the order in which they have appeared is what the part of the public which cares about me may most usefully know; and Mr. Lewes declined, on my behalf, to give any information to the editors of that work, who have had the good taste not to insert unauthenticated statements.[3]

In reply to Miss Phelps (the author of 'Gates Ajar') who said that she desired only to know something that would better enable her to illustrate the bearing of my books in some lectures which she expected to give, I stated that I was born in Warwickshire and brought up in the Church of England—the latter point having some importance merely that my sympathetic presentation of dissenters may be understood not as a prejudice of education but as an impartial judgment.[4]

Apart from this correspondence with Miss Phelps, I believe that I have in no instance given any other reply to biographical questions than, that I decline to furnish personal information.

If I ever did so, I can say without fear of its being interpreted as a hollow phrase, that a request from editors of repute transmitted so

3. For early accounts of GE in *Men of the Time* see 22 June 1861. The statement that she was "the daughter of a clergyman" appeared in the 7th ed., 1868 and the 8th, 1872. In the 9th ed., 1875, pp. 383–4, the legend was embroidered: "She is the daughter of a poor clergyman, but in early life was adopted by a wealthy clergyman who gave her a first-class education. When she left school, which happened while she was still very young, Mr. Herbert Spencer became her tutor and friend, and under his skilful training her mind was developed rapidly and broadly. She applied herself to the languages, mastering German, French, and Italian, became an accomplished musician, and familiarized herself not only with the fine arts, but also with metaphysics and logic. While in this stage she translated Strauss's 'Life of Jesus' (1846) from the fourth German edition, and soon afterwards became one of the staff of the *Westminster Review*. Here by her intimacy with Mr. John Stuart Mill and others, she became confirmed in their peculiar religious and philosophical views. Her translation of Feuerbach's 'Essence of Christianity' appeared in 1853. Subjoined is a list of her subsequent works."

4. For GE's autobiographical account given Elizabeth Stuart Phelps see 13 August 1875.

delicately through you, would be an instance that could present no obstacles, but rather, every inducement.

But I prefer that not only myself, but other authors, should be more read during their lives and have their lives left unwritten till they are dead. Perhaps you may not agree with me, but I am sure you will tolerate my difference, even if you class it as an idiosyncrasy.

With best regards to Mrs. Bancroft and yourself, in which Mr. Lewes heartily joins, I remain, my dear Mr. Bancroft,

Yours most sincerely,
M. E. Lewes.

## GE TO MME EUGÈNE BODICHON, EARLSWOOD COMMON, 16 JULY 1874

*MS:* Mr. Philip Leigh-Smith. *Extracts published:* Cross, III, 238–239, dated 17 July 1874.

The Cottage | Earlswood Common | July 16. 74.

Dearest Barbara

Your letter brings delightful news. I was in a resigned condition about you—hoping as the best thing that you were gone on a painting expedition. But it is better that everybody should be good, and that there should be no ugly corners of anxiety in your mind. And the addition of the little Baby for you to rescue and befriend is also pretty. I like much better to hear of the children already born being taken care of, than to be asked to rejoice greatly because a new one is born.

Your picture of poor Miss E[dwards] [5] is deplorable. I cannot help thinking it a misfortune that she took to writing. But it seems that the only chance of her finding dignity and independence is that she should be left to extricate herself. That chlorale is a very pernicious thing to begin taking: the doctors say that women who begin with it never leave it off.[6]

We enjoy our country peacefulness greatly, [*5 lines deleted*] George has had some headachiness, and for the last day or two it has been my turn to grumble, but I am very much stronger since I came into this pure air. I was a great wretch, you know, just before we left town.

And now I have two questions to ask of your benevolence. First, was there not some village near Stonehenge where you stayed the night? —nearer to Stonehenge than Amesbury? —Secondly, Do you know

5. Matilda Betham Edwards.

6. Dr. Matthias Liebreich of Berlin had introduced the use of chloral hydrate in 1869. Its habit-forming quality was not at first recognized.

anything specific about Holmwood *Common* as a place of residence? It is ravishingly beautiful: is it in its higher part thoroughly unobjectionable as a site for a dwelling? I ask in reference to a house which is built on the higher part of the Common—a thick-walled substantial house, but with no high trees round it.[7]

We shall be very grateful if you will answer these questions, so far as you can, by a speedy post.

It seems that they have been having the heat of Tophet in London, whereas we have never had more than agreeable sunniness, this common being almost always breezy. And the country around us must I think, be the loveliest—of its undulating woody kind—in all England.

I remember when we were driving together last, something was said about my disposition to melancholy. I ought to have said then, but did not, that I am no longer one of those whom Dante found in a Hell-border because they had been sad under the blessed daylight. I am uniformly cheerful now—feeling the preciousness of these moments in which I still possess love and thought.

I can't think who Mary Ewart [8] is. And do you know how our dear Mrs. Senior is tormented by the officials about her capital Report?

G. sends his love and I am

Always your faithful
M. E. L.

## GE TO ROLAND STUART, EARLSWOOD COMMON, 21 JULY 1874

*MS:* British Museum. *Envelope:* Master Roland Stuart | Tobermory | Mull | Scotland. *Postmarks:* PR | LONDON | 21 JY | 74; OBAN | D | JY 22 | 74; [TO]BERMORY | JY 23 | 1874. *Published:* Stuart, pp. 23–24.

The Cottage | Earlswood Cn. | July 21. 74.

My dear Roland

Thanks! you are a brave fellow for sending me your Mother's photo,[9] and have given me real pleasure. The likeness is as good as I

7. From GHL's Diary this appears to be the Old Mill House, which they considered carefully for three weeks, 12 July—3 August 1874, and finally resolved not to take.

8. Mary Ewart, daughter of William Ewart (1798–1869), who in a long career in Parliament secured many important reforms. He advocated opening museums on Sundays and the establishment of free public libraries.

9. GE asked Roland to send it 8 June 1874.

can imagine any likeness to be. So if you get the shepherd's crook laid about your back for your pretty action, you will bear it the better because you know that you not only had the good motive of giving pleasure, but were successful in giving it.

I hope you are sharing our splendid sunshine amidst your fine scenery, and enjoying your holiday to the utmost. I wonder which is the merrier of the two—you or your Mother? Please tell that dear Mother that I was very grateful to her for remembering my wish to have a photo of your profile, which I think represents you better than the front face.

You know, you are my adopted grandson, and I am concerned that you should be handsome in all ways—chiefly in that best way of *doing* handsomely, as the heroic Roland of these times. Are you practising the winding of the horn among the mountains, so that you may not be behind your predecessor and great namesake in that accomplishment?

We ate the delicious Dinan Cake as if we had been youngsters, though in fact we are aged and, just now, rather ailing. But in all other respects—pray tell my dear daughter with my love—we are thoroughly happy and are constantly bearing her in mind and heart.

Mr. Lewes sends his love to you, and I am always, dear Roland,

Your affectionate Friend
M. E. Lewes.

## GHL TO ALEXANDER MAIN, EARLSWOOD COMMON, [2 AUGUST 1874]

*Text:* Main's copy owned by Mr. John R. Sprunt. *Hitherto unpublished.*

The Cottage | Earlswood Common | Red Hill | Sunday.

My dear Main

We had rightly divined the reason of not hearing from or seeing you, and were glad for your sake that you had made the choice. Your account of the trip reassures us; there is a health of enjoyment from every line.

Our stay here has been delightful in its solitude and the beauty of the country; but has not been so beneficial to our health as might have been expected and was wished. Mrs. Lewes although better on the whole, has had no little malaise, and is not strong. She is hard at work however. My headaches and dyspepsia have been rather worse if anything since we left London—but I also am working hard and that may have something to do with it!

The revision of my second volume has turned out to be a rewriting of it—I hope to its advantage; and there is still much to be done. Therefore I do not think we shall leave England this autumn—or only for a week or two if at all. We stay here till the end of September.

As you are a lover of Wordsworth you will delight in Dorothy's Journal.[1]

Ever yours truly
G. H. L.

## GE TO MRS. EDWARD BURNE-JONES, EARLSWOOD COMMON, 3 AUGUST 1874

*MS:* Yale. *Extracts published:* Cross, III, 239.

The Cottage | Earlswood Common | August 3. 74.

Dearest Georgie

It was sweet of you to write me that nice long letter. I was athirst for some news of you, and though what you send me is not perfectly good, one has learned to be thankful for sma' mercies in this world of dreadful possibilities. That the children are well and a joy to you both, that your health has not quite broken down (of which I had some fear, remembering the terrible fluttering of your heart), and that there is this hopeful journey to Naworth in prospect, is altogether a store of "better-than-might-be's" which make my mind much easier about you than it was in its former ignorance. Life, as you say, is a big thing. No wonder there comes a season when we cease to look round and say "how shall I enjoy?," but as in a country which has been visited by the sword, pestilence, and famine, think only how we shall help the wounded and how find seed for the next harvest—how till the earth and make a little time of gladness for those who are being born without their own asking.

We are as usual getting more than our share of peace and other good—except in the matter of warmth and sunshine. Our common is a sort of ball-room for the winds, and on the warmest days we have had here we have found them at their music and dancing. They roar round the corners of our house in a wintry fashion while the sun is shining on the brown grass. Perhaps this touch of extra changefulness in the temperature from one spot to another has helped to bring on again Mr. Lewes's old dyspeptic torments. He has lost too many morn-

1. Dorothy Wordsworth, *Recollections of a Tour Made in Scotland,* A.D. *1803,* ed. J. C. Shairp, Edinburgh, 1874.

ings in headachiness, but that is the only drawback we have felt on our enjoyment of walks and long drives in this lovely country.

I hear his feet, I think, coming to ask—yes, his feet really ask me to come and walk with him.

We are not certain whether we shall stay here till the end of September, but in any case we shall not be settled at 21 N.B. until the end of October, because our house there wants cleaning, and our servants are here, so we shall have to leave them in London to brush and scour. You will not let me be without knowledge of anything good or evil beyond the everyday mark that happens to you. I am so glad of what you say about the Latin.[2] Go on conquering and to conquer[3] a little kingdom for yourself there. When one sees the foolish and the ignorant happy it is possible to doubt the good of a larger vision, but nobody ever envied narrowness of mind in misery. Always

Your loving Friend
M. E. Lewes.

## JOHN BLACKWOOD TO GE, ST. ANDREWS, 4 AUGUST 1874

*MS:* National Library of Scotland. *Extracts published: John Blackwood,* pp. 384–385.

**Strathtyrum | St. Andrews | N.B.**
August 4/74.

My Dear Mrs. Lewes

I have such good news to give of Middlemarch, Jubal, and also Spanish Gypsy that I write a line to report progress.

Of the 7/6 edition of Middlemarch we printed 3150 in May and 2100 in the latter part of June. The above are all disposed of and we have just reprinted 2100 more of which the first batch went off to Pater Noster Row the other day to supply orders. The success of Middlemarch has also exercized a benign influence on the sale of the other novels.

Of Jubal you are aware that the first edition 1609 copies is gone and we subscribed 247 of the second edition in London. Of the Spanish Gypsy I see we have sold 107 copies between December and July. This is all good and must I think make you turn to a new work with

2. Mrs. Burne-Jones had been studying Latin with Jules Andrieu (1837–84). See Mrs. George Howard to GE, 13 October 1873. (Yale.)

3. Revelation 6:2.

fresh confidence that you are not writing in vain. News of how that work is getting on will be very welcome.

I hope you are both well and enjoying this delightful weather in the country. It is charming here and even my daughter feels that there is enjoyment apart from London gaieties. As we drove through Regent St. to the Railway Station she exclaimed "Oh Papa, don't you wish we were coming in instead of going away? How bright and gay everything is." It was positively a wet foggy day.

Major Lockhart came over to us a few days ago with loud talk of shutting himself up in his room and working. The scoundrel has never been off the Links since his arrival. The other day I played a match with the Whig whip W. Adam [4] just relieved from his weary duties in the House of Commons. When we were a few holes out he exclaimed fervently, "This is a great, glorious, and noble game. There is nothing like it in the world." He was a little ahead of me at the time I think, but we were quite agreed.

In addition to the usual entertainments of the place we had a famous military week the Fife Mounted Rifles drilling in one of the Parks here. Willie turned out with them and their colonel, that mighty hunter Jack Anstruther Thomson,[5] stayed with us. You will have heard of Thomson in former days as Master of the Pytchley and also of the Atherstone. He told me a good one of Newdegate. He (T) had got a fall and broken one of the small bones of his leg. No one of course could be kinder than Newdegate, but when he had got his friend into the most comfortable possible position he began at once about the *Jesuits*. On which exclaimed the tortured Thomson, "My dear Charlie, you have done everything for me that man can until the Doctor comes and the hounds are running—pray ride on." I remember him telling me this story long ago and I never can think of it without laughing as it is so characteristic of both men.

All the world comes to St. Andrews and among others we have at present that great Oxford Don the Dean of Christ-church.[6] Liddell's

4. William Patrick Adam (1823–81), M.P. for Clackmannan and Kinross, served as Liberal whip 1874–80.

5. John Anstruther-Thomson (1818–1904), assumed the name of Thomson on inheriting from his mother Clementia Adam the estates at Charlton, Colinsburgh, Fife. He had served with the 9th Lancers and the 13th Light Dragoons and was an honorary colonel of the Fife and Forfar Imperial Yeomanry. He was M.F.H. of the Atherstone 1850–59 and of the Pytchley 1864–69. (*Annual Register,* 1904 and Burke, *Landed Gentry,* 1925, p. 1737.)

6. Henry George Liddell (1811–98), Dean of Christ Church, Oxford, author with Robert Scott of the *Greek-English Lexicon,* 1843, and *A History of Ancient Rome,* 2 vols., 1855, which GE read in Italy in 1860. She must have met him during her visit to Jowett in June 1873.

Greek Lexicon Lewes probably will know and have suffered under. He is a most agreeable old gentleman and along with his fair daughters walked round with Lockhart and me in our match yesterday. For the honour of learning I am happy to say he showed intelligence about the Game.

My son is at home for the holidays and I think you would like him. He has a strong turn for humour which he developes with much gravity.

With best remembrances to Lewes, I am always

yours truly

John Blackwood.

I cannot remember your Country address so must send this into Edinburgh to be posted. Willie is with us and he and my wife are gone out riding and I am now going to walk down to the Club to hear the Golfers retail their day's performances.

## GE TO JOHN BLACKWOOD, EARLSWOOD COMMON, 8 AUGUST 1874

*MS:* National Library of Scotland. *Mostly published:* Cross, III, 239–242.

The Cottage | Earlswood Common | August 8. 74.

My dear Mr. Blackwood

Thanks for sending me the good news. The sale of Middlemarch is wonderful out of all whooping, and considered as manifesting the impression made by the book, is more valuable than any amount of immediate distribution.

I suppose there will be a new edition wanted of the Spanish Gypsy by Christmas, and I have a carefully corrected copy by me containing my final alterations, to which I desire to have the stereotype plates adjusted.

As to confidence in the work to be done I am somewhat in the condition suggested to Armgart, 'How will you bear the poise of eminence, With dread of falling?' [7] And the other day, having a bad headache, I did what I have sometimes done before at intervals of five or six years —looked into three or four novels to see what the world was reading.[8]

In the University pulpit 22 November 1874 he referred to GE as "the greatest living analyst of human nature—not, alas! a Christian." (Newspaper cutting in letter from Mrs. Pattison to GE, 30 November 1874. Yale.)

7. "Armgart," scene ii. The MS and the published texts read "dread of sliding."

8. GHL's Diary shows that they read aloud Jane Austen's *Mansfield Park* in June and July 1874 and some of Trol-

The effect was paralyzing, and certainly justifies me in that abstinence from novel-reading which, I fear, makes me seem supercilious or churlish to the many persons who send me their books or ask me about their friends' books.

To be delivered from all doubts as to one's justification in writing at this stage of the world, one should have either a plentiful faith in one's own exceptionalness or a plentiful lack of money. Tennyson said to me, "Everybody writes so well now," and if the lace is only machine-made it still pushes out the hand-made, which has differences only for a fine fastidious appreciation. To write indifferently after having written well—that is, from a true, individual store which makes a special contribution—is like an eminent clergyman's spoiling his reputation by lapses and neutralizing all the good he did before. However, this is superfluous stuff to write to you. It is only a sample of the way in which depression works upon me. I am not the less grateful for all the encouragement I get.

I saw handsome Dean Liddell at Oxford. He is really a grand figure. They accuse him of being obstructive to much-needed reforms—but everybody accuses everybody else in that seat of learning. For my own part I am thankful to him for his share in 'Scott and Liddell' and his capital little Roman History. Apropos of books and St. Andrews, I have read aloud to Mr. Lewes, Professor Flint's volume, and we have been both much pleased with its conscientious presentation and thorough effort at fairness.

We have enjoyed the country as we always do, but we have been, for our constitutions, a little unfortunate in the choice of a spot which is the windiest of the windy. That heat which we have read and heard of has hardly been at all felt by us, and we have both suffered a little from chills which have set our organisms wrong for a week together. But Mr. Lewes is very well now, and works with much enjoyment. I, as you will perceive from my letter, am just now possessed by an evil spirit in the form of headache, but on the whole I am much the stronger for the peace and the delicious air which I take in as a conscious addition to the good of living.

I hope Miss Blackwood will not be convinced that it is Scotland which makes London delightful—that is, that she prefers London because she does not get much of it.

We have been near buying a little country hermitage on Holmwood Common—a grand spot with a view hard to match in our flat land.

lope's *The Way We Live Now,* which was appearing in monthly parts. In September they were reading *Persuasion* aloud.

But we have been frightened away by its windiness. I rather envy Major Lockhart and the rest of the Golfian enthusiasts—to have a seductive idleness which is really a healthy activity is invaluable to people who have desk work.

Yours always truly
M. E. Lewes.

## GHL TO CHARLES LEE LEWES, EARLSWOOD COMMON, 17 AUGUST 1874

*Text:* Paterson, pp. 166–167.

The Cottage, | Red Hill. | August 17, 1874.

Dearest Charles,

I went to the Priory the other day [9] and found there the Diploma of Foreign Membership to the Hungarian Academy which the President had sent me, stating in his letter that my "highly distinguished scientific merits have caused" me "to be admitted among the *celebrious* Foreign Members." The tribute is pleasant and the honour of a kind some men run after, but I cannot feel as elated as I suppose I ought.

The little Mutter has been variable in health and I do not get strong as I hoped and expected, yet getting through my work steadily enough. I must tell you of the continued sale of "Middlemarch" and the poem —the cheap edition sold over 5,000 copies in two months and is going on as brisk as ever. Our love.

Ever your
Pater.

## GE TO MRS. HARRIET BEECHER STOWE, EARLSWOOD COMMON, 23 AUGUST 1874

*MS:* Mr. Lyman Beecher Stowe. *Published:* C. E. Stowe, *Life of Harriet Beecher Stowe,* Boston, 1890, 472–473.

August 23. 74.

My dear Friend

The other day I had a letter from Mrs. Fields written to let me know something of you under that heavy trouble [1] of which such information as I have had has been quite untrustworthy, leaving me in entire incredulity with regard to it except on this point—that you and yours

9. GHL Diary, 11 August 1874.

1. Theodore Tilton had accused her brother the Rev. Henry Ward Beecher of adultery with Mrs. Tilton.

must be suffering deeply. Naturally, I thought most of *you* in the matter (its public aspects being indeterminate), and many times before our friend's letter came I had said to Mr. Lewes "What must Mrs. Stowe be feeling!" I remembered what Mr. Fields had once told me of the wonderful courage and cheerfulness which belonged to you, enabling you to bear up under exceptional trials, and I imagined you helping the other sufferers with tenderness and counsel, but yet—I felt that there must be a bruising weight on your heart. Dear honoured Friend—you who are so ready to give warm fellowship—is it any comfort to you to be told that those afar off are caring for you in spirit, and will be the happier for all good issues that may bring you rest?

I cannot, dare not write more in my ignorance, lest I should be using unseasonable words. But I trust in your not despising this scrap of paper which tells you—perhaps rather for my relief than yours, that I am always, in grateful sweet remembrance of your goodness to me and your energetic labours for all,

Yours with sincere affection,
M. E. Lewes.

We are in the country, but shall be moving to town again shortly.

## GHL TO MRS. ELMA STUART, EARLSWOOD COMMON, 25 AUGUST 1874

*MS:* British Museum. *Published:* Stuart, pp. 25–26.

The Cottage | Earlswood Common | 25 August 74.

Dear Friend

For half an hour we will *not* see you; but if you will spend the afternoon with us, you shall be received with and enfolded by outstretched arms! I told you when you went away that I counted on your being able to come again; and on Tuesday next 1 September if you find the times convenient, I propose that you leave Charing Cross at 11.15 which will bring you to Red Hill by 12.15. There I will meet you and conduct you to your loving mother, with whom you must stay till ½ past 4; and so get back to town by 5.18. However, you will understand that these hours are merely proposed on the supposition that they fall in with your other arrangements. Look into Bradshaw and propose any others—(or any other day)—and be assured that they will suit us equally well.[2] We only protest against the "Half-hours with Great Authors"—a work too snatchy for our tastes.

2. "Mrs. Stuart came to lunch and stayed till 4.30. Very interesting visit." (GHL Diary, 1 September 1874.) GHL gave her an autograph of Goethe with

Polly has been decidedly better of late, and if her Hebrew and Oriental studies were a little less absorbing and exhausting she would be what the racing men call in 'good form.'

The shepherd's crook is a faithful companion and you may be said to walk out with me every day.

God bless you.

Ever yours affectionately
G. H. Lewes.

## GHL TO ALEXANDER MAIN, EARLSWOOD COMMON, 8 SEPTEMBER 1874

*Text:* Main's copy owned by Mr. John R. Sprunt. *Hitherto unpublished.*

The Cottage | Earlswood Common | September 8. 74.

My dear Main

I quite agree with you about Tyndall's speech, and think Huxley's open to quite as much objection: both as to matter and manner.[3] I could not help regretting that my second volume was not out, or just about to appear; for I believe many readers would see in it how baseless were the exultations and the tribulations founded on the supposed *reality* of atoms. As to the Unknowable, I have a regular crusade against it, though I don't expect to be more listened to than any other unpopular teacher. What a strange perversity of speculation is that which makes men declare we cannot know a given thing because we do not know something else!

For once the round of the papers was not a fiction respecting Mrs. Lewes. She is writing what I believe will be a glorious book. I can't say the country has done her so much good as I had hoped—still she is stronger. As for me, I have had a worse time of it than in town and my rewriting (not revision alas!) of Volume 2 has been much delayed in consequence.

We go back to town on the 25th and then start for the Continent

a translation inscribed "G.H.L. to Elma Stuart, 1 Sepr. 1874." (Stuart, pp. 178–179.)

3. At the meeting of the British Association for the Advancement of Science at Belfast, 24 August 1874 John Tyndall devoted his presidential address to the relation between science and religion, maintaining the right of science to discuss such questions freely. Huxley read his address "On the Hypothesis that Animals Are Automata, and Its History," which was published in the *Fortnightly Review,* (November 1874). GHL makes "Animal Automatism" Problem III in *The Physical Basis of Mind,* the 3d vol. of his *Problems of Life and Mind,* 1877; Huxley's address is discussed in ch. 7, pp. 389–409, in which GHL rejects the materialists' purely mechanical explanation. Main's letter has not been found.

where we shall probably remain till November. But our movements are uncertain.

It is very delightful to both of us to think of you and Ritter returning with such zest and satisfaction to the works you know so well.

Ever faithfully yours
G. H. L.

## WILLIAM BLACKWOOD TO GE, EDINBURGH, 16 SEPTEMBER 1874

*Text:* Copy in Blackwood Letter Book. *Hitherto unpublished.*

45 George Street | Edinr. September 16/74.

My dear Mrs. Lewes

I have not had the pleasure of writing to you for a long time because I had nothing to trouble you with [in] a letter beyond what my Uncle had told you. Now however the inclosed Treasury order for a small sum of money on Colonial Sales of Foreign Editions of your works gives me the opportunity, as it requires your signature as George Eliot as well as our own to get the money. We have not had one for a very long time and I suspect the late Government must have pocketed several sums. It is some time now since we heard any news of you and Mr. Lewes and I have often wondered how you have been liking your Country quarters. I hope well, and that the air and quiet life have suited you both.

I have had a very jolly summer and am now well and *sound* though I have never been away from here for more than ten days and that twice only, but business has been lively and my Uncle's health and spirits have been better than I have seen him for several years. Long may he continue so I trust. I think he told you about my doings with The Fife Light Horse Yeomanry and how the Colonel, that mighty Nimrod Jack Thomson, and self and others had suffered from effects of sun, but it had splendid results and made me a new man, so I expect to enjoy some good hunting this coming season.

I am very happy to tell you that Middlemarch goes tripping along most gaily and the 2000 reprinted at end of July are all gone but a dozen or two and we have just reprinted another 2000 the first batch of which goes to London tomorrow. Jubal and Spanish Gypsy have also been selling well since last reported along with your other novels for the season of the year. I hope that your new work has been making as good progress in your hands and that we shall soon be hearing something more from you about it. . . . Post hour is up so I must conclude and with best remembrances to Mr. Lewes, believe me

Always yours sincerely
(signed) William Blackwood.

Mrs. Lewes.

## GE TO MRS. ELMA STUART, EARLSWOOD COMMON, 22 SEPTEMBER 1874

*MS:* British Museum. *Published:* Stuart, pp. 26–29.

The Cottage | Earlswood Common | September 22. 74.

Dearest Elma

Your sweet letter came yesterday. I grieve to see that it gives no address to which I could send this with a chance of its reaching you before you return to Dinan. But I please myself with writing at once—while I am musing the fire burns, and now write I with my pen.

After the letter, in the evening, came the delicate woollen things which well represent the warmth and tenderness of Elma's love. There is hardly any bodily comfort I prefer to these gossamer woollen garments which give one warmth without weight. I am also grateful that you think my words worth remembering—especially since they are sometimes enough to hinder you from marrying a man with a quiverful of those problematic blessings. Pray, if you fall in love ascertain first that the *objet aimé* is without encumbrances. If not let him find some poor governess who is well broken-in and without prospects. I have no patience with these widowers who are always expecting women to take compassion on them, and never themselves take compassion on women really forlorn. They must always have the best, forsooth—are always good enough for the best to accept. This is the fine principle of Natural Selection, they will say. I admit it, but it is also the selection of conceited gentlemen.

Little Blanche was here from Saturday till Monday morning, and was showing me the toys which a certain lady brought her—a lady who scatters her pretty gifts over the earth, like the symbolical Spring in the pictures with a miraculous cornucopia. She (Blanche) was especially delighted with her "s'an," which swam in my basin to admiration.

Mr. Lewes has just had a horrible fit of headache,[4] but is now his

4. GE and GHL went to Brighton, 16 September 1874 to visit her niece Emily Clarke. "Long walk on Parade—sitting in the sun—summer weather." The next four days he notes "Headache." (GHL Diary.)

bright self again, and is beginning to pack the books in preparation for flight homewards. He is gone off to Reigate to get labels, but I know he has love to send or keep, wherever mine goes or stays, and he delights in you, too, for your own sake—not only because you are good to me. He certainly does enjoy reading your letters, and he has no shame, as I may well have, in reading words which express the height of your affection rather than my desert. But I will not be like Coleridge and talk humility, which somehow never is active when one thinks one's audience likely to assent.

In one point, dear, you cannot be hyperbolical, and that is in believing that my strongest desire for you is that you should feel helped by me to be—what you are so well capable of being—"a joy, and blessing, and comfort and strength to others." You see I am using your own words, which are very precious to me. Only don't try what is too difficult—too great a risk of failure.

I am not too strong, though on the whole better. And this feebleness of mine makes me value very much your considerate tenderness, which is content with a silence rarely broken. I must touch on this, because I have felt particularly your delicacy in refraining from putting an address that I might not have the possibility of self-reproach in not writing. You could teach me many refinements of perfect love, which does not come altogether by nature but is acquired in the long discipline of our own need.

Good-bye, dearest Elma. I go into silence, but not that of memory, which will continually speak of you and imaginatively to you.

Your loving Mother
M. E. Lewes.

## GE TO MME EUGÈNE BODICHON, EARLSWOOD COMMON, 23 SEPTEMBER 1874

*MS:* Mr. Philip Leigh-Smith. *Hitherto unpublished.*

The Cottage | Earlswood Comm. | September 23. 74.

My dear Barbara

I have often been saying, 'Barbara is gone on her sketching expedition' or, 'This grey day will suit Barbara.' But somehow you had sent my imagination to Yorkshire. I should think Cornwall and its granite was the scenery most after your own heart.

Glad to hear good news of your establishment. Altogether you give me the impression that you have had a delightful summer. So have we.

We are not robust, but otherwise jolly—are going up to town on Friday, then into Cambridgeshire for a few days, then to France. At the beginning of November we expect to be settled in town.[4a]

George has got his 2d volume ready for the press, and we have had daily drives in lovely scenery, looking at the country through the changing months as one looks at a dear face through the changing years. The children have been to us twice from Saturday to Monday, and we have had about eight other visitors [5] for a day or half a day at rare intervals. Otherwise we have had uninterrupted quiet. You know we are not social creatures, unlike you who have always the real, breathing, talking world about you. The sketch you give me of Numa Hartog's cousin [6] is very gratifying. To hear of good young things growing up is the best of news.

I dare say you wonder that I have not done more for Girton. The fact is that we have been devoting a considerable sum of late years to the help of individual needs which are not published to the world.[7] More and more of such needs disclose themselves to one—old governesses and other beings having some claims through the memory of good received in one's youth, and who could only be helped by such special care. But you will let me know what is to be done for this nice girl.

George has had a good deal of headache but you know how elastic his nature is, and how soon he brightens when pain has left him. He sends his love with mine.

Always your affectionate
M. E. Lewes.

4a. They returned to London Friday, 25 September; visited Mr. W. H. Hall at Six Mile Bottom, 28 September—1 October; and left for France 3 October. No letters have been found during their journey, which began with a week in Paris, 4–11 October, took them by way of Soissons, Rheims, Sedan, and Dinant to Brussels, where they stayed 14-18 October. They returned to the Priory 19 October.

5. In addition to Mrs. Stuart and Roland, Mrs. Congreve, Mrs. Geddes, Lord Lytton, and John Cross are mentioned in GHL's Diary.

6. Phoebe Sarah Marks (1854–1923), afterwards Hertha Ayrton. Her cousin Numa Edward Hartog, (1846–71), son of Alphonse Hartog, French professor at Jew's College, Finsbury Square, was admitted pensioner at Trinity College, Cambridge without oath in 1865 and was Senior Wrangler in 1869, the first Jew to attain this honor. His failure to obtain a fellowship is said to have caused the removal of the disability.

7. Among her charities in 1874 were £200 to Octavia Hill and £10 to Maria Lewis, her old governess. But the largest gifts were those to GHL's family. Agnes was given about £200, and her children by Thornton Hunt, who died in 1873, received generous gifts from time to time; GHL's sister-in-law Mrs. Edward Lewes had £75; his children, especially Herbert, were helped, and a number of organizations like the Comte Fund, the Little Sisters of Hammersmith, and the Shakespeare Society were subscribed to regularly.

I was pleasantly surprised by Mr. Allingham's marriage.[8] I rejoice in his getting the editorship and in the indications that his bride is an accomplished industrious woman.

## GE TO MME EUGÈNE BODICHON, LONDON, 26 OCTOBER 1874

*MS:* Mr. Philip Leigh-Smith. *Hitherto unpublished.*

**The Priory, | 21. North Bank, | Regents Park.**
October 26. 74.

My dear Barbara

I want a housemaid with a first-rate character—our nice little Charlotte having divined in herself a genius for cooking which makes her want to be a kitchen maid. Can you help me? I know you will, if you can.

We are just come home, and after a little ramble of two or three days we shall be settled here for the winter.[9] I imagine you at Blandford Square by this time, and think it safest to send my note there. We expect to leave town again on Thursday and to return on Saturday.

In any case I hope to see you soon and shall keep all gossip till then.

Always your loving
Marian.

## GE TO MRS. ELMA STUART, LONDON, 26 OCTOBER 1874

*MS:* British Museum. *Published:* Stuart, pp. 30–31.

**The Priory, | 21. North Bank, | Regents Park.**
October 26. 74.

Dearest Elma

Edith [1] was here yesterday, the first Sunday of our presence at home, and she told us things about your health which made me grievously anxious about you. I beseech you to learn as far as possible what is

8. William Allingham married 22 August 1874 Helen Paterson (1848–1926), eldest child of Dr. Alexander Henry Paterson.

9. The day after their return from Belgium, in spite of a cold and sore throat, GE set out with GHL for Salisbury, probably in search of local color for *Daniel Deronda;* Offendene, Brackenshaw Castle, and Diplow Hall are all in Wessex, near Wanchester. They spent three days walking to Old Sarum and Stratford, and driving to Stonehenge. They returned to the Priory Friday, 23 October.

1. Edith Jemima Simcox (b. 1844.)

physiologically wise in the treatment of yourself and to act upon the knowledge. The reason why I feel strongly on this point is, that I have had hard experience how all the good in oneself and one's lot may be marred by inconsiderateness about health in the younger years when various better possibilities are still open. Please try and remember that it is a sin to waste your nights in sleeplessness, or squander your young strength in the day-time, when you have any power over the circumstances that bring about such results. I cannot bear to think of your bright spirit being ruined by the eating malaise of imperfect health.

And you have been having a serious fortnight's illness! I shall not be quite happy till I hear that you are as well as usual again, and that you are prevailed on to promise self-care for the future.

In your case, I imagine, it is hardly ludicrous to say, "Take care of yourself for the sake of others"—perhaps, remembering what you have said to me, I may venture to say in answer, Take care of your body and soul for my sake.

We came home on Friday, but are still bent on one more excursion for a week. After that, we shall be voluntary prisoners in this dim city for many months to come. Let us always know something about you.

Ever your loving
Mother.

## GHL TO MRS. ELMA STUART, LONDON, 26 OCTOBER 1874

*MS:* British Museum. *Published:* Stuart, pp. 33–35.

26 October 1874.

Dear Elma

We returned home on Friday, and yesterday Edith came, saddening us with a sad account of your health, and making your spiritual parents somewhat disposed to scold you for your imprudence!—if you were well and strong you would be scolded by me for not attending sufficiently to the ordinary rules of right 'conduct of the body'—even more important than the 'conduct of the understanding.' For the sake of others, if not your own, do bring a little of your energy and intellect to bear on the question of keeping yourself in a normal condition of health and do not play tricks with Valerian, Opium, etc.! You will perhaps retort on me that I have not practised my own precepts—but it is not so—I damaged my body by overwork and over-confidence, till it was too late to do more than patch and patch the old carcase. But I take as much pains not to get worse, as I should wish you to take not to destroy the fountain of spirits, energy, and love which still bubbles in your somewhat damaged organism. I hope to hear a better account of you soon.

We enjoyed our stay at Paris very much, owing to the splendid weather and our very comfortable quarters. We went every night to the theatre and saw *nobody!* From Paris we ran to Soissons and Sedan, Dinant, and Brussels—at the last place Mrs. Lewes caught cold which rather spoiled the effect of the holiday and now we are settling down to the old home routine with an everabiding consciousness of the fact that the climate of England is not the climate of France.

Ever your loving
G. H. Lewes.

## GHL TO MRS. ELMA STUART, LONDON, [1 NOVEMBER 1874]

*MS:* British Museum. *Endorsed:* Ocr. 1874. *Published:* Stuart, pp. 31–33.

**The Priory, | 21. North Bank, | Regents Park.**
Sunday.

Dear Elma

There is more joy in the Priory over one Elma that repenteth than over ninety-nine d——d niggers who take care of their carcasses because they have a wellfounded suspicion that no one else cares enough for them to take that task upon themselves. Therefore, dear child, take this to heart and continue virtuously in bed (or elsewhere) till your loving attendant [2] (to whom my grateful thanks, for all the love she shows you) declares you are a fit and proper person to be "at large" again. We have just returned from another week in the country [3] which has set Polly right again and now she is ready for the desk and Socicty!

Do you see the Contemporary Review in your Dinan diggings? If so, you will be interested I think in Mat Arnold's papers in the October

2. Roland Stuart notes: "'Your loving attendant' refers to a very dear friend and cousin, the Honourable Mrs. Stewart-Menzies, who is constantly referred to later in the letters as 'the guardian angel'—a title which she so richly deserved, nursing my mother with a most unselfish devotion and tender loving-kindness through long periods of illness. (p. 32.) She was Catharine Thurlow Fraser, a younger sister of Baron Saltoun of Abernethy; in 1860 she was married to John Stewart Menzies, Esq. of Chesthill, Perthshire, who died in 1867. (Burke, *Peerage,* 1894, under Saltoun.)

3. They went to Wiltshire Wednesday, 28 October, staying at Devizes, driving about looking at Bowood, Spye, Laycock and other great houses and parks, probably for details in *Daniel Deronda,* returning to London Saturday, 31 October.

and November numbers.[4] Much that he says on Religion we both think very good, and likely to have a *yeasty* effect on that strange fluid Public Opinion. I, myself cannot see how the Bible 'makes for righteousness' though I profoundly agree with him that righteousness is salvation—and is not to be sought in metaphysical refinements about a 'personal God' but is to be found in our idealization of human relations and human needs. If you don't take the Review at Dinan I will send you the number by post.

What a singular spectacle is presented by the contrast of the general tone of men's minds on this subject of Religion at the present day and that of some twenty years ago! And the progress rushes on, it does not simply move.

Your mother sends her dearest love and wishes. God bless you!

Ever yours
G. H. L.

## GE TO JOHN BLACKWOOD, LONDON, 2 NOVEMBER 1874

*MS:* National Library of Scotland. *Hitherto unpublished.*

**The Priory, | 21. North Bank, | Regents Park.**
November 2. 74.

My dear Mr. Blackwood

Since I wrote my letter to Mr. William Blackwood we have seen our son Charles, who tells us that during our absence, three weeks ago, he sent you an article of his on Mrs. Nassau Senior's Report on Workhouse Schools. I was sorry to hear that he had done so, because I feared that the article might not be suitable for the Magazine and that it might be a rule of yours to throw rejected articles at once into the Dom-daniel. We care about it particularly on account of our friend Mrs. N. Senior and her labours, and if the paper has not been already thrown out of reach I shall be much obliged if you will send it me. It is not a penny-a-lining literary affair, but an effort to put some serious social labour in the right light.

We were glad to hear from Mr. William Blackwood that you and yours are all well.

Always yours sincerely
M. E. Lewes.

4. "Review of Objections to 'Literature and Dogma,'" *Contemporary Review,* 24 (October and November 1874), 794–818, 981–1003.

## GE TO ALEXANDER MACMILLAN, LONDON, 10 NOVEMBER 1874

*MS:* Yale. *Hitherto unpublished.*

**The Priory, | 21. North Bank, | Regents Park.**
November 10. 74.

Dear Mr. Macmillan

How shall I show my gratitude for your generous gift of Mr. Masson's 'Milton'? [5] When I saw it advertised, I said inwardly, 'I should like to have that, but will not indulge myself.' I could not dream that it would come to me, like many other of the best things in the world, without my doing anything for it.

Your publishing list is to me the most tempting I ever look at, and when one sees the books one finds them in a costume that soothes the eyes with its soberness and good taste.

We are only just settled at home for the winter. I hope that you and yours are quite well.

Always yours sincerely
M. E. Lewes.

## GE TO MRS. HARRIET BEECHER STOWE, LONDON, 11 NOVEMBER 1874

*MS:* Mr. Lyman Beecher Stowe. *Published:* Cross, III, 242–244.

**The Priory, | 21. North Bank, | Regents Park.**
November 11. 74.

My dear Friend

I feel rather disgraced by the fact that I received your last kind letter nearly two months ago. But a brief note of mine, written immediately on hearing of you from Mrs. Fields, must have crossed yours and the Professor's kind letters to me, and I hope it proved to you that I love you in my heart.

We were in the country then, but soon afterwards we set out on a six weeks' journey, and we are but just settled in our winter home.

Those unspeakable troubles [6] in which I necessarily felt more for

5. David Masson, *Life of Milton, Narrated in Connection with the Political, Ecclesiastical, and Literary History of His Time,* 7 vols., London, Macmillan, 1859–1894. Vol. I, 1859, II, 1871, and III, 1873 had appeared; IV and V were published together in 1878.

6. The troubles of Henry Ward Beecher were far from ended. Tilton had sworn out a complaint 20 August 1874,

*you* than for any one else concerned, are I trust, well at an end and you are enjoying a time of peace. It was like your own sympathetic energy to be able, even while the storm was yet hanging in your sky, to write to me about my husband's books. Will you not agree with me that there is one comprehensive Church whose fellowship consists in the desire to purify and ennoble human life, and where the best members of all narrower churches may call themselves brother and sister in spite of differences? I am writing to your dear Husband as well as to you, and in answer to his question about Goethe, I must say, for my part, that I think he had a strain of mysticism in his soul,—of so much mysticism as I think inevitably belongs to a full poetic nature— I mean the delighted bathing of the soul in emotions which overpass the outlines of definite thought. I should take the "Imitation" as a type (it is one which your husband also mentions), but perhaps I might differ from him in my attempt to interpret the unchangeable and universal meanings of that great book.

Mr. Lewes, however, who has a better right than I to a conclusion about Goethe, thinks that he entered into the experience of the mystic —as in the confessions of the *Schöne Seele* [7]—simply by force of his sympathetic genius, and that his personal individual bent was towards the clear and plastic exclusively. Do not imagine that Mr. Lewes is guided in his exposition by theoretic antipathies. He is singularly tolerant of difference, and able to admire what is unlike himself.

He is busy now correcting the proofs of his second volume. I wonder whether you have headaches and are rickety as we are, or whether you have a glorious immunity from those ills of the flesh. Your husband's photograph looks worthy to represent one of those wondrous Greeks who wrote grand dramas at eighty or ninety.

I am decidedly among the correspondents who may exercise their friends in the virtue of giving and hoping for nothing again. Otherwise I am unprofitable. Yet believe me, dear Friends, I am always with lively memories of you

Yours affectionately
M. E. Lewes.

charging him with adultery; the trial began 11 January 1875 and lasted six months.

7. *Wilhelm Meister,* Book 6.

## GE TO MME EUGÈNE BODICHON, LONDON, 16 NOVEMBER 1874

*MS:* Mr. Philip Leigh-Smith. *Hitherto unpublished.*

**The Priory, | 21. North Bank, | Regents Park.**
November 16. 74.

Dearest Barbara

A prospective welcome to you! We will find you an edifying book when you come—Tylor's Early History of Mankind,[7a] if you have not read it, or something else as good. Meanwhile you ought to be in great mental vigour compared with your fellow-mortals who muddle and enfeeble themselves with reading.

I am delighted to hear so good an account of the Doctor, and I trust that your soul is at rest now from any gnawing anxieties.

I have hired a very promising housemaid,[8] found for me by our dear Mrs. Senior who—did you know?—is laid prostrate by illness and ordered to lay herself up for two or three years at least. She looks like a white angel in her little bed.

Please give my kindest remembrances to the beautiful little Aunt[9] —or rather, ask her to remember me kindly—for I think our forms of message are very conceited and ungraceful. How do we know that our kind remembrances are wanted? Whereas we do know whether we want the kind remembrances of others.

Come in for a bit of lunch at ½ past 1 some day—that is the best way of getting a chat. And then we will drive you on some errand.

Yours always
M. E. L.

7a. Edward Burnett Tylor, *Researches into the Early History of Mankind and the Development of Civilisation,* 1865. GE and GHL had finished reading it 18 August 1874. (GHL Diary.)

8. "Drove to Mrs. Nassau Senior's and to get the character of a new servant —Kate." (GHL Diary, 7 November 1874.)

9. Miss Julia Smith.

## JOHN BLACKWOOD TO GE, EDINBURGH, 19 NOVEMBER 1874

*MS:* National Library of Scotland. *Extract published: John Blackwood,* pp. 385–386.

**45, George Street, | Edinburgh.**
November 19/74.

My Dear Mrs. Lewes

When I got back from the Country last Thursday I found a most alarming pile of letters and packets of manuscript of all kinds awaiting me, but your pleasant dispatch with its most welcome news leavened the whole mass.[1] I do long to see that "Slice of M.S." which has passed into the "irrevocable." Lewes and I are both I believe good critics but it is very plain sailing when we have works such as yours to comment upon.

You will be glad to hear that Kinglake has returned for press nearly the last sheet of his Inkerman volume. It is a splendid series of pictures and will take us all back to the Crimea. In writing to him I told the good news of your novel with a sort of explanation of your mode of composition and I cannot resist copying for Lewes' delectation if not for yours his truly graceful and powerful comment. He says, "Another novel from Mrs. Lewes is really a national blessing! Why don't critics have illuminations for news so grateful instead of making believe to 'rejoice' at some absurd 'birth-day' or the accession of another Lord Mayor? What you tell me of the intellectual fermentation from which works like Middlemarch result is very interesting and makes me envy the process of disciplined thought which after the 'simmering' passes all at once into 'the irrevocable.' " There speaks a Master of English and I feel ashamed to go on with my own disjointed sentences.

We are shaking down into town life now and the *stair carpets are down.* I mildly suggested that they might have been laid down before we came but was sternly asked what effect the innumerable packing boxes and workmen's feet would have upon them. I retired. The leav-

1. GE's letter has not been found. Blackwood enclosed it in a note to Langford, 20 November 1874: "From George Eliot's letter you will see that her novel is becoming an accomplished fact." (NLS.) There are few comments on the book's progress. "Polly read all the evening the chapters she had written of Daniel De Ronda." (GHL Diary, 27 August 1874.) More was read on 11 September, and 15 and 16 November GE read over again to GHL the early chapters. GE's letter was probably sent to Blackwood when they went to the City 17 November to go over the Bank of England with John Cross. At the end of December GHL notes that "Polly has begun *Daniel de Ronda* and written about two thirds of Vol. I."

ing Strathtyrum was as usual a melancholy business and we had to leave behind Tickler, the favourite old Terrier, for whom a visit to his usual sanitarium, the keeper's lodge, was declared necessary. He was heard swearing violently as we drove through the lodge gate to the railway. Meanwhile we are not without dogs, as that rascal Jack brought down a fox terrier with him from school and left it with us. It is a perfect demon of mischief. Its first act was to tear my own copy of the monthly Magazine and then it tried to apologise to me by utterly demolishing a Cornhill. From its supposed great value it is not allowed to go into the streets yet and occupies its leisure with insane attacks upon a bear skin rug in the library. It will finish the work my nephew's rifle began in the Himmalaỹa. I see I cannot spell the word in any known form although I am printing it every month. Have you read the Abode of Snow [2]—not that it is by my nephew? I wish it was.

With best regards to Lewes and hoping to hear from you soon, I am
always yours truly
John Blackwood.

## GE TO SARA SOPHIA HENNELL, LONDON, 20 NOVEMBER 1874

*MS:* Yale. *Extracts published:* Cross, III, 244–245.

**The Priory, | 21. North Bank, | Regents Park.**
November 20. 74.

My dear Sara

How are you on this anniversary? [3] Without threat of troublesome winter cough, I trust—though colds seem to be the common lot at this season—and also with strength of body enough to enjoy the activity of your mind. I know you will let me have some news of you at this epoch, and please tell me about everything—Harriet and all other persons and things that affect your comfort.

From Mrs. Call [4] I have heard of Mr. Bray's increasing trouble with his asthma and of his visit to Bournemouth, with the conclusion that home is the best place for him. But I have heard no other particulars about the family well-being or the contrary so that any news you can tell me will be fresh.

2. After appearing serially in *Blackwood's* these articles by Andrew Wilson (1831–81) were published as *The Abode of Snow: Observations on a Journey from Chinese Tibet to the Indian Caucasus through the Upper Valleys of the Himalaya,* 1875.

3. Their birthdays.

4. "The Calls to lunch. Drove them home." (GHL Diary, 13 November 1874.)

We have spent this year in much happiness and are sorry to part with it. From the beginning of June to the end of September we had a house in Surrey, and enjoyed delicious quiet with daily walks and drives in the lovely scenery round Reigate and Dorking. October we spent in a country visit to friends and in a journey to Paris and through the Ardennes homeward, finishing off our travels by some excursions in our own country which we are ready to say we will never quit again—it is so much better worth knowing than most places one travels abroad to see. Now we are settled for the winter in the old spot. It has been a joy to us lately that our good Charles (father of two children and wearing spectacles) has been promoted to be the head of a department in the Post Office—a result of conscientious work and practical ability.[5]

We make ourselves amends for being in London by going to museums to see the wonderful works of men, and the other day I was taken over the Bank of England and to Woolwich arsenal[6]—getting object-lessons in my old age, you perceive.

Mr. Lewes is half through the proof-correcting of his second volume, and it will be matter of rejoicing when the other half is done, for we both hate proof-correcting (do you?)—the writing always seems worse than it really is, when one reads it in patches, looking out for mistakes. This is the gossip of our lives, and now give me yours.

I hear from Madame Bodichon that Miss Julia Smith has been with her at Hastings for a short time. What a beautiful, gentle old lady she is! The last time I talked to her she expressed very strongly the pleasure she had had in your society.

We have not yet read Mill's book[7] which everybody is talking about, preferring to wait so as not to be tempted into joining in the too hasty judgments which are being passed. I don't know whether you are interested in his opinions.

Please tell Cara that I shall expect soon to receive the account for the printing of her book, which I hope has gone on without let or

5. Charles Lee Lewes was promoted to First Class Clerk 31 October 1874. (Information from the Librarian and Archivist of the General Post Office.)

6. The National Gallery, 18 November; the South Kensington Museum, 19 November. At the Bank of England 17 November the "Album in which illustrious and royal visitors affixed their autographs to 1000 *l* notes was shown, and then Polly had to affix *her* autograph. Lunched at Johnnie's office and then per rail to Woolwich Arsenal—fatiguing and not very interesting." (GHL Diary.) Cf. GE's allusion to the Bank's "delicate machine for testing sovereigns" in "Shadows of the Coming Race," *Impressions of Theophrastus Such,* 1879, p. 300.

7. John Stuart Mill, *Three Essays on Religion: Nature, the Utility of Religion, Theism,* 1874.

hindrance. And give my love to her, please, and my sympathy to Mr. Bray in that worrying trial of asthma.

You all enjoyed the Handel Music in the summer?—And is the Sydenham house let again? I am so idle in correspondence myself that I don't deserve to have my questions answered, but please deal generously with me.

All possible comforts to you, dear Sara, would be among my first wishes if wishes would bring what I want.

Always your affectionate
Pollian.

## GE TO MRS. CHARLES BRAY, LONDON, 23 NOVEMBER 1874

*MS:* Yale. *Hitherto unpublished.*

**The Priory, | 21. North Bank, | Regents Park.**
November 23. 74.

My dear Cara

I am delighted to have the good news about the books. Especially I enjoy thinking that the little darkies in Hindustan will be the better for the work of your dear fair head.

Yes, I should like to have a proof (if it can be had in pages, for slips are too irritating) of Paul Bradly, just for the chance of getting anything done with it in Mrs. Schwabe's direction. She is not forthcoming just now, and may be in Italy for what I know, but she has a house in Clarges St. Piccadilly to which she comes from time to time, and I dare say she will show herself by and by. She is a dear benevolent widow, up to her chin in wealth, I suppose, and wanting to do good with it.

The plan of getting illustrations is a very happy one. I think, in the case of a book about animals, they will really help the moral effect by giving the children more vivid images of the creatures written about.

As to the printing, that is to be paid for irrespective of proceeds or profits, and is my contribution to your Society for the protection of animals.

Please thank Sara from me for her delightful letter, telling me news in her nice easy way, just as of old. In haste,

Your always loving
Marian.

## GE TO MRS. CHARLES BRAY, LONDON, 24 NOVEMBER 1874

*MS:* Yale. *Address:* Mrs. Charles Bray | 3 Barrs Hill Terrace | Coventry. *Postmark:* ST. JOHNS-WOOD | B5 | NO 24 | 74 | N.W. *Hitherto unpublished.*

November 24. 74.

D[ea]r C.

In my letter written last night I forgot to beg that you would give my affectionate return to Mrs. P.'s [8] kind greeting. Tell her that her words of remembrance are very welcome and dear to me.

M. E. L.

I had quite forgotten that I gave her that print, and am glad to find that I did so.

## GHL TO ALEXANDER MAIN, LONDON, [30 NOVEMBER 1874]

*Text:* Main's copy owned by Mr. John R. Sprunt. *Hitherto unpublished.*

**The Priory, | 21. North Bank, | Regents Park.**
Sunday.

My dear Main

We have returned from our continental trip in fairly good condition, and I am hard at work on the final proofs of Volume 2 while Mrs. Lewes advances with her new work. You need be under no anxiety about her beginning to publish until the whole is complete—or at least so much of it that no probable interruption would occur.

After leaving the country house we paid a visit in Cambridgeshire then went to Paris and through the Ardennes (visiting Sedan) to Brussels, going almost nightly to the theatre and leading a very holiday existence. The weather was transcendent. On our return home we started again for a tour through Wiltshire having long promised ourselves a sight of Salisbury plain and Stonehenge. This was a delightful tour though the weather was often wretched.

I have not seen Picton's book,[9] though your words about it will give it an interest for me should it fall in my way. I have too much to read for my own purposes—and in a quite different direction—to look after other people's speculations.

Reading the proofs of Vol. 2 is very dispiriting. All seems so dull

8. Mrs. Abijah Hill Pears.
9. James Allanson Picton (1832–1910), *The Mystery of Matter, and Other Essays,* 1873.

and incomplete. One wishes to have the whole thing rewritten—a wish checked by the knowledge that even then it would produce just the same effect! It is only by the response of other minds that one can ever feel lasting satisfaction. All I can console myself with is the consciousness that I have done my best to condense into a few chapters the best results of years of meditation. But it is not only the prosperity of a jest half of which lies in the hearer [1]—the prosperity of all writing half depends on the reader. The listener seldom brings any prepossession which will disturb the effect of the jest—but generally the reader brings his views, theories, superstitions to disturb the effect of a proposition.

Mrs. Lewes bids me send her affectionate remembrances.

Ever yours
G. H. L.

## DAVID MASSON TO GE, EDINBURGH, 1 DECEMBER 1874

*MS:* Alderman Library, University of Virginia. *Hitherto unpublished.*

10, Regent Terrace, | Edinburgh. | December 1, 1874.

Dear Mrs. Lewes,

You must let me thank you for your kind note, received two or three days ago.[2] It would have been a pleasure to me to learn in any way that you had found anything to like in the Milton book; and you have greatly increased the pleasure by taking the trouble to tell me the fact yourself. I am particularly glad too that you have fastened on that verse discussion and think it goes in the right direction. The gentleman of the "Five Iambi and nothing else" must be unique (who is he?); but the Iambic chant among even educated readers of blank verse has long troubled my soul, and I have also come upon many persons whose opinions seemed to be, as you say, that Prosody was in the beginning of things and that poets came later to be her ministers and reveal her to mortals.

With renewed thanks, and begging to be kindly remembered to Mr. Lewes, I am, dear Mrs. Lewes

Yours very truly,
David Masson.

1. *Love's Labour's Lost,* v, ii, 870

2. GE's note has not been found.

## GE TO MRS. MARK PATTISON, LONDON, 1 DECEMBER 1874

*MS:* British Museum. *Hitherto unpublished.*

**The Priory, | 21. North Bank, | Regents Park.**
December 1. 1874.

Thanks, dear Figliuolina, for your pretty and sympathetic deed.

Perhaps I shall see your smile above us in the concert room some Saturday, and then you will come and tell us everything left out of your letter. We are looking forward to the Rector's book—which is a great deal to say in these times.

Your always affectionate
Madre.

## GE TO THE HON. MRS. HENRY FREDERICK PONSONBY, LONDON, 10 DECEMBER 1874

*Text:* Cross, III, 245–250, and Magdalen Ponsonby, *Mary Ponsonby,* [1927] pp. 93–97.

**The Priory, | 21. North Bank, | Regents Park.**
*December* 10*th,* 1874.

My dear Mrs. Ponsonby,[3]

For some days after receiving your note with the photographs and accompanying papers, I was head-achy and deferred thanking you in the hope that I might bye-and-bye be able to write something more than—mere acknowledgment.

3. The Hon. Mary Elizabeth Bulteel (1832–1916), a granddaughter of Earl Grey, served as Maid of Honour from 1853 until her marriage in 1861 to Henry Frederick Ponsonby, Private Secretary and Equerry to Queen Victoria. As a girl she gave herself up to the most ardent High Church Anglicanism and thought of joining a sisterhood; but gradually her mind turned towards the agnosticism which she held the rest of her life. She was one of the original committee that founded Girton College, of which she was a member until her death. She was also one of the most active organizers of the first Trade Union for Women. See *Mary Ponsonby,* [1927], x, 227–8, xiv, xv. In Mrs. Ouvry's collection there is a 24-page letter from Mrs. Ponsonby dated October 1874 recounting her religious experience from the age of 16: She can't believe just because she wants to; "I would rather take chloral at once and deliver my soul and spirit . . . to Father Newman and say 'Let me do exactly what you have done and be at rest!'" She writes GE because she feels from her books that GE is in possession of some secret which makes it possible for her to combine sympathy for modern scientific thought with "approval for moral greatness and beauty and purity in the high ideals you would set before us."

I am deeply interested in what you have confided to me, and feel the confidence to be a strong link between us. But I fear that any such limited considerations as I could put before you, in the sort of letter which is all that I could manage to write specially to you at present, could hardly have much more efficacy than what you have found in my books, which have for their main bearing a conclusion the opposite of that in which your studies seem to have painfully imprisoned you—a conclusion without which I could not have cared to write any representation of human life—namely, that the fellowship between man and man which has been the principle of development, social and moral, is not dependent on conceptions of what is not man: and that the idea of God, so far as it has been a high spiritual influence, is the ideal of a goodness entirely human (i.e., an exaltation of the human).

Have you quite fairly represented yourself in saying that you have ceased to pity your suffering fellow-men, because you can no longer think of them, as individualities of immortal duration, in some other state of existence than this of which you know the pains and the pleasures?—that you feel less for them now you regard them as more miserable? And, on a closer examination of your feelings, should you find that you had lost all sense of quality in actions—all possibility of admiration that yearns to imitate—all keen sense of what is cruel and injurious—all belief that your conduct (and therefore the conduct of others) can have any difference of effect on the wellbeing of those immediately about you (and therefore on those afar off), whether you carelessly follow your selfish moods or encourage that vision of others' needs, which is the source of justice, tenderness, sympathy in the fullest sense? I cannot believe that your strong intellect will continue to see, in the conditions of man's appearance on this planet, a destructive relation to your sympathy: this seems to me equivalent to saying that you care no longer for colour, now you know the laws of the spectrum.

As to the necessary combinations through which life is manifested, and which seem to present themselves to you as a hideous fatalism, which ought logically to petrify your volition—have they, *in fact,* any such influence on your ordinary course of action in the primary affairs of your existence as a human, social, domestic creature? And if they don't hinder you from taking measures for a bath, without which you know you cannot secure the delicate cleanliness which is your second nature, why should they hinder you from a line of resolve in a higher strain of duty to your ideal, both for yourself and others? But the consideration of molecular physics is not the direct ground of human love and moral action, any more than it is the direct means of composing a noble picture or of enjoying great music. One might as well hope to dissect one's own body and be merry in doing it, as take molecular physics (in which you must banish from your field of view what is specifically human) to be your dominant guide, your determiner of motives, in what is solely human. That every study has its bearing on every other is true; but pain and relief, love and sorrow, have their peculiar history which make an experience and knowledge over and above the swing of atoms.

The teaching you quote as George Sand's would, I think, deserve to be called nonsensical if it did not deserve to be called wicked. What sort of "culture of the intellect" is that which, instead of widening the mind to a fuller and fuller response to all the elements of our existence, isolates it in a moral stupidity?—which flatters egoism with the possibility that a complex and refined human society can continue wherein relations have no sacredness beyond the inclination of changing moods?—or figures to itself an æsthetic human life that one may compare to that of the fabled grasshoppers who were once men, but having heard the song of the Muses could do nothing but sing, and starved themselves so till they died and had a fit resurrection as grasshoppers; and "this," says Socrates, "was the return the Muses made them." [3a]

With regard to the pains and limitations of one's personal lot, I suppose that there is not a single man, or woman, who has not more or less need of that stoical resignation which is often a hidden heroism, or who, in considering his or her past history, is not aware that it has been cruelly affected by the ignorant or selfish action of some fellow-being in a more or less close relation of life. And to my mind, there can be no stronger motive, than this perception, to an energetic effort that the lives nearest to us shall not suffer in a like manner from *us*.

The progress of the world—which you say can only come at the right time—can certainly never come at all save by the modified action of the individual beings who compose the world; and that we can say to ourselves with effect, "There is an order of considerations which I will keep myself continually in mind of, so that they may continually be the prompters of certain feelings and actions," seems to me as undeniable as that we can resolve to study the Semitic languages and apply to an Oriental scholar to give us daily lessons. What would your

3a. In *Phaedrus,* ch. 41, Plato has them become locusts.

keen wit say to a young man who alleged the physical basis of nervous action as a reason why he could not possibly take that course?

When I wrote the first page of this letter I thought I was going to say that I had not courage to enter on the momentous points you had touched on, in the hasty brief form of a letter. But I have been led on sentence after sentence—not, I fear, with any inspiration beyond that of my anxiety. You will, at least, pardon any ill-advised things I may have written on the prompting of the moment.

I hope that we shall see you before very long, and that you will always believe me,

Most sincerely yours,
M. E. Lewes.

P.S. As to duration, and the way in which it affects your views of the human history, what is really the difference to your imagination between Infinitude and billions, when you have to consider the value of human experience? Will you say that since your life has a term of threescore years and ten, it was really a matter of indifference whether you were a cripple with a wretched skin disease or an active creature with a mind at large for the enjoyment of knowledge and with a nature which has attracted others to you?

Difficulties of thought and acceptance of what is without full comprehension belong to every system of thinking. The question is to find the least incomplete.

## GE TO FREDERIC HARRISON, LONDON, 30 DECEMBER 1874

*MS:* Tinker Collection, Yale. *Hitherto unpublished.*

**The Priory, | 21. North Bank, | Regents Park.**
December 30. 74.

Dear Mr. Harrison

Is the legitimization of a son by act of Parliament so rare that it would be out of the probabilities for any Nob, or Snob who could pay for it? [4]

I make no apology for troubling you because I know by experience that you are glad to do a service.

Yours always sincerely
M. E. Lewes.

4. Was GE considering this course for Daniel Deronda, who suspected that he was the illegitimate son of Sir Hugo Mallinger?

## JOHN BLACKWOOD TO GE, EDINBURGH, 30 DECEMBER 1874

*MS:* National Library of Scotland. *Hitherto unpublished.*

3 Randolph Crescent
December 30/74.

My Dear Mrs. Lewes

I must not let the year slip away without writing all good wishes to Lewes and you in that which is now so close upon us. I do hope you are both well and facing the cold manfully. We are all well and happy, bar an obstinate little cough which keeps me off the Ice, as Curling, which next to Golf is the best game in the world, keeps one hanging about in the cold too much. I went out to the ice however yesterday to see my son and daughter skating and they were a neat little pair, though I say it. He is, I am sorry to say backward in all his studies, but he is a clever fellow. He did make me laugh this morning at breakfast. On pretext of seeing whether it would suit the ladies he had gone last night to the minor theatre here and gave a doubtful answer to his sister's question. I asked "Is it low?" "The dresses are," was his brief reply.

Will you look at a story Giannetto which begins the January number of Maga? There is only another part of it, and it strikes me as one of the most perfect stories of its kind I ever read. The writer is a young lady (23) [5] "a leddy o' high degree." In such cases one has usually to exhaust oneself in excuses, and my surprise and pleasure were great when I found this tale so good that I not only agreed to publish it as a little volume, but said I should like the readers of the Magazine to have the first of it. I shall be curious to hear what you think of it.

Pray give me any news of your approaching work and believe me

always yours truly
John Blackwood.

5. Lady Margaret Elizabeth, second daughter of the Earl of Crawford and Balcarres, married in 1870 Lewis Ashurst Majendie. "Gianetto," *Blackwood's,* 117 (January–February 1875), 1–31, 145–171.

## GHL TO WILLIAM KINGDON CLIFFORD, LONDON, [1874?]

*Text:* Mathilde Blind, *George Eliot,* 1883, p. 206.

Few things have given us more pleasure than the intimation in your note that you had a *fiancée.*[6] May she be the central happiness and motive force of your career, and, by satisfying the affections, leave your *rare* intellect free to work out its glorious destiny. For, if you don't become a glory to your age and time, it will be a sin and a shame. Nature doesn't often send forth such gifted sons, and when she does, Society usually cripples them. Nothing but marriage—a happy marriage—has seemed to Mrs. Lewes and myself wanting to your future.

6. William Kingdon Clifford married Lucy, daughter of John Lane, 7 April 1875. (*DNB.*)

# The Writing of *Daniel Deronda*

| | |
|---|---|
| *1875 January* | Frederic Harrison advises on legal problems in *Daniel Deronda.* |
| *1875 April 8* | GE and GHL dine at Lord Lytton's. |
| *1875 May 1–3* | Visit Jowett at Oxford. |
| *1875 June 17—September 23* | At Rickmansworth working on *Daniel Deronda.* |
| *1875 June 29* | Herbert Lewes dies in Natal. |
| *1875 July 8* | GHL presented to the Queen of Holland. |
| *1875 September 24—October 9* | Priory smelling of paint, GE and GHL go off to Wales. |
| *1875 October 20* | Publication of *Daniel Deronda* in 8 monthly parts decided on. |
| *1875 December 25* | GE has finished Book v; writing Book vi. |

## GE TO MR. AND MRS. ALBERT DRUCE, LONDON, 1 JANUARY 1875

*MS:* Miss Elsie Druce. *Hitherto unpublished.*

**The Priory, | 21. North Bank, | Regents Park.**
New Year's Day 1875.

Dear Friends

Let me tell you of our delight in the beautiful flowers which came an hour ago and in the friendship which sent them. Thanks seem to me somehow rather clumsy coarse things on such an occasion. I want you chiefly to know that your impulse in sending us that remembrance has been just as sweetly beneficent as you wished it to be. In haste, before going out,

Yours always affectionately
M. E. Lewes.

## GE TO FREDERIC HARRISON, LONDON, 1 JANUARY 1875

*MS:* Tinker Collection, Yale. *Envelope:* Frederic Harrison Esq. | 1 Southwick Place | W. *Postmarks:* ST. JOHNS-WOOD | B5 | JA 1 | 75 | N.W; LONDON-W. | JA | JA 1 | 75. *Hitherto unpublished.*

**The Priory, | 21. North Bank, | Regents Park.**
January 1. 75.

Dear Mr. Harrison

Many thanks for your kind reply. If you are so good as to write to me again after looking through the said lists, will you please tell me whether if A. B. were made legitimate he would as a matter of course inherit the successions or presumptive heirships of C. D.—including even the peerage—or simply the actual family estates?

Always yours truly
M. E. Lewes.

## GE TO ALEXANDER MAIN, LONDON, 2 JANUARY 1875

*Text:* Main's copy owned by Mr. John R. Sprunt. *Extracts published:* Cross, New Edition, pp. 534–535.

**The Priory, | 21. North Bank, | Regents Park.**
January 2. 1875.

My dear Mr. Main

Your New Year's affectionate greeting was very sweet and welcome to me. I missed nothing cordial and cheering in your letter except some assurance that this epoch finds you in outward peace and comfort as well as in inward steadfastness and joy in all goodness. It is your general fault to say nothing about that more solid measurable self which, however inferior and troublesome, is yet an inseparable companion of the more spiritual Alexander Main. I trust that you are free from domestic trouble and that your days are passed in satisfactory work.

On the other hand you usually want to know our bodily condition, and I can tell you now that we are both *un*usually well, having escaped cold in spite of the severe weather which has made victims of so many delicate and elderly persons.

Mr. Lewes's second volume is very nearly through the press, and he is already mastering with great zest the stores of long-gathered material for the psychological portion of his work.

You have probably heard from M. Ritter lately and have received his brochure of translations from some of the extracts made by you—translations which seem to me both careful and frequently felicitous. He sent me this little token with a charming letter yesterday,[1] which lay along with yours to gladden me when I went down to lunch. There is a quite peculiar grace in his letter-writing—do you not think so? This is the fourth year, I think, since your first letter, asking about the pronunciation of Romola, reached me in the country. How the little twig planted then has burgeoned and blossomed!—the best of blossoming being as you say the spiritual relation of conscious sympathy.

I want very much to be assured of your perpetual striving after excellence in all such ways as your life offers a path for. Because your excellence in anything is likely to bear fruit after our work is finished. You know I care as much for what is called private work as for public, and I believe in its incalculable efficacy.

1. With his letter dated Morges, Vaud, 29 December 1874 (Yale) Ritter sent 20 pages translated from Main's *Wise, Witty, and Tender Sayings . . . of George Eliot,* which he continued and published as *Fragments et pensées de George Eliot extraits et traduits de ses oeuvres,* Geneva, 1877. Main's letter, 30 December 1875 is in the NLS.

The minute hand of my clock tells me that I ought to be writing something else. This hasty note is only good for the true sign it gives of my constant regard and gratitude for your affectionate remembrance.

Mr. Lewes is below at his desk, but he has always friendly messages to you in his heart. And I am, as always,

Your sincere and affectionate Friend
M. E. Lewes.

## GE TO GEORGE SMITH, LONDON, 2 JANUARY 1875

*MS:* Sir John Murray. *Hitherto unpublished.*

**The Priory, | 21. North Bank, | Regents Park.**
January 2. 75.

Dear Mr. Smith

To be remembered by one's friends is among the best warming influences in this severe time, and I assure you that the beautiful box of Bonbons which came yesterday with your good wishes was in all senses sweet and welcome.

I think it is the thirteenth year since you first spent an evening with us in Blandford Square.[2] But I do not believe that thirteen is an unlucky number for us in any other way than by being one more than twelve—which is of consequence in the debt of years. I trust that this thirteenth year of our epoch will be to you one of unbroken health and happiness—family happiness which includes all the best things. Believe me

Always yours sincerely
M. E. Lewes.

## GE TO MRS. MARK PATTISON, LONDON, 3 JANUARY 1875

*MS:* British Museum. *Brief extract published:* C. W. Dilke, *The Book of the Spiritual Life,* 1905, p. 40.

**The Priory, | 21. North Bank, | Regents Park.**
January 3. 75.

My dear Goddaughter

A happy new year to you in the most prosperous industry! It was very dear of you to remember me and write me an interesting letter.

2. 23 January 1862.

But first about the "Isaac Casaubon." Mr. Lewes and I both cry out against the omission of that final chapter which must be needed as a spire to the edifice.[3] And it is unfair to those who buy the first edition, that such an advantage should be reserved for the second. But I suppose our crying out is in vain now. You should have called in a body of remonstrants before it was too late. What is the use of adapting good books to bad readers? Your picture of Mr. Heslop is really striking and has set me trying to imagine his strangely blended life. I should like to be able to put in the exact background and know how St. Bees'[4] looks.

We are uncommonly well—have got through the severe time without colds and are altogether as happy as two imperfect and worn mortals can be. Mr. Lewes's proofs of his second volume are to be all in by the 11th[5] and he is already busy mustering his stores for the psychological part of his work.

I enter into the Rector's weariness under his proof and revise reading. All writing seems to me worse in the state of proof than in any other form. In manuscript one's own wisdom is rather remarkable to one, but in proof it has the effect of one's private furniture repeated in the shop windows. And then there is the sense that the worst errors will go to press unnoticed!

I am glad to hear that you are so far on your way in your useful book.[6] Let us all consider ourselves privileged persons to be surviving in comfort while our fellow-men are shattered in railways and burnt at sea. Were there ever such horrors accumulated about one Christmas?[7]

Please, when you see Miss E. Smith, offer her my best remembrances and believe me

Always your affectionate
M. E. Lewes.

3. The final ch. of *Isaac Casaubon* discussing his religious attitudes is the same in the 1st ed., 1875 and the 2d, 1892.

4. In her next letter, Sunday [10 January 1875] Mrs. Pattison describes St. Bees, Cumberland: the theological college and its curious members—a broken-down cab driver, a grocer sick of spices, an Oxford man banished from College and Hall, who is married but can't get servants to stay with him because he won't let them wear flowers in their bonnets, etc. (Yale.)

5. He was still reading them 18 January 1875. (GHL Diary.)

6. *Renaissance of Art in France,* 1879.

7. On 24 December a railway wreck near Oxford killed 31 persons and a colliery exploded in Staffordshire, while 25 December news was received of the burning of the *Cospatrick,* an emigrant ship bound for New Zealand, with the loss of nearly 500. (*Annual Register,* 1874.)

## GE TO CHARLES RITTER, LONDON, 3 JANUARY 1875

*MS:* Bibliothèque Publique et Universitaire, Geneva. *Extracts published:* Cross, New Edition, p. 535.

**The Priory, | 21. North Bank, | Regents Park.**
January 3. 1875.

Dear M. Ritter

Your kind letter was among the most valued gifts of the New Year's Day. Like each former letter of yours it is made precious to me by being an expression not only of sympathy, but of a mind whose favourable judgment is a guarantee of the kind I most desire.

Both Mr. Lewes and I have read all the translated extracts and we think—always of course with diffidence as to our power of estimating the capabilities of a foreign language—that the evident care with which the meaning is rendered has been not seldom repaid by a felicity. We should both rejoice if you found satisfaction in carrying out the plan which you mention of further translation. I understand your discontent with your own rendering. No one language is completely furnished with verbal and idiomatic equivalents for another, and it is easier to produce something better than the original than what is everywhere exactly equivalent to it. Nevertheless careful translation is a beneficent work. And if there is any help toward a nobler life to be got out of a book, surely the French literature of our times has need of it!

I am delighted with what you write about my husband's books. Imagine a man as objectively absorbed as it is possible to be in the work he is doing *for its own sake,* quite free from oblique glances at minor results, knowing nothing of jealousy, and open as day to sympathy in the work of others: you have then imagined my husband. He gets more pleasure out of any work of mine than I do, and he especially enjoys the delicacy of your appreciations.

I suffer always increasingly from doubt as to the quality of what I am actually doing. Just now I am writing a new novel (which will not be ready for a long while to come), but if it were not for his firmness of opinion as to the worth of what is already written I could not carry out my intention. In this way he has always supported me—by his unreserved sympathy and the independence of his judgment.

I trust that your health is undisturbed by the severities of the winter, and that your life has as equable a flow of happiness as we susceptible mortals can reasonably expect in the vast entanglements of the world.

I am glad to think that you have some communication with our young friend Mr. Main (whom also I have never seen).[8] Your fine, experienced criticism might be of much service to him in his efforts as a writer.

Mr. Lewes unites with me in high and grateful regards towards a friend who seems to be near to us in spite of miles and mountains, and who has been among our valued possessions ever since the arrival of that letter announcing the volume of Strauss's Essays in the summer of 1872. Believe me, my dear Sir,

Always yours most sincerely
M. E. Lewes.

M. Charles Ritter.

## GE TO FREDERIC HARRISON, LONDON, 7 JANUARY 1875

*MS:* Tinker Collection, Yale. *Envelope:* Frederic Harrison Esq | 1 Southwick Place | Hyde Park Square | W. *Postmark:* LONDON-N.W | B4 | JA 7 | 75; LONDON-W. | HA | 7. *Hitherto unpublished.*

**The Priory, | 21. North Bank, | Regents Park.**
January 7. 75.

Dear Mr. Harrison

Pardon my troubling you to give me one more 'response.' I have been looking into Williams on Real Property,[9] but cannot get clear as to the frequency and strict necessity of resettlements of estates in tail. Pray give me a little light on the following case.

Sir A. B. Bart., having resettled the estate (in tail general) on his marriage, has issue, two sons C. and D.

C. remains unmarried till latish in life, while D. marries early and has a son E.

Afterwards, when this son E. is already of age, C. marries and has no other issue than three daughters.[1] What resettlements would probably have taken place?

And if E. died without issue while C. was still living, would the inheritance go to the three daughters equally, spite of the father C.?—

8. Main wrote GE 15 January 1875 that Ritter, as she supposed, had also sent him his translations. (NLS.)

9. Joshua Williams, *Principles of the Law of Real Property, Intended as a First Book for the Use of Students in Conveyancing,* 2d ed., 1849.

1. In *Daniel Deronda* Sir A. B. Bart., became Sir Francis Mallinger; C, Sir Hugo Mallinger; D, his brother, the father of E, Henleigh Mallinger Grandcourt; and the three daughters, Sir Hugo's.

the baronetcy becoming extinct—or would the whole power over the estate revert to C., so that he could resettle it as he liked? And if the estate went to the daughters would the baronetcy go off to a distant male branch?

I wish I had all knowledge so as to do without taxing your precious time. And I might have hunted further, but as that solitary hunting might be unsuccessful after all, I send this note in time (it is to be hoped) to save you from writing me two letters instead of one.

Yours always gratefully
M. E. Lewes.

## GE TO FREDERIC HARRISON, LONDON, 8 JANUARY 1875

*MS:* Tinker Collection, Yale. *Envelope:* Frederic Harrison Esq | 1 Southwick Place | Hyde Park Square | W. *Postmarks:* ST. JOHNS-WOOD | C5 | JA 8 | 75 | N.W; LONDON-W. | JA | JA 8 | 75. *Hitherto unpublished.*

**The Priory, | 21. North Bank, | Regents Park.**
January 8. 75.

Dear Mr. Harrison

I am hating myself for having caused you any extra work when you were already overladen, and especially sorry that I did not say "There is no hurry." I can wait for anything further until you are at leisure—which I imagine you will hardly be by Saturday. On almost all days we are at home again after our drive and walk by 5 o'clock, and ready to chat.

Your letter—for which I am sorrowfully grateful—contains probably as much as I shall need, but a question or two might arise which you could easily settle for me in conversation.

Pray remember that I am in no haste. I am only needing the facts prospectively, and needing them rather as ground for feeling to act on, than as materials for exact statement.

Yours always sincerely
M. E. Lewes.

## GE TO MRS. ELMA STUART, LONDON, 10 JANUARY 1875

*MS:* British Museum. *Published with incomplete facsimile:* Stuart, pp. 36–40.

**The Priory, | 21. North Bank, | Regents Park.**
January 10. 1875.

Dearest Elma

Your letter made the best part of my breakfast this morning. I *was* sorry that you had to keep your bed (though I am not consciously open to the accusation of having sent you there). But now the sorrow seems like a dispersed but once clinging mist, which has given way to the usual warm sunshine surrounding my idea of you. It is really a cordial to me to know that you are well again. And you will be good and careful henceforth, won't you?—keeping a spiritual scourge for that naughty spiritual self which afflicts its fleshly yoke-fellow. It is of no use asking advice against your sins if you don't take care of your body, and let it get distempered by fitful habits which are the makers of new sins. But I am not writing for the sake of this lecture, being inclined to believe you blameless until I have evidence of the contrary.

As to your intolerance, dear child, I like a little unselfish indignation, and think one's soul can hardly be healthy without it. Only, of course it needs constant checking by a vision of life in that other aspect —that he who hates vices too much hates men, or is in danger of it, and also may have no blame to spare for himself. If moral indignation can be well tempered with self-blame, surely it is a good thing. I am very fond of that old Greek saying that the best state is that in which every man feels a wrong done to another as if it were done to himself.[2] Better have an ideal of right-doing that makes you by chance flog a cruel Frenchman,[3] than have no ideal at all. Caring for the just and loving deed of every day in your part of Dinan carries your heart strongly to every other part of the world which in its need of love and justice is just in the same predicament, and in this way you get a religion which is at once universal and private. So I should not like to see you quite dispassionate in the presence of ugly conduct.

2. Not traced.

3. When a French road-mender was about to throw a stone at her little terrier, which was fighting with his dog, Mrs. Stuart "seized the man by his shirt-collar, and gave him a good thrashing with her dog-whip. To do the man justice, I must admit that he took his thrashing in good part and made no attempt to retaliate." (Roland Stuart's note, p. 35.)

But your trouble about your mother [4] touches me more nearly. The parting will have to come—I have known twice over at widely different ages and in quite a different way, what the final parting with a parent is. But now I imagine from your description of your mother that the solemn trial may be deferred for years: you spoke of her, I think, as having a fine strong physique, and I remember her photograph.

As for the news of us on which you insist, it is altogether good. We have both been exceptionally well this winter, and have quite escaped colds, until this morning that Mr. Lewes complains of slight sore throat. He has nearly done correcting the proofs of his second volume, and is already happy amidst the manuscript for a third. I am busy—which means not that I am doing *much* but that I am always *doing*. Small claims multiply; and that is the reason why I am obliged to restrict letter-writing as much as possible, because the various divisions of my day are so filled that the absolutely necessary answers to correspondents are all my feebleness can manage without infringing on my morning hours from 9 to 1, which are my only hours for writing. And I am writing a book—since you wish to know that, I tell it you. But I am not fond of announcing that fact, because I never feel any confidence that I can do anything until it is ready for the word, *Finis*. Always there is the possibility of breaking down, or of doing what is too poor to afflict the world with. For our world is already sufficiently afflicted with needless books, and I count it a social offence to add to them.

My best love to Roly. And I say 'Amen' to the answer you gave him about the orchard-robbing. Ask him whether he intends to steal venison because Shakspeare did? If so we will only forgive him on condition that he writes Hamlets, Macbeths, Lears and 'As-you-like-its.' I sympathize with the love of a foray, but the lads should properly have to go through a skirmish, and not carry off their spoil quite easily.

Once more, dearest daughter, keep well. And be sure always that you come to my thoughts among the blessings which life has given me—that I am

Your always mindful and loving spiritual Mother,
M. E. Lewes

Please not to let anyone read my letters except yourself.[5]

4. Dame May Anne Cumming (Fraser) Coxe, wife of Sir James Coxe, M.D. of Kinellan, near Edinburgh.

5. This postscript is omitted in Stuart and deleted from the facsimile.

## JOHN BLACKWOOD TO GHL, EDINBURGH, 11 JANUARY 1875

*MS:* National Library of Scotland. *Hitherto unpublished.*

**45, George Street, | Edinburgh.**
January 11/75.

My Dear Lewes

I have the pleasure of inclosing statement [6] of Mrs. Lewes' Works for the past year and a cheque for the balance £864-0-6d. I hope you will both be pleased with the result, which I do think very satisfactory. Middlemarch is a subject for immense congratulation. If you look at the dates of the reprints you will see the pace at which the sale has gone on and I do not hear of any symptoms of flagging yet. No previous experience could have led us to expect such a rapid and extended sale in the 7/6 form and it is most satisfactory to think that the right course has been adopted throughout with this great book.

The steady continuous sale of Jubal and The Spanish Gypsy is well and will I daresay please Mrs. Lewes quite as much as the success of their big brother. The Gypsy is just reprinted.[7]

Comparing the statement with that rendered at the same time last year will I think enable you to understand this one, but if you are in the slightest doubt about anything, write.

It gave me great pleasure to receive Mrs. Lewes' truly gratifying expression of good wishes at the turn of the year, and I hope this will find you both well. Your being threatened with gout is hard. Nobody can say of you, "Ye've wrought well for it," which is a consolatory phrase I have heard addressed to myself in early days.

I have got quit of the cold which has been bothering me almost ever since I came from the country. The final remedy was I think Musselburgh, where I went on Saturday. It came on to rain so I did not play but walked for several hours with a greatcoat and umbrella, watching a good match in a deluge of rain. I felt that I could not logically defend my conduct and I was in a horrid fright all night lest I should begin coughing, but I did not.

Willie joins me in best remembrances to Mrs. Lewes and believe me

always yours truly
John Blackwood.

H. G. Lewes Esq.

6. In Mrs. Ouvry's collection.

7. A 5th edition of 525 copies.

MIDDLEMARCH

in eight parts 5/-

| | I | II | III | IV | V | VI | VII | VIII |
|---|---|---|---|---|---|---|---|---|
| On hand Jany 1874 | 5 | 4 | 0 | 97 | 42 | 70 | 61 | 0 |

There are at present rather more than these quantities in hand in consequence of our having taken odd parts in exchange when it was politic to do so from parties who purchased more than the equivalent value of the guinea Edition.

Ditto in 4 Vols. @ 21/-

| | | |
|---|---|---|
| On hand Jany 1874 | 329 Copies | |
| Do Jany 1875 | 140 | |
| Sold | 189 | |

Ditto in one Volume

| | | | |
|---|---|---|---|
| 1874 May | Printed | 3150 Copies | |
| June | Do | 2100 | |
| August | Do | 2100 | |
| Septr | Do | 2100 | |
| Novr | Do | 3700 | |
| | | 13150 | |
| | Copies to Author and Libraries | 12 | |
| | " on hand Decr 31 | 2631 | 2643 |
| | Sold | | 10507 |

JUBAL 1st Edition

| | | | |
|---|---|---|---|
| 1874 May | Printed | | 1591 Copies |
| | Copies delivered | | |
| | Author | 21 | |
| | Reviewers etc. | 77 | 98 |
| | Sold | | 1493 |

JUBAL 2nd Edition

| | | |
|---|---|---|
| 1874 August | Printed | 1313 Copies |
| | On hand December 1874 | 838 |
| | Sold | 475 |

THE SPANISH GYPSY 4th Edition

| | | |
|---|---|---|
| 1874 January | Copies on hand | 197 |
| | All sold | |

Royalty payable on

| | | | |
|---|---|---|---|
| 189 | Copies less 25th Book Middlemarch 4 Vols. 21/- | @ 5/- | 45.10. |
| 2000 | Copies Middlemarch in one volume per agreement | | 50. |
| 8507 | Copies less 25th Book Ditto | @ 1/6 | 612.10.6 |
| 1493 | Copies less 25th Book Jubal 1st Edition | @ 1/6 | 107.11. |
| 475 | Copies less 25th Book Ditto 2nd Edition | @ 1/6 | 34. 4. |
| 197 | Copies less 25th Book Spanish Gypsy 4th Edition | @ 1/6 | 14. 5. |
| | | | £864. 0.6 |

## GE JOURNAL, LONDON, 13 JANUARY 1875

*MS:* Yale. *Published:* Cross, III, 250–251.

January 13. 1875. Here is a great gap since I last made a record! [1] But the time has been filled full of happiness. Yesterday I received from Blackwood the last year's account of Middlemarch, Jubal and the Spanish Gypsy, amounting to £860. Of Jubal a second edition was published in August and the 4th edition of the Spanish Gypsy is all sold. This morning I received a copy of the 5th edition. The amount of copies sold of Middlemarch up to December 31 is between 19 and 20,000.[2]

Yesterday I also received the good news that the engagement between Emily Cross and Mr. Otter is settled.[3]

The last year has been crowded with proofs of affection for me and of value for what work I have been able to do. This makes the best motive or encouragement to do more; but as usual I am suffering much from doubt as to the worth of what I am doing and fear lest I may not be able to complete it so as to make it a contribution to literature and not a mere addition to the heap of books. I am now just beginning the part about Deronda, at p. 234.[4]

## GE TO EMILY CROSS, LONDON, [13 JANUARY 1875]

*Text:* Copy [by Mrs. Otter?], Yale. *Hitherto unpublished.*

Dearest Emily,

I had a letter from "you know whom" last night, but I needed yours of this morning to give the finish to my joy.[5] What you say has comforted my heart and set it quite at rest. The future must always be in one sense dark, but with a deep love which enables us to be the light and bliss of another, we can never be without reason for saying "I am glad that I have lived." That is really the highest good of a wife—to be quite <certain> sure in the midst of the dimness and doubt which this difficult world surrounds us with, that there is one close to her

1. The last entry was 19 May 1874; the next is on Christmas Day 1875.

2. See also GE's Record of Literary Earnings, Appendix I.

3. Francis Otter (1832–95), eldest son of Francis Otter of Ranby Hall, Louth, Lincolnshire, B.A. 1854, Corpus Christi College, Oxford, of which he was a Fellow 1859–75, Tutor and Vice-president 1871.

4. The end of ch. 15.

5. "Otter wrote to say he was engaged to Emily Cross." (GHL Diary, 12 January 1875.)

whose life is every day the better for her. I do believe and hope that you will know this.

And please don't worry yourself about "cleverness," which is a doubtful sort of condiment or "Kitchen" to the excellent wheaten bread of a loving truthful woman's <heart> nature. Cleverness often leaves people very stupid about the best knowledge. If you were going to marry a shallow, green sentimentalist whose supposed affection might turn out to be a changeful fancy, I should wish him to get cleverness in return as the best he deserved. But you are going, I believe to marry a man of large comprehension and with that depth of feeling which means fidelity. You know how thoroughly your uncle enters into this happiness. I think he is writing to Mrs. Cross, and will ask her about the possibility of her coming to us with you. That might be too great an effort for her and I fear to urge it. Always dear child

Your loving Aunt
M. E. Lewes.

## GE TO FRANCIS OTTER, LONDON, 13 JANUARY 1875

*Text:* Cross, III, 251–252.

Your letter was a deeply-felt pleasure to me last night; and I have one from Emily this morning, which makes my joy in the prospect of your union as thorough as it could well be. I could not wish either her words or yours to be in the least different. Long ago, when I had no notion that the event was probable, my too hasty imagination had prefigured it and longed for it. To say this, is to say something of the high regard with which all I have known of you has impressed me—for I hold our sweet Emily worthy of one who may be reckoned among the best. The possibility of a constantly growing blessedness in marriage is to me the very basis of good in our mortal life; and the believing hope that you and she will experience that blessedness, seems to enrich me for the coming years. I shall count it among my strengthening thoughts that you both think of me with affection, and care for my sympathy. Mr Lewes shares in all the feelings I express, and we are rejoicing together.

## GHL TO MRS. WILLIAM CROSS, LONDON, [13 JANUARY 1875]

*MS:* Yale. *Hitherto unpublished.*

**The Priory, | 21. North Bank, | Regents Park.**
Wednesday.

Dear dear Friend

Since all that befals you of good or evil befals us you may imagine the delight with which last night we heard from Otter, and this morning the still more gratifying confirmation from Emily of her state of mind. We think him an extremely lucky fellow but we have also so high an opinion of him that long ago we used often to wish he would fall in love with one of the doves. Nothing we have heard for a long time has been such a real joy to us—as of course it is to all of you.

Now won't you bring the 'blushing bride' to see us? so that we may have a look into your dear face, which has been so long a stranger to our eyes. Come to lunch on Monday or Tuesday next or any day that will suit.[6] You may have much to do just now, but you must give us one day. Madonna sends her love and blessings

Ever yours affectionately
G. H. L.

## GE TO MRS. CHARLES BRAY, LONDON, 14 JANUARY 1875

*MS:* Yale. *Endorsed:* Mr. Fiske. *Hitherto unpublished.*

**The Priory, | 21. North Bank, | Regents Park.**
January 14. 1875.

Dear Cara

Herewith the cheque for £ 28.10.[7] I am very glad to see the specimen of the Animal World. The portrait of the dear donkey on the right hand side I am sure must be edifying. The plan of getting illustrations in this way seems to me most fortunate.

Then about the Blood. Mr. Lewes says, 'Yes, the red colour *is* rust' (until further notice).

The news of you all is very welcome—that about Sara delightful. We are very well, having gone through the severe weather without once taking cold.

6. "Mrs. Cross and Emily to lunch." (GHL Diary, Tuesday, 19 January 1875.)

7. Entered in GHL's Diary under Charities for "Mrs. Bray's book."

Mr. Fiske used to come to us sometimes while he was in England. A large-headed man with rather a good-looking face—what Milton might call a "bush with frizzy hair implicit" [8]—staring at you as if in spell-bound silence when he put out his hand to say goodbyes and altogether rather in the heavy style. Yet he is not at all a heavy writer.

I hope you got a card from me some time ago, correcting my omission to return dear Mrs. Pears's greeting in my [*The second page has been cut away.*]

## GE TO MRS. PETER ALFRED TAYLOR, LONDON, 15 JANUARY 1875

*Text:* Cross, III, 252–253.

Please never wonder at my silence, or believe that I bear you in any the less lively remembrance because I do not write to you.

Writing notes is the *crux* of my life. It often interferes with my morning hours (before 1 o'clock), which is the only time I have for quiet work. For certain letters are unavoidable demands; and though my kind husband writes them for me whenever he can, they are not all to be done by proxy.

That glorious bit of work of yours about the Home for Girls [9] is delightful to hear of. Hardly anything is more wanted, I imagine, than homes for girls in various employments—or rather for unmarried women of all ages.

I heard also the other day that your name was among those of the ladies interested in the beginning of a union among the bookbinding women, which one would like to succeed and spread.

I hope, from your ability to work so well, that you are in perfect health yourself. Our friend Barbara, too, looks literally the pink of well-being, and cheers one's soul by her interest in all worthy things.

8. *Paradise Lost,* VII, 323.
9. Young Women Servants' Temporary Home, 1 Bessborough Gardens, London.

## GHL TO MRS. ELMA STUART, LONDON, 27 JANUARY 1875

*MS:* British Museum. *Published:* Stuart, pp. 40–41.

**The Priory, | 21. North Bank, | Regents Park.**
27 January 75.

Dear Elma

You need no assurance from us that everything which befals you touches us nearly, and that we deeply sympathize with you in your present trouble.[1] It is only as a silent pressure of the hand that this comes. Words are necessarily vain, except as an indication of sympathy, in sorrows that must be borne and cannot be alleviated.

If on your way back to France you pause in London, and it would give you the slightest comfort to hear a word of love from Madonna, come with full assurance. We could give you a bed if you would like it.

Ever your loving
G. H. Lewes.

## GE TO THE HON. MRS. HENRY FREDERICK PONSONBY, LONDON, 30 JANUARY 1875

*Text:* Cross, III, 253.

I should urge you to consider your early religious experience as a portion of valid knowledge, and to cherish its emotional results in relation to objects and ideas which are either substitutes or metamorphoses of the earlier. And I think we must not take every great physicist—or other "ist"—for an apostle, but be ready to suspect him of some crudity concerning relations that lie outside his special studies, if his exposition strands us on results that seem to stultify the most ardent, massive experience of mankind, and hem up the best part of our feelings in stagnation.

1. The death of her mother, Lady Coxe, 25 January 1875.

## GHL TO MRS. ELMA STUART, LONDON, [2? FEBRUARY 1875]

*MS:* British Museum. *Endorsed:* early in <1874> 1875. *Published:* Stuart, pp. 41–42.

**The Priory, | 21. North Bank, | Regents Park.**
Tuesday.

Dear Elma

It is not to thank you for the lovely *table* (and the thoughtful tenderness of the additions) because you said I was not to thank you—and because I can't properly express on paper in blue ink what is written on my heart in red ink. It is for another purpose I write—to beg you to dismiss from your mind the very preposterous anxiety lest your visits or letters should ever be other than a delight to us. Because we seclude ourselves from acquaintance that makes us only the more glad to have friends, and you are one of the *inner circle.*

Therefore as you value my approbation, and your own peace of mind, no more of the old hesitation and reticence!

You may have your time fully occupied while passing through London. We would not stand in your way; only mind and let us have the unoccupied hours. Surely you might spend the afternoon and evening with us?[2]

Understand that you are to fix your own times, but understand also that any doubt of your presence here being otherwise than delightful to us is an offence against friendship. [Madonna sends her dearest love and a kiss.

Ever your loving
G. H. L.][3]

2. She dined with them 15 February. Three days later GHL writes: "Elma to lunch. She showed us the handkerchief with which she had wiped the tears from Polly's eyes, and henceforth has preserved as a *relic.*" (GHL Diary, 18 February 1875.)

3. This passage has been cut out of the MS. A pencil note reads: "Augt. 10. 1881. Boyd's Lodge, Malvern. The bit cut out was to put below his picture and ran thus—"

## GE TO FREDERICK LOCKER, LONDON, 6 FEBRUARY 1875

*MS:* Harvard. *Address:* Frederick Locker Esq | 25 Chesham Street | S.W. *Postmark:* ST. JOHN'S WOOD | B 5 | FE 6 | 75. *Hitherto unpublished.*

**The Priory, | 21. North Bank, | Regents Park.**
February 6. 75.

My dear Mr. Locker

It is always a real pleasure to me to see you, and we shall be very glad to make Mrs. Locker's acquaintance.[4] But at present I find a difficulty in making any appointment for a weekday. Sunday is the only day on which I can promise to be at home. I will hope that we may have the benefit of an exception to Mrs. Locker's rule. We belong entirely to our friends from ½ past 2 till 6 on a Sunday.

I am grieved to hear that gentle Mrs. Tennyson is an invalid.[5] She must be very precious to both husband and sons.

With our united best remembrances, I am always

Sincerely yours
M. E. Lewes.

## GE TO JOHN BLACKWOOD, LONDON, 7 FEBRUARY 1875

*MS:* National Library of Scotland. *Mostly published:* Cross, III, 253–255.

**The Priory, | 21. North Bank, | Regents Park.**
February 7. 75.

My dear Mr. Blackwood

Last night I finished reading aloud to Mr. Lewes the Inkerman volume,[6] and we both thank you heartily for the valuable present. It is an admirable piece of writing. Such pure, lucid English is what one rarely

4. After the death of his first wife in 1872, Locker married 6 July 1874 Hannah Jane Lampson, daughter of Sir Curtis Miranda Lampson, a native of Vermont, who had become a naturalized British subject in 1848 and was created a baronet in 1866 for his work on the Atlantic cable. In 1885 Locker added Lampson to his name.

5. Mrs. Alfred Tennyson fell ill in the autumn of 1874 and was almost entirely confined to her sofa for the rest of her life. See Hallam Tennyson, *Alfred Lord Tennyson. A Memoir,* 2 vols., 1898, II, 157.

6. *The Battle of Inkerman,* 1875, Vol. V of A. W. Kinglake's *The Invasion of the Crimea,* 8 vols., 1863–1887.

gets to read. The masterly marshalling of the material is certainly in contrast with the movements described. To my non-military mind the Inkerman affair seems nothing but a brave blundering into victory. Great traits of valour—Homeric moments—but also a powerful lack of brains in the form of generalship. I cannot see that the ordering up of the two 18-pounder guns [7] was a vast mental effort, unless the weight of the guns is to be counted in the order as well as the execution. But the grand fact of the thousands beaten by the hundreds remains under all interpretations. Why the Russians in their multitudinous mass should have chosen to retreat into Sebastopol, moving at their leisure and carrying off all their artillery, seems a mystery in spite of General Dannenberg's memorable answer to Mentschikoff.[8]

There are some splendid moments in the story—the tradition of a Minden yell, the "Men, remember Albuera," and the officer of the 77th advancing with "Then I will go by myself," with what followed, are favourite bits of mine.[1] My mind is in this anomalous condition of hating war and loving its discipline, which has been an incalculable contribution to the sentiment of duty. I have not troubled myself to read any reviews of the book. My eye caught one in which the author's style was accused of affectation. But I have long learned to apply to reviews an aphorism which tickled me in my childhood—"There must be some such to be some of all sorts."

Pray tell Mr. Simpson that I was much pleased with the new dress of the "Spanish Gypsy." I waited for this occasion of writing, to tell him so.

The first part of "Gianetto" [2] raised my interest, but I was disappointed in the unravelling of the plot. It seems to me neither really nor ideally satisfactory. But it is a long while since I read a story newer than Rasselas, which I re-read two years ago with a desire to renew my childish delight in it, when it was one of my best-loved companions. So I was a bad judge of comparative merits among popular writers. I am obliged to fast from fiction, and fasting is known sometimes to weaken the stomach. I ought to except Miss Thackeray's stories, which I cannot resist when they come near me—and bits of Mr. Trollope, for affection's sake. You would not wonder at my fasting if you knew how deplorably uncalled for and "everything-that-it-should-not-be" my own

7. By Lord Raglan, pp. 129, 374.

8. General Dannenberg ordered the Russians to retreat to avoid their complete destruction. When Prince Mentschikoff, who was nominally in command, protested, Dannenberg said: "If your Highness thinks otherwise, have the goodness to give the orders yourself, and take from me the command." (p. 434.)

1. For these episodes see pp. 308, 310, 425.

2. See 30 December 1874.

fiction seems to me in times of inward and outward fog—like this morning when the light is dim on my paper.

Always yours truly
M. E. Lewes.

## GE TO THE HON. MRS. HENRY FREDERICK PONSONBY, LONDON, 11 FEBRUARY 1875

*Text:* Cross, III, 255–256.

*Do* send me the papers you have written—I mean as a help and instruction to me. I need very much to know how ideas lie in other minds than my own, that I may not miss their difficulties while I am urging only what satisfies myself. I shall be deeply interested in knowing exactly what you wrote at that particular stage. Please remember that I don't consider myself a teacher, but a companion in the struggle of thought. What can consulting physicians do without pathological knowledge?—and the more they have of it, the less absolute—the more tentative—are their procedures.

You will see by the 'Fortnightly,' [3] which you have not read, that Mr Spencer is very anxious to vindicate himself from neglect of the logical necessity that the evolution of the abstraction "society" is dependent on the modified action of the units; indeed he is very sensitive on the point of being supposed to teach an enervating fatalism.

Consider what the human mind *en masse* would have been if there had been no such combination of elements in it as has produced poets. All the philosophers and *savants* would not have sufficed to supply that deficiency. And how can the life of nations be understood without the inward light of poetry—that is, of emotion blending with thought?

But the beginning and object of my letter must be the end—please send me your papers.

3. J. E. Cairnes reviewed *The Principles of Sociology* for the *Fortnightly:* "Mr. Spencer on Social Evolution," 23 (January–February 1875), 63–82, 200–213. Spencer appended "A Note on the Preceding Article," pp. 214–216 denying that he said evolution eliminated the need for altruistic motives.

## GHL TO ALEXANDER MAIN, LONDON, [12 FEBRUARY 1875]

*Text:* Main's copy owned by Mr. John R. Sprunt. *Hitherto unpublished.*

**The Priory, | 21. North Bank, | Regents Park.**
Friday.

My dear Main

I should be glad if the second volume contains any real food for you—mystical or non-mystical. We have observed with some surprise (not suspecting you of philosophic studies) a keen insight in such matters—probably here as elsewhere insight comes from sympathy, as, according to my doctrine, all cognition is primarily emotion. Certainly no one ever really understood an opinion until he had learned to see it as it presented itself to the mind which formulated it. I shall send you Vol. 2 in a few days. You would have had the first had I thought it likely to be so much to your taste.

Mrs. Lewes is pretty well and hard at work—despairing over it, of course,—*aliter non fit liber*—at least with her. I am and have been for some time supremely happy in my work, having got away from hated metaphysics into dear Biology and Psychology. If ever you see a duck painfully picking its way over the stones, and then, when it has reached the water, complacently wagging its tail, and turning round its head with an air of calm content at finding itself once more in its element, think of me as I *was* during the last two years, and as I *am* just now. If I wag my tail a little, don't call it conceit so much as Elemental Complacency! Mrs. Lewes told me when I wrote to you to send some pretty message from her—and I send it. You remember Quintus Fixlein in Jean Paul [4] who was all his life occupied with a work on Errata, which contained important moral conclusions, he said, and —advised the reader to draw them.

Ever yours
G. H. L.

4. GE and GHL were reading Jean Paul Richter's *Quintus Fixlein* aloud, 17 December 1870. (GE Journal.)

## GE TO FREDERIC HARRISON, LONDON, 19 FEBRUARY 1875

*MS:* Tinker Collection, Yale. *Envelope:* Frederic Harrison Esq | 1 Southwick Place | Hyde Park Square | W. *Postmarks:* ST. JOHNS-WOOD | B5 | FE 19 | 75 | N.W; LONDON-W | JA | FE 19 | 75. *Hitherto unpublished.*

21 North Bank | February 19. 75.

Dear Mr. Harrison

Apropos of the case we talked of,[5] according to your kind advice, I abstain from reading law-books and apply again to you.

B[6] has a life interest in estates which, failing male issue from him, will go to C (his nephew) as heir in tail. As you observed, men in that relation might easily hate each other. But I want certain conditions, *founded on the relation,* which would make them wish to suppress any show of dislike and would give them a mutual sense of self-interest in being friendly.

Can you give me any indications that would help me?—any probable conditions that would answer my purpose? I confine myself to the barest statement of my need, because I think that will save you trouble. If I said more I might only give you irrelevancies to be "écartées."

We have received the great vol. I of the *Politique,*[7] and last night I read Dr. Bridges' admirable rendering of the Preface and Dedication.

Always yours truly
M. E. Lewes.

## GE TO OSCAR BROWNING, LONDON, 2 MARCH 1875

*Text:* O. Browning, *Life of George Eliot,* 1890, p. 122.

Your letter shall be sacred. I am glad to know that you have made up your mind to endure and persevere—words easy to write as advice, but hard to follow out in the patient action of days, months, years. Perhaps the most difficult heroism is that which consists in the daily conquests of our private demons, not in the slaying of world-notorious dragons. Certainly it seems to me that the finest course of action you can pursue will be to impose the utmost restraint on impatience, and

5. When he and Mrs. Harrison lunched at the Priory, 17 January 1875. (GHL Diary.)

6. B is here Sir Hugo Mallinger and C his nephew Grandcourt.

7. Comte's *System of Positive Polity,* Vol. I translated by John Henry Bridges, 1875.

look at your life simply as the problem of carrying out your ideas of usefulness at Eton as far as may be without dangerous collisions.[8] To further this happiness and beneficence of your life—even apart from that question of your dear mother's feeling—you should have a precise conception of an alternative to your present task,[9] an equivalent social contribution, before you unlink yourself. But I gather that your resolution is thoroughly formed, and I rejoice.

We shall see you at the end of this fiercely menacing March. You are young enough to dare travel at that time of year which we used to find everywhere cruel, south as well as north.

## GE TO MRS. ELMA STUART, LONDON, 4 MARCH 1875

*MS:* British Museum. *Published:* Stuart, pp. 42–44.

**The Priory, | 21. North Bank, | Regents Park.**
March 4. 75.

Dearest Elma

Yes! the beautiful Saint Esprit came duly, and I must have been in a state of more than usually dulled sensibility or I should have sent on a letter to Dinan immediately that you might know of your messenger Dove being in its destined place at once on your arrival. The dulled sensibility is to be accounted for by a wrong condition of body which has been creeping over me for some time and which according to the doctor, has just declared itself as the presence of that admirable substance called 'gravel' in the place where it is least wanted—even less than in one's boots. The attack, however, has been a very slight one.[1] I lay in bed all yesterday, but this morning I am in my study chair, as usual, to receive the parcel of Elma's comfortable devices—the flannel belt, with the bit of extra flannel and sewing-silk in case of

8. A long feud with the Headmaster of Eton Dr. J. J. Hornby ended in Oscar Browning's dismissal at the end of 1875. Among the matters of disagreement were Browning's favoring the study of modern history, art, and literatures, his opinion that athletics were overemphasized, and his close personal attachment to certain pupils. For an account of the affair see H. E. Wortham, *Oscar Browning,* 1927, pp. 75–155.

9. To return to Cambridge, as Fellow of King's College.

1. GHL wrote in his Diary 28 February: "Polly walked with me in Park discussing *De Ronda.*" Dr. Andrew Clark called to see her 1 March 1875. At 4 the next morning she "had another attack of violent pain—probably from the kidney. Gave her opiate and fomentation which relieved her. Blood in her water." These symptoms lasted several days, but she came down to dinner 4 March and walked in the Park again 5 March.

need, the pattern-shirt, and the bath-slippers. I believe in Providence, and one of its many names is Elma.

I had meant to wear the Saint Esprit tonight at a musical party [2] where Joachim and all the next best to him were to play divinest music. But I am forbidden to stir out, and have to resign myself. Worn the Dove will be, if I live—and the flannel belt and the slippers. About the shirt I will report in the future. "Ever more thanks, the exchequer of the poor." [3]

I enclose with this note the autograph of Charlotte Bronte. The unlovely sarcasms with which it is wound up refer to the course taken by the "Leader" concerning the "Ecclesiastical Tithes Bill." [4] It is altogether a characteristic letter. Also I return Mrs. Anderson's prescription, which Mr. Lewes has already had made up in preparation for distant needs, promptitude being the vehicle of all his virtues—the briskest little vehicle imaginable.

I will not write more now, because my head is achy. But it comforts me to send this scrap of writing which in its way is also a winged messenger carrying the love of your affectionate

Mother.

Let us know how your health goes on.

## GHL TO ALEXANDER MAIN, LONDON, [7 MARCH 1875]

*Text:* Main's copy owned by Mr. John R. Sprunt. *Hitherto unpublished.*

Sunday.

Dear Main

Your two letters were very interesting, and your story about the Lectures immensely significant. Mrs. Lewes was very poorly when yours to her arrived. She has had another attack of stone—the pain of which is excruciating—and leaves her weak and fluttering, but she is now again getting into her usual state, and will no doubt improve after this.

2. At the Frederick Lehmanns': "Joachim, Piatti, Ries, Zerbini, and Marie Krebs; Antoinette Sterling sang. Came away at 12, but not before I heard a divine quartett by Schubert, a quintett by Schumann, Prelude by Bach, and Polonaise by Beethoven (superbly played by Mdle Krebs), a sonata for violin alone by Bach, and two songs. Talked to Lady Colvile, Louisa Courtney, Lady Castletown and Mrs. Wingfield, Lady Grant, the Harrisons, Mrs. Linton, Browning, etc." (GHL Diary, 4 March 1875.)

3. *Richard II,* II, iii, 65.

4. Charlotte Brontë's letter to GHL, dated Haworth, 23 November 1850, is published in Stuart, pp. 173–175. She was disturbed by the *Leader's* sympathy for the Catholics.

Don't expect to hear from us unless we have something special to communicate—letter writing is so onerous—but be sure of our constant regard.

Yours ever
G. H. L.

## GHL TO ALICE HELPS, LONDON [8 MARCH 1875]

*MS:* Mr. Arthur Helps. *Endorsed:* GE and GL. *Hitherto unpublished.*

**The Priory, | 21. North Bank, | Regents Park.**
Monday.

Dear Alice

A silent pressure of the hand to assure you that the calamity [5] which has fallen on you is felt by us. We know how devoted your love for your father—we know how loveable he was—nothing more to be said! [6]

## GE TO FRANÇOIS D'ALBERT-DURADE, LONDON, 20 MARCH 1875

*Text:* Copy by D'Albert-Durade in Tinker Collection, Yale. *Hitherto unpublished.*

The Priory | 21 North Bank | Regent's Park | March 20. 1875.

My dear Friend

Your words of affectionate remembrance are very sweet to me and rouse vivid pictures of that long past time [7] when I made my first severe acquaintance with sledge travelling, and when your admirable portrait of "Maman" won the agents of the Douane to a gracious behaviour. The March wind was less formidable to me then, and I had no fear of neuralgia from a moment's draught of air.

Your letter arrives propitiously in every way, except that it asks about my health at a moment when I happen to be unusually ailing. I had got through the harsh winter unusually well till about five weeks ago, when a state of malaise began which found its climax in sharp attacks of pain, attributed by my physician to gravel in the kidney.

5. Sir Arthur Helps died suddenly of pleurisy 7 March 1875.

6. The bottom of the MS has been torn away. A note in the hand of Alice Helps says: "The double autograph of G. H. Lewes and G. Eliot asked for by the Queen on seeing the letter."

7. See [26 March 1850].

The attacks have ceased,[8] but I am still out of health with occasional interruptions from headache.

I rejoice to know that dear Maman has an unclouded mind in the midst of her bodily feebleness. The sense that your life is passed beneficently for her and the others immediately around you must help to sustain you under the monotony and restriction which you enable me to imagine. I wish you happened to like whist, for in that case it would be a sedative for you equivalent to the cigar on which many men rely as a solace under all earthly trouble.

I heard of your son Alphonse from a Mrs. Sartoris who saw him at Vichy—perhaps two or three years ago.[9] She was Adelaide Kemble—a remarkable singer, who married after her first season—the daughter of Charles Kemble and niece of Mrs. Siddons. Your handsome Italian-looking son seems to have struck her agreeably. But she, poor thing, has been beaten down by the sorrow of losing her son, who was brought home dead from hunting.[1] Sorrow and age are too strong for wealth and homage of which she has abundantly.

Mr. Lewes is very busy and happy in his writing and our happiness in common seems to grow continually in spite of bodily feebleness. I am also writing, but my work "hangs fire" just now.

I write this morning immediately on receiving your letter lest anything should happen to retard my answer if I deferred it to the uncertain morrow. Whenever you are wondering at my long silence, pray imagine me with claims that fill up my days and still leave me a defaulter. Writing notes is an occupation which I am disposed to reduce as much as possible, and well-meaning Americans who are ever and anon asking me for my autograph probably think me the most churlish of celebrities, for I systematically leave their requests unanswered.

Mr. Lewes begs you and Madame D'Albert to accept his warm regards and best wishes. Assure Maman of my unfailing affectionate remembrance and believe me

Yours with faithful friendship
M. E. Lewes.

Our son Charles is highly prosperous and blessed with two dear little girls as well as with one of the best wives in the world. He advances both in worldly position and in intellectual capabilities. Lately he has

8. GE had a second sharp attack 8 March 1875. She "took a short walk for the first time," 18 March. (GHL Diary.)

9. See 29 January 1872.

1. Greville Sartoris (1840—23 October 1873) was killed by a fall from his horse —"not in the-hunting-field." (*Letters of Edward FitzGerald to Fanny Kemble,* ed. W. A. Wright, 1895, p. 35.)

been promoted to a post of much responsibility in connection with the telegraphs which our government has now taken in hand. Our son in Africa is also happily married, but we hear bad accounts of his health.

## GHL TO ALEXANDER MAIN, LONDON, [22 MARCH 1875]

*Text:* Main's copy owned by Mr. John R. Sprunt. *Hitherto unpublished.*

**The Priory, | 21. North Bank, | Regents Park.**
Sunday.

Dear Main

Mrs. Lewes, I grieve to say, continues suffering—the stone has not passed yet, nor has it fallen back altogether so as to give her peace—but she is better on the whole, and we hope in a few days she will be like herself again. Thank you for your letters.

Any criticisms and any corrections of misprints you may send will always be acceptable. But I haven't time to answer them. Probably when you have read Problem VI you will have answered your own difficulty about the cosmos.

Ever yours truly
G. H. L.

## GE TO MRS. HENRY CROMPTON, LONDON, 24 MARCH 1875

*MS:* Mr. Samuel L. Fuller. *Hitherto unpublished.*

**The Priory, | 21. North Bank, | Regents Park.**
March 24. 75.

My dear Mrs. Crompton

I am very glad that you have enabled me to correct the misstatement about your Father.[2] You must have imagined how uncomfortable I was in hearing him spoken of so inadvertently before you. Our friend of course had no knowledge of your relationship, and every one present

2. Lucy Henrietta Romilly, daughter of the Rt. Hon. John, 1st Baron Romilly (1802–74) had married Henry Crompton (1836–1904) the Positivist in 1870. The incident alluded to in this letter occurred 14 March, when Cross made some slurring allusion to Lord Romilly, who had died the previous December. According to the *DNB* Lord Romilly's cases "were somewhat often reversed on appeal. He was prone to decide causes without sufficiently considering the principles they involved and the precedents by which they were governed."

considered the disgrace of unintelligibility to lie rather in the state of our legal language than in any testator who might have fallen a victim to it.

Still it is a satisfaction to me that I can do something towards arresting a misstatement about one whose memory is so eminently dear to you. I enter fully into your feelings which would not allow you to pass over the matter in silence—indeed, I think it was your duty to write about it.

Our friend Mr. Cross had so much pleasure in talking to you that I rather pity him for having to feel that anything he had said caused you uneasiness. It was very sweet to have you near me for an hour or two.

Always yours affectionately
M. E. Lewes.

I am much better.

## GE TO WILLIAM RALSTON SHEDDEN-RALSTON, LONDON, 24 MARCH 1875

*MS:* Huntington Library. *Hitherto unpublished.*

**The Priory, | 21. North Bank, | Regents Park.**
March 24. 75.

Dear Mr. Ralston

Thanks for the feuilletons containing Tourguéneff's story,[3] which I will return when we have read it.

We are both much interested in your resolution to quit the Museum,[4] and are inclined to congratulate you. Pray let us know when the matter of the pension is decided. With health, you are sure to make yourself of value in fresh ways, but that modest certainty of £120 would be an insurance against anxiety in case of delays.

Always yours sincerely
M. E. Lewes.

3. GHL's Diary, 27 and 29 March 1875, shows that it was "Pounine et Babourine."

4. "Being of an extremely sensitive nature, as well as of a weakly constitution, he felt called upon to resign his appointment in 1875, after twenty-two years' service." (*DNB*.)

## GE TO MRS. ELMA STUART, LONDON, 24 MARCH 1875

*MS:* British Museum. *Extracts published:* Stuart, pp. 44–46.

**The Priory, | 21. North Bank, | Regents Park.**
March 24. 75.

Dearest Elma

I have made a new era of comfort for myself by devising the simplest thing possible in the way of braces to hold up my flannel and calico drawers, and I am wondering whether I have the start of you in invention so that I can actually give you a hint of ease in return for all the thoughts and stitches you have given me. This mighty birth of my mind consists of two fine flannel strips about 2½ or 3 inches wide pinned to the aforesaid garments with safety pins and crossed over the back just where a little warmth is agreeable to the marrow. They cause no cutting or pressure, and in warm weather—if such a condition should ever again occur in our part of this planet—I have reflected that the flannel may be replaced by strips of washing silk. This is the humble contribution of my intellect in the question of braces. Perhaps you have already found exactly the right thing for yourself, in which case please think of my suggestion only as the loving desire to relieve your dear hips from pressure.

I have been an invalid ever since I wrote to you until the last two or three days, but now I am recovering heart and hope. The tender attention I get might reconcile me to a month's ailing, if I were quite resigned to doing nothing and receiving all things.

Our weather has been cruelly cold. North east winds have dried up our bodily moisture and the sky has been gloomily grey. Only for the last three days has there been a promise of Spring in the air. How have you been? You must remember that until you can report yourself quite strong again, we need a more frequent reassurance about you.

The shirt, meine Liebe, will not adapt itself to my needs. I am sorry. But there are two insurmountable difficulties—the fussiness about my neck, and the difficulty of managing my other garments so as to lift them off my loins. When Edith will be able to pay her visit to you seems uncertain, but I shall not forget to burthen her with the little parcel, unless you come first to carry it back with you.

Mr. Lewes is both glad and sorry at once that he has to prepare a new edition of his Life of Goethe [5]—glad that the public has absorbed

5. George Smith wrote GHL 23 March 1875 that it was running out of print and proposed a 3d edition of 2000 copies. GHL revised the text 8–17 April, wrote

the old edition, but sorry to quit his other writing for the necessary interim. He is very well, occasional headaches excepted, and sends his love to you.

I wore the Saint Esprit on my black velvet the other day, and he was very proud of its effect. I have been too weak to be proud, but I am getting so strong again that I shall be equal to that sinning by and by.

If we could only have some sunshine! Sunshine becomes more and more of an independent joy to me—independent of everything but husband and health, which are rather weighty provisoes.

I am writing this on my knees at one corner of the evening fire, and Mr. Lewes is reading his beloved physiology at the other corner. Imagine us pausing to speak of you and wondering if there is anything else to tell you. I conclude that there is nothing but this—that I am

Your loving mother,

M. E. Lewes.

I had written a page before I found that the sheet was torn at the back.

## GE TO JOHN WALTER CROSS, LONDON, [MARCH 1875]

*MS:* Yale. *Endorsed:* March 1875. *Hitherto unpublished.*

**The Priory, | 21. North Bank, | Regents Park.**
Friday Evening.

My dearest Nephew

The deep deep joy your letter has given us! It seems for this hour as if the weight of the world's weariness and sorrow were all gone. It was good of you to write us the first word.[6]

Thanks for the sight of Miss Thornley's letter which I enclose, because it seems to be 'documentary.'

Always your affectionate Aunt

M. E. Lewes.

notes for it in May. The first proofs arrived 24 June and the last were finished 11 October. For this edition he received £250. (GHL Diary.)

6. The recovery of some member of the family?

## GE TO FREDERICK LOCKER, LONDON, 17 APRIL 1875

*MS:* Harvard. *Hitherto unpublished.*

**The Priory, | 21. North Bank, | Regents Park.**
April 17. 75.

Dear Mr. Locker

I have a most agreeable and respectful remembrance of Miss Anna Swanwick [7] and should find any incidental meeting with her pleasant. But, as you divine from my late explanation, I am obliged to restrict my reception of visits, and I shall be grateful to you if you will save me from the need to say so directly to Miss Swanwick.

I hope to hear that Mrs. Locker is safely through the troublous introduction to a new happiness.[8]

Yours very sincerely
M. E. Lewes.

## WILLIAM BLACKWOOD TO JOHN BLACKWOOD, LONDON, 21 APRIL 1875

*MS:* National Library of Scotland. *Hitherto unpublished.*

38 Albemarle Street | London W | April 21/75.

My dear Uncle

I am very annoyed to find that my letter of Monday did not reach you yesterday morning as I sent it off from here in ample time for the extra stamp post. . . . I lunched with the Lewes' and found them both rather seedy I am sorry to say. George Eliot looked especially so and Lewes afterwards told me that she had been very unwell and I was quite shocked and distressed to see her looking so aged and haggard but she cheered up and both were very pleased to see me.

I thought the sales of Middlemarch were good enough to take her a note of them and she was extremely happy at seeing them so good still. We have sold over 1200 since January 1st and the number for April is already greater than that of March. She thanked me most cordially for bringing such bright news, and I replied that I hoped she had equally good to give me about the new novel. She at once

7. From her visits to GE at 142 Strand in 1852.

8. The birth of her son Godfrey Tennyson Locker, later Locker-Lampson (19 June 1875–1946).

hung her head low and said "Oh no, it is detestable I think, but Mr. Lewes will tell you all about it when you smoke your cigar in the garden"—which he did.

Of course his opinion was quite the reverse and he said it was perfectly charming and all about English Ladies and Gentlemen and scene laid in Wiltshire. I got the title of it from him in great confidence and as a secret to be told to no one but you, not even Mr. Langford. It is Daniel DĕRōnda, and as Lewes rolled it out in a deep bass sounding voice he said "Does it not sound very grand?" I then learned that whole of Volume I was in a complete state and part one of the next volume. I suggested could I not take it down for you to read quietly before coming up, as you would then be well able to talk it over with Mrs. Lewes and give her encouragement to go on, and Lewes thought it a capital idea. As for trusting it to the Post that was not for a moment to be thought of. "What would we do if it were lost and it could never be rewritten?"

When she joined us Lewes proposed it as my suggestion very nicely; if you had seen her face of horror and fright and meek expression you would have been startled. It was one of the most striking scenes I have ever seen and for a minute or two she would not speak. She seemed just to tremble at the idea of the M.S. being taken from her as if it were her baby; and by degrees she assented, and I am to go on Sunday or day before I start North for it. . . .

Lewes was also very strong upon the Inkerman Volume and described it as quite the most wonderful literary performance of its class he had ever read. They walked half way back with me and we had altogether a most pleasant chat. . . .

Best love to all.

Ever your affectionate nephew
William Blackwood.

## JOHN BLACKWOOD TO GE, EDINBURGH, 22 APRIL 1875

*MS:* National Library of Scotland. *Extract published: John Blackwood,* p. 387.

**3 Randolph Crescent**
April 22/75.

My Dear Mrs. Lewes

Willie tells me he has had a long and most interesting visit at the Priory, the only drawback to which was that you were complaining of not feeling well and being depressed. I have seen that depression on you before at periods when other authors would have been crowing and flapping their wings without the solid reason which I am sure you have for doing so. I am quite elated at the prospect of Willie bringing down so large a portion of your new Novel and I feel your sending the M.S. to me in this way as a thing to be proud of. Curiously enough I was walking about with Theodore Martin yesterday when talking about you and Lewes; he mentioned how devoted the Queen was to your works, especially Adam Bede.[9] So I told him how you had given me the M.S. of first volume of Adam with strict injunctions not to read it until I could do so quietly at home and how I utterly disobeyed orders by peeping into the first pages on the top of the omnibus where Lewes deposited me at Kew and fastening upon it the moment I left King's Cross next morning until I finished my reading with delight before I reached Newcastle when night was setting in.

This is what is called Preaching Thursday here, and Edinburgh is not a lively place to me when 45 George St. is shut up, and although my wife and daughter have been affable and kind they evidently feel me a sort of intruder.

I shall go now and have a walk into the country which is beginning at last to look bright and spring like. I hardly expect to be up in London until after the middle of May. One reason of my detention strikes me as peculiarly ludicrous. Our old butler who has been with us for 15 years is leaving us, and it is thought that I should be here when his successor comes. Now I am utterly useless about household affairs and would be most justly sat upon if I attempted to lift up my voice on the subject. With best regards to Lewes

always yours truly
John Blackwood.

9. In the Royal Library at Windsor Castle there is a copy of *Adam Bede,* 5th ed., 1859 upon the fly leaf of which the Queen has written: "Victoria. Begun at Balmoral Sept: and finished at Windsor Oct: 1859." There is also a copy of the Tauchnitz edition of *Romola,* 1863, bound in a typical Florentine binding of white parchment and extra-illustrated with photographs of Florence. Sir Owen Morshead, the Librarian, wrote me, "I do not doubt that Queen Victoria read it while staying at the Villa Palmieri just outside Florence."

## GHL TO WILLIAM BELL SCOTT, LONDON, 1 MAY [1875]

*MS:* Mrs. Gilbert McCoy Troxell. *Hitherto unpublished.*

**The Priory, | 21. North Bank, | Regents Park.**
1 May

Dear Scott

Your beautiful volume [1] arrived last night and was duly welcomed. My heart goes out to you and it; but I shall not be able to read it for some time, being just now not only desperately busy with many things besides work, but having all my reading time absorbed in the wearisome toil of going through more than 20 volumes of German dreariness—indispensable!—for the new edition of my Life of Göthe—a hateful task, though I cannot but be grateful for the necessity of a new edition. Curiously enough the bringing out the cheap and abridged 'Story of G's Life' has so *encreased* the demand for the larger book that 600 copies of it went off last year.

We are off today to Oxford on a brief visit to Jowett, but shall be home again next Sunday.

Ever yours affectionately
G. H. L.

## GHL DIARY, OXFORD AND LONDON, 1–5 MAY 1875

*MS:* Yale. *Hitherto unpublished.*

**Saturday 1 May 1875**

Wundt.[2] Finished revision of Problem I. Went to Oxford on a visit to Jowett. Bowen and Lord and Lady Lansdowne the other guests, but at dinner and evening, each day there were several interesting people.[3]

1. *Poems. Ballads, Studies from Nature, Sonnets, etc.*, 1875. This copy inscribed "G. H. Lewes, from his ancient friend W. B. Scott, April 1875," was sold at Sotheby's, 27 June 1923, item 557.

2. Wilhelm Max Wundt (1832–1920), *Vorlesungen über die Menschen-und Thierseele, 1863.*

3. Most of the people they met on this visit were Balliol men, friends and pupils of Jowett. Henry Charles Keith Petty-FitzMaurice, the 5th Marquis of Lansdowne (1845–1927), who married in 1869 Lady Maud Hamilton, youngest daughter of the Duke of Abercorn. John William, Lord Ramsay (1845–87), son of the 12th Earl of Dalhousie. Henry John Stephen Smith (1826–83), mathematical tutor. Henry Parry Liddon (1829–90), Canon of St. Paul's, London, and Vice-principal of St. Edmund's Hall. Lady Elizabeth Emma Proby, daughter

Lord Ramsay, Sir H. Maine, Henry Smith, Cannon Liddon, Lady Claud Hamilton and her daughter, Mr. Abbott (paraplegic), Mr. Esquith, Mr. Tatton, Mr. Symonds, Mr. Gore, Two Japanese, Mrs. Pallavicini, Mr. Roper, and others. Very pleasant talk and some good stories. . . .

**Sunday 2 May 1875**

Called on Henry Smith, Rolleston and the Pattisons—at the latter house saw Nettleship, Neubauer, Jefferson, Mills, Thursfield, etc. Went over the Museum with Rolleston rapidly.

**Monday 3 May 1875**

But this morning at 4 Polly awoke me with the painful news of a fresh attack of her stone. The pain lasted till 6.30 Then she got better and we came home.

**Tuesday 4 May 1875**

Polly became very unwell at night though without return of the pain. She stayed in bed all day. I sat with her and wrote letters. London Library and called on the Calls whom I drove in the Park. Then sat the rest of the day with Polly.

**Wednesday 5 May 1875**

Polly better this morning but not well enough to get up. Read Wundt, Menschen und Thierseele. Problems. Walk in Park. Dr. Clark came to see Polly at 3. Went to Chemist's and drove in Hyde Park. Found Polly up on my return. Read Scott's Poems to her. Düntzer Charlotte von Stein.[4]

of the 3d Earl of Carysfort, who was married in 1844 to Lord Claud Hamilton, and had three daughters, the eldest of whom married Professor Tyndall in 1876. Evelyn Abbott (1843–1901) distinguished himself at Balliol as a scholar and athlete. In 1866 a fall over a hurdle injured his spine and completely paralyzed his legs. Elected a fellow and tutor at Balliol in 1874, he was "the mainstay of the administration and teaching of his college" until his death. He edited Jowett's *Life and Letters*. Herbert Henry Asquith (1852–1928), also elected a fellow of Balliol in 1874. John Addington Symonds (1840–93), a pupil of Jowett in 1858. Charles Gore (1853–1932), later Bishop of Worcester, Birmingham, and Oxford. Thomas Godolphin Rooper (1847–1903), B.A. Balliol, 1870, was private tutor to the 11th Duke of Bedford. George Rolleston (1829–81), Linacre Professor of Anatomy and Physiology. Either Henry Nettleship (1839–93), who had been a fellow and tutor at Lincoln 1862–68, or his brother Richard Lewis Nettleship (1846–92), a fellow of Balliol 1869–92. Adolf Neubauer (1832–1907), sub-librarian of the Bodleian, where he catalogued the Hebrew MSS. John Cordy Jeaffreson (1831–1901), inspector of MSS for the Historical MSS Commission 1874–87. Lawrence Heyworth Mills (1837–1918), Orientalist, Professor of Zend Philology at Oxford after 1887.

4. (Johann) Heinrich Joseph Düntzer, *Charlotte von Stein, Goethe's Freundin*, Stuttgart, 1874.

## LESLIE STEPHEN TO GE, CAMBRIDGE, 6 MAY 1875

*MS:* Alderman Library, University of Virginia. *Hitherto unpublished.*

Cambridge | 6.5.75.

Dear Mrs. Lewes

I have been at Cambridge for a few days and have taken the opportunity to ask a few questions as to the resignation of scholarships problem.[2] The result is as follows—Sidgwick confirms my opinion that such a combination as you suggested would be impossible at Trinity. I find, however, that the following case actually happened at Trinity Hall (my college) and might happen, I presume, at other colleges. A. was first in the examination in May and B and C were bracketed second. A. left the University before October, i.e. the end of the vacation and his scholarship was thereupon divided between B and C.

The objection which occurs to me in regard to using this precedent is this: that the first scholarship was in this case worth about £50 a year and the second worth £30. If therefore A had left the University for the benefit of B, he would only have secured for him £20 a year extra. This, or something like this, would be the ordinary case and the sacrifice seems too small to be worth making.

There is, however, another case which not only may, but frequently does happen and which might, I think, answer your purpose, if otherwise suitable. At all the colleges, now, it is customary to give exhibitions to youths on entrance, and these are sometimes of sufficient value to be really important to a poor man, say, £50 to £70 or even £80 a year. A successful candidate often declines to take one of these when it is offered to him, and in that case it is given, as a matter of course, to the second in the examination. I have heard of a scholarship of £50 a year being thus passed on through two or three candidates.

The ordinary motive, of course, is that the successful candidate

2. GE was planning ch. 16, in which Daniel Deronda spends a year at Cambridge. She finally made him fail to win a mathematical scholarship because he had spent most of his time helping Hans Meyrick prepare for his classical scholarship. In his *George Eliot,* written for the English Men of Letters series, 1906, p. 191 Sir Leslie Stephen remarks that GE "took great care to give an accurate account of the incidents of Cambridge life. I have always fancied—though without any evidence—that some touches in Deronda were drawn from one of her friends, Edmund Gurney, a man of remarkable charm of character, and as good-looking as Deronda. In the Cambridge atmosphere of Deronda's day there was, I think, a certain element of rough common sense which might have knocked some of her hero's nonsense out of him."

thinks that he can get something better elsewhere. Perhaps he has done better than he expected and fancies that he will have a chance for some exhibition which he had previously supposed to be beyond his powers; or he might have expected to get the first exhibition and has only received an offer of the second. Anyhow the case is a common one; and, if your hero is not forced to be already an undergraduate when the case occurs, he might refuse the scholarship without causing any particular remark and with the certainty that it would be given to his friend. He might say, for example, that he wished to go to another college or not to go to the University at all.

I hope this may be of some service to you. I shall be glad to answer any other questions to the best of my ability when I have the pleasure of seeing you again.[3]

Yours very truly,
L. Stephen.

## GE TO MRS. WILLIAM SMITH, LONDON, 10 MAY 1875

*Text:* Cross, III, 256–257.

We cannot believe that there is reason to fear any painful observations on the publication of the memoir in one volume with 'Gravenhurst' and the Essays.[4] The memoir is written with exquisite judgment and feeling; and without estimating too highly the taste and carefulness of journalists in their ordinary treatment of books, I think that we may count on their not being impressed otherwise than respectfully and sympathetically with the character of your dear husband's work, and with the sketch of his pure elevated life. I would also urge you to rely on the fact that Mr Blackwood thinks the publication desirable, as a guarantee that it will not prove injudicious in relation to the outer world—I mean the world beyond the circle of your husband's especial friends and admirers. I am grieved to hear of your poor eyes having been condemned to an inaction which, I fear, may have sadly increased the vividness of that inward seeing, already painfully strong in you. There has been, I trust, always some sympathetic young companionship to help you—some sweet voice to read aloud to you, or to talk of those better things in human lots which enable us to look at the good of life a little apart from our own particular sorrow.

3. Stephen called at the Priory Sunday, 16 May 1875.

4. Blackwood published the privately printed memoir of William Smith with *Gravenhurst* and some essays, 1875.

## GE TO MRS. EDWARD BURNE-JONES, LONDON, 11 MAY 1875

*MS:* Yale. *Mostly published:* Cross, III, 257–258.

**The Priory, | 21. North Bank, | Regents Park.**
May 11. 75.

Dearest Mignon

The doctors have decided that there is nothing very grave the matter with me,[5] and I am now so much better that we even think it possible I may go to see Salvini in the Gladiator tomorrow evening.[6] This is to let you know that there is no reason against your coming, with or without Margaret, at the usual time on Friday.[7]

Your words of affection in the note you sent me are very dear to my remembrance. I like not only to be loved but also to be told that I am loved. I am not sure that you are of the same mind. But the realm of silence is large enough beyond the grave. This is the world of light and speech, and I shall take leave to tell you that you are very dear to

Your faithfully affectionate
M. E. Lewes.

## GE TO MRS. PETER ALFRED TAYLOR, LONDON, 14 MAY 1875

*Text:* Cross, III, 258.

You are right—there is no time, but only the sense of not having time: especially when, instead of filling the days with useful exertion,

5. There were recurrent attacks until 9 May, when Dr. Andrew Clark and Sir James Paget "both came and after examinations pronounced it not serious—merely excess of uric acid." She did not get up till dinner, thus avoiding the Sunday visitors, who included "Alexander Bain and his wife, Lady Colvile, Mrs. Mark Pattison, Sanderson, Mrs. Sitwell, Mr. Flower of Stratford and Dr. Willis, Mr. Paterson (the bore), Du Maurier, Champneys, Hinton, the Harrisons, Lady Claud Hamilton and her daughter. Lady Claud stayed till six talking mostly of Polly and looking at the m.s. of Adam Bede and Spanish Gypsey." (GHL Diary, 9 May 1875.)

6. They saw Salvini's Othello twice, 7 and 19 April and were greatly moved by both performances. "Polly came home in a fever of excitement." But in *Il Gladiatore,* a melodrama by Altenheim (1841), they "were greatly disappointed with him. He seemed as poor as he was fine in Othello." (GHL Diary, 17 May 1875.) Salvini reawakened GHL's interest in the stage; he appended "First Impressions of Salvini. 1875" to the reprinted essays *On Actors and the Art of Acting,* 1875.

7. There is no record of this call; on Friday "We both went to Tunbridge to see the house." (GHL Diary 14 May.) For several years Friday seems to have been set apart for the Burne-Joneses, who came less frequently on Sundays.

as you do, one wastes them in being ill, as I have been doing of late. However, I am better now, and will not grumble. Thanks for all the dear words in your letter. Be sure I treasure the memory of your faithful friendship, which goes back—you know how far.

## JOHN BLACKWOOD TO MRS. JOHN BLACKWOOD, LONDON, 19 MAY 1875

*Text: John Blackwood,* p. 387.

The Burlington, May 19, 1875.

I went yesterday by appointment to lunch with the Leweses, where I was most cordially welcomed. She is looking pale and a little languid, but that was to be expected under the interesting circumstances, as she delivered to me a volume of MS.[8] which I am yearning to sit down to. As I left she said, "Now bring me a particular account of Jack. Nobody is more interested in the house of Blackwood than I am." I had told her I was going to Storrington to-morrow to see him.[9]

## JOHN BLACKWOOD TO GE, LONDON, 20 MAY 1875

*MS:* National Library of Scotland. *Hitherto unpublished.*

The Burlington | May 20/75. 10 a.m.

My Dear Mrs. Lewes

I congratulate you. It is splendid. I could not get settled down to your M.S. until ½ past 8 and I made a night of it. At first I began to try to read quickly but I found that was even more utterly out of the question than usual with your books and I soon settled down to calm leisurely enjoyment reading line by line and constantly turning back again to make sure that I had *got it all.* I paused and enjoyed myself so much that although it was 3 o clock in the morning when I went to bed I had only got through ½ the volume!!!!

I must be off to train and again congratulating you

always yours truly
John Blackwood.

8. "Blackwood to lunch. He carried off vol. 1 of Daniel Deronda." (GHL Diary, 19 May 1875.)

9. John Blackwood was being tutored for Oxford. He matriculated at Christ Church 13 October 1876 but did not take a degree.

## JOHN BLACKWOOD TO GE, LONDON, 25 MAY 1875

*MS:* National Library of Scotland. *Extracts published: John Blackwood,* pp. 391–392.

The Burlington | May 25/75.

My Dear Mrs. Lewes

Reading the whole and rereading many parts of the first volume of Daniel Deronda has more than confirmed the admiration and delight with which I wrote and spoke to you after my first happy sitting over your M.S. That first night I really felt like a glutton dallying over his feast and not reading at all with my usual rapid stride.

The first scene in the dreary gorgeous German gambling saloon with the gamblers all looking so like each other about the eyes and mouth is to the life, and poor Gwendolen's "enraged resistance" [1] is so true. Her want of early associations with home and the very "stars" a part of it is beautifully touched.[2] Mr. Gascoigne's pleasant easy tone that made the world "a manageable place of residence" [3] is very fine.

Gwendolen seeing Mrs. Arrowpoint's folly and not perceiving that she was showing her own hand to the old lady is so like a clever young creature.[4] I did not know what a hold the mermaid witch had got of me until I felt inclined to kick Herr Klessmer for his criticism on her singing [5] and I did not forgive him until I saw him with his hat "on his hair" [6] when a laugh took away all angry feeling. I knew what must happen to Rex but I was very sorry for him when the blow came [7] and her tears afterwards give me a hope that her creator is going to be merciful to the witch. She is a fascinating witch and I shall not be able to help feeling for her if she does get into "a swamp, satin shoes" and all. She had "no objections to be adored" [8] and was hardly entitled to the feeling. That is a magnificent illustration of yours about circumstances weighing upon characters such as hers like the weather upon the Harvests.

There is something very impressive in the way that fear froze that wild wilful heart on the sudden fall of the pannel and disclosure of that horrid picture.[9]

The glimpse of the little blacksmith [1] who came to the help of Rex

1. *Daniel Deronda,* 1876, I, 10. (ch. 1.)
2. I, 32. (ch. 3.)
3. I, 53. (ch. 3.)
4. Ch. 5.
5. I, 80. (ch. 5.)
6. I, 181. (ch. 10.)
7. I, 144. (ch. 7.)
8. I, 122. (ch. 7.)
9. Mrs. Glasher's interview, I, 274. (ch. 14.)

1. Joel Dagge, I, 126. (ch. 7.)

is a perfect picture. I know the little rascal as well as if I had been in the habit of giving him sixpences for years.

Ladies' necks like "leisurely lilies if they took to motion" [2] is a singularly happy idea. I am afraid there are few necks like that but we have all seen some.

Grandcourt is a most original character and he and Deronda promise to be a grand contrast in your picture. Gwendolen takes Grandcourt up admirably about "pleasures and follies left off" [3] and his sudden fit of numbness when he thinks he is within certain reach of his object is so true to nature.

There is somewhere as passage about false air of dæmonic strength in commonplace unregulated people who know not how to direct their force that has made a great impression on me, but if I tried to refer to all the passages that have done that I should never finish my letter, as when they recur to me I turn to the M.S. and pass some time reading them and the context.

You tell the Tale of Deronda's goodness and that of the stray Jewish Maid so straightly and so simply that no feeling of doubt or improbability arises, and I quite agree with Mrs. Mer[r]ick that Miriam's mother must have been good, as "wheaten bread does not come from naught." [4] Sir Hugo is always good and his placid reflections upon good birth like those of a man after a good dinner contrast happily with Deronda's sensitive but terrible fears on that subject.[5] That "grim walled slice of a house" [6] that the Merricks have is a happy and consoling thought in the midst of the wilderness of grim looking small houses that really cons[t]itute London. How often one has looked at them with a kind of shuddering pain as to what life could be to the inhabitants, but you have given an interior that leavens the whole mass.

Again I beg to congratulate you on this most auspicious opening of another immortal work [7] and believe me

always yours truly
John Blackwood.

2. I, 176. (ch. 10.)
3. I, 198. (ch. 11.)
4. II, 38. (ch. 20.)
5. Ch. 16.
6. I, 356. (ch. 18.)
7. This list of admired touches is longer than usual in consequence of a visit GHL paid Blackwood while it was being written. "I showed him what I was doing. He said: 'Do go on. You have no idea how much good that will do her. She has more faith in your judgment than in that of any one else.' His own judgment, he says, she naturally enough considers may be biassed, but I must say I have never found him wrong on the subject." (*John Blackwood,* p. 388.)

## GE TO ALEXANDER MAIN, LONDON, 26 MAY 1875

*Text:* Main's copy owned by Mr. John R. Sprunt. *Extracts published:* Cross, New Edition, pp. 539–540.

**The Priory, | 21. North Bank, | Regents Park.**
May 26. 75.

Dear Mr. Main

Your letters are always "a good message from a far country," [8] and we value every assurance you give us of your welfare or of our share in furthering it.

Our plans for the year do not now include a journey to the Continent, which Mr. Lewes had only thought of as a sanitary measure for me. What we are bent on is, to spend the next four or five months quietly in the country, working and breathing the fresh air. There is an unexpected hitch about a house which we had thought ourselves sure of, but if this difficulty can be surmounted we shall leave London next week.[9] I cannot yet tell you our country address, but we always have letters sent on to us from this house.

After an interval of improved health in which I had a pleasant visit to Oxford, some chill caught there revived the old discomforts, but the doctors have decided that there is really nothing at all serious the matter with me, and on the whole I resign myself to the conviction that my ailments have not the dignity of being dangerous. The worst of it is that I have wasted a great deal of time over them.

Mr. Lewes is very bright and enjoying in spite of occasional headachiness, and he will soon have finished the revision of his Goethe for a new edition. He is going, I think, to send you a spare copy of the "Academy" which contains a sympathetic notice of his 2d volume. I fear you are right in believing that it would be difficult to get a copy of the dear little old original Biographical Hist[ory] of Philosophy.[1] Pocket editions of solid books, such as one can carry three or four of without being conscious of a burthen, are now getting delight-

8. Proverbs, 25:25.

9. GHL's Diary for May 1875 records intensive house-hunting. He went with GE to Reigate, 20 May and looked at three houses; on one of them—at Wray Park—GHL made an offer of £175 for four months. But 27 May he was looking at one at Redhill and 28 May another, the Elms at Rickmansworth, which they took.

1. Main wrote 25 May 1875 of his plan to go to the Highlands, taking a 1-vol. Shakespeare, GE's *Poems,* the *Sayings,* and Browning's last work; if he could find the "original two wee volumes of the *Biographical History of Philosophy*" he would take them too.

fully abundant in France. But our system of publishing seems not to admit of agreeable cheapness in the form of books.

We have been much interested lately in seeing Salvini, a genuinely great actor, play Othello. And on Monday we are hoping to see him in Hamlet. I wish you could have the same enjoyment. Great art, in any kind, inspirits me and makes me feel the worth of devoted effort, but from bad pictures, bad books, vulgar music, I come away with a paralyzing depression.

Mr. Lewes is going to republish some interesting little Retrospects of Actors which he wrote nearly ten years ago in the Pall Mall Gazette. He remembers Edmund Kean—who you know died in 1832.[2]

I wish I had time to think of something better to tell you, but I hear the footstep of a visitor to lunch and must close my poor dispatch. It will have answered your question about our movements and also it will have assured you that you are always one of the valued possessions in our spiritual estate.

Ever yours faithfully
M. E. Lewes.

## GE TO FREDERIC HARRISON, LONDON, 1 JUNE 1875

*Text:* Typed copy, Coventry and Warwickshire Collection, Coventry City Libraries. *Extracts published:* Cross, III, 258–259.

June 1. 75.

Dear Mr. Harrison

If you could some day this week or the beginning of next, allow me half an hour's quiet tête-à-tête, I should be very much obliged by such a kindness.

I could call on you at 3 o'clock on any day except Saturday, or if it would be easier for you to come to me, I should be at home always at 5 o'clock, again with the exception of Saturday.

The trivial questions I want to put could hardly be shapen in a letter so as to govern an answer that would satisfy my need. And I trust that the interview will hardly be more troublesome to you than writing.

I have mentioned the hours of 3 and 5, but if you could specify any other hour on any day (before the 16th when we leave town)[3] I could

2. Edmund Kean (1787—15 May 1833) is the subject of ch. 1, *On Actors and the Art of Acting,* 1875.

3 They took possession of the Elms 17 June.

accommodate myself to your appointment either for my visit or yours.

I hope when you learn the pettiness of my difficulties you will not be indignant, like a great doctor called in to the favourite cat. With best remembrances to Mrs. Harrison.

Yours always truly
M. E. Lewes.

## GE TO FREDERIC HARRISON, LONDON, 2 JUNE 1875

*Text:* Typed copy, Coventry and Warwickshire Collection, Coventry City Libraries. *Extracts published:* F. Harrison, *Memories and Thoughts,* 1906, p. 149.

June 2. 75.

Dear Mr. Harrison,

Herewith the statement you have kindly allowed me to send. It occurs to me that in my brief fragmentary chat with Mr. Bowen [4] he had gathered Sir H. to be a tenant in tail coming of age, so that his father could make no disposition without his consent; but even then I don't see why he, Sir H., should have objected to a settlement in the given sense. Do you? This question has reference simply to my alarms about apparent improbabilities.

Yours thankfully
M. E. Lewes.

It is required to know the longest possible term of years for the existence of the following conditions.

1. That an estate, for lack of a direct heir, should have come into the possession of A (or of a series—A, a, a′—if that were admissible).

2. That subsequently a claim should have been set up by B on a valid plea of nearer kinship.

3. That B should have failed in his suit from inability to prove his identity, over which certain circumstances (already fixed) have cast a doubt; and should have died soon after.

4. That B's daughter, being an infant at the time of his death, should have come to years of discretion and have a legal claim on the estate.

---

These are the essentials as closely as I can strip them. The last, viz. the legal claim of B's daughter, might be dispensed with, if the ade-

4. See 1–5 May 1875.

quate stretching of the time is not to be obtained by any formula of conditions. The moral necessities of the situation might be met by the fact of injustice and foul play towards B; but I should prefer the legal claim, if possible.

You see, I should be glad of as large a slice of a century as you could give me, but I should be resigned if I could get 40 years.

## GE TO ALICE HELPS, LONDON, 7 JUNE 1875

*MS:* Mr. Arthur Helps. *Hitherto unpublished.*

**The Priory, | 21. North Bank, | Regents Park.**
June 7. 75.

The Pocket is perfect, my sweet Providence, and will be a comfort to me in my earthly pilgrimage for a long while. The touch of colour is a charming device.

Loving thanks, dear. I should never have got anything comparable to this without your care for me. The feather-like lightness is the chief requisite for me. I could not carry a wallet at my side with an antique silver clasp either for duty or pleasure.

Be sure to write and let us know of your affairs and intentions before long. Your poor dear face, which we have been used to see so lively, has made a new memory of itself with the shadow of sorrows upon it.[5]

Ever yours affectionately
M. E. Lewes.

## GE TO FREDERIC HARRISON, LONDON, 9 JUNE 1875

*MS:* Tinker Collection, Yale. *Envelope:* Frederic Harrison Esq | 22 The Cedars | Putney | S.W. *Postmarks:* ST. JOHNS-WOOD | C 12 | JU 10 | 75 | N.W; LONDON-S.W | EN | JU 10 | 75. *Hitherto unpublished.*

**The Priory, | 21. North Bank, | Regents Park.**
June 9. 75.

Dear Mr. Harrison

I am deeply obliged to you for the full and lucid paper you have written me.

By going back and altering a detail or two in what I wrote some

5. "Alice Helps to dinner." (GHL Diary, 4 June 1875.)

time ago, I think I shall be able to make out all I want, by using the possibility of exchange between Sir H. and G.[6]

I suppose that the possible son whose rights cannot be infringed does not disappear from the legal scene until the death of the possible father, who if one wife died could marry any number of wives in succession. He is rather troublesome to me. But I hope that through your kindness I may be able to understand what were the family affairs of my personages—for such understanding is necessary to my comfort, if not to the true relation of that part of their history which I undertake to write. Always

Sincerely and gratefully yours
M. E. Lewes.

## GE TO EMILY SUSANNAH CLARKE, LONDON, 12 JUNE 1875

*MS:* Mr. C. E. Clarke. *Hitherto unpublished.*

The Priory, | 21. North Bank, | Regents Park.
June 12. 75.

Dearest Emily

I am sorry to think of your losing so healthy a change as a visit to Scotland during the Summer Holidays, but the sweet duties of gratitude cannot be neglected without a still greater loss, and you will at least have the relief of rest with your friend Madam Monsigny.

Next week we go into the country for the summer and autumn—or part of autumn—to a house at which our address will be | The Elms | Rickmansworth | Hertfordshire. | I am longing much for the country hoping that it will make me stronger, for I have no good report to give of my health during these last three months. Apart from health all has been well with us.

I wish we had been able to manage a little visit to Brighton for a day and a night this spring, for it would have been a great satisfaction to me to have a kiss and a chat with you. But I have been so delicate and so liable to suffer from the slightest draught, that we have been discouraged from railway journeys in which we must have had that undesirable companion the North-East Wind.

I am surprized to hear that our old friend Dr. Kittermaster [6a] is still living. The kind old man would be sadly grieved to know of the

6. Sir Hugo Mallinger and Grandcourt.

6a. James Kittermaster, M.D. (1790?–18 June 1877). See 10 April 1840. Edward Clarke was Emily's eldest brother. Cf. 12 November 1854.

trouble about Edward in whom he took so friendly an interest. You can hardly expect to hear from that unfortunate Brother, and perhaps silence is the least painful condition in relation to him.

The bit of newspaper you sent me about Dr. Ruge[7] gratified me highly. It is an honour to his fellow-countrymen that they do him honour. I hope that you keep up your connection with Frau Ruge, and are not too much exhausted by other work to have a little appetite for German studies.

All blessings on you, dear. Your Uncle unites with me in love.

Ever your affectionate
Aunt Polly.

## GE TO FREDERIC HARRISON, LONDON, 15 JUNE 1875

*Text:* Typed copy, Coventry and Warwickshire Collection, Coventry Public Libraries. *Envelope,* Tinker Collection, Yale: Frederic Harrison Esq | 1 Southwick Place | Hyde Park Square | W. *Postmarks:* ST. JOHNS-WOOD | C5 | JU 15 | 75 | N.W; LONDON-W | A | JU 15 | 75. *Published:* F. Harrison, *Memories and Thoughts,* 1906, p. 149.

June 15. 75.

Dear Mr. Harrison

I must write to tell you my joy that on further study of your "document" I find in it precisely the case that will suit the conditions I had already prepared. I mean the case that "Sir H. might ardently desire a particular house and property, locally part of the settled estates or not, to leave to his widow and daughters for their home and residence, etc."[8] Clearly I have a special Providence to whom my gratitude is due, and he is the able conveyancer who has drawn up said document.

We are in the pangs of preparation for starting to-morrow morning.[9]

Always yours sincerely,
M. E. Lewes.

7. Arnold Ruge (1803–80), radical political and philosophical writer, edited at Halle and Dresden various journals which were suppressed by the governments. A member of the Frankfurt National Assembly in 1848, he fled to England in 1849 and settled as a teacher and writer at Brighton, where Emily had lived since 1873.

8. In ch. 15 Sir Hugo is led "to dwell on a plan which had grown up side by side with his disappointment of an heir; namely, to try and secure Diplow as a future residence for Lady Mallinger and her daughters, and keep this pretty bit of the family inheritance for his own offspring in spite of that disappointment." (*Daniel Deronda,* 1876, I, 288.)

9. They left 17 June 1875: "Started at 9.30 for our House at Rickmansworth. Mr. Kenyon there to receive us. The day occupied with unpacking and reading proofs." (GHL Diary.)

## GE TO FREDERIC HARRISON, RICKMANSWORTH, 18 JUNE 1875

*MS:* Tinker Collection, Yale. *Envelope:* Frederic Harrison Esq | 1 Southwick Place | Hyde Park Square | London | W. *Postmarks:* RICKMANSWORTH | C | JU 18 | 75; F | WATFORD | JU 18 | 75; LONDON-W. | F7 | JU 19 | 75. *Hitherto unpublished.*

The Elms | Rickmansworth | June 18. 75.

Dear Mr. Harrison

Thanks for the additional important paper received this morning. In the statement grounded on the act, 1833, the words: "Every *tenant for life* whether in possession, remainder, contingency or otherwise can *dispose of lands entailed* as against all persons whose estates come *after* his, saving the rights of all persons whose estates come *prior* to his"—are clear to me considered as a warrant and limitation for G's side of the transaction with Sir H.

But in other relations the wording puzzles me, because it seems in contradiction with the inability of a *tenant for life* to do anything in the way of disposal without the consent of his extant successor. Of course there is no real contradiction and you need not trouble yourself to explain if, as I imagine, there is nothing to affect my previous conception of the case between Sir H. and G.

That conception is, that Sir H. is tenant for life, and can dispose of no lands, without the consent of G. who is tenant in tail, and who, if he chooses, could have his own right or anybody else's except that of Sir H's (legally) possible son.

Is it also correct to conceive that G's ability to dispose of the entailed lands would cease on the birth of a son [10] to himself, that son's existence as tenant in tail constituting his father's interest a tenancy for life?

Or is it that every right of succession included in the settlement is a mere tenancy for life? —But if so, what becomes of the limiting distinction by which a tenant for life has his hands tied, while his successor may bar the entail?

You understand that my difficulty lies in the *wording* above cited, which seems to nullify the distinction between a life-interest and absolute possession. But do not worry yourself to answer unless there be danger of a practical qui pro quo on my part.

Always gratefully yours
M. E. Lewes.

10. Henleigh Glasher, Grandcourt's illegitimate son, who becomes his heir. (Chs. 13, 49.)

P.S. on second thought:

I *should* like to be clear on that point—whether after G. had a son born to him on his approaching marriage, his power of parting with his right over the portion of entailed property would cease until the son came of age and could concur.

## GHL TO CHARLES LEE LEWES, RICKMANSWORTH, [24 JUNE 1875]

*MS:* Mrs. Carrington Ouvry. *Endorsed:* 24 June 1875. *Extracts published:* Paterson, p. 167.

The Elms Rickmansworth | Thursday.

Dearest Charles

Enclosed is a note to Mr. M. from the Mutter if Gertrude likes to present it and try her eloquence on him, but from all we have seen or heard, he is not at all a likely person to be moved in that direction (the names of the Duke of W. and Lady Burdett Coutts would have more influence than any abstract idea of "the people") and the Mutter feels so little personal sympathy with him that she cannot write to him more fully. No one else occurs to us. Indeed desirable as the proposed Park [11] may be—especially to those who live near it—I fear that so large a sum could not be gained for a park so near Regent's Park and Hampstead Heath. But there is no knowing what ingenious advocacy may effect.

We enjoy this place vastly—the drives surpass those of Reigate, and we have a park opposite in which we can walk, and a lovely park ten minutes distant in which we can drive. The weather has been fine and mild, not warm. The Mutter is certainly better, but not so strong as I could wish and perhaps will not be quite herself while this book is on hand, which gets on very slowly and with constant despondency. I am much the same—except that I too feel the benefit to my work of the long uninterrupted peace.

You will have my book in a few days and have already I suppose had a proof of Goethe.[12] *No hurry* with those proofs.

11. Gertrude Lewes's sister Octavia Hill was trying to save the fields near the Swiss Cottage from being built over. Though her effort failed, the movement she started later developed into the National Trust. Mr. M. is Alfred Morrison. See 13 August 1875.

12. *On Actors and the Art of Acting,* 1875, consisting chiefly of his articles in the *Pall Mall Gazette,* 1865–67. *The Life and Works of Goethe,* 3d ed., 1875 was revised 23 March—28 May. The proof began to arrive 24 June 1875. (GHL Diary.)

Love to you from both—Mutter wishes me to apologize for her not writing.

Ever your loving
Pater.

## GHL TO MARY FINLAY CROSS, RICKMANSWORTH, 8 JULY 1875

*MS:* Miss Emily Cross. *Hitherto unpublished.*

The Elms, Rickmansworth, Saturday July 8th 75.

Dearest Niece

Your bright letter was like a gleam of sunshine (much needed in these rainy days) with its pleasant picture of the Aachen group—Johnny's flirtations with Sulphur Springs and Dutch Dolls (to whom my compliments with the whispered addition that Johnny "is not a Prussian having been born at Chelsea"—dass Sie es wissen!) Florie's caricaturings, and Germanizings with wild outbursts of British audacity in throwing herself among genders and inflexions!—and Eleanor drawing in the shade, making her observations on the passing world, with stray thoughts in the direction of Aunt and Uncle!

I should have acknowledged it at once but I thought I would wait till after Lady Airlie's [1] Garden Party that I might give you an account of it, there being absolutely nothing else of new. Know then that being invited to meet the Queen of Holland,[2] and finding I could run up to town comfortably after lunch, and be back home again by 8, I arrayed myself in my 'war paint,' and presented myself at Airlie Lodge. To my surprise I found that the Queen had expressed a special wish that I should be presented to her, so immediately on her arrival that ceremony took place. You must imagine a pale plain elderly woman of somewhat feeble and certainly unenchanting aspect—and opposite her stands—The Matchless! Then this dialogue ensues.

*Queen.* Very glad to see you, Mr. Lewes. I saw you in 1871 [3] at Florence. You were there were you not?

1. Henrietta Blanche, 2d daughter of Lord Stanley of Alderley, was married in 1851 to the 6th Earl of Airlie. She was a sister of Lyulph Stanley, Lady Amberley, and Mrs. George Howard. She had taken up GHL in 1867.

2. Queen Sophie (1818–77), daughter of William I of Wurtemburg and 1st wife of William III, King of the Netherlands. GHL's Diary, 8 July 1875 gives an account of the presentation in almost the same words.

3. The date is clear both here and in the Diary. GHL had not been in Florence since 1869, but naturally did not correct Her Majesty.

*The M.* I was, your Majesty.
*Q.* You were pointed out to me at the theatre, you and your wife. Lady Airlie (not having caught the word 'Florence' or because 'Weimar' was running in her head, we having been talking of it when the Q. arrived) "Mr. Lewes says they were so very kind to him at Weimar."
*Q.* (*with something like fretful impatience*) I don't want to hear about Weimar! (*loftily*) I have done with them. (*Family quarrel*)— So you like Weimar, Mr. Lewes? (*a touch of sarcasm in the tone*)
*The M.* Well, your Majesty, I was very happy there and much interested in everything.
*Q.* It's a very ugly place. You can't say it's beautiful!
*The M.* No, not beautiful—certainly not like Florence.
*Q.* Oh! Florence is charming. (*a pause*) I admire your writings—as to your wife's, all the world admires them.
Here the Matchless bows, and begins to think 'when will this come to an end.' Lady Dillon [4] and Jenny Lind [5] were brought up to be presented, and this seemed an opening for escape, so I whispered to Mrs. Howard, "May I consider the audience over?" "Yes, if you are bored." "I am." "Then come and talk with me." Accordingly we slipped on to the lawn, and though I saw, I did not again approach her majesty.

It was a brilliant sight that garden dotted with lovely women and lovely dresses (with some *not* so lovely!) and celebrated men and 'nobs.' [6] I enjoyed an hour and a half of it; and came away wondering whether I had produced anything like the same impression on Royalty that Royalty had produced on me.

We stay here till the middle of October; we have not taken the house for more than that time; but perhaps shall go to the seaside or

4. Sarah Augusta, daughter of Alexander Hanna, was married in 1856 to Theobald Dominick Geoffrey Lee Dillon, 15th Viscount Dillon.

5. Jenny Lind-Goldschmidt (1820–87), Swedish soprano, became a British subject in 1859 and spent her remaining years in England. In his Diary GHL describes their conversation: "Jenny Lind begged I might be introduced to her, and held my hand, pressing it fervently while she poured forth admiration of the Goethe, and explanations of why she had not liked to answer my letter to her until she could do it fully in person. As I have always felt an instinctive antipathy to her I did not respond to her warmth, and for the first time in her life, I suppose, she got no compliments." (GHL Diary, 8 July 1875.) GHL had written her about her experience of somnambulism, 26 December 1869.

6. "The George Howards, Browning, Oscar Browning, Spencer, Sir H. Thompson, Hamilton Aidé, Lyulph Stanley, Lady and Maude Stanley, Mrs. Lane Fox, Lord Stanhope etc. Lady Egerton of Tatton when I was introduced vowed she had dined with me at Mrs. Mildmay's—(she hadn't). Lady Clementina Mitford—quite a Gainsborough or Sir Joshua—charmed me with her beauty. Introduced also to Mrs. Tennant, who introduced me to her pretty daughters." (GHL Diary, 8 July 1875.)

to Paris while the Priory is getting itself cleaned. We are having the Drawing Room redecorated and *restored,* and the outside Roman cemented. You don't say how long 'die Kur' is to last—with that debauchery of six glasses before breakfast I should prophesy that a Kur would be a Kuriöse Erscheinung! (There's a pun!!!)

The dear Aunt sends her love to Nieces and Nephew to which ditto do is subscribed by

The Matchless.

## GE TO MRS. MARK PATTISON, RICKMANSWORTH, 16 JULY 1875

*MS:* British Museum. *Hitherto unpublished.*

The Elms, | Rickmansworth | July 16. 75.

My dear Figliuolina

The sad account of you brought me by Mr. Newton [7] before we left town haunts me more and more importunately. Are you better? Pray, if you can, write me a few words to assure me of that happier fact. I cannot bear to think of your not having been able to sleep without that insidious Chloral. Tell me that you are sleeping naturally and well. Or if there is only bad news to be told, let me know, that I may sympathize with what is actual, instead of imagining your circumstances falsely.

Yours with affectionate anxiety
M. E. Lewes.

## GHL TO ALEXANDER MAIN, RICKMANSWORTH, 22 JULY 1875

*MS:* The late Arthur Pforzheimer. *Hitherto unpublished.*

The Elms | Rickmansworth, Herts. | 22 July 75.

My dear Main

We concluded from your silence that you were on your walking tour.[8] It was quite well that you hadn't my book [9] in your knapsack,

7. Charles Thomas Newton, calling at the Priory, Sunday, 13 June 1875, brought word that the gout which had attacked Mrs. Pattison in the hand early in June 1875 had rapidly developed into arthritis, and that "she was threatened with complete stiffening of all the joints. In August she was despatched to Wilbad in the Black Forest, where a severe course checked the evil." (C. E. Dilke, *The Book of the Spiritual Life,* 1905, p. 44.)

8. See 26 May 1875.

9. *On Actors and the Art of Acting,* published 3 July 1875. GHL is too mod-

for it would have been quite unworthy of its porterage. It is a mere trifle—reprints of papers written between 1851–67.

You need not send me the 'Theory of Knowing' (though thanks for the intention) the author sent it me on its publication.[1]

In spite of the vile weather we have had during the last fortnight, the peace of our country life has had a most beneficial effect on Madonna, who begins to look like her own sweet self again, and is hard at work on a glorious book—which she is as dejected over as usual! We see no one—absolutely no one; but read, write, drive and ramble in sweet security and unvarying happiness.

I ran up to town the other day for a garden party at Lady Airlie's where I was to meet the Queen of Holland, who had expressed a wish to see me. The interview was flattering, of course; but not interesting. The cock having scratched up an uneatable pearl reflected that a simple grain of millet ferait mieux son affaire. I agreed with the cock—a single ganglionic cell—well isolated—would have pleased me better than the biggest crown in christendom. I am hard at work on the 'Physical basis of Mind,' with ever increasing clearness, and consequent enjoyment. We shall stay here till the end of September, and then most likely go somewhere to the coast as I have a few questions to put to the molluscs.

We were not a little startled and interested at the revelation of your chance phrase "my sisters"—we had no suspicion of there being such tender belongings. How reticent you have been about yourself!

You may be interested to know that my son Charles has an article in the new number of the Edinburgh Review on the education of Pauper children.[2] To our great satisfaction he has not gone into feeble literature but from time to time has written in the Spectator and such on social subjects.

Madonna sends her kindest regards.

Ever your faithful
G. H. Lewes.

est about his work. Mrs. Ouvry assures me that Sir John Gielgud considered it "*the* handbook for actors."

1. John Cunningham, *A New Theory of Knowing and Known,* published by Blackwood, 1874.

2. "The Education of the Children of the State," *Edinburgh Review,* 142 (July 1875), 89–110, a defence of Mrs. Nassau Senior's report against the attacks of Edward Carleton Tufnell, a former inspector of Poor Law Schools in London. Charles had offered it to Blackwood 9 October 1874. (NLS.)

## ELIZABETH STUART PHELPS TO GE, EAST GLOUCESTER, 27 JULY 1875

*MS:* Berg Collection, New York Public Library. *Hitherto unpublished.*

East Gloucester | Massachusetts. | July 27. 1875.

My dear Mrs. Lewes:

I am quite conscious that in my endeavor last year to learn from you *exactly* how to treat in my lectures the biographical aspects of the author, I blundered so far as to be misunderstood, if not indeed to give you positive offence.[6] And yet I trust so far to your quick perceptions and kind heart as to venture once more to ask a favor of you—the last time that I shall trouble you, I hope, in this way.

If I am found by my physicians strong enough, I am to read these long-delayed lectures early in October next; [7] the whole course being upon George Eliot.

Now I make a "point" in one lecture, where, in reading such passages from your letter as <you> I felt authorized to use, I want to lift the letter in my hand, that the boys and girls may see it at the audience-distance. The whole *motif* of one of my pet sentences hangs upon the act—and you can fancy my dismay at going one day to my travelling-bag where I had packed your two letters with valuable money papers for safe keeping, to find that my little travelling-flask of brandy had leaked out and ruined them both. I think I would rather have lost the money! But there they are—illegible; and the best chemical advice gives me no hope of restoring them. Here then is my bold request: I enclose a copy of the extracts [8] which I so much want. If you felt quite willing to rewrite them and send them back to me, I shall gratefully appreciate it. If you do not, I am sure that you will not. My address will be for a month or more, as above.

I was at Mrs. Stowe's pretty Florida home this winter, for a little; I like to hear one great woman speak of another as she spoke of you. I am, Madam,

Yours sincerely,

Elizabeth Stuart Phelps.

I took the liberty of sending you the little volume of my verses [9] just out; though I do not think largely of them myself, nor expect others to.

6. This part of the correspondence has not been found.

7. At Boston College. They were not given till 1876. See her letter to GE, 1 December 1876. (Yale.)

8. One sheet of these extracts in Miss Phelps's hand is at Yale.

9. *Poetic Studies,* Boston, 1875.

## GHL TO JOHN BLACKWOOD, RICKMANSWORTH, 29 JULY 1875

*MS:* National Library of Scotland. *Hitherto unpublished.*

The Elms | Rickmansworth | Thursday 29 July 75.

My dear Blackwood

Mrs. Lewes' correspondents are of course not grateful to me for relieving her of her task of writing them. But unless I did so her valuable time and strength would have to be largely used up; and as we don't put racers into Hansom cabs so we mustn't let *writers* do the work of correspondents.

The Deluge has passed; our river running so quickly at the end of the garden has *not* overflowed its banks and floated us into Space (with G.H.L. *à l'instar de Cæsar* holding aloft *her* Commentaries!) [1] but like a sober, well-conducted river has kept the even tenor of its way so that we have not had to make a raft of our dining table. While the deluge lasted, Mrs. Lewes continued getting stronger, but now has taken a chill, which affects her throat [2]—I hope not seriously. Meanwhile the *Commentaries* have been developing into deeper and deeper interest. It is true I am snubbed for being 'cockaloop' about them, and for not adopting the despondent view of *other people*—but on that subject my estimate of the estimate of *other people* is that it isn't worth two peas!

Your account of Cheneys [3] was not exaggerated, and we were willing to take on your authority the character of the beer. But Cheneys is only one of the lovely drives hereabouts—they have but the one defect of being too hilly, and of not having enough of wild country and commons.

I'm glad you agree with the dramatic criticisms—a subject on which a d——d deal of nonsense is written and spoken. —We were so pleased with your picture of the dogs, and the arrival of "the boy." [4] Mrs. Lewes begs me to say she thoroughly sympathizes with you there, and that we both think a deficiency of scholastic brilliancy the smallest possible defect where there is good honest heart and brain—*those* are the levers of this world! This is how we have felt about our own boys.

We are complete hermits here—not a soul have we seen or spoken

1. Suetonius tells the story in his *Divus Iulius*. During July 5.32 inches of rain fell in London—more than twice the average.

2. "Went up to town to take Polly to the dentist—he removed her tooth and gave her hopes of quiet till October." (GHL Diary, 28 July 1875.)

3. A village five miles northeast of Rickmansworth.

4. His son John Blackwood.

to. I had to rush up to town one day to a garden party at Lady Airlie's because the Queen of Holland had expressed a wish that I should be presented. I hope her majesty found the interview more interesting than I did! —Except that, and twice rushing to the Priory to get books (it's no use taking down a bookcase—one never thinks of the right books!) my days have been passed in the most delicious peace and uniformity and work has advanced proportionately.

Ever yours truly
G. H. Lewes.

## GHL TO GEORGE JACOB HOLYOAKE, RICKMANSWORTH, 1 AUGUST 1875

*MS:* Yale. *Hitherto unpublished.*

The Elms, | Rickmansworth | 1 August 75.

My dear Holyoake

Mrs. Lewes would *very* much like to have your book.[5] We are here for the summer leading the lives of Hermits whose devotions are not to the next world. The uninterrupted peace is very favorable both to health and work. We see no one—absolutely no one. Les jours se suivent et se ressemblent! I did one day run up to town because the Queen of Holland had expressed a wish that I should be presented to her, but except that august (and uninteresting) audience I have given no sign of myself (yes, I ought to add to a dentist) beyond what spiritual presence—through no 'medium' I hope!—may have effected.

From your note I gather you have been suffering from your eyes—let me hope that it is over now—or at least in a fair way to be so!

Ever yours faithfully
G. H. Lewes.

## GE TO MRS. PETER ALFRED TAYLOR, RICKMANSWORTH, 9 AUGUST 1875

*Text:* Cross, III, 259–260.

We admire our bit of Hertfordshire greatly; but I should be glad of more breezy common land and far-reaching outlooks. For fertility,

5. George Jacob Holyoake (1817–1906), *A History of Co-operation in England,* 2 vols., 1875–79. GE probably contributed £5 to the public subscription to procure Holyoake an annuity; a note of this amount appears among the gifts to charity in GHL's Diary, April 1875. Holyoake's ashes are buried near GHL and GE in Highgate Cemetery.

wealth of grand trees, parks, mansions, and charming bits of stream and canal, our neighbourhood can hardly be excelled. And our house is a good, old, red-brick, Georgian place, with a nice bit of garden and meadow and river at the back. Perhaps we are too much in the valley, and have too large a share of mist, which often lies white on our meadows in the early evening. But who has not had too much moisture in this calamitously wet cold summer?

Mr Lewes is very busy, but not in zoologising. We reserve that for October, when we mean to go to the coast for a few weeks. It is a long while since I walked on broad sands and watched the receding tide; and I look forward agreeably to a renewal of that old pleasure.

I am not particularly flourishing in this pretty region, probably owing to the low barometer. The air has been continually muggy, and has lain on one's head like a thick turban.

## GE TO MME EUGÈNE BODICHON, RICKMANSWORTH, 13 AUGUST 1875

*MS:* Mr. Philip Leigh-Smith. *Hitherto unpublished.*

The Elms | Rickmansworth | August 13. 75.

My dear Barbara

As to weather you are better off than we are. The last ten days and nights have brought us frequent rain which we try to be thankful for because it is not continuous as it was in the calamitous time of July. Our nice old house is unfortunately in a valley much given to mists, and my health has I think been the worse for it. I am much satisfied with your news about yourself, which had been too long waited for.

We have had a trouble, prepared for by a long-standing anxiety. On the 29th of June our poor Bertie died at Durban, where he was staying for the sake of sea-air and medical attendance. The sad news only reached us last Sunday, when we were hoping that we might soon get a letter to tell us of his being able to rejoin his wife. He leaves two little children, the youngest an infant boy, born in May. It is a comfort that we are able to provide for the wife and children, but the consequent claims (in these next months when there will be debts and expenses of uncertain amounts) prevent me from doing what I should like to do, namely, to supply the needed £100 for the new rooms at Girton.[6]

6. See Barbara Stephen, *Emily Davies and Girton College,* 1927, p. 303.

It will be worth while to send the information to Mrs. Alfred Morrison [7]—it can do no harm. But she made no response at all when I sent former circulars to her; she is now ill, and her husband a most unsympathetic mortal. I am determined not to appeal to him again in any way. I lately gave an introduction to Gertrude that she might try to interest him in keeping open the Hampstead fields, and she found the interview a great *crux*.

I am glad to think that Miss Edwards has got into the right groove. —But poor Mr. Sylvester! [8] It is saddening to think of him beginning anew at 64—driven from what he is first-rate in, and setting himself the difficult task of being second-rate in something else. One longs helplessly to be of use to such a man.

Poor Bertie had been suffering from the glandular disease of which he showed symptoms when a boy, but which he appeared to have completely outgrown. He had become a splendidly strong man before he went to Natal and continued so till about three years ago, when he began to complain of neuralgia. His death was immediately caused by an attack of bronchitis.

We return to town on September 23. but go off again in two or three days to the Coast—Bournemouth I believe, till about the end of October.

Ever yours lovingly
M. E. L.

7. Alfred Morrison (1821–97), wealthy collector of works of art and autographs, married in 1866 Mabel, daughter of the Rev. R. S. C. Chermside. They began to call at the Priory in 1872, and twice GHL records going to see their collections at 16 Carlton House Terrace: "Called on the Morrisons to see Houdon's bust of Voltaire and their pictures. Bored by being shown all their splendours and rarities: each the 'finest in the world.'" (GHL Diary, 21 March 1872.) On the second visit, 9 May 1874, he and GE were shown a wonderful watercolor by Albrecht Dürer of a bird's wing.

8. James Joseph Sylvester (1814–97), mathematician, had resided at St. John's College, Cambridge, but as a Jew could not take his degree until after the passing of the Tests Act in 1872. Long before then he was recognized as one of the foremost mathematicians of the time. He was Professor of Mathematics at the University of Virginia, 1841–1845 and at the Royal Military Academy, Woolwich, 1855–1870. In the interval he practised law and worked as an actuary. In 1877 he went again to America as the first Professor of Mathematics at the Johns Hopkins University and in 1883 returned as Savilian Professor of Geometry at Oxford. The mistake about his age was Mme Bodichon's. See Hester Burton, *Barbara Bodichon,* [1949], p. 74.

## GE TO ELIZABETH STUART PHELPS, RICKMANSWORTH, 13 AUGUST 1875

*Text:* Copy found among Mr. Cross's papers, Yale. *Hitherto unpublished.*

The Elms | Rickmansworth | Herts. August 13. 75.

My dear Madame

I am happy to be able to remedy the little accident to your paper by copying the passages you have extracted from my former letter.[9]

"I certainly feel a strong disgust for any readiness to satisfy that idle curiosity which, caring little for the study of an author's works, is pleased with low gossip about his private life and personal appearance. Of every writer worth reading it may be said

"He gave the people of his best;
"His worst he kept; his best he gave."[1]

Can we be too severe on the spirit which neglects the "best," and eagerly accepts details called biographical, which would be worthless even if they were accurate?

Every sentence of your letter assures me that you are at one with me on this point. . . .

It is interesting, I think, to know whether a writer was born in a central or border district—a condition which always has a strongly determining influence. I was born in Warwickshire, but certain family traditions connected with more northerly districts, made those districts a region of poetry to me in my early childhood.

I was brought up in the Church of England, and have never joined any other religious society, but I have had close acquaintance[2] with many dissenters of various sects, from Calvinists and Baptists to Unitarians.

I never—to answer one of your questions quite directly—I never had any personal acquaintance with J. S. Mill—never saw him, to my knowledge, except in the House of Commons; and though I have studied his books, especially his Logic and Political Economy, with much benefit, I have no consciousness of their having made any marked epoch in my life.

Of Mr. Herbert Spencer's friendship I have had the honour and advantage for twenty years, but I believe that every main bias of my mind

9. Neither this letter nor the one it answered has been found.

1. Tennyson, "You Might Have Won the Poet's Name," line 25.

2. The copy Miss Phelps sent to be copied reads "but I have close personal acquaintance."

had been taken before I knew him. Like the rest of his readers, I am of course indebted to him for much enlargement and clarifying of thought." [3]

Let me add to this transcription that I felt no offense from your second letter to me. As far as I can recall the circumstances, I think I remained silent from a want of health and leisure which obliges me to restrict my correspondence. I can sympathize from experience with the cause which has hindered you from working as you wished to do, and I should rejoice to know that your physical delicacy is of a kind from which you may be completely restored.

We are in a country house for the summer, and for that reason I have not seen the poems you have kindly sent us, most packets for us being allowed to remain in town.

I see that I wrote (automatically) 'dear *Madame*' at the beginning of my letter. If that looks chill and formal to you, believe that it does not represent my feeling which is that of sympathetic as well as respectful regard.

Yours, dear Miss Phelps, sincerely
M. E. Lewes.

## GE TO JOHN WALTER CROSS, RICKMANSWORTH, 14 AUGUST 1875

*MS:* Yale. *Extracts published:* Cross, III, 260–261.

The Elms | Rickmansworth | August 14. 75.

Dearest Nephew

What a comfort that you are at home again and well! [4] The sense of your nearness had been so long missing to us that we had begun to take up with life as inevitably a little less cheerful than we remembered it to have been formerly, without thinking of restoration. I trust you will soon feel settled in your old place and gradually effacing any undesirable signs of your long absence.

My box is quite dear to me, and shall be used for stamps, as you recommend, unless I find another use that will lead me to open it and think of you the oftener. You revile it, but to my taste it is exceedingly pretty, and has that charm of a box to me—a lid with a

3. The remarks on Mill and Spencer are intended to counter the ridiculous statements about her relation to them in *Men of the Time,* 9th edition, 1875. See 15 July 1874.

4. Cross had been abroad for six weeks.

hinge, so that I can open and shut it without trouble. It is very precious to me that you bore me in your mind and took that trouble to give me pleasure—in which you have succeeded.

We have lately had a sorrow in the death of our youngest son Herbert, whom you have heard us speak of as Bertie. For a long while we have been in anxiety about him on account of a sad change in his health. From having been splendidly muscular and altogether vigorous he had become reduced by what he reported to be neuralgic pains. It now appears that a tendency to glandular disease which had shewn itself in his early boyhood had returned and rapidly developed itself, so that every one of his glands was enlarged. He went to Durban for the sake of sea air and medical advice, but while there an attack of bronchitis hastened his death. He has left a widow and two children, one of them an infant boy born in May last. He was a sweet-natured creature—not clever, but diligent and well-judging about the things of daily life, and we felt ten years ago that a colony with a fine climate, like Natal, offered him the only fair prospect within his reach. What can we do more than try to arrive at the best conclusion from the conditions as they are known to us? The issue, which one could not foresee, must be borne with resignation—is in no case a ground for self-reproach, and in this case, I imagine, would hardly have been favourably altered by a choice of life in the old country.

Our house here is rather a fine old red brick Georgian place, with a lovely bit of landscape, but I think we have suffered the more from the rainy close weather because we are in a valley and can see the mists lie in a thick white stratum on our meadow. Mr. Lewes has been on the whole flourishing and enjoying, writing away with vigour, and making a discovery or theory at the rate of 1 per diem.

Of your unfortunate Aunt you must expect no good. She has been in a piteous state of debility in body and depression in mind. Her book seems to her so unlikely ever to be finished in a way that will make it worth giving to the world that it is a kind of glass in which she beholds her infirmities.

That expedition on the Thames would be a great delight if it were possible to us. But our arrangements forbid it—our loving thanks to Mr. Druce as well as to you for reviving the thought. We are to remain here till the 23d of September, then to fly through town, or at least only perch there for a night or so, and then go down to the coast while the servants clean our house. Mr. Lewes looks forward to a little renewal of his old zoologizing pleasures at the coast, and at present we expect that Bournemouth will be our destination.

Let us have news of you all again soon. Let us comfort each other while it is day, for the night cometh——

Our best love to all the dear ones now mustered together. I hope this change of weather in which we are glorying both for the country's sake and our own will not make Weybridge too warm for Mrs. Cross.

Always your affectionate Aunt
M. E. Lewes

## GE TO THE HON. MRS. HENRY FREDERICK PONSONBY, RICKMANSWORTH, 19 AUGUST 1875

*Text:* Cross, III, 261–263.

I don't mind how many letters I receive from one who interests me as much as you do. The receptive part of correspondence I can carry on with much alacrity. It is writing answers that I groan over. Please take it as a proof of special feeling that I declined answering your kind inquiries by proxy.

This corner of Hertfordshire is as pretty as it can be of the kind. There are really rural bits at every turn. But for my particular taste I prefer such a region as that round Haslemere—with wide furzy commons and a grander horizon. Also I prefer a country where I don't make bad blood by having to see one public house to every six dwellings—which is literally the case in many spots around us. My gall rises at the rich brewers in Parliament and out of it, who plant these poison shops for the sake of their million-making trade, while probably their families are figuring somewhere as refined philanthropists or devout evangelicals and ritualists.

You perceive from this that I am dyspeptic and disposed to melancholy views. In fact I have not been flourishing—but I am getting a little better; grateful thanks that you will care to know it. On the whole the sins of brewers, with their drugged ale and devil's traps, depress me less than my own inefficiency. But every fresh morning is an opportunity that one can look forward to for exerting one's will. I shall not be satisfied with your philosophy till you have conciliated necessitarianism—I hate the ugly word—with the practice of willing strongly, willing to will strongly, and so on, that being what you certainly can do and have done about a great many things in life, whence it is clear that there is nothing in truth to hinder you from it—except you will say the absence of a motive. But that absence I don't believe in, in your case—only in the case of empty barren souls.

Are you not making a transient confusion of intuitions with innate ideas? The most thorough experientialists admit intuition—*i.e.,* direct impressions of sensibility underlying all proof—as necessary starting-points for thought.

## GE TO MRS. ELMA STUART, RICKMANSWORTH, 2 SEPTEMBER 1875

*MS:* British Museum. *Published:* Stuart, pp. 46–49.

The Elms | Rickmansworth | Herts. September 2. 75.

My dearest Elma

We both think that the idea of your writing a detailed story of your self-initiation as a wood-carver is one to be carried out without delay. I should imagine that many girls and women might be helped through your experience, directly or indirectly. And if your loving heart makes it a necessary condition to your doing the good work, that you should mention me (with due discreetness) I will not raise any obstacle. Only we must not see what you write beforehand. Neither Mr. Lewes nor I must have anything to do with it. This is quite absolute. You have a perfect right, my sweet daughter, to say what you think fit (I have confidence in your sense of fitness) about any relation my writings may have had to your history. My writings are public property: it is only myself apart from my writings that I hold private, and claim a veto about as a topic. And I particularly object to Mr. Lewes's having any cognizance of what you choose to say. If you cannot trust your own judgment, consult some dispassionate friend—friends are not wanting in dispassionateness as critics of the praise given to some one else, and what your overflowing heart prompts is sure to have a sound of eulogy which, as your fervent countrymen would say, will seem "strong enough," i.e. quite tremendously strong to your friendly critic. I don't of course mean that you will write any direct praise, but that your grateful ardour may easily seem to others more than George Eliot deserves.

But write your paper with a vision of the idle women's needs before you.[4a]

Your spiritual mother has been a sadly dispirited mother of late, with a distaste for herself and her doings which would make life heavy

4a. Though the article was written and reprinted, I have been unable to find it. See 3 March 1876.

if it were not borne up by soft strong wings of affection—tender husband's affection. You must have known much in your shorter but often difficult life of that double, reflected depression in which one is constantly wondering how much is bodily feebleness, how much mental anxiety. But since you say nothing of your health I am hoping that you are stronger—though I fear your silence is not good evidence. Have you left off naughtily working too long at night? And do you encourage sleep in all rational ways? Please to bear in mind that in being careless about your nerves you are endangering your 'precious soul.'

We shall leave this place on the 23d. It will be time to do so, for the autumn mists on our meadows would not be sanitary. I suppose we shall go down to the coast while our London house is being cleaned, and perhaps I shall be quickened into more vigour by that change. I have constant cheerfulness by my side in my other self. He works with delight, and on the whole has been much better in this summer abode than in the last, at Redhill.

I am much comforted that you are no longer in anxiety about Roland. Please offer my loving remembrances to him, and tell him that the Eau de Cologne has seemed much more desirable to me since he became my purveyor. But my consumption does not go on so fast as his kind care in providing. Always, dearest Elma,

Your loving Mother
M. E. Lewes.

## GHL TO JOHN BLACKWOOD, RICKMANSWORTH, [11 SEPTEMBER 1875]

*MS:* National Library of Scotland. *Hitherto unpublished.*

The Elms | Rickmansworth | Saturday.

My dear Blackwood

You were kind enough to say you would send Mrs. Lewes The Abode of Snow [5]—if it has not already been sent to the Priory will you please order it to be sent here?, as she wishes to read it aloud of an evening.

The book gets on slowly amid usual depression. Her health does not improve and when we leave this—on the 22d—I propose taking

5. Andrew Wilson (1831–81), *The Abode of Snow. Chinese Tibet to Indian Caucasus,* published by Blackwood, 1875 after serialization in *Blackwood's.* They read it aloud 16–21 September. (GHL Diary.)

her to Wales for a complete holiday in hopes that rest and bracing air may set her up.

I am hard at work and tolerably well. What superb weather we have at last. You must have too many letters to write for me to wish for any reply to this unless you have something special to say.

Ever yours truly
G. H. L.

## GHL TO JOHN WALTER CROSS, RICKMANSWORTH, [17 SEPTEMBER 1875]

*MS:* Yale. *Envelope:* J. W. Cross Esq | Weybridge Heath | Weybridge | Surrey. *Postmarks:* RICKMANSWORTH | C | SP 18 | 75; B | WATFORD | SP 19 | 75; WEYBRIDGE STATION | SP 20 | 75. *Hitherto unpublished.*

The Elms, Rickmansworth | Sunday.

My dear Nephew

From aunt and self all good wishes rest upon the new Firm! [6] I won't say may you get your deserts as *that* may be a whipping; but may you be as prosperous as rational desires can prefigure!

I wish I could give better accounts of Madonna; but this low lying Thames Valley is decidedly enervating, and added to her depression of spirits, it has counteracted even the splendid weather we have had of late. We shall only stay one day in town and then start for the Welsh Mountains. Perhaps their bracing air (and complete idleness) may set her up for the winter. Nor can I give much better accounts of your's truly. Our life is so unvaried here that there is absolutely nothing to write about except health! Yes, by the way, there was one variety the other day in the escape from what might have been a serious accident. Madonna was coming to meet me at the Watford Station on my return from town,[7] when a runaway horse in a brewer's cart, dashed up against ours—broke our shaft and strained the springs but did no other damage! When I learned about it you can imagine "the turn" it gave me. Madonna was perfectly calm throughout, and not really frightened.

It is sad to hear of dear Emily not getting strong again. Why is love so little therapeutic? and why are nice people so seldom strong?

6. Cross, Benson and Co., commission agents, 38 Cornhill. His partner was Robert Benson.

7. GHL's most recent visit to London was 4 September 1875. This episode is not mentioned in his Diary.

Charles and Gertrude are at St. Moritz and write rapturously of the Engadine and the weather. Our dearest love to all

Ever yours
G. H. L.

## GE TO MRS. WILLIAM CROSS, RICKMANSWORTH, 19 SEPTEMBER 1875

*MS:* Yale. *Hitherto unpublished.*

The Elms | Rickmansworth | September 19. 75.

Dearest Mrs. Cross

I write to you on a little errand of my own, and will not pretend to be less self-seeking than I am. Two years ago, or more, our dear "jeunesse" Florence [8] told me that her doctor had given her a delightfully soothing pink ointment for the skin. If she has the prescription still by her, I should be very grateful for it.

Having frankly made use of you, let me say that I love you for something else than your usefulness to me, and shall be doubly grateful if you will pour me out a few sentences about yourself. It is too long since I had that gift of friendship from you, perhaps because my silence has deserved silence in return.

Perhaps Nephew John has told you that we go up to town on Thursday, and set off again into Wales on the Saturday—only for a brief space, at the end of which we shall settle down for the winter. [*The rest of the page has been cut away.*]

## GE TO PHOEBE SARAH MARKS, RICKMANSWORTH, 21 SEPTEMBER 1875

*Text:* Evelyn Sharp, *Hertha Ayrton,* London, E. Arnold, 1926, pp. 37–38.

The Elms | Rickmansworth | September 21, 1875.

My dear Miss Marks,—

I enter with the keenest interest into your needs—so does Mr. Lewes —and we are longing to see some avenue of light on the probabilities of your finding what will meet the rather difficult conjunction of requisites, especially as to salary and freedom from dogmatic prejudice.[9]

8. Florence Nightingale Cross (1857–1915), later Mrs. Henry Weston Eve.

9. While preparing herself to enter Girton College, Miss Marks was also looking after an invalid sister, earning a living for both by giving lessons. In the summer of 1875 her health broke down. Having sent her sister away to school, she was free to seek a position as governess. GE gave her £10 in May. (GHL Diary.)

I have written to one lady, who I know will help us if she can. But I think I must give up the attempt to interest any one else until I have the opportunity of personal intercourse with our friends. I only send this hurried note to let you know that you have our sympathy, and that we shall be rejoiced if that sympathy can turn into practical usefulness. I certainly should have held it an advantage for you if you could have managed to make the necessary money by separate lessons and classes. The difficulties of the resident situation seem to me great.

We leave this place on Thursday and are then going on a journey; [1] but I hope we shall be at the Priory again by the middle of October.

Yours always most sincerely,
M. E. Lewes.

## GHL DIARY, SHREWSBURY, 24 SEPTEMBER 1875

*MS:* Yale. *Hitherto unpublished.*

Left at 10 for Shrewsbury and found I had left my Guide Book behind, so as soon as dinner was ordered at the Raven went to Telegraph for it. We rambled about the old town in the rain delighting in the picturesque old houses and the views from the heights and bridge. After dinner learned that Sir James Paget and family were in the hotel—sent in my card and Sir James at once came to us and dragged us to their room which was *full* of young men and the family. Passed a very pleasant evening with them—singing and chat.

## GE TO JOHN BLACKWOOD, LONDON, 10 OCTOBER 1875

*MS:* National Library of Scotland. *Extracts published:* Cross, III, 264–265.

**The Priory, | 21. North Bank, | Regents Park.**
October 10. 75.

My dear Mr. Blackwood

I behaved rather shabbily in not thanking you otherwise than by proxy for the kind letter you sent me to Rickmansworth, but I had a

1. GE and GHL returned to the Priory 23 September 1875. Finding the drawing room still unpapered and the whole house smelling of paint, they set out the next morning for Shrewsbury. After three days there they went on for brief stays at Aberystwith, Barmouth, Dolgelley, Carnarvon, Llanberis, and Chester, reaching home 9 October to find "the Priory still in the hands of the paper hangers!" During their trip GE read aloud Jane Austen's *Emma,* Dickens's *Uncommercial Traveller,* Turgenev's *Nouvelles Moscovites* and *Récits d'un chasseur,* and Sterne's *Sentimental Journey.*

'bad time' down there and did less of everything than I desired. Last night we returned from our trip—a very lively word for a journey made in the worst weather—and since I am on the whole the better for a succession of small discomforts in hotels and struggling walks taken under an umbrella, I have no excuse for not writing a line to my neglected correspondents.

You will laugh at our nervous caution in depositing our MSS at the Union Bank before we set out. We could have borne to hear that our house had been burnt down provided no lives were lost, and our unprinted matter, our œuvres inédites, were safe out of it.[2]

About *my* unprinted matter—Mr. Lewes thinks it will not be well to publish the first part till February.[3] December he says will be too soon for the necessary arrangements with America, and January he maintains is a bad month for publishing anything, whereas February is altogether eligible. The four first monthly parts are ready for travelling now. I am a little uncertain about the way the quantities will turn out, but I have divided these two volumes to the best of my calculation. I found that the first volume—i.e. the first two parts—would turn out enormously thick on my first plan of division, and have therefore revised the arrangement.

It will be well to begin the printing in good time so that I may not be hurried with the proofs, and I must beg Mr. Simpson to judge for me in that matter with kind carefulness.

I can't say that I am at all satisfied with the book or that I have a comfortable sense of doing in it what I want to do, but Mr. Lewes *is* satisfied with it and insists that since he is as anxious as possible for it to be fine I ought to accept his impression as trustworthy. So I resign myself.

I read aloud "The Abode of Snow" at Rickmansworth to our mutual delight, and we are both very much obliged to you for the handsome present. But what an amazing creature is this Andrew Wil-

2. Mrs. Gerald Porter describes how on one occasion when she and her father were calling, GE "said that she was very anxious about the safety of the MS. of 'Deronda,' and wanted to have it back, but dared not trust it to the post-office. My father said he could not bring it himself next day, but could send it by a trusty messenger (the footman). At this she quailed. 'Oh, he might stop at a public-house and forget it.' We assured her such a lapse had never been known to occur. 'Then might he not, if he were the sort of high-minded Bayard we described, be very likely to stop and help at a fire? This was a contingency we had never contemplated, and finally, after much laughter, we promised her that some member of the family should place the MS. in her hands, and as a matter of fact I think my mother drove over with it to her the next morning." (*John Blackwood*, pp. 388–389.)

3. *Daniel Deronda* appeared in 8 monthly parts, February–September 1876.

son to have kept pluck for such travelling while his body was miserably ailing! One would have said that he had more than the average spirit of hardy men to have persevered even in good health after a little taste of the difficulties he describes. The account of the *dandi* [4] seems something like a cruel punishment of criminals in ancient Tartary.— Also I found last night, and read, Principal Tulloch's Sermon,[5] besides Mr. Simpson's budget of Dutch and Australian [6] Correspondence, which Mr. Lewes takes charge of.

I wonder if Scotland has continued to have the advantage over us in weather. Wherever we have been, notwithstanding the rain, the trees show little sign of autumnal changes, and if we could have a fortnight of sunshine it would be the most delicious bit of the year for the country—where I imagine you will feel settled till the end of the month. I hope that you are all well enough to enjoy it thoroughly.

Yours always sincerely
M. E. Lewes.

## GE TO FRANÇOIS D'ALBERT-DURADE, LONDON, 13 OCTOBER 1875

*Text:* Copy by D'Albert-Durade, Tinker Collection, Yale. *Hitherto unpublished.*

The Priory | 21 North Bank | Regent's Park | October 13. 75.

My dear Friend

On my return to town the other day I found your kind letter with the volume obligingly presented to me by Mr. Gustave Revilliod.[7] Pray offer him my best thanks and say that I have an interest in oriental literature which makes the gift especially acceptable.

Your letter is a delightful assurance that you have been having much family happiness, and I can imagine the pretty picture made by the grandparents with the two younger generations. What a comfort that Madame D'Albert, in spite of bodily weakness, is able to share such joys of heart and mind!

To us the summer brought sorrow in the death of our son Herbert who, you may remember, was settled in South Africa. He had for some

4. Wilson describes (pp. 132–133) being carried in a dandi, slung from a bamboo between two natives who found him too heavy and actually cried at the difficulty over the Rúhang Pass.

5. John Tulloch, *Religion and Theology. A Sermon for the Times*, published by Blackwood, 1875.

6. Negotiations for the Australian and Dutch rights to *Daniel Deronda.*

7. Eugène Revillout (1843–1913), archeologist and bibliophile, *Vie et sentences de Secundus, d'après divers manuscrits orientaux,* Paris, 1873.

time been in delicate health, and we were afraid of urging him to come to England because his disease was of a nature to be encouraged by our fitful climate. This death is all the sadder because he was very happily married and has left a deeply attached young wife to sorrow for him. Hardly a month before his death she had had a second child—a fine little boy. Our consolation is that we are at least able to provide for them in the worldly sense—but for her, poor dear, there is no present consolation. They felt peculiarly united, leading unseparate[d]ly a retired life and being all in all to each other.

Apart from this loss our life has been as much blessed as usual, our son Charles and his family being a constant source of satisfaction to us and our own domestic joy having no flaw except the accustomed infirmities of health which we must not expect ever to be free from.

We spent the summer in the country according to our habit, but our situation was rather too low, and I think we suffered some depression of vitality from a rather close and over moist atmosphere. But we have been and are still very busy, Mr. Lewes being engaged on the third volume of Problems, and I on a long book, the first part of which will perhaps appear in the beginning of February.

We old people cannot help regretting the beautiful old Geneva, enclosed in its harmless fortifications. But the changes you describe are such as we have to witness in all prosperous towns—in Dresden, for example—which used to have a clear heaven above it and quiet amusements within the streets and beyond them where one could sit and hear the best music without being overcrowded. The last time we were there the times had changed all that. Everywhere there is a prosperous crowd to be amused, and the tastes of the crowd are not yet refined, so that Art must condescend to please the low average. This condescension is painfully marked in our huge rich London; but of late we have been a little cheered [by] a revived interest in the Shakespearean drama to counterbalance Offenbach.

Mr. Lewes begs me to offer his best remembrances to Madame D'Albert and yourself, and I am as ever both to her and you

Your affectionate friend
M. E. Lewes.

## GE TO [?], LONDON, 13 OCTOBER 1875

*MS:* Bodleian. *Hitherto unpublished.*

**The Priory, | 21. North Bank, | Regents Park.**
October 13. 75.

Dear Madam

I thank you for obeying the impulse to write to me.

Such words as yours are the strongest, the most precious of encouragements. It is beyond what I could have hoped that in the freshness of such a sorrow as yours, any words of mine could be cherished as companions.

Yours with deep sympathy
M. E. Lewes.
(George Eliot)

## GHL TO ALEXANDER MAIN, LONDON, 13 OCTOBER 1875

*Text:* Main's copy owned by Mr. John R. Sprunt. *Hitherto unpublished.*

Wednesday 13th October 75.

My dear Main

On our return home your letter smiled at us amid a pile of circulars and notes. The return was from Wales, and *not* Mürren—so you see the papers have been as accurate as usual, and our interview with the Archbishop must have taken place in the presence of a "Special Correspondent." [7a] I had hoped the mountain air would brace us both—but we had little sun, and *gales* in lieu of "air," blustering day and night, and diversified with storms, so that our journey was a mull and made us long for the "comforts o' the saut market." Now we are fixed for the winter and ready to resume work, not indeed as strong as one could wish, but yet well enough to jog on.

Among the letters was the enclosed which I thought would interest you on account of your share in it. Send it me back. Madonna is always deeply gratified by such evidence that her work has not been in vain. I have too many letters to write to expatiate.

Ever yours truly
G. H. L.

7a. Main's letter has not been found.

## GE TO MRS. MARK PATTISON, LONDON, 18 OCTOBER 1875

*MS:* British Museum. *Hitherto unpublished.*

**The Priory, | 21. North Bank, | Regents Park.**
October 18. 75.

My poor dear Figliuolina

Alas, I had been making pictures of you to myself in Oxford again, cured and tasting your ordinary life with hard-won freshness, and your letter has just brought me what I must consider very bad news. How gladly would I comfort you! but the attempt to give comfort by words in such trouble as yours would be an impertinence and a mockery. Even if I sat by you I should keep silence and trust to your knowledge that I am enough acquainted with bodily suffering to enter with fellow-feeling into your heavier trial. I think much of the Rector too, and of the way in which his loneliness must enter into your sadness under the condemnation to exile.[8]

That you are having your violin sent with your papers is a pleasant proof of your power to use all your ten fingers. And I build some hope on the general liability to error in doctor's prophecies. The complexity of the subjects they pronounce upon makes it no disgrace to them when things turn out better as well as worse than they expected, and I have known, as I dare say you have, as many instances of the "better" as of the "worse."

As to Nice, I compassionate you with some knowledge of the place, though only through short visits. But there are other places that would do as well, if you are obliged to go south for other winters—not perhaps places with much art in them, but still preferable as a variety. You must consider the Southern map, and if you are a good sailor, you may get to some scenery fresh enough to be something of a substitute for the Art above Nature, which Nature makes.

I hope that the Rector has some work in hand of the absorbing kind —a work of like value with the 'Isaac Casaubon.' That is the best refuge in domestic privation. And *you* will carry on the woof of work begun. You see I am determined to think of you as cheerfully as I can, being too much inclined to despond about my own doings to afford despondency about my friends.

8. Still suffering from arthritis, Mrs. Pattison was advised to remain away from England during the winter. She went to Aix-les-Bains for the autumn and then to Nice. (C.W. Dilke, *The Book of the Spiritual Life*, 1905, p. 44.)

There is nothing to tell you, except that we are just come back to town and are unable to sit in the drawing-room for the smell of paint. I have not been well through the last four months, and a rainy fortnight's excursion into Wales was not greatly curative. The weather is now brightening, and we have had a couple of autumnal days with clear air and a sharp edge of cold.

Our only real ground of sadness lately has been the death of our youngest son, who was settled (and married) in S. Africa. He was a dear good fellow, and thoroughly happy in his marriage, so that his death seems an extinction of nothing but joy—not at all of a counterbalancing evil. His young widow has two tiny children, and it is our comfort to be able to provide for them.

Always when one looks beyond one's own lot there is some evident reason for taking one's share of trouble as not excessive, when it is something short of agony. But I fear that your long, wearisome endurance of pain which eats itself into every cranny of mind and body may have sometimes seemed to you to deserve the name of agony. I have been thinking a great deal lately of such cases as Auguste Thierry's, who with paralyzed limbs which obliged him to be carried about like a bundle, made his life precious to himself and others, and was really an enjoying creature.[9]

Mr. Lewes joins me in sympathy and affectionate wishes.

Always your faithfully attached
M. E. Lewes.

## JOHN BLACKWOOD TO GE, ST. ANDREWS, 18 OCTOBER 1875

*Text:* Copy in Blackwood Letter Book. *Hitherto unpublished.*

Strathtyrum | St. Andrews October 18/75.

My Dear Mrs. Lewes

You will think me very ungrateful for not having at once answered your pleasant and most welcome letter. I got it in Edinburgh when I was in a whirl of business, after which I had to pay a visit in a country house, very pleasant but not conducive to writing, and since I came home on Saturday I have been obliged to sit doggedly at an enormous M.S. about which a friend is coming from the other end of the Island tonight to consult with me. Thank God I have finished the reading and

9. Jacques Nicolas Augustin Thierry (1795–1856), French historian, was blind as well as paralysed from 1830 till the end of his life.

the great pile of M.S. is lying beside me *face* downwards. However the M.S. was I am happy to say worth reading. I am sorry Rickmansworth did not suit you better, but it is a comfort that the "trip" to Wales has done some good. Your happy phrase of trip being too lovely an epithet for such an expedition reminds me of May cruises in the rainy West Highlands when I devoutly wished myself at Randolph Crescent or Strathtyrum all the time.

I am delighted to hear of the two volumes being ready for the printer and I sympathise with your feeling in taking the "Plate Chest" to your bankers before you started. Who has got such a plate chest? Mr. Simpson was energetic in his applause of the precaution and begged me to tell you that we have a fire proof room at 45 George Street where he would carefully deposit the precious M.S. and dole it out to the printers.

I think Lewes is right about February being the best month to begin publication. The active world of London is then drawing together and although I do not think it greatly matters when such a Ship as yours is launched it is well to have the buzz of talk open at headquarters at once. The main thing of course is not to hurry or harass you. It would be better to begin publication in the dog days than do that in any degree. From the state of progress however in which I am happy to think "Daniel Deronda" is, I see no fear of the start in February being too soon.

You had better send the M.S. as soon as may suit you and we shall return proofs at any time that may be most easy to you for correction. From reading the first volume, which privilege has ever since made me feel rather ahead of the rest of the world, I am quite sure Lewes who has seen more is right, and you may dismiss those fears that so easily beset you as to not having hit your mark. The scope and merits of that first volume are wonderful.

As to form I do not think we can do better than follow Middlemarch only making the publication monthly as the audience are more ready.

I am very glad the Abode of Snow pleased you so much as it will be an immense gratification to the Author to hear of praise from you. How he got over those fatigues is not the least remarkable part of the story as physically he seems to have no more muscle than a jelly fish and he is a queer fish but a very big fish in mind and energy. Some 20 years ago when quite a youngster he wrote a paper for me which indicated genius and I wrote to him saying so and urging him to go on. He became however a kind of wandering waif and only hearing of him vaguely for years I feared he had gone to the bad—when after many days the prodigal son returned and produced this admirable series of papers.

We are suffering here from very wild stormy weather and I fear it is not over yet. Yesterday at lunch we heard the guns signaling a ship in distress in the Bay and of course my wife and daughter insisted on sallying forth with me. Their two slight figures perched in a hurricane of wind and rain on one of the dunes by the seashore watching the struggling ship would have made a picture. The ship drifted away from us and finally went ashore on a sand bank south of the Tay opposite. All lives were saved.

We intend to remain here until about the 10th of November and I am in hopes of good weather after this fearful week.

Always yours truly
(Signed) John Blackwood.

## GE TO MRS. PETER ALFRED TAYLOR, LONDON, 20 OCTOBER 1875

*Text:* Cross, III, 265–266.

The arrangements as to the publication of my next book are already determined on. Ever since 'Adam Bede' appeared, I have been continually having proposals from the proprietors or editors of periodicals,[1] but I have always declined them, except in the case of 'Romola,' which appeared in the 'Cornhill,' and was allowed to take up a varying and unusual number of pages. I have the strongest objection to cutting up my work into little bits; [2] and there is no motive to it on my part, since I have a large enough public already. But, even apart from that objection, it would not now be worth the while of any magazine or journal to give me a sum such as my books yield in separate publication. I had £7000 for 'Romola,' but the mode in which 'Middlemarch' was issued brings in a still larger sum. I ought to say, however, that the question is not entirely one of money with me: if I could gain more by splitting my writing into small parts, I would not do it, because the effect would be injurious as a matter of art. So much detail I trouble you with to save misapprehension.

1. One of them recorded in GHL's Diary is a letter from Porter and Coates of Philadelphia "offering 1500 £ for the advance sheets of Polly's new novel." (10 July 1874.)

2. Mrs. Taylor's inquiry was probably on behalf of her husband, who had become owner of the *Examiner* in 1874.

## JOHN BLACKWOOD TO GHL, ST. ANDREWS, 3 NOVEMBER 1875

*Text:* Copy in Blackwood Letter Book. *Hitherto unpublished.*

Strathtyrum | St. Andrews November 3/75.

My dear Lewes

The arrival of the two volumes was a great event in 45 George St. and my nephew tells me they were after a careful inspection carried off to the fire proof room in the loving arms of Simpson.

The Proofs now begin to arrive here and I wait instructions from Mrs. Lewes or you as to times and quantities in which she wishes them sent to her. Proof of the first sixty four pages is what I have got and of course I could not resist reading at once. To read was to renew pleasure and I found my first impression of the wonderful skill and power of the opening more confirmed.

We have said nothing directly about terms but my understanding, subject to your approval, is that we should begin at the same price and pay the same lordship as with Middlemarch.

My nephew as well as my wife and daughter, who have had the privilege of looking into these 64 pages, are as much delighted as I am. I hope Mrs. Lewes is pretty well and that the sending off these two volumes of Daniel Deronda has been a relief to her. Give her my best regards and congratulations to her.

Always yours truly
(Signed) John Blackwood.

G. H. Lewes Esq.

## GHL TO JOHN BLACKWOOD, LONDON, [4 NOVEMBER 1875]

*MS:* National Library of Scotland. *Hitherto unpublished.*

**The Priory, | 21. North Bank, | Regents Park.**
Thursday.

My dear Blackwood

She was much pleased to hear that the second reading was not a falling off. She is decidedly better in health since our return, but proceeds very slowly and despondingly with volume 3. Non fit aliter!

As to terms, yes, the old Middlemarch both price and lordship. May the success be as great! [3]

I am curious to hear how volume 2 will affect you and whether you find a crescendo of interest.

I am going to Cambridge next week to work in the Physiological laboratory [4]—but have a wretched account to give of myself. Nervous exhaustion has for some weeks entirely prevented work and I am only now feebly beginning again.

Ever yours truly
G. H. Lewes.

John Blackwood.

## GE TO JOHN BLACKWOOD, LONDON, 10 NOVEMBER 1875

*MS:* National Library of Scotland. *Hitherto unpublished.*

**The Priory, | 21. North Bank, | Regents Park.**
November 10/75.

Dear Mr. Blackwood

I want your opinion about the length of the four first Parts of D. D. Mr. Simpson sends me word this morning that Pts. III and IV make respectively 170 and 175 pp. Pts. I and II being 191 and 180. My original division made the two first parts considerably longer—Pt. I ending at the end of the Archery Ball, and Part II at the end of Mirah's story.[5] But I found that by this arrangement, the first part would be more than 220 pp. and the second at least 190—making the 1st vol. tremendously thick. But I fear that the present division may make the two first parts—the impression from which is of course supremely important—rather poverty-stricken in point of matter.

What do you think? As to the III and IV Parts—there are two Books of Middlemarch which are 175 and 176 respectively, but they don't

3. On each of the 8 Books of *Middlemarch,* which sold for 5/, GE received a lordship of 2/. At this time the book had brought her more than £8000. (See Appendix I.)

4. GHL Diary, 9 November 1875: "Went down to Cambridge by the afternoon train and took fly to Shelford on a visit to Michael Foster. [Francis Maitland] Balfour, Langley, and Martin to dinner. Glorious physiological talk. At night attacked with the fiercest cramp I ever had." 10 November: "All day from 9 to ¼ past 4 in the Laboratory working with Foster on frogs and snails—capital talk the while. Lunched at Dew Smith's, and came home by 7.30 to find Vivian [Lewes] there, who dined with us."

5. The original arrangement divided the story after chs. 11 and 22; as published Book I ends with ch. 10 (188 pages), Book II with ch. 18 (172 pages), Book III with ch. 27 (185 pages), and Book IV with ch. 34 (173 pages).

come together. The question of course is rather of matter in relation to interest than in relation to quantity.

If you are for the larger size of Parts I and II and Mr. Lewes concurs, (he is this morning at Cambridge) I could throw the *same* amount into Parts III and IV—not less, I fear, because of the difficulty as to properly dividing the subject matter. Unhappily I cannot drill myself into writing according to set lengths.

Charging 5s per Book makes me dreadfully afraid of giving the Public too little for its money. On the other hand, Too Much is the most thankless form of generosity. Please give me your ideas.

Always yours sincerely
M. E. Lewes.

The 2 first volumes would preponderate in the one case—the 2 last in the other.

## JOHN BLACKWOOD TO GE, ST. ANDREWS, 10 NOVEMBER 1875

*MS:* National Library of Scotland. *Extract published: John Blackwood,* p. 392.

**Strathtyrum | St. Andrews | N.B.**
November 10/75.

My Dear Mrs. Lewes

I send proof of the first 256 pages of Daniel Deronda and I know not how to express my admiration. The reading in type transcends even the impression the M.S. had left upon me. In print one can turn back so much more easily to re-enjoy the splendid turns of thought, wit, and expression which adorn every page and had hardly been fully appreciated at the first perusal. *Stupendo,* that often misused Italian phrase, could never be so rightly applied as here.

That wicked witch Gwendolen is perfectly irresistible, new and yet so true to nature, like all the other characters. Her running mental reflections after each few words she has said to Grandcourt are like what passes through the mind after each move at a game, and as far as I know a new device in reporting a conversation.[6] A cautious speaker

6. *Daniel Deronda,* ch. 11. Dr. F. R. Leavis fixes on the same device of "psychological notation" in this part of the novel. "What later novelist has rendered the inner movement of impulse, the play of motive that issues in speech and act and underlies formed thought and conscious will, with more penetrating subtlety than she? It is . . . one of the distinctive characteristics of her mature style." (*The Great Tradition,* New York, George W. Stewart, [1948], pp. 102–103.)

will here learn that his pauses may also give his interlocutor an advantage.

Uncle Gascoigne is a perfect picture and echoes all over with human nature. His wife, daughter, and Rex are charming, and I did feel for Rex in his terrible prostration. That morning ride with Gwen [7] is a picture, and I see you could not resist the wish that they might gallop away and be happy together. The witch will I hope be saved ultimately but you alone must decide.

In the drawing room here my wife, daughter, and nephew have been reading the proofs and the sort of exclamations are "splendid," "glorious" etc. Having read so much more of the wondrous tale than they have I am ordered to be reticent in my expression of opinion about the characters but up to this point our agreement is perfect. Mr. Simpson too, who has been reading the proofs in Edinburgh, writes in a perfect ecstasy of praise. That wretch Gwen has evidently taken the veteran bachelor by storm.

The verdict among us all here is that you are fairly outdoing Middlemarch and I need say no more. The finish of every character however briefly touched is perfectly wonderful and I should have liked to have heard Gwen giving the Curate's "Perdition catch my soul." [8]

Those sworn "horse coursers," my wife and nephew, suggest that poor Primrose's *knees* were not likely to have been broken by such a fall as you describe *in a field*.[9]

I remember pausing at the use of the word dynamic in the very first sentence and I am not quite sure about it yet as it is a *dictionary* word to so many people.[1] I know no other word however that would so powerfully and strictly convey your meaning. I think I see Klesmer at the Archery meeting,[2] and how you have touched off a whole class in Lush. Miss Arrowsmith is charming, but Gwen's comparison of the relative effect of their charms is perfectly true.

7. Ch. 13.

8. Gwendolen declares that Mr. Middleton would say it in the same tone as "Here endeth the second lesson." (ch. 6.) *Othello,* III, iii, 90.

9. GE accepted the suggestion. The MS and proof sheets read: "in crossing a rough pasture, where coarse tufted grass concealed some treacherous holes, Primrose fell as into a trap, broke his knees, and undesignedly threw Rex over his head." (ch. 7.) The printed text (I, 125): "in the search for a gate, along a lane lately mended, Primrose fell, broke his knees, and undesignedly threw Rex over his head."

1. "Was she beautiful or not beautiful? and what was the secret of form or expression which gave the dynamic quality to her glance?" The word was not new. Emerson used it in *English Traits,* 1856 ("their dynamic brains"), and Tyndall, Spencer, and others used it earlier than GE.

2. Ch. 10.

Mrs. Davilow is truly affecting and effective in her helplessness and slaving.

I was sorry to hear from Lewes that he was so poorly and I hope his visit to Cambridge has done him good. This is our last week here for the season and we have bright clear frosty weather which makes the Links most enjoyable.

With hearty congratulations, Believe [me], Dear Mrs. Lewes

always yours truly

John Blackwood.

As I finish this letter the rest of volume one comes in so I inclose it also and promise myself the pleasure of reading it tonight. The proof goes in separate packet.

## GE TO CHARLES LEE LEWES, LONDON, 11 NOVEMBER 1875

*MS:* Yale. *Published:* Paterson, p. 168.

**The Priory, | 21. North Bank, | Regents Park.**

November 11. 75.

Dearest Boy

Many thanks for the list. It has been just the thing in reminding me of 'Al piè d'un Salice' and of 'Per pietà.' [3] The latter was an early love of mine. I picked it out with delight in Knight's collection when I had no one else's taste as a finger-post, and there is a peculiar pleasure in finding one's independent impressions afterwards warranted by the best judgments. 'Che farò' and 'Ho perduto' I have already used in 'Mr. Gilfil's Love Story' [4]—having heard Johanna Wagner sing them at Berlin when in her glory there.

Pater came back to dinner yesterday after a very pleasant 'Schmaus' of Physiology at Cambridge. Best love to all from

Your loving

Mutter.

You have not said whether Gertrude has got back her voice, but I gathered that she had from what she said of the effect the air at St. Maurice had upon it.

3. Mirah Cohen sings Beethoven's "Per Pietà non dirmi addio," (*Daniel Deronda*, ch. 32; 1876, I, 310) as a result of Charles's suggestion. In the MS "She sang Schubert's 'Adieu,' filling out its long notes. . . ."

4. "Che Farò senza Eurydice?" from Gluck's *Orfeo*, III. In *Scenes of Clerical Life*, 1858, I, 202, GE describes both this and "Ho Perduto il bel sembiante" as from *Orfeo;* in later eds. the latter is ascribed to Giovanni Paesiello.

## GE TO MME EUGÈNE BODICHON, LONDON, 12 NOVEMBER 1875

*MS:* Mr. Philip Leigh-Smith. *Hitherto unpublished.*

**The Priory, | 21. North Bank, | Regents Park.**
November 12. 75.

Dearest B.

Mr. Lewes has been ailing, but is better. I, ditto.

You are a very out-of-London-staying friend, but we shall not have forgotten you by December.

I have not had time yet to write to Miss Marks. If you are writing to her, I wish *you* would tell her to come to me. I am at home at 5 every day except Saturday, or if she could come at ½ past 2 on some Sunday, we could chat before anyone else came [5]—or if she could come some weekday at ½ past 1 and lunch with us?

I am worried by having to write small notes.

Ever your loving
Marian.

## JOHN BLACKWOOD TO GE, EDINBURGH, 17 NOVEMBER 1875

*MS:* National Library of Scotland. *Hitherto unpublished.*

**45, George Street, | Edinburgh.**
November 17/75.

My Dear Mrs. Lewes

In regard to the division of the parts you are by far the best judge and I lean to what you now propose which would make the first volume end with the close of Mirah's story and the explanation of Deronda being at Leubrunn which draws this whole tale and dramatis personæ together.[6] As it stands the first part ends very well with the introduction of Grandcourt to Gwendolen but is of course more complete after the Archery Ball [7] and as a windup to the second part Mirah's most touching narrative to dear old Mrs. Meyrick is necessary to waken up the full interest in the little wanderer.

Practically if there is to be a difference in the thickness of the

5. Miss Marks came Sunday, 21 November 1875. (GHL Diary.)

6. Ch. 20. In the proofs Book II closes with ch. 19, originally the concluding pages of ch. 18.

7. Ch. 10 and ch. 11.

volumes it is well that the two first should have the preponderance, and in this case unless I am utterly mistaken by the time the public have reached the third volume they will be too happy to take and pay for whatever you give. Divide as you think best without regard to the outward aspect of the volumes. I enclose 180 pages more and I think I need only say that my admiration has gone on at a fastly crescendo rate. The interest goes on and on mounting and then it is a series of perfect little dramas. Every touch makes a picture.

I do not like to remark upon particular beauties, as when I turn back over the leaves I see that I would be omitting to comment upon something equally good in the next page. The only plan would be to mark with a pencil as one read but that would interrupt the pleasure and after all it would only be a running *bene bene* BENISSIME. The point to which I have read you will see is the wondrous scene where Gwendolen accepts Grandcourt.[8] You kept me uncertain up to the last moment as to whether it was to be Yes or No. I had not the heart to tell her to say No and send the bright creature to be "looked over" by Mrs. Mompert and all the hopeless gloom she foresees so clearly. This feeling in my mind proves I think the surpassing skill of your workmanship.

My wife and daughter have not yet had an opportunity of reading this part and I am very curious to see how it strikes the ladies but I think I can guess.

To return to business details we think here that the first part should be published about the 15th of January so as to give the Newspapers time to speak out before the meeting of Parliament.

On another point there is a difference of opinion among us. Mr. Simpson holds strongly, and my nephew inclines, for an interval of two months between the four first parts at any rate, as it takes the public a long time to digest and fully appreciate the value of such food and talk to their neighbours about it as we found with Middlemarch. I on the contrary am in favour of only one month's interval as our audience is much more ready than it was for Middlemarch and I am afraid of the two months giving the Librarians a better opportunity of starving their supplies.

There can be no better judge of such a point than Lewes. Will you ask him also to write to me with form of advertisements which should begin to appear now. Should we let loose any gossiping paragraph? I am not fond of such things but it will be done in spite of us and as the name Daniel Deronda does not give the idea of such a thorough picture

8. Ch. 27, the end of Book III.

of English life we had better put them on the right and most popular scent.

We left Strathtyrum on Monday with weeping and wail in spite of the weather which had been most eccentric. On Saturday to make the most of her last day my daughter skated in the morning and in the afternoon rode on nice soft roads. We had a fortnight of hurricane and rain, then a week of bright clear frost and afterwards a hurricane which only lasted 24 hours. The tides were exceptionally high and the sacred links were invaded. On the Sunday afternoon we walked down to look at the sea which was coming in grandly. Of course all the dogs accompanied us on this farewell walk and one of the little terriers barking and splashing gallantly through the shallow water surrounding the (usually) small burn which crosses the links went headlong into the burn itself. The scene would have amused you. I have heard many a golfer swear at his ball getting into this burn but I am sure [no] direr oath than Tory's (the pet's name) when he found himself suddenly heels over head in four feet of water. However he struggled gallantly up the walled side of the burn and saved me from walking in to the rescue.

always yours truly
John Blackwood.

## GE TO JOHN BLACKWOOD, LONDON, 18 NOVEMBER 1875

*MS:* National Library of Scotland. *Extracts published:* Cross, III, 266.

**The Priory, | 21. North Bank, | Regents Park.**
November 18. 75.

My dear Mr. Blackwood

Your enjoyment of the proofs cheers me greatly. And pray thank Mr. Blackwood for his valuable hints on equine matters. I have not only the satisfaction of using these hints—I allow myself the inference that where there is no criticism on like points I have made no mistake.

As to the division Mr. Lewes has made up his mind decidedly—he will tell you to what effect, among the other points about which he is writing to you.

I should be much obliged to Mr. Simpson—whom I am glad that Gwendolen has captivated—if he would rate the printers a little about their want of spacing. There are really some lines where the words all run into each other as in an ancient Greek inscription. I am anxious that my poor heroes and heroines should have all the advantage that paper and print can give them.

Has the colour of the wrapper been at all discussed? The lettering I want to have large, simple Roman.

It will perhaps be a little comfort to you to know that poor Gwen is spiritually saved, but "so as by fire." [9] Don't you see the process already beginning? I have no doubt you do, for you are a wide-awake reader.

But what a climate to expect good writing in! Skating in the morning and splashy roads in the afternoon is just typical of the alternations from frigid to flaccid in the author's bodily system, likely to give a corresponding variety to the style.

I leave all other questions to Mr. Lewes's letter.

Yours always truly
M. E. Lewes.

## GHL TO JOHN BLACKWOOD, LONDON, [18 NOVEMBER 1875]

*MS:* National Library of Scotland. *Hitherto unpublished.*

Thursday.

Dear Blackwood

I agree with you entirely on the question of monthly rather than bi-monthly issues. But although there would be some advantages in issuing number 1 on the 15 or later of January—(though announcing it for the 1 February) yet I have doubts as to whether that would interfere with the American reprint. I suppose they must not publish on 1 January—if we only come out on the 15th—and if we come out on the 15th we do not give them the fair start for February 1. As it is a question of 1500 £ [1] you will see that it is worth considering. If there is no objection to their appearing on January 1, then it might be well to anticipate the opening of Parliament by a few days. But on consideration the 15th seems to me too early since it will make six weeks

9. I Corinthians 3:15.

1. GHL had been corresponding with Harpers since 13 August 1875 about the sale of early sheets of *Daniel Deronda.* He received a telegram from them 23 November agreeing to pay £1700 for the North American rights. They published it in two editions, one at a low price; and though the book was pirated in twenty-cent series as soon as it was complete, Harpers' editions sold extensively. See J. H. Harper, *The House of Harper,* New York, 1912, pp. 388, 446.

between 1 and 2. The newspapers might have their copies earlier than the public.

I have read and reread the parts with a view to decide as to their divisions and come to the decided conviction that the present arrangement is on the whole the best—except that I throw the last five pages of volume I on to the opening of volume II.[2] At each close there is a strong *expectation* excited the best of all closes. The end of the scene in Mrs. Meyrick's moves me so that I can't patiently read the few pages which follow—they come as anticlimax but would open volume 2 quite pleasantly.

We are so pleased that you continue to like the book. It gets better and better and what it will be at last!

Yes, the gossipping paragraph will be good as advertisement and a hint as to the subject will serve to correct that absurd rumour about American life.[3] It takes so much advertizing to make the public alive to the fact of a new work's existence so that a little preliminary notice is always good.

Ever yours
G. H. Lewes.

Antæus it is said recovered his lost vigour whenever he touched the earth. I seem to have recovered some of mine on handling my old friends the frogs—I was at work in the Cambridge laboratory last week, and now I can write of a morning!

## GE TO MRS. ERNST LEOPOLD BENZON, LONDON, 19 NOVEMBER 1875

*MS:* Library of Congress. *Hitherto unpublished.*

**The Priory, | 21. North Bank, | Regents Park.**
November 19. 75.

My dear Mrs. Benzon

Since it is a pleasure to your kind feelings to give me the beautiful scarf, it cannot but be a pleasure to me to wear it for your sake. And I think it will last my life, for I am fond of these silky meshy things washed and washed again.

2. Chapter 19. GHL's suggested division was followed. Ch. 19 was made from the last pages of ch. 18.

3. "A Report is going the round of the papers that 'George Eliot has a new novel in preparation, illustrating American Life.' The first part of the statement is, we believe, true; the second part is undoubtedly incorrect." (*Athenaeum,* 18 September 1875, p. 373.)

That was true friendship to refuse a letter of introduction to us. Pray go on and do likewise unless there happen to be an exceptionally charming applicant.

The penitent sinner sends his love and I am always

Yours affectionately
M. E. Lewes.

## GE TO MRS. ELMA STUART, LONDON, 19 NOVEMBER 1875

*MS:* British Museum. *Mostly published:* Stuart, pp. 49–50.

**The Priory, | 21. North Bank, | Regents Park.**
November 19. 75.

Dearest Elma

I am too busy to write a letter. This is not a letter—it is a wail at your silence. How can you leave your parent so long in ignorance about you?

And if I had time to write, I should tell you that you seemed to misunderstand that letter of mine from Rickmansworth long ago, in which I said that we must not see the paper you wot of before publication. You spoke of 'trouble'—excused yourself from the suspicion that you intended to give trouble. That was rather cruel. As if trouble for your sake would not be very sweet to my good husband, if not my indolent or selfish self! The grounds of my prohibition were quite remote from the question of trouble. I shall explain them more fully when we see you.

Write me a few words at least, to assure me that you are well—that Roland is causing you no anxiety—that all things are peaceful with you.

We long to have some assurance that you love us still. But whether or not, I am as ever,

Your faithfully affectionate
Mother.

I am having some trial shirts made, or rather, according to your nomenclature, fine long chemises, differing from your pattern only in having no double thickness about the neck. I am hoping for much comfort from them. I should mention that we *have* heard of you once of late, as a fairy godmother sending a box of toys.

GE TO SARA SOPHIA HENNELL,
LONDON, 20 NOVEMBER 1875

*MS:* Yale. *Extracts published:* Cross, III, 267.

**The Priory, | 21. North Bank, | Regents Park.**
November 20. 75.

My dear Sara

I get my head from under the pressure of other matters, like a frog from under the water, to send you my November greeting. My silence through the rest of the months makes you esteem me the more, I hope, seeing that you yourself hate letter-writing—a remarkable exception to the rule that people like doing what they can do well, if one can call that a rule of which the reverse seems more frequent, namely, that they like doing what they do ill.

All the intimations I have gathered about you this year have made me imagine you able to share in much active enjoyment, and I trust that you have been one of those who have escaped bodily suffering from the inflictions of weather-changeableness. Since I saw Cara in the late Spring I have heard nothing about any of you, so that the least little bulletin will be acceptable.

We have gone through much since that time. Our son Bertie—a sweet-natured fellow, who had married very happily in Natal—has died of bronchitis superadded to a return of the glandular disease which he had been subject to as a child, but which he appeared long ago to have outgrown, having become an athletic young man. His widow has her second child, still an infant. It is our comfort that we are able to provide for them. We are naturally the more solicitous about Charles, the only one left. He is now thoroughly well, but the boys seem all to have inherited an untrustworthy physique.

We stayed till nearly the end of September at the house we had taken in Hertfordshire: after that we went into Wales for a fortnight and were under umbrellas nearly the whole time. Mr. Lewes has been suffering from lack of nervous energy, but he is recovering his usual power of work and enjoyment of work, having had an excursion to Cambridge to make physiological experiments with Prof. Michael Foster as a crowning means of invigoration after iron and phosphorus and pancreatic emulsion.

Mr. Lewes had a letter from Mr. Call the other day which told us the sad news that poor Mrs. Call remains as much as ever a sufferer from rheumatism after a long course of treatment at Aix. The letter did not tell us what we hear from other sources—that Frank is going to be married. Is that true? [4]

And how is Harriet under advancing age? [5] I should like much to know that you have no painfully increasing cares on her behalf. Indeed, if you will take the kind trouble to tell me, I should like to know of everything in which your health and comfort are concerned.

I wonder if you all remember an old governess of mine who used to visit me at Foleshill—a Miss Lewis? I have found her out; she is living at Leamington, very poor as well as old, but cheerful—and so delighted to be remembered with gratitude.[6] How very old we are all getting! But I hope you don't mind it any more than I do. One sees so many contemporaries, that one is well in the fashion. The approach of parting is the bitterness of age.

It would sweeten this birthday very much dear Sara, to be assured that it finds you in serenity—undisturbed by illness or care.

Please give my love to Cara and Mr. Bray.

Always your affectionate
Pollian.

## GHL TO JOHN BLACKWOOD, LONDON, [22 NOVEMBER 1875]

*MS:* National Library of Scotland. *Hitherto unpublished.*

Monday.

My dear Blackwood

The question of division into parts has greatly 'exercised' us latterly but finally we have come to a decision and abide by that already existing in the proofs. Accordingly I telegraphed this morning to cancel Mrs. Lewes's letter of yesterday.[7]

"George Eliot's New Story of English Life—DANIEL DERONDA—will appear in Eight Monthly Parts. The first part to be published on February 1."

4. Frank Spenser Hennell was married 6 June 1876 to Miss Amy Murray (d. 1941).

5. Harriet Hennell died in her 71st year, 21 November 1875, the day after this letter was written.

6. Learning Maria Lewis's address somehow, GE wrote her in September 1874, sending £10, which, Maria said, "came opportunely." (22 September 1874. Yale.) Payments of £10 appear in GHL's Diary each November, 1874–1877; his death in November 1878 may have interrupted the series, but the payments are noted in GE's Diary November 1879 and 1880.

7. GE's letter has not been found.

That is the *kind* of announcement I should suggest, but leave you and Mr. Simpson to improve on it. I don't know how the gossip paragraph should read. It may as well say that the new book like 'Middlemarch,' is a story of English life but of *our own* day, and dealing for the most part in a higher sphere of Society.[8]

We are so pleased that Klesmer has laid hold of you. The coincidence of your experience is very interesting—only last night I was telling Madonna that I thought she was doing a real service to many a misguided girl and youth in thus plainly setting forth the arduousness and difficulties of a career so facile in imagination.

Yours truly
G. H. L.

## GE TO WILLIAM ALLINGHAM, LONDON, 30 NOVEMBER 1875

*MS:* Privately owned. *Envelope:* W. Allingham Esq | 12 Trafalgar Square | Chelsea | S.W. *Postmark:* ST. JOHNS WOOD | B 2X | NO 30 | 75. Published in *Letters to William Allingham,* ed. H. Allingham and E. Baumer Williams, 1911, p. 177.

**The Priory, | 21. North Bank, | Regents Park.**
November 30. 75.

Dear Mr. Allingham

The fact of your editorship gives a pleasant persuasiveness to the invitation you have sent me. But just now I am absorbed and could not entertain one additional proof.

I had heard with joy of Baby as an expectation, but an actual Gerald [9] come of age after perils makes joy all the safer.

Pray accept and offer to your wife my warm congratulations. But I shall owe Master Gerald a grudge if he greatly hinders Mamma's pencil. He is Posterity but—Wer machte dann die Mitwelt Spass? [1]—

Always yours truly
M. E. Lewes.

8. The *Athenaeum,* 27 November 1875, p. 709 prints this sentence almost verbatim.

9. Gerald Allingham, born 8 November 1875.

1. Goethe, *Faust,* Part I, Vorspiel, line 77.

## GE TO MRS. ERNST LEOPOLD BENZON, LONDON, 30 NOVEMBER [1875]

*MS:* Library of Congress. *Hitherto unpublished.*

**The Priory, | 21. North Bank, | Regents Park.**
November 30.

Dear Mrs. Benzon

I dare say it is of no consequence to you—but lest you should stay in one half hour because I said that Mr. Lewes hoped to pay you a visit today, I write (I hope in time) to tell you that he is in bed with sore throat and cannot leave the house today.[2]

Excuse this fuss.

I am ever affectionately
M. E. Lewes.

## GE TO ALICE HELPS, LONDON, 30 NOVEMBER 1875

*MS:* Mr. Arthur Helps. *Hitherto unpublished.*

**The Priory, | 21. North Bank, | Regents Park.**
November 30. 75.

My dear Alice

Mr. Lewes is to take me, else I should have been glad of your sweet guardianship in going to see 'Iolanthe.' [3]

I have not been able to deserve your remembrance in any way except by often thinking of you. This I have done, but I have not had ten spare minutes to spend in telling you of it. We came home about the middle of October, but, to our annoyance, found a smell of paint in the drawing room which obliged us to live for three weeks in my study.

We are now at large in the house as usual, and there is no one we should like to see better than you, if it were not unreasonable to wish

2. "Stayed in bed with sore throat and headache till 12. Read first instalment of Trollope's 'Prime Minister.'" (GHL Diary, 30 November 1875.)

3. Helen Faucit played Iolanthe, the blind princess in *King René's Daughter,* tr. by Theodore Martin from the Danish of Henrik Hertz. The performance at the Haymarket, 9 December 1875, was for the benefit of the Royal General Theatrical Fund.

that you should come so far in the cold with[out] [4] some duteous zeal to warm you on the way.

Only remember that you have two cordial friends in this corner, whom your presence will gladden.

Mr. Lewes is ailing. I am not more dowdy than usual.

Always yours affectionately
M. E. Lewes.

## JOHN BLACKWOOD TO GE, EDINBURGH, 30 NOVEMBER 1875

*MS:* National Library of Scotland. *Hitherto unpublished.*

**45, George Street, | Edinburgh.**
November 30/75.

My Dear Mrs. Lewes

You would get proof of all the M.S. we have last week, which brings us to the end of the second volume. I have been reading and rereading and always with increased wonder and admiration. As I read I constantly lean back in my chair to make sure that I am taking in all the beauty of the thought and feeling. It is like inspiration and you may rest assured that you are writing one of the most remarkable Books that ever was produced by man or woman. I know nothing like it.

It seemed hard to be torn away from Gwendolen after she read that "horrible" letter and Grandcourt came down "dressed for dinner," [5] but so exquisitely do you work the other chain of your story that one is speedily as engrossed as ever. Where did you get your knowledge of the Jews? But indeed one might say that of all your characters, so life-like and human are they. That Jew boy [6] is a little marvel and in the midst of their substantial kindliness Mordecai being helped to "the tails" of the whitings [7] is irresistible.

Simpson tells me he sent you yesterday specimens of cover papers which he has gathered in all directions. I rather lean to the pearl grey which he told me is the name of the colour.[8] At home we have constant discussions as to what is going to happen and who Deronda is, all be-

4. Another hand has added "out" to this word.

5. Mrs. Glasher's letter sent with the diamonds, ch. 31.

6. Jacob Alexander Cohen, the precocious six-year-old son of the pawnbroker, ch. 33.

7. 1876, II, 357; ch. 34.

8. The gray wrapper was used.

ing spoken of as living beings, but I must not tell you of our speculations.

When you are ready we shall be glad to stereotype so as to return type. It seems confoundedly prosaic to mention such things in connection with such a book.

always yours truly
John Blackwood.

## GHL TO JOHN BLACKWOOD, LONDON, [1 DECEMBER 1875]

*MS:* National Library of Scotland. *Hitherto unpublished.*

**The Priory, | 21. North Bank, | Regents Park.**
Wednesday.

My dear Blackwood

We both think the cover chosen quite perfect and the lettering exactly what Mrs. Lewes wished. Let the *back* correspond in style and plainness.

Your admiration is very cheering to her, and I must add that your taking so heartily to the Jewish scenes is particularly gratifying to me, for I have sometimes shared her doubts on whether people would sufficiently sympathize with that element in the story. Though I have reflected that [as] she formerly contrived to make one love Methodists, there was no reason why she should not conquer the prejudice against the Jews.

You are surprised at her knowledge of the Jews? But only learned Rabbis are so profoundly versed in Jewish history and literature as she is—and this will not only make a Rembrandtish background to her dramatic presentation, but I suspect will rouse all the Jews of Europe to a fervor of admiration for the great artist who can—without disguising the ludicrous and ugly aspects—so marvellously present the ideal side of that strange life. Lydgate in Middlemarch conquered all the medical profession—and Mordecai will in like manner conquer all the Jews. What a stupendous genius it is! I have heard of several of our great surgeons expressing their astonishment how any one not bred to the medical profession and practising in the country could have painted such a picture as Lydgate—and yet her *direct* knowledge has been very slight.

I return proofs of the first volume for *press.* My fourth reading has intensified my admiration and I begin to think that the book will be a great success even for her.

Ever yours
G. H. L.

Have you seen Trollope's first part?[9] And do you think we ought to adopt as wide a margin to look handsome or keep to the old size for the sake of uniformity?

## GHL TO GEORGE SIMPSON, LONDON, [6? DECEMBER 1875]

*MS:* Yale. *Hitherto unpublished.*

**The Priory, | 21. North Bank, | Regents Park.**
Monday.

O Moltke of Edinburgh! This last move has surprised even our expectations! We think however that since there is no possible competitor to fall back upon, we had better not scare the Melbourne people by asking more than they gave before after a hard fight. £200 will be very acceptable from them and we might miss all by asking for more.[1]

Yours truly
G. H. Lewes.

## JOHN BLACKWOOD TO GE, EDINBURGH, 14 DECEMBER 1875

*MS:* National Library of Scotland. *Hitherto unpublished.*

**45, George Street, | Edinburgh.**
December 14/75.

My Dear Mrs. Lewes

I was very sorry to see by a note from Lewes to Simpson that in the change of weather you had caught a bad cold, but I hope the steady continuance of the milder weather has put you all right again.[2] It has

9. *The Prime Minister,* published in monthly parts, November 1875—June 1876.

1. GE's account shows payments of £200 each for the Australian reprints of *Middlemarch* and *Daniel Deronda.* See Appendix I and 31 May 1876.

2. The note has not been found. In his Diary, 9 December 1875 GHL notes: "Polly upstairs with bad cold. I read aloud to her George Sand 'Le Marquis de Villemer.'" GHL's own health was more alarming: "After dinner while dozing in my chair felt a strange pressure

enabled me to golf and my wife and daughter to ride, both things conducive to the family health and happiness.

I often wonder how you are getting on with the Great Book and I never venture to ask how far you have got with your wondrous tale of human life.

Mr. Langford evidently felt so left out in the cold while we were all full of Daniel that I told Simpson to send him a copy of the sheets for private perusal. He returned them to me with an excellent rapturous letter which may be summed up in his own statement that when he finished the second volume he felt inclined to "rush up to the Priory and throw himself on his knees before you." The idea of the tableau is amusing, but the same genuine feeling will be shared by many, so great is the mastery of the book.

Mr. Simpson has arranged with the Australian paper but could not get them above the £200.

You will be glad to hear that Middlemarch is going on selling and there is also good life in The Spanish Gipsy and Jubal.

Hoping soon to get good accounts of your health, believe me

always yours truly
John Blackwood.

A two volume 8° life of Heine [3] has been sent to me and I propose to send it to Lewes if he has not got a copy. I inclose a poetic letter from Lockhart to me which may amuse you and has intensely delighted the golfing world.[4]

## GE TO JOHN BLACKWOOD, LONDON, 15 DECEMBER 1875

*MS:* National Library of Scotland. *Published:* Cross, III, 267–269.

**The Priory, | 21. North Bank, | Regents Park.**
December 15. 75.

My dear Mr. Blackwood

Your letter is an agreeable tonic—very much needed, for that wretched hindrance of a cold last week has trailed after it a series of

inside the ears accompanied by inability to move or speak. Thought paralysis had come on or Death. But it passed away, leaving only a sense of Indigestion behind." (Diary, 14 December 1875.)

3. William Stigand (1825–1915), *The Life, Works, and Opinions of Heinrich Heine,* 2 vols., London, Longmans, Green, 1875.

4. A long letter in rhymed doggerel entitled "A Voice from the Rhineland," by Laurence Lockhart, describing his dream of the golf at St. Andrews is published in *John Blackwood,* pp. 190–192.

headaches worse than itself. An additional impression like Mr. Langford's of the two volumes is really valuable as a sign that I have not so far failed in relation to a variety of readers. But you know that in one sense I count nothing done as long as anything remains to do, and it always occurs to me that the worst difficulty is still to come. In the sanest, soberest judgment, however, I think the third volume (which I have not yet finished) would be regarded as the difficult bridge. I will not send you any more M.S. until I can send the whole of Vol. III.

We think that Mr. Simpson has conducted our Australian business admirably. Remembering that but for his judgment and consequent activity we might have got no publication at all in that quarter, we may well be content with £200. I am quite satisfied too with the prospect of the wrapper, which I think will be just what I wanted.

Mr. Lewes has not got the life of Heine and will be much pleased and obliged by your gift.

Major Lockhart's lively letter gives me a longing for the fresh breezy life and fine scenery it conjures up. You must let me know when there is a book of his, because when I have done my own I shall like to read something else by him. I got much pleasure out of the two books I did read.[5] But when I am writing, or only thinking of writing fiction of my own, I cannot risk the reading of other English fiction. I was obliged to tell Anthony Trollope so when he sent me the first part of his Prime Minister, though this must seem sadly ungracious to those who don't share my susceptibilities.

Apparently there are wild reports about the subject-matter of Deronda—among the rest, that it represents French life! But that is hardly more ridiculous than the supposition that after refusing to go to America I should undertake to describe society there.

It is wonderful how Middlemarch keeps afloat in people's minds. Somebody told me that Mr. Henry Sidgwick said it was a bold thing to write another book after Middlemarch, and we must prepare ourselves for the incalculableness of the public reception in the first instance. I think I have heard you say that the chief result of your ample experience has been to convince you of that incalculableness.

I congratulate you on your return to golf and Mrs. and Miss Blackwood on the delight of riding, which helps to compensate for the loss of Strathtyrum.

Always yours truly
M. E. Lewes.

5. *Doubles and Quits,* 1869, and *Fair to See,* 1871.

What a blow for Miss Thackeray—the death of that sister[6] to whom she was so closely bound in affection.

## GE TO MRS. ELMA STUART, LONDON, 20 DECEMBER 1875

*MS:* British Museum. *Published:* Stuart, p. 51.

**The Priory, | 21. North Bank, | Regents Park.**
December 20. 75.

Dearest Elma

The pretty blue and white letter (style parfait) arrived safely in the hands of the faithful post, and has already kept my feet warm for several days.[7] You have just fitted my feet—I like plenty of room and feel any pinching in my body as a pinching of my thought.

Thanks, sweet daughter. I wish I could say that we are well, but we live in hope of being better.

Always your loving
Mother.

## GE JOURNAL, LONDON, 25 DECEMBER 1875

*MS:* Tinker Collection, Yale. *Extracts published:* Cross, III, 269–270.

June 15 or 17 we went to a house we had taken at Rickmansworth. Here in the end of July we received the news that *our dear Bertie had died on June 29th.* Our stay at Rickmansworth, though otherwise peaceful was not marked by any great improvement in health from the change to country instead of town—rather the contrary. We left on September 23 and then set off on a journey into Wales which was altogether unfortunate on account of the incessant rain. After our return I grew better and wrote with some success—G. worse, and consequently he consulted Dr. Reynolds, whose prescriptions seem to have answered so that he has recovered his usual power of enjoying work.

For the last three weeks, however I have been suffering from a cold and its effects so as to be unable to make any progress. Meanwhile, the 2 first volumes of Daniel Deronda are in print and the first Book is to be published on February 1.—I have thought very poorly of it myself throughout, but George and the Blackwoods are full of satisfaction

6. Harriet Marian Thackeray, first wife of Leslie Stephen, died suddenly in London 28 November 1875.

7. The MS is clear.

in it. Each part as I see it before me *im Werden* seems less likely to be anything else than a failure, but I see on looking back this morning —Christmas Day—that I really was in worse health and suffered equal depression about Romola—and so far as I have recorded, the same thing seems to be true of Middlemarch.

I have finished the vth Book, but am not so far on in the vith as I hoped to have been, the oppression under which I have been labouring having positively suspended my power of writing anything that I could feel satisfaction in.

## GHL TO JOHN BLACKWOOD, LONDON, 27 DECEMBER 1875

*MS:* National Library of Scotland. *Hitherto unpublished.*

**The Priory, | 21. North Bank, | Regents Park.**
27 December 75.

My dear Blackwood

I hope it isn't a mocking sound in your ears to be saluted with "a merry Christmas." It is in ours; unless we are understood in Froissart's phrase as taking our pleasure "moult tristement." Mrs. Lewes has been much out of sorts and overpowered with gloom and apprehension which no 'reasoning' has power to dispel. But she is getting better again. I have had a diffused sense of the universe being a vague headache. Fortunately we have accepted no invitations, so that we need not be troubled by 'festivities.' 'Deronda,' advances very slowly—but superbly. By the way we have not seen a proof of title page and motto [8]—will you order it to be sent? It should appear with part I.

I suppose you will now begin to advertize energetically; and if the *Times* could be persuaded to notice the 1st part that would be worth 50 £ of advertizing. 'Middlemarch' they did not notice until their notice came too late for any good effect. They used always to notice Thackeray and Dickens's first numbers.

Your advertizing agent might soon begin to canvass for Part I. A good show would help to make the part look more important.[9]

The life of Heine you were kind enough to send me I couldn't read. I looked into it here and there, but read blockhead and blunderer in

8. Six and one-half lines of blank verse by GE beginning "Let thy chief terror be of thine own soul," facing the title page.

9. Books I and II each had 16 pages of advertisements.

very 'round text,' and so closed the volumes with a sigh. It was a task to have tested high abilities. Why do the dull dogs always lay hold of subjects specially demanding wit and lightness of touch?

Mrs. Lewes begs me to remember and add her kindest regards to Mrs. Blackwood, Miss Blackwood and Willie as well as to her 'old friend J. B.' Nor should good Mr. Simpson be omitted.

Ever yours truly
G. H. L.

## GHL TO MARK PATTISON, LONDON, 27 DECEMBER 1875

*MS:* Bodleian. *Hitherto unpublished.*

**The Priory, | 21. North Bank, | Regents Park.**
27 December 75.

My dear Rector

Last night Mrs. Lewes read aloud your remarkable paper on Philosophy at Oxford [1] and I must scribble you a line to say how delighted and gratified we were with it. Not only is it a valuable contribution to the history of our time but will help to form sound ideas on that *most important* of all reforms—reform of the theory of Education. There are other splendid passages—passages such as Burke would have delighted in. Notably that one beginning "there was no light on the arena" etc. and the description of the prizeman with his "moral palor." [2] This latter portion of the essay was particularly pleasing to Mrs. Lewes because confirming something she has written in her new book; and we were both not a little gratified at the telling reference to 'Problems.' [3]

This last reminds me that I attributed to your friendly interest the very gratifying notice of Problems in the Sat. Rev.[4] which contained an objection I was glad to have pointed out—not that I thought it touched a weak point in the system, but it did disclose an oversight in the exposition.

We hope you have better tidings of Mrs. Pattison. Mrs. Lewes has

1. In *Mind,* I (January 1876), 82–97.

2. A discussion of the Oriel fellows—Keble, Arnold, Newman, Whately, who wrestled in the dark, imperfectly acquainted with the condition of their own England. (p. 84). "But in the average Oxford prize-man we too plainly recognise the symptoms which indicate that he has suffered from the forcing house; mental pallor, moral indifferentism, the cynical sneer at others' effort, the absence in himself of any high ideal." (p. 94)

3. P. 96.

4. *Saturday Review,* 4 September 1875, pp. 301–302.

been very suffering lately, but is better again. Don't neglect us whenever you are in town and free.

Yours truly
G. H. Lewes.

## JOHN BLACKWOOD TO GHL, EDINBURGH, 28 DECEMBER 1875

*MS:* National Library of Scotland and Mrs. Carrington Ouvry. *Hitherto unpublished.*

**45, George Street, | Edinburgh.**
December 28/75.

My Dear Lewes

It gives me much pleasure to receive your letter today and most cordially do I and all your friends here respond in warm good wishes to Mrs. Lewes and you. I often wish she could hear some of our home talk about Daniel as it might lighten some of her despondent views. We speak of the book and the characters as of realities, and the exquisite selfishness of Grandcourt's complaint that Mrs. Glasher had made him feel quite unwell that morning has so tickled us that a reference to that scene [5] is applied to all unreasonable complaints.

Simpson showed me a comprehensive scheme of advertising and "billing" Deronda and I have no doubt he is carrying it out energetically. He is not here today owing to a slight touch of cold and I am sending him your letter as I know your kind message will be very grateful. I have desired Title pages to be set for your approval.

I have already sounded the glories of Deronda in the Times direction and I have very little doubt they will notice the first part at once.

Inclosed I have the pleasure of sending a cheque £333-1-6d being the royalty for the year on Middlemarch, Jubal, and The Spanish Gypsy as per accompanying memorandum.[6] You will I hope join me in thinking it very satisfactory, especially as regards Middlemarch and the Gypsy. Jubal I think ought to sell more.

I am sorry to hear the Life of Heine is so worthless. The compiler must I think be a literary gentleman who was introduced to me some years ago and wrote submitting a list of a dozen subjects all of which he was equally ready to handle. It would have required an intellectual giant with even a few of the subjects proposed, so I intimated that my

5. At the end of ch. 30. (1876, II, 271.)

6. The memorandum is in Mrs. Ouvry's collection.

hands were full or did not answer at all. I must find you some better book.

This is a fine bright day and instead of golfing I am actually going to drive into the country with my wife to make a Christmas call.

The *approach* of this season generally makes me very dull as it recals so many so very dear who are gone, but when the time comes I feel as of old and our dinner party on Saturday was very bright. My nephew joins me in all good wishes to you both.

ever yours truly
John Blackwood.

Royalty payable on

| | | | |
|---|---|---|---|
| 4059 | Copies less 25th Book Middlemarch, 1 vol. | 1/6 | 292. 5.6 |
| 205 | Copies less 25th Book Jubal, 2nd Edition | 1/6 | 14.15.6 |
| 361 | Copies less 25th Book Spanish Gypsy 5th Edition | 1/6 | 26. 0.6 |
| | | | £333. 1.6 |

## GHL TO MARK PATTISON, LONDON, 28 DECEMBER 1875

*MS:* Bodleian. *Hitherto unpublished.*

**The Priory, | 21. North Bank, | Regents Park.**
28 December 75.

My dear Rector

I know the state you describe but too well. *Don't let it go on.* It is anaemia—perhaps caused by or at any rate complicated by inaction of the liver. The irritability is a certain index of anaemia—the depression probably hepatic. But get Acland [7] or Rolleston [8] to have an examination. Probably a tonic and rest will be all necessary if taken in time. But cerebral anaemia is not to be prolonged without evil!

How grieved we are both for her sake and yours to hear of Mrs. Pattison!

Ever yours
G. H. L.

7. Henry Wentworth Acland (1815–1900), Regius Professor of Medicine at Oxford 1858–94.

8. George Rolleston (1829–81), Linacre Professor of Anatomy and Physiology at Oxford, 1860–81.

## GHL TO JOHN BLACKWOOD, LONDON, [29 DECEMBER 1875]

*MS:* National Library of Scotland. *Hitherto unpublished.*

**The Priory, | 21. North Bank, | Regents Park.**
Wednesday

My dear Blackwood

Your checque and agreeable letter arrived this morning. The sales are indeed satisfactory and promise for Deronda, who I suspect will have a much larger public. The Jews alone would constitute an energetic propagandist party, for never have they been idealized and realized so marvellously before.

Since I wrote Mrs. Lewes has been better. But 'tis a frail vessel of Venetian glass! Your amusing account of Stigand is just what might have been conceived. But I must tell you that I am far too deeply engrossed with nerve centers to pay attention to anything else—my strength is small and it is all absorbed by my work. It is rarely I can even read Maga!

Yours ever
G. H. L.

## GHL TO WILLIAM BLACKWOOD, LONDON, [30 DECEMBER 1875]

*MS:* National Library of Scotland. *Hitherto unpublished.*

**The Priory, | 21. North Bank, | Regents Park.**
Thursday.

My dear Willie

We agree with your uncle about the subtitle which although useful for the advertisement is superfluous to any one holding the book in his hand who would see at once it was a story of modern English life.[9]

Mrs. Lewes was much pleased at your pleasure in the book. I read her your letter while she lay in bed suffering severe pains in the stomach. Yesterday I gave account of her to your uncle!

Ever yours
G. H. L.

9. There is no subtitle in the MS or printed texts.

# The Publication of *Daniel Deronda*

| | |
|---|---|
| *1876 February 1* | *Daniel Deronda*, Book I published. |
| *1876 February 6* | GE ill again. |
| *1876 February 14–18* | GHL has lumbago. |
| *1876 March 13–24* | At Halls' house at Weybridge, returning to the Priory for Sundays. |
| *1876 March 31* | GHL a founder of the Physiological Society. |
| *1876 May 18* | GE and GHL dine at Lady Portsmouth's. |
| *1876 May 20–22* | Visit Jowett at Oxford. |
| *1876 May 31* | GHL presented to King of the Belgians at Lord Houghton's. |
| *1876 June 8* | *Daniel Deronda* finished. |
| *1876 June 10* | GE and GHL leave for France and Switzerland. |
| *1876 June 17–25* | At Aix-les-Bains. |
| *1876 July 5–22* | At Ragatz. |
| *1876 August 3–25* | At Klönthal and St. Blasien. |
| *1876 September 1* | Return to London. Last book of *Daniel Deronda* published. |
| *1876 October 4–7* | Visit Halls at Six Mile Bottom; go to Newmarket. |
| *1876 October 19* | Blackwood offers £4000 for 10-year lease of copyrights. |
| *1876 November 9* | GHL takes chair at Physiological Society dinner. |
| *1876 November 24* | GE accepts a royalty arrangement for Cabinet edition. |
| *1876 December 6* | GE and GHL purchase the Heights at Witley. |
| *1876 December 24–28* | Visit the Crosses at Weybridge. |

## GE TO THE HON. LADY SEBRIGHT, LONDON, 1 JANUARY 1876

*MS:* The Countess of Iddesleigh. *Hitherto unpublished.*

**The Priory, | 21. North Bank, | Regents Park.**
January 1. 1876.

Dear Lady Sebright [1]

Many thanks for your kind remembrance of us. We are hermits, and rarely know anything of the world except through the stragglers from the crowd, who visit our cell.

But I hope that our going to you at Beechwood is not a necessary condition to your finding your way hitherward again on a Sunday when you are in town. Of late I have been invalided by cold and the sequel of small miseries that a cold usually leaves behind. We should be relieved to hear that Lady Castletown's health is re-established. The last news we heard of her was, that she was at Fontainebleau, still in a very delicate state.

Mr. Lewes begs to be remembered by you kindly in spite of our unsociable habits, and we both hope to exchange opinions with you in the spring on the Italian actors who are coming to lighten our theatrical darkness.

Always yours sincerely
M. E. Lewes.

## GHL TO ALEXANDER MAIN, LONDON, 2 JANUARY 1876

*Text:* Main's copy owned by Mr. John R. Sprunt. *Hitherto unpublished.*

**The Priory, | 21. North Bank, | Regents Park.**
2 January 76.

My dear Main

May the blessed sun shine on you through the year! It won't—but never mind—let the moral sun shine instead.

Your friends here have but a poor account to give of themselves. It has been an unfortunate year for both of us as regards health—(in

1. Olivia Amy Douglas FitzPatrick, youngest daughter of Lord Castletown, was married in 1865 to Sir John Gage Saunders Sebright, Bart. They lived at Beechwood, Dunstable, Hertfordshire.

every other respect we have nothing but blessings) and we have not had the advantage of a recuperant holiday. Wales under an umbrella was not bracing!

The great book proceeds slowly but superbly. She has not yet finished the 3rd volume, and is in the usual gloom of despondency and diffidence which is not more than momentarily lightened by my and Blackwood's admiration.

Your Glasgow enthusiast interested me and I felt inclined to say with Spontini [2] when Berlioz praised him hyperbolically, "Il a du talent —comme critique!"

We had a most charming letter from M. Ritter a little while ago, in which to our surprise he speaks of you as a correspondent from whom it is difficult to get a word! I fear he will be sadly put out when he finds that no reprint of Daniel Deronda will appear in Germany until the end of the year. We don't fancy English tourists supplying themselves with Tauchnitz or Asher's editions.

I am getting on slowly with the "Physical Basis of Mind" [3]—condensing the mass of material and trying to put it into a shape intelligible as well as interesting to the general reader.

Have you seen the new periodical *Mind?* The article by Pattison on philosophy at Oxford is very valuable and extremely well written. Altogether for a first number the periodical presents a most hopeful aspect. Mrs. Lewes sends her best wishes.

Ever yours
G. H. L.

## GHL TO JOHN BLACKWOOD, LONDON, 10 JANUARY 1876

*MS:* National Library of Scotland. *Hitherto unpublished.*

**The Priory, | 21. North Bank, | Regents Park.**
January 10/76.

My dear Blackwood

I observe that you have not *billed* the Contemporary or Fortnightly Reviews; the former has become a very important organ circulating among probable buyers of Deronda, and I think that in the next number

2. Gasparo Spontini, Conte di Sant' Andrea (1774–1851), composer of operas.

3. *Problems of Life and Mind,* 2d series, 1877.

at any rate a bill might be inserted with effect[4]—better late than never! Mrs. Lewes is better again, and the third volume is oh! so grand![5]

I think of reproducing some half dozen of the illustrations which appeared in the 'Physiology of Common Life' in my 3rd volume.[6] Would you object to let Trübners have casts of them? I haven't quite determined the point, nor the figures to be chosen; but I should be glad to have the casts if you see no objection.

I believe you bind the proofs of Mrs. Lewes's books? I am preserving them for you.

Ever yours
G. H. L.

## GHL TO WILLIAM BLACKWOOD, LONDON, [12 JANUARY 1876]

*MS:* National Library of Scotland. *Hitherto unpublished.*

**The Priory, | 21. North Bank, | Regents Park.**
Wednesday.

My dear Willie

Last night we were not a little disturbed by a telegram from New York saying that Deronda had not reached and wanting to know by telegraph at what date it had been dispatched. I anticipated it would have been in their hands ten days ago and I particularly explained to Mr. Simpson the reasons for sending it earlier than he suggested. Harpers may not unreasonably say we have not fulfilled our part of the contract, and as the sum they pay is exceptionally large this may lead to difficulties which can only be obviated by our postponing publication till March. In this sense I telegraphed to you this morning, requesting you to let them know by telegram at *what date* the proofs were dispatched and whether *they wished* the publication postponed until March. This would be a great bore—but one must not give them an opening for not carrying out the contract. There is still time to make the change.

We were very sorry to hear of your uncle's being laid up—celà lui ressemble si peu!

Was not he and were not you surprised at the news of the Vice-

4. The announcement appears in the succeeding issues of both.

5. See GE Journal, 25 December 1875.

6. *The Physical Basis of Mind* reproduces 26 drawings in "Problem II. The Nervous Mechanism."

royalty?[7] In some respects the appointment is a good one. But I can't picture Robert as Governor General. When one has patted and petted a boy it is so hard to think of him as a Viceroy!

Yours truly
G. H. L.

## GHL TO WILLIAM BLACKWOOD, LONDON, [12 JANUARY 1876]

*MS:* National Library of Scotland. *Hitherto unpublished.*

**The Priory, | 21. North Bank, | Regents Park.**
Wednesday night.

My dear Willie

The enclosed[8] just arrived. You will see what just cause of complaint the Harpers have and how inexcusable the delay must appear to them. I have written to say (what I hope you conveyed in your telegram) that at any inconvenience to us the publication should be postponed till March if they desired it.

Meanwhile to prevent any recurrence of such cases will you please to ask Mr. Simpson to arrange that Harpers have Part II *at once* and each succeeding part at least one month in advance of publication?

Yours truly
G. H. Lewes.

Did your telegram to New York put the question distinctly as to postponement? If not please send one to that effect.

## GHL TO JOHN BLACKWOOD, LONDON, [14 JANUARY 1876]

*MS:* National Library of Scotland. *Hitherto unpublished.*

**The Priory, | 21. North Bank, | Regents Park.**
Friday.

My dear Blackwood

Mrs. Lewes has been greatly worried about this Harper business, because they will not unreasonably feel that we have not acted up to our promise. Giving so exceptionally large a sum for early sheets they

7. Robert, Lord Lytton was appointed Governor-General of India in January 1876.

8. A second telegram from Harpers saying that the early sheets of *Daniel Deronda* had not arrived.

had a right to expect to have their convenience consulted and I promised them the sheets as soon as they were ready. Nor was there any valid reason for not letting the sheets go; and I cannot explain how the prompt and considerate Simpson disregarded my last letter to him on the subject wherein I explained why Harpers wanted the sheets earlier and that I wished them to be sent. Even now, neither he nor you have mentioned the *date* at which they were dispatched—so as in some sense to relieve Mrs. Lewes's anxiety. You both merely say the sheets have been sent. Nor do you say whether you have asked Harpers if they wished publication postponed. This is absolutely important to keep to our contract—otherwise the sheets may have arrived too late or not at all—and we should then have no claim whatever on them. I should like the postponement as little as you but it would be the only fair course. Please telegraph to me on the two points of date and postponement.

Will you also please have Part II sent at once, and make a note that each succeeding part be sent off on the 20th of each month—thus giving them a full month in advance?

As we are in this state with Harper's we must not issue the book before the 20th and press copies 25th. Otherwise it will reach America too soon. We have determined *not* to reprint at all in Germany until our sale in parts has been exhausted, namely in October next.

Will you send a copy to Main? I haven't included him in my list because Mrs. Lewes said you always sent to him.

Ever yours truly
G. H. L.

## JOHN BLACKWOOD TO GHL, EDINBURGH, 14 JANUARY 1876

*Text:* Copy in Blackwood Letter Book. *Hitherto unpublished.*

45 George Street | Edinburgh January 14/76.

My Dear Lewes

We have today telegraphed to Harper's according to your instructions asking them whether they wished the publication of Deronda postponed until March. We did not do so in Telegram we sent on Wednesday as our doing so seemed merely suggesting this awkward step to them. I hope sincerely they will not propose the delay and if they reflect I hardly think they will.

I am excessively vexed that the proofs had not been sent at the time, but unless Harper's were going to publish long before the end of the month the delay can only cause a very trifling inconvenience. Their note too does not seem to indicate anything more than inconvenience and I think you are troubling yourself too much about the matter.

I do not think you reflect sufficiently upon the extreme danger of a copy getting afloat too early in that country where I suppose it could be reprinted in all directions. However I have sent off part today as you direct. I am sorry they are going to publish Deronda in their Magazine [9] as there will be greater difficulty in keeping it out of this country than if it appeared as an independent publication.

Hoping that this little trouble will blow over pleasantly and not interfere with the launch of the goodly ship, I am

ever yours truly

(Signed) John Blackwood.

Frost has come back upon us and really I think it agrees better with my cold than the milder weather.

## GHL TO JOHN BLACKWOOD, LONDON, [17–19 JANUARY 1876]

*MS:* National Library of Scotland. *Hitherto unpublished.*

**The Priory, | 21. North Bank, | Regents Park.**
Monday.

My dear Blackwood

Your letter this morning removes a load of anxiety. Since Harper's did not wish postponement there can only have been inconvenience—and that I will explain to them with expressions of my regret.

I have asked Langford to come and lunch with us on Tuesday to discuss details about issue of copies etc.

Ever yours truly

G. H. L.

Wednesday

This was enclosed in an envelope to my sister in law. The telegram since arrived was a great comfort. Langford was with us yesterday.

9. Book I of *Daniel Deronda* appeared in *Harper's New Monthly Magazine,* 52 (February 1876), 425–459.

## JOHN BLACKWOOD TO GHL, EDINBURGH, 20 JANUARY 1876

*Text:* Copy in Blackwood Letter Book. *Hitherto unpublished.*

45 George Street | Edinburgh January 20/76.

My dear Lewes

By a letter from Langford today I see that you and he propose we should send Deronda to the weekly press from here on the 25th and to the Daily Press on the 27th, but so many of the weekly are connected with the Daily Press that I do not think it would be safe to make the distinction. So if you agree I propose to post all the Press copies from this on the 25th with a request that reviews should not appear before Saturday. I hope Mrs. Lewes is pretty well and that I shall soon be gladened by the sight of Volume 3.

A very clever young contributor of mine Julian Sturgis [1] has asked me for an introduction to Mrs. Lewes and you but I hesitate about intruding upon her at present. He is an immense favourite of mine and you will I am sure be charmed with him. He is American by birth but I could not point out a better type of what Eton and Oxford can produce than this young fellow.

I had a most amusing letter from Lockhart yesterday and he excuses himself for not having sent Christmas greetings because he did not like to send his "good wishes" without a specimen of his "good works." He will I think be able to take the field with a novel in spring.

ever yours truly

(Signed) John Blackwood.

I wonder that blunder of putting letters into wrong envelopes does not occur oftener.

1. Julian Sturgis (1848–1904) wrote John Blackwood, 17 January 1876: "Is George Eliot in town? Would she mind knowing me? If not, would you ask her to let me call?" (NLS.) For an account of him see *Who Was Who.* William Blackwood brought him to the Priory 6 February.

## GE TO DR. JOSEPH FRANK PAYNE, LONDON, 25 JANUARY 1876

*MS:* Mrs. Evelyn Payne Murphy. *Envelope:* Dr. Payne | 6 Savile Row | W. *Postmark:* LONDON-N.W | 7 L | JA 31 | 76. *Hitherto unpublished.*

**The Priory, | 21. North Bank, | Regents Park.**
January 25. 76.

My dear Dr. Payne

No word of your unspeakable loss had reached me.[1] But of your Father's illness I heard quite lately after I had written a letter of introduction to him which happily there proved to be no need of sending. Your words about him let me hope that your care will end in his restoration.

You could have done nothing to touch me with more keenness—to move me more deeply, than your writing that letter to me in October. I say so at once on reading it, that you may know I am bearing it in mind even if I keep silence for the present in relation to that supreme subject—how far the religion of the future must be one that enables us to do without consolation, instead of being what religion has been (I think pervertingly) held—chiefly precious as a source of consolation.[2]

Your letter will have associated you with questions which are the most frequently in my thoughts—questions which are my chief prompters to write anything at all. But my writing is simply a set of experiments in life—an endeavour to see what our thought and emotion may be capable of—what stores of motive, actual or hinted as possible, give promise of a better after which we may strive—what gains from past revelations and discipline we must strive to keep hold of as something more sure than shifting theory. I become more and more timid—with less daring to adopt any formula which does not get itself clothed

1. The death of his mother Eliza, wife of Joseph Payne, 12 October 1875, aged 68. (*Pall Mall Budget,* 23 October 1875, p. 38.) The long letter to which this is a reply was written 17 October 1875, but not sent till January; it is in Mrs. Murphy's possession.

2. "You have, I know, touched a very noble chord in 'Jubal' as to the function of death in human life. This I can accept fully; but it does not make me less long to see those I loved again. A long separation would have the same effect on life. If you can say one word to lighten this dark subject, how happy I should be. But let me not put it as an individual wish. It is the longing of all freethinkers now that I am trying to express, and this, as traditional religion decays (if it does) will be the yearning of all mankind. Death is the great problem which man will have to grapple with again; unless we are to believe, not in no God, but in a bad one."

for me in some human figure and individual experience, and perhaps that is a sign that if I help others to see at all it must be through that medium of art.

It is true that I am not very well, and I am just now liable to feel my weakness the more because I am haunted by the fear that everything is done worse in consequence.

That is why I write this note at once. I dare not promise myself to answer your letter as I should like to do for the next month or two, and pray trust in me so far as to believe that my silence however protracted will not be one of forgetfulness.

Please offer my sympathy to Mr. Payne, if there happens a suitable occasion. It will be a joy to us if you can before long come again and tell us that he is better.[3]

Most sincerely yours
M. E. Lewes.

## GHL TO JOHN BLACKWOOD, LONDON, [28 JANUARY 1876]

*MS:* National Library of Scotland. *Hitherto unpublished.*

Friday.

My dear Blackwood

You are quite right about sending to Dailies and Weeklies at the same time. Indeed your proposition was exactly the one I submitted to Langford, though not on your grounds. There must be no favoritism shown.

By the way, indisposed as I am to look at criticism I should be glad to see what the dailies except the *Times* say of the first part—if Mr. Simpson will kindly send them. Mrs. Lewes is but so so and gets on slowly and anxiously, but I hope soon to send you volume 3.

Although we are rather shy of making new acquaintances unless they are really pleasant we should of course be glad to see any one of whom you speak so favorably as of Mr. Julian Sturgis. If he will come some Sunday he will be welcome.

Enclosed my list of presentation copies. My sister in law's address I will forward you by post, when I get it. The letter missent to you was to ask her where she had moved to now her son is appointed chemist to the Wellington College.[4]

3. He called Sunday, 20 February 1876. (GHL Diary.)

4. Vivian Byam Lewes (1852–1915).

Langford tells me that we shall see Willie shortly. Perhaps he may take back the precious m.s.!

Ever yours truly
G. H. Lewes.

## GHL TO WILLIAM BLACKWOOD, LONDON, [30 JANUARY 1876]

*MS:* National Library of Scotland. *Hitherto unpublished.*

**The Priory, | 21. North Bank, | Regents Park.**
Sunday.

Dear Willie

I write to warn you against any mention [5] of criticisms that may have appeared on Deronda—Mrs. Lewes is so easily discouraged and so ready to believe and exaggerate whatever is said against her books that I not only keep reviews from her but do not even talk of them to her. When people sometimes speak indignantly of objections that others have made they little know how it depresses her, and therefore whenever the subject is approached I step in if I can to stop their mouths.

Ever yours
G. H. L.

## GHL TO ALEXANDER MAIN, LONDON, [31 JANUARY 1876]

*Text:* Main's copy owned by Mr. John R. Sprunt. *Hitherto unpublished.*

**The Priory, | 21. North Bank, | Regents Park.**

My dear Main

If the editor does not print both your articles [6] it will assuredly not be because they don't deserve it—they are admirable—but because he hasn't space for them. On the first topic he has a note from me, (at his request) in answer to Bain, and as we take the same line he may think yours superfluous carrying of coals to the Newcastle depôt.

In a letter from Ritter we received the other day he plaintively

5. William Blackwood came to lunch 31 January 1876.

6. Main replied, 6 February 1876, that the editor of *Mind* [Croom Robertson] would insert his 2nd paper and let the 1st lie over till he saw GHL's reply to Bain to decide if anything further needs urging on that side. (NLS.)

remarks that you haven't written since May last. Now this book is appearing I daresay you will feel the impulse to *s'fogársi* on it to him.

Yes, what you say about Mrs. Lewes's happiness in her work is true—the pain is there but it is delicious pain after all; and the deep feelings she creates in others react upon herself and make her prize her power.

Tomorrow you will have the "Spoiled Child." [7]

Ever yours
G. H. L.

## GHL TO JOHN BLACKWOOD, [LONDON, 1 FEBRUARY 1876]

*MS:* National Library of Scotland. *Hitherto unpublished.*

Tuesday.

Dear Blackwood

By to-day's mail registered I send Part 6 for printers to begin on; part 7 will follow in a few days.

I hope—in fact I am sure—that you and Mr. Simpson are highly gratified with the brilliant start of D.D. And as to the grand idea of the placards I am almost tempted to carry it further and walk down Bond Street with one pinned on my brow as a phylactery!

Mrs. Lewes was horribly depressed on Saturday, feeling as she said "quite guilty and that every one would be despising her feeble performance." However Willie's cheering news and assurances and the Times [7a] and other voices revived her spirits yesterday. I hear nothing but a chorus of praise and delight—but that of course. I take good care that nothing comes to her ears or eyes that would sound or read like objection, being so well aware of how she would lay hold of it as proof of her forebodings being justified. And I don't let her see even the enthusiastic criticisms, for many reasons.

Will you please ask Mr. Simpson to put down on my list of presentation copies the name of E. S. Pigott | 28 South Bank | N.W. and send him No. I? My sister in law has not yet sent me her address, so I can't give Mr. Simpson that.

I am curious to know how the third volume will strike you.

We were so pleased to hear of your being yourself again and so sorry to hear that Mr. Simpson still suffers from his bronchial affection.

Ever yours truly
G. H. L.

7. Book I of *Daniel Deronda*.
7a. By A. I. Shand, 31 January 1876, p. 6e.

## GE TO MRS. CHARLES BRAY, LONDON, 3 FEBRUARY 1876

*MS:* Yale. *Endorsed:* Lewes on Vivisection. *Hitherto unpublished.*

**The Priory, | 21. North Bank, | Regents Park.**
February 3. 76.

Dear Cara

How is it that your sight is troubling you? Unless there is some inflammation, the right glasses would surely make seeing easy to you. Have you taken pains to get the right glasses? Pray when you come to town consult an oculist. Our young Charles, only 33, was slightly short-sighted and used only occasionally a pince-nez. Feeling a little increased trouble in seeing he went to Liebreich, who told him that he was injuring his eyes by wrong treatment and prescribed spectacles which he now constantly wears. I remember that you used years ago to complain of weariness in using your eyes, and I fear that you have suffered for want of the right aids. Don't wear glasses *telles quelles* but consult about getting the right ones.

Please tell me whether it would be the least comfort and convenience to you if we were to advance the £40 for your "Morals" [8] so that you could await Nelsons' payment without anxiety—if I understand you rightly in supposing that they have accepted the work. The fact of the Sydenham house having stood empty for a year must have hampered you sadly. I think it is the first time you have been so long unfortunate with the letting or not-letting—is it not?

Thanks for the little blue-coated Paul Bradley. The illustrations do look a little worse in this form than when one saw them indulgently on the pages of the Animal World.[9] The doggie watching the gap is the least objectionable. The clergyman is of the namby-pambiest "description."

Mr. Lewes gave evidence on the subject of Vivisection before the Committee of Inquiry, and has corrected the proofs for the Blue Book.[1] He thinks it good that there should be a strong check from public opinion, but <thinks> that hardly any legislative measure on the subject can be taken without doing more harm than good. Your

8. Caroline Bray, *The Elements of Morality, in Easy Lessons for Home and School Teaching,* eventually published by Longmans, 1882; 2d ed., 1888.

9. The illustrations for *Paul Bradley* are taken from *The Animal World,* published by Partridge in folio, 1870–71.

1. GHL was examined before the Royal Commission on Vivisection, 15 December 1875, and corrected the proofs of his examination 23 December. (GHL Diary.)

quotation from the 'Science Primer' [2] shocks me very much. Mr. Lewes knows Michael Foster, who is in many respects an admirable man—but men, like societies, have strange patches of barbarism in the midst of their 'civilization.' There are facts in almost everybody's habits for which they "have eyes but see not." [3] Let us be thankful for any anointing that will make us see better. But one wishes that the advocates of good would be a little more scrupulous in their modes of advocacy.

Our daughter-in-law and grandchildren are not coming to England—at least there is no thought of that at present. She was brought up in the colony. And the little boy is still an infant. The little girl is a very lively 'Marian.'

With best love to all
Your affectionate
M. E. L.

## JOHN BLACKWOOD TO GE, EDINBURGH, 24 FEBRUARY 1876

*MS:* National Library of Scotland. *Brief extract published: John Blackwood,* p. 393.

**45, George Street, | Edinburgh.**
February 24/76.

My Dear Mrs. Lewes

The revise of Book v was sent to you last night and the Printers will soon have proof of Book vi ready. Book fifth is very wonderful. There is a feeling of thunder in the air that inspires awe, and I do not think the boldest critic that ever dashed off daily and weekly reviews would go in at it lightly. Grandcourt is hateful and one reflects with grim satisfaction that the Furies have entered his house.

Poor Gwendolen, her penance has begun. One sees now why you brought out so strongly that element of nervous terror in her character.

The gravity of the Book is admirably relieved by the touches you throw in. Sir Hugo's little attempts at mild humour and the perfect description of the old abbey [4] tell famously. Then the little house at Chelsea is so true to itself when the mighty Klesmer appears to decide the destiny of Mirah.[5] Of Mordecai I feel that it would be presump-

2. Michael Foster, *A Course of Elementary Practical Physiology,* which probably shocked Mrs. Bray with such directions as: "Prepare surface sections of a cat's or dog's gastric mucous membrane, which has been taken warm from the body. . . ." (3d ed., 1878, p. 108.)

3. Mark 8:18. GE must also have recalled GHL's experiments in his study of the nervous system.

4. Ch. 35.

5. Ch. 39.

tuous to speak until one has read more, and I daresay that puzzling and thinking over that phase of the Tale has been the cause of my not having written to you sooner.

I suspect we would need to get back a Titian to put him and Deronda on canvas as you have done them upon paper.[6] There is something excessively quaint in the conjunction of two such extremes of Jewish nature as that little Jacob and Mordecai.[7] I am determined to enjoy Book VI quietly at home, so did not look into the M.S. beyond a page or two before sending it into the printing office.

Mr. Langford writes that he is keeping Lewes informed of the subscription for Book Two and I think it is very satisfactory. Here the numbers are about equal to what the trade had taken at first of Book One and bought since, which is satisfactory. Willie would I daresay tell you that I had a pleasant letter from Mr. Alden,[8] the Editor of Harper's Magazine. You may probably have heard from him since he had read Book One. He seems to wish the Books earlier than the date Lewes named, which was to be in their hands a month sooner than the date of publication of their Magazine. There is no objection if they can keep them safe, but a month does seem plenty of time.

With many congratulations and good wishes, I am

always yours truly
John Blackwood.

## GE TO JOHN BLACKWOOD, LONDON, 25 FEBRUARY 1876

*MS:* National Library of Scotland. *Extracts published: John Blackwood,* p. 393.

**The Priory, | 21. North Bank, | Regents Park.**
February 25. 76.

My dear Mr. Blackwood

The printers did their work with remarkable correctness on Book V. I think the most serious misprint was 'change' for 'charge.'

With respect to the sending of the sheets to America Mr. Lewes agrees with you that the month beforehand is ample. He wrote Harpers to that effect some time ago, in reply to their acknowledgment that they had received Book II. All the signs that have reached us seem to

6. "I wish I could perpetuate those two faces, as Titian's 'Tribute Money' has perpetuated two types presenting another sort of contrast." (*Daniel Deronda,* 1876, III, 175; ch. 40.)

7. Ch. 38.

8. Henry Mills Alden (1836–1919).

imply that Deronda is received with more interest than Middlemarch, but I am rather muddy as to the relation of total sales,[9] though Mr. William and Mr. Langford have kept us informed on details.

I thought it likely that your impressions about Mordecai would be doubtful. Perhaps when the work is finished you will see its bearings better. The effect that one strives after is an outline as strong as that of Balfour of Burley [1] for a much more complex character and a higher strain of ideas. But such an effect is just the most difficult thing in art —to give new elements—i.e. elements not already used up—in forms as vivid as those of long familiar types. Doubtless the wider public of novel-readers must feel more interest in Sidonia than in Mordecai. But then, I was not born to paint Sidonia.[2]

We are going to dine with Lord and Lady Lytton tomorrow to say a long farewell.[3] It had seemed to us unlikely that we could have a glimpse of them, but I am very glad to have a parting remembrance—which to us old folk has that aspect of being final that begins to predominate in all partings. I am reminded of age by the fact that Mr. Lewes has been laid up with lumbago and is still rickety.

We had not heard that the editor of Harper's Magazine had written to you agreeably, but I suppose it is he who has diligently sent American notices in newspapers, one of which I think Mr. Lewes said was ably done. One newspaper passeth away and another cometh,[4] but we must remember that the writing which does this brief office is often a more difficult industry than work of more lasting value. Reviewers are fellow men towards whom I keep in Christian feeling by not reading them. But Mr. Lewes thinks they have treated me very well, though Mr. Langford hints a disposition to grumble.

Yours always truly
M. E. Lewes.

9. Of *Daniel Deronda,* Book I, 5250 copies were printed in January 1876, 2100 in February, and 1575 in March, making a total of 8925. By June 7287 copies had been sold. See 13 July 1876.

1. In Scott's *Old Mortality.*

2. The mysterious and romantic Jew who dominates Disraeli's *Coningsby.*

3. Lord Lytton left England 1 March 1876 to take office as Governor-General of India. He did not return until May 1880. (*DNB.*)

4. Cf. Ecclesiastes 1:4.

## GHL TO JOHN BLACKWOOD, LONDON, [27 FEBRUARY 1876]

*MS:* National Library of Scotland. *Hitherto unpublished.*

**The Priory, | 21. North Bank, | Regents Park.**
Sunday.

My dear Blackwood

I was very sorry to find from your last that you did not take cordially to Mordecai—sorry because *I* think it on the whole one of the greatest of her creations, (and of course one likes to have one's admiration reflected in the admiration of others)—but mostly sorry because I knew it would damp her. It has cast a gloom over her already desponding mind; she feeling that the public will in general share your imperfect sympathy. All along this has been her vision of the effect which this presentation of the Jewish ideal would have; and I have vainly combated it. But whether it is liked or disliked do it she must and will.

The great success of Part I and the confidence exhibited by the booksellers *ought* to encourage her, but doesn't. She knows that her gloom is foolish, but this knowledge can't displace the feeling. What a blessing a little of the author's self satisfaction would be to her!

Last night we dined with the Lytton's to say good bye. Poor Lady Lytton is far from well and Robert is certainly not in a promising state for India and official work.[5]

I have been laid up with severe lumbago, which is now gone at last.[6] Mrs. Lewes is better again, but until volume four is finished one can't hope for more than a slight improvement.

Ever yours
G. H. L.

5. The only other guest mentioned in GHL's Diary was John Morley.

6. The attack came 14 February after he had been "to see [H. R.] Octavius Sankey's *Preparations of the Brain* on a new method. Walked home through the snow, and after lunch was seized with the most violent *Lumbago* I have ever known. It was with difficulty I was got to bed and there I remained all **Tuesday 15 February 1876**" and for 3 days more. (GHL Diary.)

## JOHN BLACKWOOD TO GHL, EDINBURGH, 29 FEBRUARY 1876

*MS:* National Library of Scotland. *Hitherto unpublished.*

**45, George Street, | Edinburgh.**
February 29/76.

My Dear Lewes

I had a pleasant letter from Mrs. Lewes on Saturday and note from you today and I only wish they contained better accounts of both your healths but I trust better weather and the continued most cheering reception of Deronda will help to put you soon right.

As Mrs. Lewes says she has got a little confused about the total number sold, I have had the memorandum I inclose made up which will be about accurate.

The sale of Book 2 is greatly more than that of Book one at the corresponding date last month and in the course of March I hope he will quite overtake Book 1. Mudie has not yet sent in for the second supply 250 that he took of Book 1 but from the demand on the part of the public Langford feels confident he must have it immediately.

From the state[ment]s you have of Middlemarch you will see that Deronda has already got ahead of his great predecessor.

The impression the book is making is enormous and the small cavillers will only do good by exciting discussion and helping on the overwhelming verdict against them.

On the whole the Critics are behaving very well, and I only wonder those who take little exceptions venture, on the imperfect state of their information, to do anything but cry hurrah over the splendid banquet that is opening before them. If Mrs. Lewes heard the excited speculations over Mordecai among the privileged few here who have read Book v she would be more than satisfied with the impression her wonderful Jew is making. The printers promise Book 6 tomorrow and I hope proofs will be ready to post for you but I am not quite certain.

I am very sorry to see what you say of Lady Lytton's health and also that you do not think him looking very fit. I do hope all will go well with them. A sort of comparative coolness had arisen between him and me, but as I felt that it arose from his being so much in the hands of poor Forster, who was always an unfriend to Blackwoods, it did not interfere with my warm regard to Lytton and his charming wife.

Write soon to tell me how you both are.

ever yours truly
John Blackwood.

Should we repeat Motto on the back title of each volume of Deronda.[7]

## GHL TO ALEXANDER MAIN, LONDON, 1 MARCH 1876

*Text:* Main's copy owned by Mr. John R. Sprunt. *Hitherto unpublished.*

**The Priory, | 21. North Bank, | Regents Park.**
1 March 76.

My dear Main

Your sympathy is so genuine and the insight which springs from sympathy so unerring that in spite of its hyperbolical expression it cheers and strengthens Mrs. Lewes—too much given alas! to despair and doubt. All the ringing chorus of praise which echoes from afar does not stifle her doubt; but is nevertheless very pleasant to her. The success of Deronda already seems to surpass that of Middlemarch and I am persuaded that it will increase with each monthly part. To my mind it is the greatest work she has done.

She is still in very feeble health I am sorry to add, and there seems no chance of her getting better now till the book is finished and we get away to the Continent. I also have been laid up with severe lumbago, headache and liver and the "Problems" have been getting on slowly in consequence. The third volume will not be sent to press until the autumn because I want it to have the benefit of her reading before printing it. Two things I hope this volume will effect—namely a sweeping away of much superstition respecting the nervous system, and a final quashing of the automaton theory.

I am glad you liked 'Animal Studies." I have not looked at it since it was published—now several years ago—but it was written with almost as much gusto as "Seaside Studies"—the book of all my books which was to me the most unalloyed delight.

7. The motto appears on the half title verso facing the title page of each of the four volumes.

We went last Thursday to hear Liszt's Oratorio [8]—mainly out of regard for Liszt; but partly also out of curiosity as to this specimen of the music of the future—so in spite of its being an *evening* concert we went and suffered (physically) in consequence. Then to add to the ill effect we dined out on the day after at the Lyttons, to say good bye to them, before they go to India. We are very fond of them both; and so far were glad to have a last farewell; but dining out doesn't suit us, and we have both been limp since.

Ever yours
G. H. L.

## JOHN BLACKWOOD TO GHL, EDINBURGH, 2 MARCH 1876

*MS:* National Library of Scotland. *Extract published: John Blackwood,* pp. 393–394.

**45, George Street, | Edinburgh.**
March 2/76.

My Dear Lewes

I had to go out of Town this morning and have only time to write a line before post hour to say that I read Book Six last night and have unbounded congratulations to send to Mrs. Lewes. She is *A Magician.* It is a Poem, a Drama, and a Grand Novel.

One cannot rightly read Deronda while people are talking and moving about, so I did not get fairly begun until I went to my dressing room where it kept me reading, thinking, and admiring until past three a.m. The book is *A Work* in itself, and I do not wonder at the creator of such work feeling exhausted and nervous, but she may dismiss all anxiety as to what the world will think and feel satisfied that she has transcendently carried out her purpose.

There is no doubt about the marvellous Mordecai and oh that Cohen family! The whole tribe of Israel should fall down and worship her. I must read again before venturing to write to her. When I finished the part at ½ past three I grudged very much not being able to go with Deronda to see his Mother. The suspense is great.

ever yours truly
John Blackwood.

8. "The Legend of St. Elizabeth." In his Diary, 24 February, GHL wrote: "Went to concert Liszt's *Elizabeth of Hungary*—wearied by its want of melody and absence of true expression. Home at 11.30."

## GHL TO JOHN BLACKWOOD, LONDON, 3 MARCH 1876

*Text: John Blackwood,* p. 388.

The Priory, March 3, 1876.

Dear Blackwood,

Your note has been as good as a dose of quinine. As the drooping flower revives under the beneficent rain, so did her drooping spirits under your enthusiastic words.

## GE TO MRS. MARK PATTISON, LONDON, 3 MARCH 1876

*MS:* British Museum. *Hitherto unpublished.*

**The Priory, | 21. North Bank, | Regents Park.**
March 3. 76.

Dearest Figliuolina

When the Rector said that you had twenty-seven unanswered letters on your desk I despaired of hearing from you again. That makes your letter all the welcomer. And besides, the news you send me is better than the intimations beforehand had allowed me to hope. The best element in it is the cheerfulness of its tone, but after that it is really a solid good that you are now able to think of moving northward and getting the new mental stimulus that you must be sorely in need of at the end of your long banishment. Such a nurse and general care-taker as you describe in your matronly-bodied Burgundian is a "mercy." I had thought with some alarm for you of the "French courier-nurse" having once seen an unlucky speculation of that kind.

I wish you could have seen the collection of Walker's pictures.[9] They were worth enduring the suffocation prepared for me by the crowd of beholders. I came away headachy but enriched more than one can well be by a miscellaneous exhibition which compels one to see the world through twenty different minds in quick succession. One day we encountered your good friend Miss E. Smith in the crush at this 'gallery,' and we talked of you less cheerfully than we should have done if I had then had your courageous letter.—We are hoping to get away to the continent by the end of May, but I hope also you will have risen

9. Frederick Walker (1840–75). GHL went to Deschamp's Gallery to see his pictures 24 January, 1 and 10 February 1876. GE was probably with him the first time, when he remarks, "Room very crowded." (GHL Diary.)

above the horizon here before that time. You will find us looking thin and ghastly.

The Rector's article in 'Mind' on Philosophy at Oxford pleased us mightily by its vigorous portrait of the Prizeman.[1] He spoke with husband's pride of your having written your last article on the Life of Voltaire [2] without any books at hand.

Burne Jones goes on transcending himself and is rising into the inconvenient celebrity which is made up of echoes as well as voices. I do hope he will be urged into having a collection of his pictures in a separate little gallery for a time, so that his admirers might point to the reason for the faith that is in them.[3]

I have no news worth telling. We go to our one amusement of the Saturday concert, our friends come to see us on a Sunday, and lately we have said goodbye to the Lyttons with many longings for his and her good in their new, distant, trying honours. She is expecting another Baby in August, and one hopes it may be a boy to soothe the poignant memories of the lost ones.[4]

Mr. Lewes begs you to think "without contempt" of his kind regards and sympathetic wishes as of a fellow-creature to whom also gout is not alien, making him occasionally cry out in the night as if a crab had hold of his foot. Rain, rain, rain here, and unhealthy mugginess in quick alternation with cold, upsetting the liver and bodily comfort generally of

Your affectionate
Madre.

1. See 27 December 1875.

2. I have not found this article.

3. This hope was realized in 1877 when by invitation of Sir Coutts Lindsay he exhibited eight pictures at the opening of the Grosvenor Gallery. "From that day he belonged to the world in a sense that he had never done before, for his existence became widely known and his name famous." (Lady Burne-Jones, *Memorials of Edward Burne-Jones,* 2 vols., 1904, II, 75.)

4. Victor Alexander George Robert Lytton was born at Simla, 10 August 1876. (Burke, *Peerage,* 1880, p. 788.)

## GE TO MRS. ELMA STUART, LONDON, 3 MARCH 1876

*MS:* British Museum. *Published:* Stuart, pp. 51–53.

**The Priory, | 21. North Bank, | Regents Park.**
March 3. 76.

Dearest Elma

Thanks for the sweet violets and still sweeter letter, which promises delightful things—the best being that you will come over in April and see your parent who is hanging to life by a very indifferent loop of flesh. Imagine us both as ghastly as possible, that the sight of us may not shock you too much.

I wrap myself already in the new plaid that is being woven for me, and take its soft tissue as a symbol of gentle affection. As to the reprints,[5] dear child, it was like your warm heart to get them done, but *they must be destroyed, please.* You could not hinder the suspicion that we had prompted the distribution—that would be the immediate conclusion of ordinary minds, and would by and by become their absolute statement. I have not read the article. Mr. Lewes carefully protects me from reading about myself, and as soon as I know that there is an article on me in any periodical, I wait till it is cut out before I take up the print for other reading. But Mr. Lewes reads everything about me that comes in his way, and he thought, with you, that the said account of me in the *W.*[6] was well written and done in an excellent spirit. He read aloud to me two sentences. But the details of fact are quite erroneous, except the Liggins story, which is correctly told.

As to the Table, the photograph shows a great beauty, but our own are beauties too of which we are very proud, and we don't see why you should have the trouble of packing and bringing anything better in exchange. Pack and bring yourself, my daughter. You will cheer greatly the heart of

Your anxious and affectionate
Mother.

Our love to Roland, of whom we hope to hear the best news when you come.

5. I have not succeeded in finding Elma Stuart's article either in periodical form (see 2 September 1875) or in the reprint.

6. This seems not to be a reference to the *Westminster Review.*

## JOHN BLACKWOOD TO GE, EDINBURGH, 6 MARCH 1876

*MS:* National Library of Scotland. *Hitherto unpublished.*

**45, George Street, | Edinburgh.**
March 6/76.

My Dear Mrs. Lewes

On Saturday I got the inclosed note and sent the reply, the substance of which I have scrawled on at the end of the note. On Sunday came your note to Mr. Simpson on the same subject. It is a laughable coincidence, and not the least curious thing to me is that I should not only have taken the trouble to reply but have kept a memorandum of what I said. Simpson is writing to you what measures he is taking to stop if possible your corrector's correspondence.[7]

The sales during the last three days of last week were most satisfactory, and as we have a note from Mudie today ordering the extra 250 of Book II it is as I predicted overtaking Book I while B. one is still marching on. Since I wrote to Lewes my copy of Book VI has been in the hands of my wife and daughter. They are deeply, I may say solemnly, impressed.

always yours truly
John Blackwood.

## JOHN BLACKWOOD TO GE, EDINBURGH, 16 MARCH 1876

*MS:* National Library of Scotland. *Hitherto unpublished.*

**45, George Street, | Edinburgh.**
March 16/76.

My Dear Mrs. Lewes

Sales for the last day or two have been steady but hardly worth reporting and the mute eloquence of the enclosed note touched me so much when Simpson laid it before me with a smile that I said I would send it to you. From the memo. there are purchases, obviously for buyers of the book, not for mere library readers. Book Two is coming up hand over hand upon Book One and must now be between two and three hundred of its predecessor.

7. See [18] March 1876.

Critics both public and private amuse me by their complaint that they do not quite understand Gwendolen. Did they wish you to lay down a chart of her character and fate on the first page? Did they ever *fully* know any human being at a first meeting or even after years of acquaintance? The objection is in reality the highest compliment, being in fact the plainest confession of the interest excited. I hope you have both enjoyed your expedition to the country [8] and returned with renewed health and spirits. The weather has I fear been against you. We have frost and snow here today, but Willie has gone out to hunt and I saw other maniacs passing the window in red coats as I was dressing.

always yours truly
John Blackwood.

## GE TO JOHN BLACKWOOD, LONDON, [18] MARCH 1876

*MS:* National Library of Scotland. *Published:* Cross, III, 274–275.

**The Priory, | 21. North Bank, | Regents Park.**
March 17.[1] 76.

My dear Mr. Blackwood

We have just come in from Weybridge, but are going to take refuge there again on Monday for a few days more of fresh air and long breezy afternoon walks. Many thanks for your thoughtfulness in sending me the cheering account of sales. I find one—also from Mr. Langford carrying the good news up to the last moment—this morning being marked 25 of B. II.

Mr. Lewes has not heard any complaints of not understanding Gwendolen, but a strong partizanship for and against her. My correspondence about the misquotation of Tennyson [2] has quieted itself since the fifth letter. But Mr. Reeve,[3] the Editor of the Edinburgh, has written me a very pretty note taxing me with having wanted insight into

8. The W. H. Halls lent them their house at Weybridge for two or three weeks. They went Monday, 13 March 1876 and stayed till Friday, 24 March except for the Saturday and Sunday, which they spent at the Priory.

1. GHL's Diary shows that they went to the Priory 18 March and returned to Weybridge 20 March.

2. GE quoted from memory the motto to ch. 17: "This is true the poet sings, | That a sorrow's crown of sorrow | Is remembering happier things," ascribing it to Tennyson's *In Memoriam.* An erratum slip was inserted before the half-title of Book III quoting the passage correctly from *Locksley Hall.*

the technicalities of Newmarket, when I made Lush say 'I will *take* odds.' Mr. Reeve judges that I should have written 'I will *lay* odds.' [3] On the other hand, another expert contends that the case is one in which Lush would be more likely to say 'I will take odds.' What do you think?—I told Mr. Reeve that I had a dread of being righteously pelted with mistakes that would make a cairn above me—a monument and a warning to people who write novels without being omniscient and infallible.

Mr. Lewes is agitating himself over a fifth reading of Revise, B. VI, and says he finds it more interesting than on any former reading. It is agreeable to have a home criticism of this kind. But I am deep in the Fourth Vol. and cannot any longer care about what is past and done for—the passion of the moment is as much as I can live in.

We have had beautiful skies with our cold, and only now and then a snow shower. It is grievous to read of the sufferings elsewhere from floods.

Always yours sincerely
M. E. Lewes.

## GHL DIARY, LONDON, 24–26 MARCH 1876

*MS:* Yale. *Hitherto unpublished.*

**Friday 24 March 1876**

Delboeuf.[4] Problems. Walked with Emily and Eleanor on St. George's Hill. Superb weather. After lunch we went there again with Eleanor and started at 3.40. Came home to find Dr. Andrew Clark had sent me a present of a Writing Pad of novel construction. Dressed and went to dinner party of 18 at Mrs. Benzon's: Joachim, Fraülein Krebs,[5] Browning, Leighton, the Lehmanns etc. After dinner Joachim and Krebs played—she superbly—and Fraülein Löwe [1] sang Schumann. Agreeable evening. Home at 12.15.

**Saturday 25 March 1876**

Delboeuf. Problems. Wrote 6 letters and had a turn. Concert: Joachim and Mad. Schumann. Spohr's Quintett and Schumann's grand

3. Henry Reeve (1813–95). In later printings this sentence at the very end of ch. 13 reads "I will lay odds."

4. Joseph Rémy Léopold Delbœuf, *Théorie générale de la sensibilité*, Brussels, 1875.

5. Marie Krebs (1851–1900), pianist, daughter of Karl Krebs (1804–80).

1. Sophie Loewe (1848–1926), soprano, sang in London from 1871 to 1877, when she married W. von Glehn.

quintett, superbly played. Read the papers and at ¼ to 8 went to dinner party at the Pagets': present Lord and Lady Blachford,[2] Sir Garnett and Lady Wolseley, Miss Lawrence (surgeon's daughter),[3] the fiancé of Miss Paget, two of the sons, Sir James and Lady P. Delightful party. We were both charmed with the Wolseleys, especially with him and were pleased that he asked if they might be allowed to call.[4] Home at 12.

**Sunday 26 March 1876**

Sick last night and headache to-day—the usual consequences of dinner parties! Polly also headachy and unable to work. We had a couple of hours walk in the Park and came back somewhat better. Mrs. and Miss Huth, Charles, Prof. and Mrs. Beesley, Mrs. Orr, Mrs. F. Lehmann, Lord Houghton. Went to bed soon after dinner.

## GE TO MARY DICKENS, LONDON, 29 MARCH 1876

*MS:* Dr. Eric Millar. *Hitherto unpublished.*

**The Priory, | 21. North Bank, | Regents Park.**
March 29. 76.

Dear Miss Dickens [5]

I am very much obliged to you for remembering my request and letting me know in such good time the first night of "Queen Mary." [6]

Mr. Lewes unites with me in thanks and kind regards.

Yours sincerely
M. E. Lewes.

2. Frederic Rogers, 1st Baron Blachford (1811–89).

3. Sir William Lawrence, 1st Baronet, (1783–1867), surgeon to St. Bartholomew's Hospital 1824–65, had a son and two daughters.

4. See 14 April 1878.

5. Harry and Mamie Dickens were among the guests at a large dinner party given by the Frederick Lehmanns 12 March 1876. (GHL Diary.) She was the novelist's elder daughter (1838–96).

6. Tennyson's play was published in 1875; it was first played at the Lyceum 18 April 1876.

GE TO MME EUGÈNE BODICHON,

LONDON, 30 MARCH 1876

*MS:* Mr. Philip Leigh-Smith. *Extracts published:* Cross, III, 275–276.

**The Priory, | 21. North Bank, | Regents Park.**
March 30. 76.

My dear Barbara

Your letter was a most welcome assurance that no evil had befallen you on the voyage which was made in what to us was horribly blustering weather. I had said to Mr. Lewes, 'She will perhaps send me a post card by and by'—so that your letter with more details than a card could have carried, was doubly acceptable as something better than what I had counted on.

I am delighted to know that nature and the weather are enjoyable to you and your companions altogether sympathetic, still more that the Doctor was glad to receive you all and that your object in taking the journey is likely to be answered. Also, I am well pleased that Deronda touches you. I *wanted* you to prefer the chapter [7] about Mirah's finding, and I hope you will also like her history in Part III which has just been published.

We want very much to get away, but I fear we shall hardly be able to start till the end of May. At present we think of the Maritime Alps as a destination for the warm summer, if we have such a season this year, but we shall wander a little on our way thither and not feel bound to accomplish anything in particular. Meanwhile we are hearing some nice music occasionally, and we are going to see Tennyson's Play which is to be given on the 15th.[8] The occasion will be very interesting and I should be sorry to miss it.

I have not seen or heard anything of Miss Marks since you left. I trust that all is going on well with her.[9] Apropos of her and all other subjects, will you kindly remember that we shall be out of reach of ordinary letters after May?

We have been getting a little refreshment from two flights between Sundays to Weybridge, where Mr. and Mrs. Hall lent us their house and servants. But we have had the good a little drained from us by going out to dinner two days in succession. At Sir James Paget's I

7. Ch. 17.
8. i.e. the 18th.
9. She was studying Greek in preparation for her examination for the Girton scholarship. (Evelyn Sharp, *Hertha Ayrton,* 1926, p. 48.)

was much interested to find that a gentle-looking, clear-eyed, neatly-made man was Sir Garnet Wolseley and I had some talk with him which quite confirmed the impression of him as one of those men who have a power of command by dint of their sweet temper, calm demeanour and unswerving resolution. The next subject that has filled our chat lately has been the Blue Book on Vivisection, which you would like to look into.[1] There is a great deal of matter for reflection in the evidence on the subject, and some good points have been lately put in print and conversation that I should like to tell you of if I had time. Prof. Clifford told us the other Sunday that Huxley complained of his sufferings from "the profligate lying of virtuous women." [2] I am scribbling at the fag end of the day, being short of time not so much because of work as because of my feebleness which makes me incapable of getting through it.

Best, affectionate remembrances to your sister and Miss Blythe. And kind regards to the Doctor from both of us. George unites in love to you. I hope we shall hear of your being safe in England before we set off.

Yours always
Marian.

## GHL DIARY, LONDON, 31 MARCH 1876

*MS:* Yale. *Extract published:* Kitchel, pp. 276–277.

**Friday 31 March 1876**

Horwicz.[3] Problems. Prof. Preyer [4] of Jena to lunch. Drove him in the Park to show him "the swells." Called on Mrs. Geddes. Went to a conference of physiologists at Burdon Saunderson's: [5] Huxley, Sharpey,[6]

1. *Digest of Evidence Taken before the Royal Commission on the Practice of Subjecting Live Animals to Experiments for Scientific Purposes,* 1876. GHL's testimony, pp. 41–42, describes his methods. He thinks the amount of pain caused is very small, and, while admitting society's right to restrict experiments, fears that a law will hinder physiology.

2. Miss Sophia Jex-Blake, having failed her medical examination at Edinburgh, suggested in a letter to the *Times* that the paper had been unfairly marked. Huxley, to whom the paper had been referred, replied in the *Times,* 8 July 1874, explaining that his prejudice was in favor of admitting women to the practice of medicine.

3. Adolf Horwicz, *Psychologische Analysen auf physiologischer Grundlage,* appeared in parts, 1872–78. GHL was reading "Denklehre."

4. Wilhelm Thierry Preyer (1841–97) taught at Jena 1867–88.

5. John Scott Burdon-Sanderson (1828–1905), at this time Professor of Practical Physiology and Histology at University College, London.

6. William Sharpey (1802–80) had retired after 38 years as Professor of Anatomy and Physiology at University College, London.

Pavy,[7] Marshall,[8] Humphry,[9] Ferrier,[1] Lauder Brunton,[2] etc. It was agreed to form a Physiological Society and I was asked to be one of the Council.[3] The question was discussed of what steps should be taken with regard to the Vivisection Report, and it was agreed to let the Government quietly understand that we would not oppose a Bill framed in the spirit of that Report.

## GHL TO WILLIAM BLACKWOOD AND SONS, LONDON, 10 APRIL 1876

*MS:* National Library of Scotland. *Address:* Messrs. W. Blackwood and Sons | 45 George St. | Edinburgh. *Postmark:* LONDON-N.W | A 3 | AP 10 | 76. *Hitherto unpublished.*

The Priory, 10 April.

Part VII goes by this post; and VIII will I hope soon follow.

Langford's news is very cheering. All well.

G. H. L.

## JOHN BLACKWOOD TO GHL, EDINBURGH, 10 APRIL 1876

*Text:* Copy in Blackwood Letter Book. *Hitherto unpublished.*

45 George Street | Edinburgh April 10/76.

My dear Lewes

I was greatly pleased to hear from Simpson that there was something due to you on our old transaction The Physiology of Common Life. In 1862 we paid you for all the Stock on hand as you will see by statement rendered at that time. Since then we have reprinted odds and ends of numbers to make complete sets of the book and inclosed cheque £66.5.9 pays for them as per accompanying statement. We have about a thousand complete copies on hand which move slowly.

7. Frederick William Pavy (1820–1911). Lecturer on Physiology at Guy's Hospital.

8. John Marshall (1818–90), Professor of Clinical Surgery at University College.

9. George Murray Humphry (1820–96), surgeon, Professor of Human Anatomy at Cambridge.

1. David Ferrier (1843–1928) whose study localized functions and opened the way for brain surgery.

2. Thomas Lauder Brunton (1844–1916).

3. The provisional committee that drew up the Society's rules. See Sir Edward Sharpey-Schafer, *History of the Physiological Society during Its First Fifty Years 1876–1926,* 1927. Biographical sketches of many of the founders are given, pp. 17–40.

Mr. Langford, I doubt not, keeps you well posted as to sales of Daniel and they are I think most satisfactory and Books two and three keep so well up with Book one. I confess however that I expected more of a spirt in sale but I think the closing scene of Book Four, I mean the Jewel scene, will set all the world talking. There is immense puzzlement as to what the author is going to make of Gwendolen, which is a good thing and none are more sorely baffled than the Newspaper critics.

While writing to you it occurs to me that I did not reply to Mrs. Lewes' last pleasant letter but I do not think there was any point requiring an answer. However I shall write to her very soon.

We had three lovely warm days but today it has gone back to East wind and snow.

ever yours truly
(signed) John Blackwood.

## GHL TO JOHN BLACKWOOD, LONDON, 11 APRIL 1876

*MS:* National Library of Scotland. *Hitherto unpublished.*

11th April 76.

Homme de relations charmantes!

Just time to acknowledge your checque for 66.5.9. Tell Mr. Simpson the oftener he repeats *that* kind of research the higher will be his position in the mind of

Yours ever
G. H. Lewes.

Yesterday I sent Part VII.

## GE JOURNAL, LONDON, 12 APRIL 1876

*MS:* Yale. *Published:* Cross, III, 276–277.

April 12. On February 1 began the publication of Deronda, and the interest of the public, strong from the first, appears to have increased with Book III. The day before yesterday I sent off Book VII. The success of the work at present is greater than that of Middlemarch up to the corresponding point of publication. What will be the feeling of the public as the story advances I am entirely doubtful. The Jewish element seems to me likely to satisfy nobody.—I am in rather better health, having perhaps profited by some eight days' change at Weybridge.

## JOHN BLACKWOOD TO GE, EDINBURGH, 17 APRIL 1876

*MS:* National Library of Scotland. *Extract published: John Blackwood,* p. 394.

**45, George Street, | Edinburgh.**
April 17/76.

My Dear Mrs. Lewes

Proofs of Book Seven go to you by this post. I can hardly venture to speak about it and as for criticism, I should as soon think of regaling you with comments upon one of the great Greek Tragedies. This Book is so powerful as to be very terrible. What a pain must have been Deronda's in that interview with his mother [4] and how directly and simply does the language bring it home to the reader.

I was nearly as uneasy as Deronda while Gwendolen went on with her confession.[5] The words of old Elspeth in the Antiquary came irresistibly to my mind: "An' Murder tirlit at the door if it cam na' ben." [6]

No wonder Deronda felt "worn" [7] at the close of the interview. I can hardly imagine any one reading without being carried away and feeling upset, and what must be the strain of thinking and writing out such a scene. Much as I know of the conscientious pain and anxiety you go through in the construction of your great works, I never felt more deeply and sympathisingly with you in your labours than I did last night in reading this Book 7 of Daniel, and it was for the second time, as I had not been able to resist reading the M.S. before I sent it into the Printing Office. But the glory is great and I trust the labour with this work is nearly over.

I think I hear and see Lewes over the proofs and hoping this may find you well and happy, I am

always yours truly
John Blackwood.

P.S. I must tell you I sent for a Hebrew Dictionary to look up the word tephillin [8] but to my shame I could not make out the letters and the dunderhead of a German who compiled the book had not given a relative table of English and Hebrew letters.

4. Chs. 51, 53.
5. Ch. 56.
6. Scott, *The Antiquary,* ch. 40 reads "tirl'd at the door-pin."
7. At the end of Book VII GE describes Deronda as "worn in spirit by the perpetual strain of this scene."
8. Tephillin, the phylacteries with verses inscribed on them, are mentioned in ch. 51, Book VII, p. 27.

You were quite right as to Lush saying he would "take odds." He was not in such a happy and sanguine state as to say he would lay odds, but as to that you are the only judge, as you alone knew his exact feelings.

## GE TO JOHN BLACKWOOD, LONDON, 18 APRIL 1876

*MS:* National Library of Scotland. *Published:* Cross, III, 277–280.

**The Priory, | 21. North Bank, | Regents Park.**
April 18. 76.

My dear Mr. Blackwood

It was better than I expected to receive the proof of Book VII. so soon in this Easter time. And your sympathetic letter is a welcome support to me in the rather depressed condition which has come upon me with a whole week's internal disorder, from the effect, I imagine of a chill taken in the sudden change from mildness to renewed winter.[9] You can understand how trying it is to have a week of incompetence at the present stage of affairs. I am rather concerned to see that the part is nearly a sheet smaller than any of the other parts. But Books V and VI are proportionately thick, and Mr. Lewes insists that B. VII is thick *enough*.[1] It seemed inadmissible to add anything after the scene with Gwendolen, and to stick anything in, not necessary to development, between the foregoing chapters, is a form of 'matter in the wrong place' particularly repulsive to my authorship's sensibility.

People tell us that the book is enormously discussed, and I must share with you rather a neat coincidence which pleased us last week. Perhaps you saw what Mr. Lewes told me of—namely, that the Spectator opined that the scenes between Lush and Grandcourt were not 'vraisemblable'—were of the imperious feminine, not the masculine character.[2] Just afterwards Mr. Lewes was chatting with a (man) friend who, without having read the Spectator or having the subject in the least led up to by Mr. Lewes, said that he had been at Lady Walde-

9. "Polly unwell and kept in bed. Sat with her the greater part of the day—read aloud papers and Macaulay's Life." (GHL Diary, 15 April 1876.) The next day she was "rather better, but still headachy."

1. Books V and VI came to 196 and 197 pages respectively; Book VII was only 162.

2. "Mr. Grandcourt shows to Lush rather the kind and degree of insolence which a proud and selfish woman would show to a dependent, than what a *man* who has at least passed through the public discipline of school and college life, would be likely to show." (*Spectator*, 8 April 1876, p. 464.)

grave's [3] where the subject of discussion had been 'Deronda' and *Bernal Osborne,*[4] delivering himself on the book, said that the very best parts were the scenes between Grandcourt and Lush. Don't you think that Bernal Osborne has seen more of the Grandcourt and Lush life than that critic has seen?—But several men of experience have put their fingers on those scenes as having surprizing verisimilitude, and I naturally was peculiarly anxious about such testimony where my construction was grounded on a less direct knowledge.

We are rather vexed, now it is too late, that I did not carry out a sort of incipient intention to expunge a motto from Walt Whitman which I inserted in Book IV. Of course the whole is irrevocable by this time, but I should have otherwise thought it worth while to have a new page, not because the motto itself is objectionable to me—it was one of the finer things which had clung to me from among his writings —but because, since I quote so few poets, my selection of a motto from Walt Whitman might be taken as the sign of a special admiration which I am very far from feeling.[5] How imperfectly one's mind acts in proof reading! Mr. Lewes had taken up Book IV yesterday to re-read it for his pleasure merely, and though he had read it several times before, he never till yesterday made a remark against taking a motto from Walt Whitman. I, again, had continually had an 'appetency' towards removing the motto and had never carried it out—perhaps from that sort of flaccidity which comes over me about what *has been* done, when I am occupied with what *is being* done.

People in their eagerness about my characters are quite angry, it appears, when their own expectations are not fulfilled—angry, for example, that Gwendolen accepts Grandcourt etc. etc. One reader is sure that Mirah is going to die very soon and I suppose will be disgusted at her remaining alive. Such are the reproaches to which I make myself liable. However, that you seem to share Mr. Lewes's strong feeling of Book VII being no falling off in intensity, makes me brave. Only, end-

3. Mary Dorothea Palmer, daughter of Lord Selborne, was married in 1874 to Sir William Frederick Waldegrave, Earl Waldegrave.

4. Ralph Bernal Osborne (1808–82), M.P. 1841–1874, "for many years one of the recognised wits of politics." (*DNB.*)

5. As motto for ch. 29 GE used two lines from Whitman's "Vocalism." Her acquaintance with his poems dated from 1856, when she quoted a few lines in reviewing the 1st edition of *Leaves of Grass* in the *Westminster Review.* Perhaps Lady Strangford or Whitman's most ardent admirer Mrs. Gilchrist had stimulated her interest more recently. Her regret at having used the motto sprang from an attack on Whitman in the *Saturday Review,* 18 March 1876, pp. 360–361, which declared that "although there is a small *coterie* of persons in this country who are not ashamed to confess their liking for Whitman's nastiness, his own countrymen have universally repudiated him." GHL's Diary for 1876 lists under Charities £2 for Walt Whitman.

ings are inevitably the least satisfactory part of any work in which there is any merit of development.

We are going tonight to see the first representation of "Queen Mary" which is a literary and dramatic epoch. It is perhaps not likely to be played again, for without transcendant acting of Mary's part the performance will be dreary, and I fear there is no chance of transcendant acting.[6]

Always yours truly
M. E. Lewes.

I forgot to say that the tephillin are the small leather bands or phylacteries inscribed with supremely sacred words, which the Jew binds on his arms and head during prayer. Any periphrasis which would be generally intelligible would be undramatic, and I don't much like explanatory foot-notes in a poem or story. But I must consider what I can do to remedy the unintelligibility.

The printers have sadly spoiled the beautiful Greek name Kalonymos, which was the name of a celebrated family of scholarly Jews transplanted from Italy into Germany in mediaeval times. But my writing was in fault.[8]

## GE TO MRS. ELMA STUART, LONDON, 29 APRIL 1876

*MS:* British Museum. *Published:* Stuart, pp. 52–55.

**The Priory, | 21. North Bank, | Regents Park.**
April 29. 76.

Dearest Elma

You grieve your mother by dwelling on your innocent bit of hyperbole as if it were a sin. We are not so dull as to require every word to be literal or else to have an elaborate commentary. I am sorry now that I made that drollery about the writing the occasion of a remark which was entirely precautionary, and referred to *possible* words that might drop from you in the liveliness of conversation, without the least sense of mischief in anything that had been actually said. It was

6. At the Lyceum with Kate Bateman as Mary and Henry Irving as Philip. "All the interest and excitement of a First Night. Play horribly acted throughout—not one of them able to *speak*." (GHL Diary, 18 April 1876.) G. W. Smalley sat next to GE. For his account of her comments see his *London Letters*, 2 vols., 1890, I, 288.

8. In the proofs the name appears as Kalongmos.

my awkwardness to link my caution about the servant's ear with your innocent exaggeration, which, I observed, had raised a smile.[1]

We should have been mere blockheads to have supposed that your words had done any harm, even if you had expressly directed them against book-writing instead of letter-writing. Were we not "present company"?—and had we not had our patent to write for you? And does not that quick-eared servant know that you think too much of us? So pray dismiss the subject forever from your soul, and save your penitence for a real transgression.

The petticoat is very beautiful, after the beauty of petticoats—perfect in colour and in texture far better than any bat's wing I have ever been indulged with. It is not *par* for Elma's presence and tenderness, but it is a pretty message from her.

My ailings having got worse rather than better, Mr. Lewes insisted on sending for Dr. Andrew Clarke, and he is trying to make me less good-for-nothing by feeding me up and making me drink Burgundy. It seems that my usually strong pulse has got sadly flagging.

We were disappointed not to see you again. Thank Roly for his pretty letter to me. I and my other self greet you with warm affection, and shall be glad to have news of you from Scotland.

Always your loving Mother
M. E. Lewes.

Lady Claud Hamilton spoke with pleasure of having seen you, that Sunday you were in Albemarle St.

## GHL TO MARK PATTISON, LONDON, 1 MAY [1876]

*MS:* Bodleian. *Hitherto unpublished.*

**The Priory, | 21. North Bank, | Regents Park.**
1 May.

My dear Pattison

The bearer of a letter of introduction to me from M. Ribot,[2] intends paying a brief visit to Oxford and wishes to pay his respects to

1. "Charles Gertrude and the two children with Elma Stuart and Roly to lunch." (GHL Diary, 22 April 1876.)

2. Théodule Armand Ribot (1839–1916), French psychologist, author of *L'Hérédité psychologique,* Paris, 1872, *La Philosophie de Schopenhauer,* 1874, and *La Psychologie anglaise contemporaine,* 1870, in which the work of Mill, Spencer, GHL, and others is paraphrased. He was founder and editor of *La Revue philosophique,* 1876.

the Rector of Lincoln. His name is M. Gérard,[3] of the École Normale, and you will find him greatly interested in English philosophical literature.

Yours ever
G. H. Lewes.

## GE TO ALEXANDER MAIN, LONDON, 2 MAY 1876

*MS:* Parrish Collection, Princeton. *Mostly published:* Cross, New Edition, pp. 549–550.

**The Priory, | 21. North Bank, | Regents Park.**
May 2. 76.

Dear Mr. Main

Having a leisure half hour unexpectedly this afternoon I use it in writing to you, rather than trust to the time nearer our departure, which may be filled with small details of preparation. Even if you had not asked me, it would have been my impulse to send you a few lines, that I might thank you, with more directness than through my husband's report, for all your affectionate sympathy and for the painstaking appreciation with which you continually cheer me. Generally it is not good for me to be much within hearing of what is said about my books until they are at a good distance from their birth and I am in the dispassionate mood towards them of a hen towards her feathered chickens. But some genuine signs of understanding which assure me that I have not missed my aim are a helpful blessing, and you are one who can give such signs. Still, I shall be glad to take flight into the privacy of travel, as we hope to do at the beginning of June. We both need repose.

Are you not sometimes made rather desponding by the reading of newspapers and periodicals? One cannot escape seeing and hearing something of political and literary criticism in one's need to know what one's fellow-men are doing, and all information is given in a soup of comment. The ignorance, the recklessness, the lack of any critical principles by which to distinguish what is matter of technical judgment and what of individual taste, the ridiculous absence of fundamental comparison while hardly any judgment is passed without a futile and offensive comparison of one author with another—'Tired of all this,' I sometimes shrink from every article that pretends to be critical—I mean of other people's productions, not of course my own, for you know I am well taken care of by my husband and am saved from getting my

3. M. Gérard called 30 April 1876, "sent us by Ribot." (GHL Diary.)

mind poisoned with print about myself. You who are young may hope to do something towards making periodical writing a genuine contribution to culture, and I am glad to think you have found access for your thoughts with Mr. Ribot and Mr. Robertson.[4] Mr. Lewes has been much pleased with your ready and acute perception of philosophical and scientific bearings.

I trust that all is well with you in more material and domestic matters. We get great pleasure now from the thought of young lives filled with joyous activity. We too are unspeakably happy in our activity, but we have the drawback of increasing susceptibility to fatigue. I am often painfully anxious about Mr. Lewes's health—the anxiety that one must pay as the price of loving greatly.

This letter says little that I should like to say, but let it have a symbolic significance and stand as an indirect sign that I am always

Yours with sincere regard
M. E. Lewes.

## GE TO MRS. HARRIET BEECHER STOWE, LONDON, 6 MAY 1876

*MS:* Mr. Lyman Beecher Stowe. *Published:* Cross, III, 280–283.

**The Priory, | 21. North Bank, | Regents Park.**
May 6. 76.

My dear Friend

Your letter [5] was one of the best cordials I could have. Is there anything that cheers and strengthens more than the sense of another's worth and tenderness? And it was that sense that your letter stirred in me, not only by the words of fellowship and encouragement you give directly to me, but by all you tell me of your own feeling under your late painful experience. I had felt it long since I had heard of your and the Professor's well-being, but I need not say one word to you of the reasons why I am not active towards my distant friends except in thought. I *do* think of them, and have a tenacious memory of every little sign they have given me.

Please offer my reverential love to the Professor and tell him I am

4. George Croom Robertson (1842–92), editor of *Mind,* printed three letters by Main defending GHL's *Problems of Life and Mind:* 1 (April 1876), 292–294; (July 1876), 431–434; and (October 1876), 566–567.

5. An extremely long letter dated 18 March 1876, published in C. E. Stowe, *Life of Harriet Beecher Stowe,* Boston and New York, 1890, pp. 473–482, devoted mostly to the affairs of Henry Ward Beecher.

ruthlessly proud that I kept him out of his bed. I hope that both you and he will continue to be interested in my spiritual children. My cares for them are nearly at an end and in a few weeks we expect to set out on a continental journey, as the sort of relaxation which carries one most thoroughly away from studies and social claims. You rightly divine that I am a little overdone, but my fatigue is due not to any excess of work so much as to the vicissitudes of our long winter, which have affected me severely as they have done all delicate people. It is true that some nervous wear, such as you know well, from the excitement of writing, may have made me more susceptible to knife-like winds and sudden chills.

Though you tenderly forbade me to write in answer to your letter I like to do it in these minutes when I happen to be free, lest hindrances should come in the indefinite future. I am the happier for thinking that you will have had this little bit of a letter to assure you that the sweet rain of your affection did not fall on a sandy place.

I make a delightful picture of your life in your orange grove—taken care of by dear daughters. Climate enters into *my* life with an influence the reverse of what I like to think of in yours. Sunlight and sweet air make a new creature of me. But we cannot bear now to exile ourselves from our own country,[6] which holds the roots of our moral and social life. One fears to become selfish and emotionally withered by living abroad, and giving up the numerous connexions with fellow-countrymen and women whom one can further a little towards both public and private good.

I wonder whether you ever suffered much from false writing (about your biography and motives) in the newspapers. I dare say that pro-slavery prints did not spare you. But I should be glad to think that there was less impudent romancing about you as a *citoyenne* of the States than there appears to be about me as a stranger. But it is difficult for us English who have not spent any time in the United States to know the rank that is given to the various newspapers, and we may make the mistake of giving emphasis to some American journalism which is with you as unknown to respectable minds as Reynolds's newspaper with us.[7]

When we come back from our journeying I shall be interesting myself in the MS.S and proofs of my husband's third volume of his Problems,

6. Mrs. Stowe wrote that she hoped *Daniel Deronda* "will bring you enough to buy an orange grove in Sicily, or somewhere else, and so have lovely weather such as we have."

7. George William MacArthur Reynolds (1814–79), edited *Reynolds's Weekly Newspaper* from 1850 until his death. At C. L. Lewes's suggestion Cross changed this in proof to read "a low-class newspaper."

which will then go to press, and shall plunge myself into the mysteries of our nervous tissue as the Professor has been doing into the mysteries of the middle ages.[8] I have a cousinship with him in that taste—but how to find space in one's life for all the subjects that solicit one? My studies have lately kept me away from the track of my husband's researches and I feel behindhand in my wifely sympathies. You know the pleasure of such interchange—husband and wife each keeping to their own work, but loving to have cognizance of the other's course.

God bless you, dear Friend. Beg the Professor to accept my affectionate respect, and believe me always

Yours with love,
M. E. Lewes.

## GHL TO JOHN BLACKWOOD, [LONDON, 9 MAY 1876]

*MS:* National Library of Scotland. *Hitherto unpublished.*

Tuesday.

My dear Blackwood

What do you say to the enclosed proposition. It was made some time ago but I declined, not seeing what convenience it could be to Harper to have proofs he was unable to use, and if he had proofs a month in advance that was surely ample. In spite of what I send he returns to his point. We don't care two straws about having the money paid all at once, though we should like to oblige him, if it involved no risk or inconvenience to you and us. Consult on this and let me know the result. Send me a sentence I can copy for Harper.

Part IV seems to have drawn blood everywhere. How could it fail? The Jewish element has also been more generally popular than we expected. I am curious to see how volume 3 will be received.

Mrs. Lewes continues very feeble, despondent and incredulous of being able to finish effectively. She gets on slowly with part VIII. In a few days I shall send you the early chapters to have them set up so that no delay may keep us in England. I long so to get her away!

We are going to Oxford on the 20th on a visit to Jowett. This is always delightful, but very exciting and I fear it will help to delay the completion.

Ever yours
G. H. L.

8. Calvin Stowe was reading Johann Joseph Görres, *Die Christliche Mystik,* Regensburg, 1836–1842.

## GHL TO WILLIAM HALE WHITE, LONDON, [9 MAY 1876]

*Text:* Copy by Mrs. William Hale White. *Hitherto unpublished.*

**The Priory, | 21. North Bank, | Regents Park.**
Tuesday.

Dear Sir

Mrs. Lewes is so much occupied just now that I relieve her from all correspondence that is not exclusively personal. She [asks] me to say that she perfectly well remembers you and she hopes I may be successful in my application to a publisher on Mr. Maccall's behalf.[9] I shall endeavour to see one in the next two or three days and see if any translation is to be had. Should you not hear further from me you will conclude that I have not been successful.

Yours truly
G. H. Lewes.

W. Hale White Esq.

## GE TO MRS. ELMA STUART, LONDON, 10 MAY 1876

*MS:* British Museum. *Mostly published:* Stuart, pp. 55–57.

**The Priory, | 21. North Bank, | Regents Park.**
May 10. 76.

Dearest Elma

I am wearing the elastic belt and nothing can be more soothing in the way of woollen. But my husband, who has been wearing the same sort of thing for some time, finds that this loose web stretches enormously and will not shrink in washing. If so, that absence of strings which in the first instance mitigates the misery of dressing would by and by become a torment. Qu'en dis-tu? In any case, I get pleasure out of your pretty thoughtfulness—always spiritually, and in the present moment physically.

As to our going away, it will not be before the 31st, and we shall probably be obliged to stay some days later. We cannot be certain of the day. I have been again ailing (in the old renal way for the last few

9. From a letter that came from GHL the following day Mrs. White copied a sentence: "I saw Mers. Chapman and Hall today and spoke of Mr. Maccall as a translator." GHL's Diary records a call on Chapman Wednesday, 10 May 1876.

days); nevertheless I have been seduced into accepting some invitations —first, for the sake of music, and secondly for the interest of meeting certain people. They are all for next week, winding up with Oxford on the 20th. After that, I hope to remain at home.

About the Maritime Alps, dear, set your mind at rest. We shall stay nowhere unless we find comforts—the expedition up the heights will be worth doing if we resolve to come down again the next day. And the place recommended to us has an excellent hotel. We are not bound to any programme and shall stay or go according to enticement.

Poor Edith [10] is at length come home (I have not seen her), leaving her mother better and only waiting at Paris with her son for the most convenient Boulogne boat.

You know that you will be welcome whenever you can come to us, but if you take the long journey from Scotland you will hardly go back again, but meet the prayers from Dinan and go home.

Mr. Lewes is braving the east wind, doing errands in town, else he would send his love.

Your always affectionate
Mutter.

## JOHN BLACKWOOD TO GHL, EDINBURGH, 11 MAY 1876

*MS:* National Library of Scotland. *Extract published: John Blackwood,* p. 396.

**45, George Street, | Edinburgh.**
May 11/76.

My Dear Lewes

I shall be glad to oblige Messrs. Harper by letting them have proofs of Deronda sooner, although neither from their explanation nor my own knowledge of printing can I understand what convenience it can be to have the proofs more than a month or at most two before hand. The point to be strictly stipulated is no publication before the appearance of the book in this country. Any such forestalling would be a very serious thing.

I inclose a most pleasant statistical table of the sales of Daniel up to the present time. The closeness with which the sale of the successive numbers keeps up to the sale of the first Book indicates most satisfactorily

10. Edith Simcox had two brothers: George Augustus (1841–1905), and William Henry (1843–89), both of Queen's College, Oxford. William was Rector of Weyhill, Hampshire, 1869–85.

how firm and enduring is the hold that the work is taking. I never recollect a case in which the sale of a work published in a serial form kept so closely up to the first start. Many buy a first part of a popular work from curiosity and then drop it, contenting themselves to read afterwards as opportunity may serve, but Deronda has evidently hooked his fish at the first start and is keeping him steadily on the line all through the run. You will have observed too from the tables sent to you at different times what a steady back sale there has been.

I knew that book IV must tell tremendously. Jews are not generally popular pictures in fiction, but then look how they are served up. They never have been so presented before like human beings with their good and their evil, their comic and their tragic side. In the midst of triumph it is distressing to hear of Mrs. Lewes feeling so feeble. I do hope the expedition to Oxford will do her good. I am looking forward with great pleasure to seeing you both next week, as I am going up to London on Monday but I have to go out of town on Tuesday so that it will be Wednesday or Thursday before I can come to you. A letter written tomorrow or Saturday will still find me here. My wife and daughter are not going with me this time so I am going into bachelor quarters at 14 Arlington St. where the old waiter Henry who took entire charge of me at the Burlington for some 15 years has got a lodging house.[1] I had not been well at all, suffering from that confounded thing called the mucous membrane, but a week at Strathtyrum has put me all right again. Hoping soon to see you both well and flourishing

ever yours truly
John Blackwood.

I am puzzling greatly as to how Mrs. Lewes is to wind up in one more book and I am certain the public after reading book 7 will sympathise with me in wishing that there were to be more. Indeed I see symptoms already that the public would gladly have it prolonged to any length she wished.

1. In the *Post Office London Directory* for 1876 and for 1878 13–14 Albemarle St. is listed under the name of George Salmon. Henry may have been manager.

## GE TO MRS. HENRY JOACHIM, LONDON, 13 MAY [1876]

*MS:* Yale. *Envelope:* Mrs. Joachim | 25 Phillimore Gardens | Kensington | W. *Postmarks:* ST. JOHNS WOOD | C 12 | MY 13 | 76 | N.W; LONDON-W | DA | MY 13 | 76. *Hitherto unpublished.*

**The Priory, | 21. North Bank, | Regents Park.**
May 13.

Dear Mrs. Joachim [2]

Hardly any invitation could have been pleasanter to us than the one you have kindly sent us. But unhappily we have already accepted two invitations for next week—on Monday and Thursday [3]—and on Saturday we go to Oxford. Our infirm bodies, which have lately been suffering from various forms of cold, will not allow us to venture on more dissipation than we have already incurred for next week. It was very good of you to think of us.

Mr. Lewes who is just now in bed with lumbago, sends a mysterious message which I am to beg you to deliver to your Husband, namely, 'that he is curious about the cigars.' He adds, more clearly, his best regards. Believe me

Sincerely yours
M. E. Lewes.

## GE TO MME EUGÈNE BODICHON, LONDON, 15 MAY [1876]

*MS:* Mr. Philip Leigh-Smith. *Hitherto unpublished.*

The Priory 21 N.B. | May 15.

My dear Barbara

I have not written to you this long while because I was uncertain about your movements. But yesterday Miss Rintoul [4] got me the information that you were in England and sent for letters to B[landford] Sq.

2. Henry Joachim was a wool broker in Basinghall St. (*Post Office London Directory,* 1876.)

3. GHL Diary, Monday, 15 May 1876: "Dined at the F. Lehmanns': Mr. and Mrs. Rudolph [Lehmann], Sir Coutts and Lady Lindsay, Heilbut, Leighton, and *Rubinstein.* Very pleasant. In the evening a large gathering and Rubinstein played Beethoven, Chopin, Schumann, and his own compositions. Stupendous playing. Home a little after 12." For the dinner at the Earl of Portsmouth's see 18 May.

4. Miss Henrietta Rintoul is listed among the 19 visitors on Sunday, 14 May 1876. (GHL Diary.)

I would have followed your indication about Miss Marks, but for the continuous bad health which has made my inevitable engagements too much for me. (I don't know her address, but I could have sent a letter for her to Miss Townsend).[5] And now I have no time to make an appointment for her to come to me on a week-day, while the remaining Sundays before we go away are likely to be too crowded for me to have any conversation with her. Perhaps when you see her you will mention, if it seems desirable, that I should have wished much to see her if I had been in possession of health and leisure.

We want to get away at the beginning of June. I suppose you are not coming to town. So take my parting benediction, believe in my stedfast love, and send me word, if you can, that all things have gone on well from the last accounts up to the present time.

We go to Oxford on Saturday, for the Sunday. After that I should be glad if we had no more than one Sunday at home.

Always your loving
Marian.

## GHL TO WILLIAM BLACKWOOD, LONDON, [18 MAY 1876]

*MS:* National Library of Scotland. *Hitherto unpublished.*

**The Priory, | 21. North Bank, | Regents Park.**
Thursday.

Dear Willie

By this post I send you the first half of m.s. of Part VIII which please have set up at once—also Part VII for press.

As we have agreed to let Harpers have all that is in type of D.D. at once and the rest as soon as ready, will you kindly mention that to Mr. Simpson.

Mrs. Lewes I'm sorry to say is very unwell—but we are to have your uncle in half an hour and he will tell you all.

Ever yours
G. H. L.

5. Isabella Frances Vere Townshend (1847–82), one of the first students at Girton College, was an artist, a great admirer of the Pre-Raphaelites.

## JOHN BLACKWOOD TO WILLIAM BLACKWOOD, LONDON, 18 MAY 1876

*MS:* National Library of Scotland. *Brief extract published: John Blackwood,* p. 372.

14 Arlington St. | May 18/76.

My Dear Willie . . .

Langford is in great form and I think looking better since his gout. He is thinner but not too much pulled down by any means. . . .

Larrie Oliphant came in immediately after breakfast and we had a very long chat and laugh. He has a scheme for a paper which I shall work hard to get him to write, the autobiography of a joint stock company.[6] It might take the tide. . . .

I had a long and most pleasant visit to Charles Reade. He is a thorough gentleman and we shall pull together like men. When I left I said I was so glad we had come together at last and he replied "The good fortune is mine." When I went in, an old lady bustled out of the room.[7] He was busy writing and said I found him like a good boy at his work.

From him I went to the Priory where I was rapturously received and remained for about an hour and a half. She was looking a little worn and I think Lewes fidgets her in his anxiety both about her and her work and himself. She says she never reads any review, but she certainly hears plentifully all that is said or written in London on the subject of Deronda. She remarked that it was hard upon her that people should be angry with her for not doing what they expected with her characters, and if people were no wiser in their speculations about more serious subjects such as theories of creation and the world than they were about the characters one poor woman was creating it did not say much

6. In 1874 Laurence Oliphant joined the Direct United States Cable Company and in coaching a bill through the Dominion legislature learned from Jay Gould and others the secrets of commercial "rings," some of which he revealed in the "Autobiography of a Joint-stock Company," *Blackwood's,* 120 (July 1876), 96–122.

7. In February 1876 Reade proposed through Langford the publication in *Blackwood's* of his new novel *The Woman Hater.* The fastidious John Blackwood hesitated, remembering the scandalous attacks on *A Terrible Temptation,* published by Chapman and Hall in 1871. Reade answered his objections one by one, and in April Blackwood agreed to publish the story. It appeared anonymously between June 1876 and June 1877, when Blackwood reprinted it in 3 vols. The best account of their negotiations is found in Malcolm Elwin, *Charles Reade,* [1931], pp. 291–314. The old lady was Mrs. Laura Alison Seymour (1820?–1879), who had lived with Reade since 1855. See Léone Rives, *Charles Reade, sa vie, ses romans,* Toulouse, 1940, ch. 7.

for human wisdom. These are not her exact words but the meaning was how vain and foolish was the wisdom of the wise with their dogmas about what they could not know.

She did not wish me to read in M.S. here, so told me she had sent M.S. of portion of book off to Edinb. Have it up soon.

Is part 4 of C. Reade not ready yet?

ever yours affectionately
John Blackwood.

## GHL DIARY,
## LONDON AND OXFORD, 18–22 MAY 1876

*MS:* Yale. *Hitherto unpublished.*

**Thursday 18 May 1876**

Lussana e Lemoigne.[8] Problems. Blackwood to lunch—full of the success of Deronda. We dined at Lady Portsmouth's [9]—present Lord Carnarvon (who took Polly down), Lord and Lady Abercromby, Lord Ramsay, Lord O'Hagan, Grant Duff, Adams the astronomer, Meredith Townsend, Lady Catherine and Lady Lilly. Very pleasant talk with Lord O'Hagan and Lady Portsmouth. Lady Catherine said to me what a delight it was to see Polly's "saintly face again." Home at 11.15.

**Friday 19 May 1876**

Lussana e Lemoigne. Problems. Park. Mrs. Pattison and Mrs. Burne Jones. Dr. Andrew Clarke called to see Polly and prescribed for my throat. Middlemarch.

**Saturday 20 May 1876**

Lussana. Wrote letters and pottered. Went on a visit to Oxford—to Jowett. Mr. and Mrs. George Howard, Mr. Charles Howard,[1] Mr.

8. F. Lussana and A. Lemoigne, *Fisiologia dei centri nervosi encefalici,* 2 vols., Padua, 1871.

9. Isaac Newton Wallop, 5th Earl of Portsmouth, married in 1855 Lady Eveline Herbert, sister of the 4th Earl of Carnarvon (1831–90). Among the other guests listed are Thomas, 1st Baron O'Hagan (1812–85), Lord Chancellor of Ireland; Mountstuart Elphinstone Grant Duff (1829–1906); John Couch Adams (1819–92), discoverer of Neptune; Meredith White Townsend (1831–1911) of the *Spectator;* and the Earl of Portsmouth's eldest daughters, Lady Catherine Henrietta Wallop, who in December 1876 married Charles George Milnes Gaskell, and Lady Eveline Camilla Wallop.

1. Charles Wentworth George Howard (1814–79), father of George James Howard.

and Mrs. J. A. Symonds, and Mr. and Mrs. Ilbert[2] the other guests. Supped at New Hall—part-singing by the choir—very sweet.

**Sunday 21 May 1876**

Fatiguing and exciting day. Called on Rolleston.

**Monday 22 May 1876**

Returned home by 2.30. The Howards and Lord Aberdare[3] came with us. Had a walk in Park with Polly and went to Mummery. 'Middlemarch.' Letter from Lord Lytton—full of hope and visions of great things to be done, but sadly disappointed with the official help he receives. Red tape!

## GHL TO JOHN BLACKWOOD, LONDON, [23 MAY 1876]

*MS:* National Library of Scotland. *Hitherto unpublished.*

**The Priory, | 21. North Bank, | Regents Park.**
Tuesday.

My dear Blackwood

We have no *objection* to offer; but you can understand how very reluctant Mrs. Lewes would be to say a word in favor of such a scheme,[4] or of anything else that tended to her glorification. When you have read his article you will best be able to judge of the advisability or non-advisability of the proposal.

Mrs. Lewes was so poorly after the dinner on Thursday at the Portsmouths (though she enjoyed it greatly) that she determined *not* to risk the Oxford visit and I wrote to Jowett to say as much, but happily

2. Courtenay Peregrine Ilbert (1841–1924), an intimate friend of Jowett and his literary executor, was Bursar of Balliol, 1870–74, when he married Jessie Bradley.

3. Henry Austin Bruce, 1st Baron Aberdare (1815–95), Home Secretary 1868–73, was raised to the peerage in 1874 when he became Lord President of the Council.

4. Edward Dowden (1843–1913), Professor of English Literature at Trinity College, Dublin came to the Priory 9 April 1876. At GHL's suggestion he wrote John Blackwood 16 May proposing to enlarge his essay on GE in the *Contemporary Review* for August 1872 "into a book to be named *George Eliot: A Critical Study,* of the size of one Book of *Daniel Deronda,* and that it should be published by you on October 1st, one month after the appearance of the last part of the novel, and for the same price, 5/-, as a Book of *Daniel Deronda.* I should go through the novels and poems in chronological order, from *Scenes from Clerical Life* to the story now appearing." (NLS.) See also 12 October 1876 and 13 January 1877.

about 12 on Saturday she felt so much better that she agreed to go, and has come back certainly none the worse for the lionizing.

We have friends on Wednesday and Thursday—and on Saturday we go to the Philharmonic. I know of no other movements; but tell you of these lest you should be contemplating a run up on those days.

Yesterday we had a long letter from the Viceroy full of hope and energy, but with bad news of his health. To-day I met Salvini at dinner.[5]

Ever yours truly

G. H. L.

## GHL TO WILLIAM BLACKWOOD, LONDON, [30 MAY 1876]

*MS:* National Library of Scotland. The 1st paragraph has been initialed "W.B." and the 2d "G.S." for George Simpson's attention. *Hitherto unpublished.*

**The Priory, | 21. North Bank, | Regents Park.**
Tuesday.

Dear Willie

By this post I send another batch of Deronda which please have set up at once. The next final batch we shall probably get you to send after us when we are in Italy whither we shall go as soon as the last page is written.

Meanwhile will you please order casts of the woodcuts specified on the accompanying list to be made and sent to Trübner and Co. 59 Ludgate Hill who will pay the expence. They are for my new volume.

Your uncle has deserted us for Oxford so we haven't seen him again.

Ever yours

G. H. L.

## WILLIAM BLACKWOOD TO GHL, EDINBURGH, 31 MAY 1876

*Text:* Copy in Blackwood Letter Book. *Hitherto unpublished.*

45 George Street | Edinburgh May 31/76.

My Dear Mr. Lewes

I have the pleasure of announcing the safe arrival of another batch of Deronda and I have instructed Printers to try and have proofs ready

5. At Mrs. Benzon's. Hallé, Browning, the Rudolph Lehmanns, and Miss Julia Cartwright were among the guests.

to post you tomorrow. I am very anxious to read this thrilling portion which I could not resist from running my eye through.

Mr. Simpson is attending to your wishes about the Casts of the Woodcuts for your new Volume. Mr. Simpson has also handed me the enclosed cheque for £100 from the proprietors of the Melbourne Argus [5a] for permission to print Daniel Deronda in its columns. They remitted cheque for the additional £100 last month which makes payment in full of the arrangement made by Mr. Simpson on your behalf and is now discharged by us by enclosed cheque for £100 on Coutts and Co. Hoping both cheques will reach you safely believe me

Ever yours truly

(Signed) William Blackwood

P.S. When my Uncle has got his Oxford anxiety off his mind I have no doubt you will see him often and speedily. This is the day and a nice "Derby day" for Jack too. He will know result of exam tomorrow.

G. H. Lewes Esq.

## GHL TO WILLIAM BLACKWOOD, LONDON, [1 JUNE 1876]

*MS:* National Library of Scotland. *Hitherto unpublished.*

**The Priory, | 21. North Bank, | Regents Park.**
Thursday.

My dear Willie

Your letter with the two welcome checques received this morning. In two or three days now I hope to send the last pages of the incomparable novel and then we shall fly—not before the flight has become deeply needed. Mrs. Lewes is much worn and is in a very ticklish state, and I am no better for a great dose of dissipation lately, which however I closed last night by a tremendous crush at Lord Houghton's to meet the King of the Belgians. As his Majesty wished to make Mrs. Lewes's acquaintance Lord Houghton was much put out by her not going. I was presented and found his Majesty amiable and uninteresting. We conversed in French, English and German on the Life of Goethe, Italy, Belgium, and the difficulties of pronouncing English (which he does very well) [6] and I was glad enough to be released and give place to others

5a. According to Mr. C. A. McCallum, Chief Librarian of the Public Library of Victoria, Melbourne, *Daniel Deronda* appeared in the *Australasian* from 25 March 1876 to 31 March 1877.

6. In his Diary GHL adds: "not say-

who were so eager to bask in the royal smile. One *can't* feel comfortable with such grandeurs, however suave and complimentary they may be.

It took me 25 minutes to get down stairs, such was the crowd coming and going. And I should not have got my carriage for a couple of hours had I not acted as my own link boy.

I suppose your uncle will turn up tomorrow or Saturday.

Ever yours
G. H. Lewes.

Wm. Blackwood Esq.

## GE TO JOHN WALTER CROSS, LONDON, 3 JUNE 1876

*MS:* Yale. *Envelope:* J. W. Cross, Esq. | Weybridge Heath | S.W. *Postmarks:* LONDON-N.W | K Y | JU 5 | 76; WEYBRIDGE-STATION | B | JU 5 | 76. *Published:* Cross, III, 283–284.

The Priory | June 3. 1876.

Dearest Nephew

The useful 'Companion' which your loving care has had marked with my initials will go with me to be a constant sign of the giver's precious affection which you have expressed in words such as I most value.

Even success needs its consolation. Wide effects are rarely other than superficial and would breed a miserable scepticism about one's work if it were not now and then for an earnest assurance such as you give me that there are lives in which the work has done something to 'strengthen the good and mitigate the evil.'

I am pursued to the last with some bodily trouble—this week it has been sore throat and aching mouth. But I am emerging, and you may think of me next week as raising my "Ebenezer." [7]

Love and blessings to you all from

Your affectionate Aunt
M. E. Lewes.

ing anything significant, but also not saying anything silly. Very affable. Young, tall, and well looking, the star on his breast the only difference from other gentlemen."

7. The stone set up by Samuel to mark the victory of Mizpeh. I Samuel 7:12.

## GE JOURNAL, LONDON, 3 JUNE 1876

*MS:* Yale. *Published:* Cross, III, 283.

June 3. Book v published a week ago. Growing interest in the public and growing sale, which has from the beginning exceeded that of Middlemarch. The Jewish part apparently creating strong interest.

## GHL TO WILLIAM BLACKWOOD, LONDON, [3 JUNE 1876]

*MS:* National Library of Scotland. *Hitherto unpublished.*

**The Priory, | 21. North Bank, | Regents Park.**
Saturday.

My dear Willie

Please have a slip inserted in Part VI of the enclosed erratum.[8] On Monday I shall despatch more m.s. which you will have set up at once so that we may get proof on Thursday morning—we start on Friday.

Your uncle came yesterday and brought the glad tidings of the dark horse 'Jack' having been well in at the winning post! [9]

Yours truly
G. H. L.

## GE TO MRS. ELMA STUART, LONDON, [4 JUNE 1876]

*MS:* British Museum. *Published:* Stuart, pp. 57–58.

The Priory | Sunday Evening.

Dearest Elma

I have been rather melancholy ever since you left,[1] that your visit was spoiled. For me, at least; because I could not say one word to you of my gratitude for all your goodness to me in sending me deliciously warm things from Scotland and thinking of me in all tender ways. Also,

8. "Erratum" in Book v Page 34, line 12, *for* "Ashtaroth" *read* "Ashtoreth." It was inserted before the sub-half-title of Book VI.

9. "Blackwood to lunch." (GHL Diary, 2 June 1876.) John Alexander Blackwood matriculated at Christ Church, 16 October 1876.

1. "Mrs. Stuart and Mrs. Menzies, Charles, Anthony Trollope, Dr. Allen Thomson and his daughter-in-law [Mrs. John Millar Thomson], Du Maurier, Mrs. Strachey, Rudolf and Mrs. Lehmann, Dr. Payne." (GHL Diary, 4 June 1876.)

this sense of hurry and uneasiness made me *distraite* when I was parting with you, and you may have thought my manner coldly preoccupied when I was really feeling annoyed that your visit was ending without my having had any opportunity of showing you what was in my heart. And it is all without remedy now!

The most satisfactory part of an unsatisfactory business is that I made the acquaintance of gentle Mrs. Menzies.

These useless words are written as a relief to myself—before going to bed. Perhaps it may be a needful explanation of my general dulness that I had some aching of the gums all the afternoon—an unpleasant symptom which has been teazing me for the last week. Such are the griefs of

Your loving mother
M. E. Lewes.

## GHL TO MRS. ELMA STUART, LONDON, [5 JUNE 1876]

*MS:* British Museum. *Endorsed:* June 1876. *Mostly published:* Stuart, pp. 58–59.

**The Priory, | 21. North Bank, | Regents Park.**
Monday.

Dear Elma

Your visit was so horribly spoiled yesterday owing to the loud and insusceptible Trollope that you must bring Mrs. Menzies to dine here on Wednesday at 6.30. It is the only time we shall be free, and even then Charles and Gertrude will be with us—but you won't mind them perhaps and we shall have you for a good long spell.[2]

*Did* I mind being kissed before company? La belle demande! As well ask if we object to the flowers with which you brighten our table.

Did I tell you that the King of the Belgians particularly wished to make Madonna's acquaintance and she wished—he might get it! However I had an interview with H.M. in German French and English on Life of Goethe, Italy, Belgium, and English pronunciation. He was very amiable and not silly—which for a crowned head is something!

Now don't be engaged on Wednesday and do come!

Yours ever
G. H. Lewes.

2. The Charles Leweses came to dinner. "In the evening Mrs. Stuart and Mrs. Menzies came in to say goodbye. Went to bed at 10." (GHL Diary, 7 June 1876.)

I open this to say Madonna has tried on the hester but finds it scarcely a bit lighter than the one she has, and she wants something very much lighter. Her thanks all the same. I send it back with this. She is this moment painting her gums with your lotion.

## JOHN BLACKWOOD TO WILLIAM BLACKWOOD, LONDON, 6 JUNE 1876

*Text: John Blackwood,* pp. 394–395.

14 Arlington Street, June 6, 1876.

After we came out of the City we went to the Priory. She was not visible, being in the agonies of the wind up and suffering from face-ache. We had, however, a most pleasant lunch with Lewes and Miss Helps, daughter of Arthur Helps, who was there. Lewes said his wife was writing with tears in her eyes, and I do not wonder at it. That portion of the proof which I received to-day certainly made me weep.[3] There is a simplicity and power about it that has not been reached in my time.

## GHL TO WILLIAM BLACKWOOD, LONDON, [7 JUNE 1876]

*MS:* National Library of Scotland. *Endorsed:* pp. 145 to 159 to be ready this evening for last post if wanted. Will be ready for 2d post and proof will be posted per W.B. *Hitherto unpublished.*

Wednesday.

My dear Willie

Your checque and Lukin's bill[4] arrived this morning. By this post I send all but the closing chapter. Please telegraph its receipt—the proofs need not be sent until the final chapter is added, and then you can send them to me | Poste Restante | Paris. I couldn't register the last letter because it was Whitmonday and no office was open.

Ever yours
G. H. L.

3. GHL was equally susceptible. In his Diary, 7 June 1876 he wrote: "Polly read me last chapter but one of Deronda, and with hot eyes and a sense of having been beaten all over I walked out with her in Park." 8 June: "Deronda finished at last. Polly read the closing chapter after lunch and we then went to Mr. [John Howard] Mummery for final revision of teeth."

4. The cheque was £20 from van Druten, completing the sum of £40 for the Dutch translation of *Daniel Deronda.* The bill was for the casts of the woodcuts in *The Physiology of Common Life* ordered [30 May 1876] for *Problems of Life and Mind.*

## GHL TO JOHN BLACKWOOD, LONDON, [9 JUNE 1876]

*MS:* National Library of Scotland. *Endorsed:* G. S. *Hitherto unpublished.*

Friday.

Dear Blackwood

Io triumphe! The last pages were dispatched yesterday—and thrilling they were! But the delight of seeing her free from the terrible strain is inexpressible. We start tomorrow morning and in case I do not see you I leave with you the proofs corrected by her which I believe you wish to preserve. You will hear from her or me when we are settled.

Yours ever
G. H. Lewes.

## GHL TO MRS. ELMA STUART, LONDON, [10 JUNE 1876]

*MS:* British Museum. *Address:* Mrs. Stuart | Les Buttes | Dinan | La France. *Postmark:* ST. JOHNS WOOD | C S | JU 10 | 76 | N.W. *Published:* Stuart, p. 60.

The Priory, Saturday.

Dear Elma

Our trunks are packed and the carriage at the door but Madonna thinks it would gladden your heart to know that after all the lotion *was* of use in allaying the irritation of her gum.

Ever yours
G. H. L.

## JOHN BLACKWOOD TO GHL, LONDON, 10 JUNE 1876

*MS:* National Library of Scotland. *Extract published: John Blackwood,* p. 395.

14 Arlington St. | Piccadilly June 10/76.

My Dear Lewes

I got "The End" today. Grand, glorious, and touching are too mild words for this last book. In fact criticism and eulogism are out of place. I feel more than ever what I have often said to critics: "Bow and accept with gratitude whatever George Eliot writes." [4a]

4a. He wrote Langford, who had felt some qualms about Book v: "she is so great a giant that there is nothing for it but to accept her inspirations and leave criticism alone." (*John Blackwood,* p. 392.)

The situation of Gwendolen and Deronda is so new too and oh so delicately handled. I felt inclined to burst into the room and prevent Lapidoth from stealing the ring,[5] but the great author knew better and shut the door on the beast for ever.

Give her my best love, respect, and congratulations. It troubled me to see her sitting pale and tired in her carriage at the door yesterday.[6] and I fear I did not say half what I wished to say, but Mrs. Lewes sees every thing and would I trust see what I felt. No wonder she felt tired and unwilling for company, but I earnestly hope that the change across the Channel is already beginning to tell for good.

I intended to have gone to Scotland on Monday, but Delane who has been very ill presses me so earnestly to come to see him at Ascot for a couple of days that I cannot leave without seeing my old friend and companion. So if you write to me address here.

ever yours truly
John Blackwood.

My guardian angel "Henry" had brought me some note paper which is so much thinner than my own that I find I have written on two sheets of it.

## GE JOURNAL, 10 JUNE–1 SEPTEMBER 1876

*MS:* Yale. *Published:* Cross, III, 285.

June 10.—We set off on our journey, intending to go to San Martino Lantosc in the Maritime Alps. But I was ill at Aix,[7] where the heat had become oppressive, and we turned northwards after making a pilgrimage to Les Charmettes—stayed a few days at Lausanne, then at Vevey, where again I was ill; then by Berne and Zurich to Ragatz, where we were both set up sufficiently to enjoy our life. After Ragatz to Stachelberg, the Klön-Thal, Schaffhausen, St. Blasien in the Black Forest, and then home by Strasburg, Nancy, and Amiens, arriving September 1.

5. Ch. 68.
6. "Packed up and wrote letters. Called on Pigott and on Blackwood; found B. at lunch with Mrs. Oliphant, Major Lockhart, and Miss Blackwood. Did a little shopping and drove in Park." (GHL Diary, 9 June 1876.)
7. Their travels are described in detail in GHL's Diary.

## GHL TO CHARLES LEE LEWES, MACON AND AIX-LES-BAINS, 15–16 JUNE 1876

*Text:* Paterson, pp. 169–170.

Macon. | Friday, June 15, 1876.

Dearest Charles,

Just come in tired from our ramble about this town, which closed with a visit to the house where Lamartine [8] was born, I make use of the interval before dinner to send you word of our doings and sufferings.

We gave up our first notion of lingering on our way to Paris in order to be able to go to the Russian church there. When we arrived we were dismayed to find that it was *Race week* and all the hotels were crowded. After driving about from one hotel to another in an *open* carriage, the weather being wintry, we at last got good rooms at the Hôtel des Deux Mondes. Our visit to the Russian church was well worth making a push for. The Archduke Michael [9] and his Duchess were there and had probably brought their own choir. At any rate the singing was more exquisite than any we have ever heard. There was a boy who sustained and died away on one note more like Jenny Lind in her prime.

The Mutter was not well enough for any amusements so we dined cosily at a café.[1] Next morning we walked to the Poste Restante for the final proofs—after shopping, both with headaches—we drove in the Bois de Boulogne for two hours, corrected proofs [2] and went to see "L'Étrangère," a most interesting and engrossing piece and the acting very fine, especially Coquelin and Sarah Bernhardt.

Hôtel de l'Europe, | Aix les Bains. Saturday Afternoon, 4 p.m.

I resume my narrative in our new quarters. The journey here today was delicious—though long—six hours. We have had difficulty in getting rooms and must quit them on the 21st. They are extremely pleasant, looking on to a sweet garden and as quiet as one could wish, so the prospect of moving is not agreeable. We are ravished with the as-

8. Alphonse de Lamartine (1790–1869).

9. The Grand Duke Michael (1832–1909), brother of Czar Alexander II, and the Grand Duchess Olga Féodorovna (1839–91).

1. But GHL went to the Odéon and saw *Les Danicheffs,* a new comedy by Pierre de Corvin-Kroukowski and Dumas fils.

2. GHL has condensed two days into one. The proofs arrived 12 June—a triumph of speed for typesetters and post! —and GHL read them "as we sat in the Tuileries gardens." That evening they went to the Théâtre Français to see *La Cigale chez les Fourmis.* The next day they drove in the Bois and corrected the proofs at home afterwards, and then to Théâtre again to see *L'Étrangère,* the new comedy by Dumas fils.

pect of Aix under this delicious light, the air is soft and balmy, the mountains look in upon us through our windows in a most inviting manner, if the baths suit us we shall stay some days. But it is uncertain whether we shall remain in this hotel.

We both long for a little quiet solitude *à deux.*

Our love to Gertrude and the chicks.

Your loving
Pater.

## GE TO JOHN BLACKWOOD, RAGATZ, 6 JULY 1876

*MS:* National Library of Scotland. *Extracts published:* Cross, III, 285–287.

Hof-Ragatz | Ragatz | July 6. 76.

My dear Mr. Blackwood

After much travelling and almost continual bad health we seem to have reached the right place for our health and comfort, and as we hope to stay here for at least a fortnight I have begun to entertain selfish thoughts about you and the possibility of having news from you. Our month's absence seems long to us—filled with various scenes and various ailments—but to you, I daresay, the request for a letter to tell us what has happened will seem to have come before there is anything particular to tell.

On our arriving at Aix the effect of railway travelling and heat on me warned us to renounce our project of going to the Maritime Alps and to turn northward, so after resting at Aix to be ill and get better, we went to Chambéry just to make a pilgrimage to Les Charmettes,[3] and then set our faces northward, staying at beautiful Lausanne and Vevey for a week and then coming on by easy stages to this nook in the mountains, where we begin to think there is a chance of our getting an appetite and recovering the flesh we have been losing. In spite of illness, however, we have had much enjoyment of the lovely scenery we have been dwelling in ever since we entered Savoy, where one gets what I most delight in—the combination of rich, well-cultivated land,

3. "Our first glimpse of the uninteresting town was dispiriting but after a ravishing walk of 3 hours and through shady lanes to the Charmettes, with a visit to Rousseau's rooms, we were glad to have come." (GHL Diary, 25 June 1876.) They read Rousseau aloud all summer. They bought *Les Confessions* at Aix-les-Bains 20 June, finishing it 12 July. *Émile* and *La nouvelle Héloïse* followed.

friendly to man, and the grand outline and atmospheric effects of mountains near and distant.

This place seems to be one of the quietest Baths possible. Such fashion as there is, is of a German unimposing kind, and the King of Saxony,[4] who is at the twin hotel with this, is I imagine a much quieter kind of eminence than a London Stock-broker. At present the company seems to be almost exclusively Swiss and German, but all the appliances for living and carrying on the "cure" are thoroughly generous and agreeable. We rose at five this morning, drank our glasses of warm water and walked till ¼ to 7, then breakfasted and from ½ past 8 to 11 walked to Bad Pfäffers and back again, along a magnificent ravine where the Tamina boils down beneath a tremendous wall of rock and where it is interesting to see the electric telegraph leaping from the summit, crossing the gulf, and then quietly running by our roadside till it leaps upward again to the opposite summit.

Mr. Lewes has read his Times when he has had an opportunity, so we have known that Servia has declared war against Turkey, and that Harriet Martineau is dead, as well as George Sand.[5] But you may consider us as generally ill-informed and as ready to make much of a little news as any old provincial folk in the days when the stage coach brought a single London paper to the village Crown or Red Lion.

I should like to know whether you have had any further communication with modest Mr. Dowden, the Dublin professor. I have no opinion about his proposal, but I think the man himself is worthy of attention and regard.

It is well we provided ourselves with some books before getting here, for the shops seem to be of the usual watering-place order, and the windows are furnished with the same French novels that we have been seeing from Paris onward.

I hope that Book VI does not show a diminished sale. Your letter which met us with the proof at the Poste Restante, Paris, was very welcome and cheering to me.

Our Son is our only correspondent at present, reading or sifting our letters and letting us know the obliging propositions of American editors (and English) to furnish the public with our biographies etc. etc. Doubtless the biographies will be given whether we furnish the facts or not—and we certainly shall not.

4. King Albert (1828–1902) commanded the army of the Meuse in the Franco-Prussian War.

5. Serbia and Montenegro declared war on Turkey 30 June 1876; Harriet Martineau died 27 June and George Sand 8 June.

By and by, you are probably in town now with Mrs. and Miss Blackwood. If so, I hope that you are having as much sunshine as we are having, with only moderate heat. Our weather has been uniformly splendid since we left Paris, with the exception of some storms which have conveniently laid the dust.

Mr. Lewes unites with me in kind regards, and I am always

Yours most truly
M. E. Lewes.

## GHL TO CHARLES LEE LEWES, RAGATZ, 6 JULY 1876

*MS:* Mrs. Carrington Ouvry. *Hitherto unpublished.*

Hof Ragatz—Ragatz 6 July 1876.

Dearest Charles

At last we have found a resting place, and I hope a turning point for our health, which at last became such as to create uneasiness in my mind. Headache and diarrhœa which clung to us with an occasional interval of respite from Paris to Bonn, became further complicated by the Mutter's *renal* troubles (with blood!) which alarmed me, though there was no severe pain, only constant nerve [?] pain which had no pleasant promise! However that—as well as my diarrhœas—seem to have taken themselves to "fresh fields and *bowels* new" (if the parody may be allowed!)

I wrote to you from Chambéry—a letter and a postcard. After having delighted in Les Charmettes there was nothing to detain us; and it was well we left, for the weather changed to steady rain, and as the outlook on the street from the hotel was not attractive, a headachy Mutter wouldn't have enjoyed a sojourn there. By the time we reached Lausanne the weather cleared somewhat. I may say at once that we have been most fortunate in our weather. Rain has always fallen during the night on our journeys. We got a superb salon at Lausanne with views of the Lake from all our windows. We stayed there from Monday to Thursday, greatly charmed with the place, and having good walks amid the gardens and woods of the suburbs. On Thursday we went to Vevey, and there had a gorgeous salon with blue satin curtains and all other idle splendours, and a balcony over the lake (price 20 frs. asked 30; but there was no one in Vevey). We were disappointed with Vevey —not comparable to Lausanne; but still it had its charms; and we went of course to Clarens and Chillon. On Monday we went to Bern, and were both surprised on rambling about to find it so much more imposing and attractive than we remembered it. Great changes have been made as I dare say you noticed when you were last there. We sat on the terrace; but no afterglow! Tuesday we went to Zurich, and here for the first time we found all the good rooms occupied; but much as we grumbled at *the* room (on ground) we got, we were contented to have come to the Baur au lac for the sake of the garden and the delicious evening view of the lake we had. Wednesday we got here.

Such is the order of our movements. I say nothing of the lovely scenes we have been contemplating, nor of the enjoyment we have had (mitigated by mucous membranes!) for I am writing in a hurry, and don't feel up to a 'gombo.' [6] Enough to say that our small experience of this place is highly promising. The Bergluft though exquisite is not so bracing as I was led to expect, but the temperature is very agreeable and our rooms delightfully cool. Food good. Music three times a day. Guests not fashionable but German and Swiss mostly. King and Queen of Saxony are at the twin hotel; but they will, it is to be hoped, not find out our presence, and no one *else* shall with any result to themselves!

We got up at 4.50 this morning were out at 5.20; drank two glasses of warm tasteless water, walked in the country for an hour. Breakfasted at 7. Walked from 8.20 to 11.15 up the ravine of the Tamina very like the Via Mola—a glorious walk—tier upon tier of mountain sheer over the boiling torrent, with many waterfalls and one or two Staubbachs—frisches Luft, a surprising (and normal) sense of vigour in our limbs and lightness in our minds—the sweet serenity once more visible in the Mutter's face—all seemed as if now at last we were going to begin the much desired journey in search of health!—I haven't had a bath yet but the Mutter who had one yesterday while I unpacked says it's very nice and I shall experiment in half an hour, to ensure an appetite for dinner. There is drinking water for mucous membranes and bath for gout, rheumatism and general out of orderness.

What effect is Part VI having? Do you hear? I like it better than any of the preceding parts.

If you wouldn't mind the trouble of writing you might send Johnnie Cross word of our whereabout and say we should like to have a word from him. Mutter's love to both of you

Ever your
Pater.

6. "Composition" was so pronounced by a master at Hofwyl.

GE TO MRS. NASSAU JOHN SENIOR,
RAGATZ, 12 JULY 1876

*MS:* National Library of Scotland. *Hitherto unpublished.*

Hof Ragatz | Ragatz | July 12. 76.

My dear Friend

I think that if I had had the choice of the friend who should write me a letter "to be forwarded" I could not have chosen more for my own pleasure than fate has chosen for me in bringing me your dear letter which we have just read together. I have quite hungered these many months for some account of you—how your health was going on—what you meant to do about your future residence—and any detail that could give me an idea how life was bearing itself towards you. I am glad to hear that you are going to Chelsea,[7] because I remember that you had a longing to look on the river, and since we have taken to driving along the embankment I too have become attached to that part of London, and you will be delightfully within reach.

It was your impulse to help us that made you write, and if we were still in London we would run down to Yarmouth for the sake of seeing you as much as the desirable house,[1] which seems quite miraculously cheap and since it pleases your taste, I am sure is pretty. But we crossed the Channel on the 10th of June and after a month's wandering in which I had been constantly out of health, we settled here under conditions that seem to promise a recovery of health and strength. Ten days ago we thought that we should be obliged to hasten home again for the sake of getting invalids' comforts, but now we hope to remain abroad, as we intended, until the end of August, going higher as the weather gets warmer. So there is no chance of our taking the train at Waterloo in time to hinder the old tradesman from buying Monks! Most grateful thanks to Mrs. Hughes and you for laying out that pretty plan. I should grieve to miss the chance of the house, if the Isle of Wight were quite compatible with our purposes about a country home. We *do* desire, above all earthly possessions of a material sort, a house in the country to which we could go, not simply in summer, but from time to time throughout the year. To be everything we want, the

7. Mrs. Senior wrote GE 30 June 1876, "We've left Elm House for a cheaper house, 4 Lindsey Houses, Old Chelsea." (Yale.)

1. A charming house at Yarmouth, Isle of Wight, which Mrs. Senior was taken to see "on my bed on wheels."

house should be within easy reach from London—we should even not object to a place so near as High Barnet. We went once to see Mrs. Barrington's house, but found that it had not comforts enough for us old people. This was our first sight of High Barnet and we were much pleased with the aspect of the neighbourhood, though I should prefer Surrey or Kent if it were possible to get anything snug enough in those regions. You will think of us again as you have done already if among your many friends you hear of some one who has a house to part with of the sort we should like—not grand, but comfortable, and as little as possible like a suburban villa.

Your words about my writing, dear friend, are among the gifts of life which I count the most precious to me. My dear husband read them aloud to me, and cried with happiness as he read them. You know he feels these things more keenly for me than I feel them for myself. The words are worth the more to me because they come from you—what you say or write I have always felt to be genuine, and to come from something deeper than transient effusiveness. Especially I care for what you say about Mordecai.

Please admire the energy with which we are seeking health. We rise at ¼ past 5, dress quickly, set out on our walking and water-drinking expedition, and remain out till near seven, when we breakfast. Then we read till ½ past 8, then we set out again on a walk which lasts about 2 hours and a half, return and drink water again, then rest, and lunch at 12. At ½ past 3 we take our baths, at 5 we dine, and the rest of our time is chiefly spent in my reading aloud or in our sauntering and sitting within hearing of the band. We make no acquaintances, and indeed the company, though numerous, is almost invisible. The king and queen of Saxony are here, but we see no signs of their distinguished presence, and the "Gäste" whom we do see are of an unassuming German-Swiss aspect. All this suits us admirably, and is a sort of continental holiday-making rather difficult to get in these days. Probably by the beginning of August there will be a rush of Germans and English, but we shall be gone elsewhere.

Mr. Lewes tells me to say on his behalf that the prospect of having you for a neighbour would be a recommendation to any house. He sends his loving homage to you. I am sorry to say that he too has been sadly ailing since we left home, but he is feeling the benefit of our present discipline, and in fact we are as happy now as two mortals ought to desire to be in this world of difficulties—enjoying our double life in delicious quiet, without a single care on our minds. Ought we to grumble that we are thin and rickety?

I have written immediately on receiving your letter which Charlie enclosed for me, but I trust that you would immediately interpret any delay in your getting an answer from me at any time as a sign that I was not at home. Your image will be with us often in our walks. All blessings be with you, dear friend, and believe that the thought of you has always been a gain to me since I have known your sweet face.

Your affectionate
M. E. Lewes.

## JOHN BLACKWOOD TO GE, ST. ANDREWS, 12 JULY 1876

*MS:* National Library of Scotland and Mrs. Carrington Ouvry. *Hitherto unpublished.*

**Strathtyrum | St. Andrews | N.B.**
July 12/76.

My Dear Mrs. Lewes

I am delighted to receive your letter from Ragatz and to learn that you have there found a quiet peaceful retreat likely to do you good after your giant labours. You were, I am sure, quite right to abandon the knocking about in Railways, and seek a quiet spot where you can have pleasant walks and rest.

First as to the Book. I think the sale of Book VI is fully up to that of its predecessors, but I send this letter into Edinburgh that Willie may put in a Memorandum of what have been sold since the 30th of June. At that date a Memorandum was made up to show the exact state of matters. It is a very healthy show and will I hope afford you both pleasure.

I propose to pay you in cash now to your Banker's £2000 or on your return home [2] as you may wish and the balance £2052.16/- by Bill at 6 Mos. from 30th June.

On some sudden rise in sale we had, I see, printed rather too many of Book One, but I hope we shall work them all out and any way it will be a very trifling overstock on so large a sale.[3]

The public continue all abroad as to what your finale is going to be, and it was great sport to me in London that I could decline all discus-

2. The receipt from the Union Bank of London, Charing Cross Branch, dated 2 August 1876, acknowledges "£2000. for credit of G. H. Lewes Esq. also P/ Note for £2052.16.- in his favour." (NLS.)

3. In March a third printing of Part I of 1575 copies.

sion of the Book because I knew so much more than the rest of the world that I would be arguing at an unfair advantage. I used to say accept what you get when it comes and be thankful. Delane said at Ascot, "If I proclaim in the Strand here is the one man who has read the whole of Daniel Deronda, the ladies will tear you in pieces unless you tell them some lies or make a clean breast of it."

There will I know be disappointment at not hearing more of the failure of Gwendolen and the mysterious destiny of Deronda, but I am sure you are right to leave all grand and vague, and the real disappointment of your public will be that their monthly food for interesting thought and speculation is stopped.

I stayed in London rather longer than I intended in order to go to see Delane at Ascot and I am happy to say I found him better than I expected, but he has been very unwell and should take a rest. You may imagine how tired I was of my bachelor life when I resisted the most pressing invitation to stay the week at Delane's and came off to the North after the first day's racing.

My wife and daughter really did not come up to London this time and seem rather pleased with themselves now. They threaten me with an expedition to the Highlands when my heart will be, not there but on the Links. The hardest thing for my daughter to miss in London was an invitation from Lady Salisbury [4] to a small dancing party to meet the Prince and Princess of Wales, which followed me down here. Golf goes on a pace. Tom Morris the ex-champion, of whom you have heard me tell, was invited to Liverpool last week to play a match before the Duke of Connaught. He reports the Prince "a most pleasant frank Gentleman." Old Tom is a capital judge of such matters, and I would rather take his opinion on the point than that of any courtier.

I thought the deaths of Miss Martineau and George Sand would touch you. That generation is indeed wearing to an end now.

The ladies send their best regards to you. The weather is pleasant and they are enjoying their rides.

I am interested to hear that you were at Aix and Chambery, very familiar places once to me. My eldest brother was laid up at Aix with a raging fit of Asthma so long and bad that the Doctors gave up all hope, and many a melancholy hour did I pass by the Lac de Bourget. In despair we carried him into his carriage and drove to Chambery. In the ten miles drive that most fickle complaint left him and he got out at the Hotel du Petit Paris suffering only from extreme weakness.

4. Georgina, eldest daughter of Sir Edward Hall Alderson, was married in 1857 to Viscount Cranborne, who in 1868 succeeded his father as 3d Marquis of Salisbury (1830–1903).

I wonder if the Petit Paris still exists. I always think of it and Chambery with a blessing.

I have a hope that the deplorable fighting will not spread beyond the Turkish Provinces. The Powers are all afraid and jealous of each other, which gives the best hope of Peace. With best regards to Lewes, I am always

yours very truly
John Blackwood.

| | *Presentation Copies and Reviews* | *Odd Books gratis and Trade 25 as 24* | *Sold* | *On hand* | *Total Numbers* |
|---|---|---|---|---|---|
| Book I | 121 | 303 | 7287 | 1214 | 8925 |
| Book II | 121 | 257 | 6903 | 302 | 7613 |
| Book III | 123 | 282 | 6783 | 162 | 7350 |
| Book IV | 121 | 281 | 6744 | 204 | 7350 |
| Book V | 109 | 281 | 6758 | 202 | 7350 |
| Book VI | 108 | 252 | 6053 | 1200 | 7613 |
| | 703 | 1686 | 40528 | 3284 | 46201 |

40528 Books at Royalty of 2/ each £4052.16-

[*Added in pencil*] 15553
8 | 61754
7719
June 76

## WILLIAM BLACKWOOD TO GE, EDINBURGH, 13 JULY 1876

*Text:* Copy in Blackwood Letter Book. *Hitherto unpublished.*

45 George Street | Edinburgh July 13/76.

My dear Mrs. Lewes

I was delighted to see your letter to my Uncle and hear that both you and Mr. Lewes had begun to recover your appetites and were having pleasant walks and scenery that was to your liking. I have no later news than the 11th of the month to send you of Deronda but that is most satisfactory and healthy. On that date Mr. Langford reported the following sales of Daniel Deronda at 37 Paternoster Row

| | | |
|---|---|---|
| June 1 to 30 | Book 1 | 113 |
| | " 2 | 76 |
| | " 3 | 73 |
| | " 4 | 46 |
| Book 5 to June 30 | | 6094 |
| 6 to July 11 | | 5957 |

and before the month is out I feel pretty sure Book VI will have tied with Book V. Our

Sales here continue very steady and we are well up with the other Books.

Trusting this finds you continuing to improve in health and strength and with best remembrances to Mr. Lewes

ever yours sincerely

(signed) William Blackwood.

## GHL TO JOHN BLACKWOOD, RAGATZ, 17 JULY 1876

*Text: John Blackwood,* pp. 396–397.

Hof Ragatz, 17th *July* 1876.

Your pleasant and welcome letter found us both greatly improved in health and spirits by our stay here. Mrs. Lewes is quite another woman, and is recovering her colour and contour—*not* before they were wanted. Her appetite is good, and we walk four hours amid the woods and up the easy mountain-sides—bathe, eat, read, and idle—"letting the world fleet by as in the golden time." [5] Not a single word have we exchanged with any one above the rank of a waiter or shopkeeper—and don't miss the "charms of society," about which some people talk so glibly as indispensable to existence. In the woods of a morning she has taken to instruct me in Hebrew,[6] and we waken the echoes with our laughter sometimes at my blunders and attempts at Israelitish eloquence!

Mrs. Lewes desires her very best remembrances to all (with especial thanks to Willie for his agreeable note), and hopes you have been enjoying your trip into the Highlands. I have had some notion of going there too when we come back, and visiting the Brit. Association at Glasgow, but this is at present very vague.

## GE TO JOHN BLACKWOOD, LONDON, 2 SEPTEMBER 1876

*MS:* National Library of Scotland. *Published:* Cross, III, 287–289.

**The Priory, | 21. North Bank, | Regents Park.**
September 2. 76.

My dear Mr. Blackwood

We reached home only last night. After we left Ragatz our wanderings became too changeful and uncertain in their direction for me to

5. Cf. *As You Like It,* I, i, 24.

6. They had just finished Rousseau's *Confessions,* which GE had been reading aloud. "During our walk Polly began to give me lessons in Hebrew—reviving our old Spanish days." (GHL Diary, 12 July

venture on writing to you with any indication of our coming whereabout, and since the beginning of August our Son has been taking his holiday in the country, so that we arrive as strangers and foreigners to all home affairs, the fortunes of D. D. included.

We had scarcely taken our much-needed dinner before a parcel was brought in which proved to be D. D. in the four bound volumes,[7] and various letters with other "missiles" as an acquaintance of mine once (quite naïvely) called his own favours to his correspondents—which have at present only gone to swell a heap that I mean to make acquaintance with very slowly. Mr. Lewes, however, is more eager than I, and he has just brought up to me a letter which has certainly gratified me more than anything else of the sort I ever received. It is from Dr. Hermann Adler,[8] the Chief Rabbi here, expressing his "warm appreciation of the fidelity with which some of the best traits of the Jewish character have been depicted by" etc. etc. I think this will gratify you too.

We are both the better for our journey, and I consider myself in as good case as I can even reasonably expect. We can't be made young again and must not be surprized that infirmities recur in spite of mineral waters and air 3000 feet above the sea-level. After Ragatz we stayed at Stachelberg and Klönthal—two lovely places where an English face is seldom seen. Another delicious spot, where the air is fit for the gods of Epicurus, is St. Blasien in the Schwarz-wald, where also we saw no English or American visitors, except such as "übernachten" there and pass on. Amidst all the loveliness of forest and mountain, Mr. Lewes has had frequent attacks of headache and severe cramp: still, he is stronger than he was, and we have done exploits in walking, usually taking four or five hours of it daily.

I hope that you and yours have kept well, and have enjoyed the heat rather than suffered from it. I confess myself glad to think that this planet has not become hopelessly chilly. Draughts and chills are my enemies, and but for them I should hardly ever be ailing. The last de-

1876.) The next day he was studying the Hebrew alphabet, and other lessons are noted for a few days. Apart from such indications of their reading the entries during the next six weeks, though detailed, are not of great interest.

7. Part VIII was published in September 1876. Soon after Blackwood bound up 348 sets of the parts in a 4-vol. edition that sold for 42/. All but 35 of these had been sold by January 1877.

8. Hermann Adler (1839–1911), born at Hanover and educated at University College, London, after studying at Prague and Leipzig became Principal of Jews' Theological College, London in 1863, and in the following year first minister of Bayswater Synagogue. According to the *DNB* he was Delegate Chief Rabbi for his father Nathan Marcus Adler in 1879 and Chief Rabbi 1891–1911. With his letter to GE, 23 June 1876 (Yale), he sent a copy of the *Jewish Messenger* with his review of *Daniel Deronda.*

lightful effect of a draught has been to cause me a ridiculously swelled eyelid, so that I get up in the morning with a piteous, dropsical aspect, and am rather alarmed lest one eye should get into the habit of being smaller than the other—not liking to offend the prejudices of my fellow-creatures in that way.

The four volumes look very handsome on the outside. Please thank Mr. William Blackwood for many kind notes he wrote me in the days of M.S. and proofs—not one of which I ever answered or took notice of except for my own behoof.

Always yours truly
M. E. Lewes.

## GE TO FRANÇOIS D'ALBERT-DURADE, LONDON, 2 SEPTEMBER 1876

*Text:* Copy by D'Albert-Durade in Tinker Collection, Yale. *Hitherto unpublished.*

The Priory | 21 North Bank | Regent's Park | September 2. 76.
My dear Friend

While you have been wondering at my silence and explaining it by my occupation in writing, we have been far away, getting mountain air and drinking mineral waters, out of reach of all correspondents as well as all visitors. "Daniel Deronda" was finished several months ago, and we set off with the intention of going to a much recommended spot among the Maritime Alps, but the effect of the June heat on our way to Italy warned us to change our course and turn northward. We have found much benefit from our stay at Ragatz, Stachelberg and other places, not too much haunted by our fellow-countrymen, in the east of Switzerland and in the Schwarz Wald and are now in our usual place with a sense of more than usual strength. But we arrived only last night, and I have not yet attempted to read the heap of letters which lie awaiting me. Your writing, discerned on an uppermost envelope, gave me a reason for selecting it from the heap, and I hope that you will take this answer in the very first morning of my recovered home-life as a sufficient refutation of the demon's hint that I am in danger of forgetting you, especially as I see that your letter is dated only the 28th.

You perceive that we have been escaping the evil attendant on the exceptional heat, which I confess has given me a cheerful reassurance that this planet is not yet in circumstances too chilling to allow of summer heat any more. Meanwhile the harvest has profited by it. But

I can well imagine that you have found your imprisonment in the white heat of town houses particularly trying to you—the languor consequent on it being likely to increase that depression you speak of. I feel for you, dear friend, in your life of monotonous effort. But still, you have what I regard as the very strongest motive—the most fortifying consciousness under the difficult task of living, namely the sense that your life is absolutely necessary to the comfort of another and a cherished being.

Pray give my love to my venerated "Maman" and assure her that I am proud and thankful to be allowed a continual place in her memory. We are altogether happy and prosperous and must not in the midst of so many blessings beyond our share complain that we get more and more liable to infirmities of body and susceptible to the least disturbance.

I am glad that you have found some pleasure and interest in "Daniel Deronda." The writing of it was a great excitement to me and wore me down to a very low point. I had hardly a day of good health while it was in progress. But now it is all behind me, and when I open it again I shall seem to be making a fresh acquaintance with it.

You will not wonder that I write in a brief hasty way. I hardly now can write [a] letter otherwise—correspondence being a claim that eats away too much time. My husband keeps Madame D'Albert and yourself in his best regard and remembrance, and I am always, dear friend

Yours with sincere affection
M. E. Lewes.

## GE TO EMILY SUSANNAH CLARKE, LONDON, 4 SEPTEMBER 1876

*MS:* Mr. C. E. Clarke. *Hitherto unpublished.*

**The Priory, | 21. North Bank, | Regents Park.**
September 4. 76.

Dearest Emily

On returning home from a three months' journey on the Continent I found your letter among the large heap awaiting me. It was written, I see, on the 12th of July, when I had already been a month away and was on the other side of Switzerland, at Ragatz, taking walks and waters in order to get up my strength. I felt very sorry, after I had left home on the 10th of June, that I had not managed to send you a letter, as I had had it in my mind to do. The many details I had to occupy my attention, and my failing strength, caused me to forget what was not at all a matter of indifference to me. I thought of my omission very soon after I had left England, but for a long while I was so poorly that the news I had to tell would not have cheered you, and afterwards I imagined you enjoying your holidays in some place away from Brighton.

Enough of myself and my leaving-undone what I ought to have done. I am very well now, and we are hoping that before the pleasant autumn weather is all gone we shall get down to Brighton for a day to see your dear face, and hear all the little things that you could tell us in conversation so much better than in writing. I long to see you again.

I gather from your letter that you have had only a week of change from your Brighton air this summer, and that grieves me. I want to inquire into your finances and plans for other holidays. Pray go on studying your German. It may be of great use to you in many ways. I think Wednesday used to be your half holiday—is it so still?

The last letter you wrote me before I went away contained the news of Walter's engagement,[1] and I imagine that the marriage must have taken place by this time, though it has not occurred to you to mention the fact.

All blessings on you, dear Child. If you saw the many letters I have to open, you would not suppose that my silence to you implies any want of love and care for you. But now I shall be more at liberty, and shall not be in danger of neglecting you any longer. Mr. Lewes sends his best love to you, and unites with me in all tender wishes for you.

Ever your loving and faithful
Aunt Polly.

## GHL TO WILLIAM HALE WHITE, LONDON, 5 SEPTEMBER 1876

*Text:* Copy by Mrs. William Hale White. *Hitherto unpublished.*

**The Priory, | 21. North Bank, | Regents Park.**
5th September 76.

My dear Sir

On our return home we find the very acceptable present you have sent Mrs. Lewes, with the graceful letter which preceded it. She is

1. Walter Pearson Evans (1846–1920), son of GE's brother Isaac, married in 1877 Miss Constance Grace Mackie (1849–1931).

much touched at your having thought of gratifying her by the portrait of her old favorite; and although I am glad to hear that Mr. Maccall has had work placed in his hands, I cannot recognize in my own slight share in that business anything more than a simple duty of comradeship to a fellow worker, not at all deserving of the generous acknowledgment you made.[1a]

Very truly yours
G. H. Lewes.

## JOHN BLACKWOOD TO WILLIAM BLACKWOOD, ST. ANDREWS, 5 SEPTEMBER 1876

*MS:* National Library of Scotland. *Hitherto unpublished.*

**Strathtyrum | St. Andrews | N.B.**
September 5/76.

My Dear Willie

It would not do to let Deronda go out of print in its present form so soon, and we must be ready to make up *setts* so reprint cautiously as you propose.[2]

The rearrangement of the lease of the works is a puzzling question. We must be pretty bold about it.

ever yours affectionately
John Blackwood.

1a. For White's relations with GE see Wilfred Stone, *Religion and Art of William Hale White ("Mark Rutherford")*, Stanford, [1954], pp. 193–194.

2. The Blackwood records show the printings of *Daniel Deronda* in parts in 1876:

| Part I | Part II | Part III | Part IV | Part V | Part VI | Part VII | Part VIII |
|---|---|---|---|---|---|---|---|
| Jan. 5250 | Feb. 6825 | Apr. 7350 | Apr. 6825 | May 7350 | June 7613 | July 7613 | Aug. 7913 |
| Feb. 2100 | Mar. 525 | Aug. 350 | May 525 | Aug. 300 | Ang. 300 | Aug. 300 | |
| Mar. 1575 | June 263 | Sept. 100 | Aug. 300 | Sept. 100 | | | |
| | Aug. 200 | | Sept. 100 | | | | |
| | Sept. 150 | | | | | | |
| 8925 | 7963 | 7800 | 7750 | 7750 | 7913 | 7913 | 7913 |

## GE TO MME EUGÈNE BODICHON, LONDON, 6 SEPTEMBER 1876

*MS:* Mr. Philip Leigh-Smith. *Envelope:* Madame Bodichon | Scalands Gate | Hawkhurst | Sussex. *Postmarks:* LONDON-N.W | C 1 | SP 6 | 76; HAWKHURST | A | SP 7 | 76; ROBERTSBRIDGE | A | SP 7 | 76. *Published:* Cross, III, 289–290.

21 North Bank | September 6. 76.

My dear Barbara

We got home again last Friday, much strengthened by our journey, notwithstanding vicissitudes. I suppose you will not be in town for ages to come, but I let you know that I am here in case you have anything to say to me by letter—about "objects."

We gave up going to the Maritime Alps. When we were on our way as far as Aix-les-Bains, I got ill, and we almost thought we must return home. We wended northward again, and by slow stages reached Ragatz, which answered for us both, especially for me. After leaving Ragatz we still kept in eastern Switzerland in high vallies unvisited by the English, and in our homeward line of travel we paused in the Schwarz-Wald, at St. Blasien which is a *Luft-Kur,* all green hills and pines with their tops as still as if it were the abode of the gods.

But imagine how we enjoy being at home again, in our own chairs, with the familiar faces giving us smiles which are not expecting change in franc pieces!

We are both pretty well, but of course not cured of all infirmities. Death is the only physician, the shadow of his valley the only journeying that will cure us of age and the gathering fatigue of years. Still, we are thoroughly lively and 'spry.'

I hope that the hot summer has passed agreeably for you and not been unfavourable to your health or comfort. Of course a little news of you will be welcome, even if you don't particularly want to say anything to me.

Always your loving
Marian.

GHL TO [CLEMENT MANSFIELD INGLEBY],
LONDON, 6 SEPTEMBER 1876

*MS:* Folger Library, Washington. *Hitherto unpublished.*

**The Priory, | 21. North Bank, | Regents Park.**
6 September 76.

Dear Sir

Mrs. Lewes has been much interested in Mrs. Meredith's [3] letter but neither she nor I can in the least make clear to ourselves what is its special object, what Mrs. Meredith wishes Mrs. Lewes to do. Is it to interest herself with a publisher for the contemplated work? As her friend you are probably acquainted with her wishes. That is why I trouble you.

Just returned from 3 months absence I find a monticule of letters to answer!

Yours truly
G. H. L.

JOHN BLACKWOOD TO GE,
ST. ANDREWS, 7 SEPTEMBER 1876

*MS:* National Library of Scotland. *Hitherto unpublished.*

**Strathtyrum | St. Andrews | N.B.**
September 7/76.

My Dear Mrs. Lewes

I am so glad to think of you safe and well in England again and to hear that you have both enjoyed and benefited by your expedition. Your walking feats are worthy of Golfers. The details you will have got of the sales of Deronda would I think assist to make your return home pleasant. They are indeed most satisfactory and have I trust come up to Lewes' expectations and yours. The sale in the 4 vols. has not been large, but after such a triumphant run in the Numbers, that was not to be expected in the present form.

The praise of the Chief Rabbi is truly gratifying and the most convincing evidence that your intuitions as to Jewish character are as true as all the world admit them to be when you are painting your own countrymen and women. It is almost impossible to make a strong Jewish element popular in this country and it was perfectly marvellous to see

3. Mrs. Louisa Anne Twamley Meredith. See 7 November 1878.

how in your transitions you kept your public together. Anti-Jews grumbled but went on. I could not hear whether Disraeli gave any utterances on the subject.

We have had a wonderfully fine summer here but of late Scotland has been asserting herself and rain, cold winds, and fog have reappeared among us. You give a most enticing description of St. Blazien but St. Andrews Links on a fine day leave no room for envy at least in a Golfer's mind.

We are all very well and regret that the pleasant summer is slipping away from us, but we generally have a fine autumn and there are to be extra festivities at the end of the month, as Prince Leopold [4] is coming to take the chair as Captain of the Club. The discussions at the Club as to how things are to be arranged would make a play. The main difficulty is want of room, as you cannot dine 200 men with a Club room that will only dine 95. Mr. Melville aged 79 has solved this as to the dinner by deciding that senior members are to have the preference. The young ladies wonder whether this is to hold good as to the Ball.

I am writing a line to Lewes and believe me

always yours truly
John Blackwood.

I hope the suffering eye lid is better. Such little things do worry. You would have the ardent sympathy of my son Jack, the close of whose holidays have been darkened by the dentist and a swelled face.

I inclose a note which came yesterday from Mrs. W. Smith. She evidently feels the Book. Look at the Wordsworth Strathmore narratives to which she alludes in present month's Magazine.[5] Mrs. Wordsworth is a delicate, still pretty looking woman. How she survived those horrible hardships is a miracle. I never saw a more remarkable case of "the back being made for the burden."

4. H. R. H. Prince Leopold George Duncan Albert (1853–84), Queen Victoria's 4th and youngest son, had just left Oxford with an honorary D.C.L.

5. C. F. Wordsworth and Mrs. Wordsworth wrote accounts of the wreck of the "Strathmore" 1 July 1875 in the Crozet Islands; they were rescued by an American whaler in January 1876. See *Blackwood's* 120 (September 1876), 317–342.

## GE TO MRS. CHARLES BRAY, LONDON, 8 SEPTEMBER 1876

*MS:* Miss Kate C. Savage. *Envelope:* Mrs. Bray | 3 Barrs Hill Terrace | Coventry. *Postmark:* LONDON-N.W | SP 8 | 76. *Hitherto unpublished.*

21 North Bank | September 8. 76.

My dear Cara

We got back to our nest at the end of last week, and remembering that when I saw you you were not without anxieties, I am anxious to have some news of you. How is Mr. Bray's health? How is everything that touches your comfort?

We are much the better for our travel, which has lain in a direction other than we intended on setting out. When we got to Aix-les-Bains I was taken ill, the heat was already rather fierce in that region, and we felt that it would be unwise to go father south. In order to get on to the cool heights of the Maritime Alps we must have gone into hot depths. So we turned northward and by slow stages got at last to Ragatz, which proved a place of healing and invigoration. The last two months of our absence were spent entirely in the north-east of Switzerland and in the Black Forest—out of the English tracks. We saw but one acquaintance, and he was a Berlin publisher.[6] It is pleasant to be back in London when "nobody" is here.

I hope that the unusual old-fashioned heat has not been unfavourable to any one of your trio. Every detail about you will be acceptable. I think you are under a promise to tell me honestly of any outside good or evil.

My best love to Sara. It is a pity the spirit moves her so seldom to write letters, seeing that she writes them so charmingly. But I am the last who should wonder at such abstinence. In reading a heap of letters, I am preoccupied with calculating how few I can make my answers.

We shall be so glad to hear that the summer weather has been benignant to Mr. Bray's lungs. Our "often infirmities"[7] make us sympathetic about all bodily ills.

Always your affectionate
Marian.

6. "Herr [Albert] Cohn (late of Ashers) spoke to us at dinner. The first acquaintance we have stumbled on. Told him to keep our presence a secret." (GHL Diary, 23 July 1876.)

7. I Timothy 5:23.

## GE AND GHL TO MRS. ELMA STUART, LONDON, 12 SEPTEMBER 1876

*MS:* British Museum. *Published:* Stuart, pp. 60–64.

**The Priory, | 21. North Bank, | Regents Park.**
September 12. 76.

Dearest Elma

We think you will like to know that we are at home again, and are strengthened by our travel. At first we were unfortunate. When we arrived at beautiful Aix, where I promised myself that I should get well upon the rich greenth penetrated by sunlight, I fell really ill, and we soon saw that we must give up the Italian project. So we presently turned northward (after a visit to Chambéry and a pilgrimage to 'Les Charmettes') and we even feared that we must wend slowly home. But after lingering a little too long about Lake Leman we resolved to try Ragatz, and even the getting on to rather higher ground in our journey thither did me good. Ragatz itself began to set me up, and when I tell you that every day, during the greater part of our three months' absence, we walked about five hours, beginning our exercise before breakfast, you will perhaps be sceptical as to my want of health and strength. After Ragatz, we tried Stachelberg and the Klön-thal, keeping away from the usual haunts of the English and Americans. Then we went by Schaffhausen on to the Schwarzwald and lingered at St. Blasien, a *Luft-kur* which might also be called a *Ruhe-kur,* so still are the pine-tops against the serene heavens. Our journey home was made very slowly, lest we should tire our poor bodies into invalidism again, and we arrived only a week ago. Mr. Lewes, notwithstanding fluctuations, revisitings of cramp and too frequent headaches, is on the whole much stronger and is pronounced to look better than he did three months ago. We really enjoyed our fresh vision of the mountains, and our walks by the shady sides of great torrents, or in the stillness of the pine-woods, or in the open sunshine among grassy places. And the little inconveniences of sojourn in hotels have given new zest to our home comforts—but I need not tell you things which are in the history of every mortal who has a home and has once travelled away from it. The best travel is that which one can take by one's own fireside, in memory or imagination.

But whether at home or abroad, "thy woollens are ever with me." (The quotation marks have reference not to the Bible, but to my thoughts, which I this morning uttered aloud to Mr. Lewes.)

And how are you? and how is Roly—how is sweet Mrs. Menzies? The thistle tea-service is not, I trust, felt to be a vanity, but helps the cheerfulness of tea-time. Tell me all about yourself.

We are as happy as life can make us. On Saturday we went to see our children in their Kentish cottage,[8] which they have built to themselves on a glorious, high common where they have a far-stretching country below them and a wide sky, the sunset red behind the heather in front of their little drawing-room window. I drank tea out of the pretty tea-cup that you made a present of to Blanche—that having been a pleasure prepared for me in her mind, under her Mamma's inspiration.

Mr. Lewes sends his love with mine. We shall both look for your handwriting on the backs of letters until we have been satisfied with news of you.

Ever your affectionate mother
M. E. Lewes.

Madonna has not told you how often your name was on our tongues often suggested by the fact that your *stick*—the famous vine!—was in my hands as we clomb the mountain sides. Nor has she told you how she began to teach me Hebrew, and how in consequence we made the woods astonished at the uncouth sounds of my bungling attempts at speaking the language of Mirah and Mordecai.

G. H. L.

## EMILY DAVIES TO ANNIE CROW, LONDON, 24 SEPTEMBER 1876

*Text:* Barbara Stephen, *Emily Davies and Girton College,* London, Constable, 1927, pp. 184–186.

September 24, 1876.

I mentioned that I was going to see [Mrs. Lewes] yesterday. I went late in the afternoon and found them at home. They have been abroad in Switzerland and the Black Forest, and have not been long back. They were going on to Italy, but Mrs. Lewes was so ill that they thought it better to stay in the cooler parts. She was ailing all the time she was writing her book and very much knocked up at the end. This Mr. L. told me before she came in. She said herself that she had had rather a bad two years, having had much pain in the hip, which was new. I asked if it was sciatica and she said it was not, and did not seem to know what it was. She is much better now.

8. The Warren, Crockham Hill, near Edenbridge.

The talk was chiefly on Morals. It came in this way. Something being said about M. Thiers, Mr. Lewes repeated a bon mot of Royer Collard's—'M. Guizot *sait* la morale; M. Thiers ne la connait pas.' I threw out that really to know morals would be about the highest possible attainment. Mrs. L. did not agree. She thought people generally knew that there was a better and a worse thing to do. Then I told her of a controversy as to whether Morals should be taught as a lesson in schools, and that a friend of mine (Adelaide) [9] was going to do it. She said at first that she thought it would be a most dangerous thing to do, but explained afterwards that she meant that, if it was as a set of dry maxims. Such lessons as Adelaide proposes she thinks may be very useful and interesting, and went into what they should be with zest. She spoke of truthfulness as *the* most important thing to teach—that it should be explained how important it is as the basis of mutual confidence. She said she thought she had succeeded 'with these servants, by talking to them,' in making them understand this, but it was the first time she had ever succeeded with any servants. Usually they only see the harm of falsity in the form of injury by backbiting.

She would not admit the difficulty of deciding when truth ought to be spoken and when not. I instanced keeping secret the authorship of a book. She thought that might be done by refusing to answer questions, but Mr. L. agreed with me that often that is as good as telling, and maintained that denial in such a case was not lying. He said he had himself said No, flatly, when he had been asked about the authorship of her books. She said she did not know that he had,[1] and did not support his view. She thought pains should be taken to avoid situations in which truth cannot be told, so as to keep up the habit of truthfulness. She thinks you are not bound to say all that you think, but would use as a test, whether your silence would lead to action being taken under a false impression. In teaching, she would ask the children to say for themselves *why* it is right to speak the truth, etc. She was anxious that my friend should impress upon them the wide, far-reaching consequences of every action, as a corrective of the common feeling that it does not signify what we do—and on the other hand how society reacts upon us, and how much we owe to it. People are always asking, *Why* should I do what is good for society? What is society to me? The answer

9. Adelaide Manning, secretary of the Froebel Society, founded in 1874, was planning a series of lessons for Miss Leighton's School, a small boarding school for girls 15 to 19, drawn largely from the millocracy, rich and profoundly ignorant. (p. 186.)

1. See [12 February 1859].

is that if it were not for the accumulated result of social effort, we should be in the state of wild beasts.

Something was said about 'Assuming life to be a blessing.' I asked if we were entitled to assume that, and she said, Certainly not, in talking to people who deny it, and she knew several people who think it a curse. But she says that so long as you don't commit suicide, you must admit that there is a better life, and a worse life, and may try for the better. Some deny even this, but when you come to such stupid scepticism as that it's no use talking to them.

She hoped my friend would teach the girls not to think too much of political measures for improving society—as leading away from individual efforts to be good, I understood her to mean. I said I thought there was not much danger of that with girls. It is so much more inculcated upon them to be good and amiable than anything else. She said, was there not a great deal among girls of wanting to do some great thing and thinking it not worth while to do anything because they cannot do that? I said there might be, but I had not come across it. What I had met with more was not caring to do anything. She said, Yes, no doubt stupidity prevails more than anything. Then she hoped my friend would explain to the girls that the state of insensibility in which we are not alive to high and generous emotions is stupidity, and spoke of the mistake of supposing that stupidity is only intellectual, not a thing of the character—and of the consequent error of its being commonly assumed that goodness and cleverness don't go together, cleverness being taken to mean only the power of *knowing*. Mr. L. put in, 'and of expressing.'

Mr. L. was taking an active part in the conversation all the time, but what I have repeated is hers, except when he said something that seemed to express her views, and in which she was concurring. At this stupidity stage I thought I had staid long enough and came away promising to try to remember to tell my friend what she had said.

## GE TO HAIM GUEDALLA,[2] LONDON, 26 SEPTEMBER 1876

*MS:* Jewish Museum, London. *Hitherto unpublished.*

**The Priory, | 21. North Bank, | Regents Park.**
September 26. 76.

Dear Sir

I thank you heartily for your kind letter, with the copies of your pamphlet and of the Hebrew newspaper.

No response to my writing is more desired by me than such a feeling on the part of your great people, as that which you have expressed to me. It is something more than an interesting coincidence—it is a deeply felt encouragement to me, that at the date you mention, last winter, when I happened to be writing precisely that scene at the club, your practical judgment was occupied with projects not in disagreement with my conceptions.

I remain

Sincerely yours
M. E. Lewes.

H. Guedalla Esq.

## GE TO HAIM GUEDALLA, LONDON, 2 OCTOBER 1876

*MS:* Jewish Museum, London. *Extracts published: Anglo-Jewish Letters,* ed. Cecil Roth, 1938, p. 311.

**The Priory, | 21. North Bank, | Regents Park.**
October 2. 76.

My dear Sir

I have just received your letter of yesterday [3] with the accompanying pamphlet.

2. Haim Guedalla (1815–1904), a communal worker, wrote GE from 40 Connaught Sq., 25 September: "I take this opportunity to express my admiration of the profound talent shewn and my indebtedness to you as one of the heads of the Jewish Community for having represented us in so favourable a light and in so attractive and scholarly a manner before the world." (Yale.)

3. Guedalla wrote from Ramsgate, 1 October 1876, thanking her for her letter and asking if he might send a copy of it to the *Jewish Chronicle* along with an extract from his Hebrew translation of the club scene in *Daniel Deronda,* originally published in a Jewish paper in Lemberg, East Prussia. The pamphlet he sent was one on Turkish finance in which GE might see that he contemplated last November a vision of Syria again in the hands of the Jews.

Your request that my former letter to you may be published in the Jewish Chronicle I am obliged to refuse, for reasons which I trust you will not misunderstand.

I have a repugnance to anything like an introduction of my own personality to the public which only an urgent sense of duty could overcome. But over and above this feeling I have a conviction founded on dispassionate judgment, that any influence I may have as an author would be injured by the presentation of myself in print through any other medium than that of my books. False statements are frequently made both in British and American newspapers about my history and opinions, but I shall never break silence in an effort at contradiction until I perceive that some one else is being injured by those falsities in any way that my protest can hinder.

It is my function as an artist to act (if possible) for good on the emotions and conceptions of my fellow-men. But, as you are aware, when anyone who can be called a public person makes a casual speech or writes a letter that gets into print, his words are copied, served up in a work of commentary, misinterpreted, misquoted, and made matter of gossip for the emptiest minds. By giving occasion for more of this frivolous (if not vitiating) kind of comment than already exists in sickening abundance, I should be stepping out of my proper function and acting for what I think an evil result.

All this seems a great deal to say à propos of that brief note to which your request has reference, but I have said it in order that you may not suppose my refusal to rest on any but general grounds. If I could consent to the publication of my letters at all, I should certainly consent to the publication of what I wrote to you. I think that I used no expression which my feelings would not induce me to amplify. I remain, my dear Sir,

Sincerely yours
M. E. Lewes.

H. Guedalla Esq.

## GE TO MME EUGÈNE BODICHON, LONDON, 2 OCTOBER 1876

*MS:* Mr. Philip Leigh-Smith. *Envelope:* Madame Bodichon | Scalands Gate | Robertsbridge | Hawkhurst. *Postmark:* ST. JOHNS WOOD | C 5 | OC 2 | 76 | N.W; HAWKHURST | A | OC 3 | 76; ROBERTSBRIDGE | A | OC 3 | 76. *Published:* Cross, III, 290–291.

21 N.B. | October 2. 76.

My dear Barbara

My blessing on you for your sweet letter which I count among the blessings given to me. Yes. Women can do much for the other women (and men) to come. My impression of the good there is in all unselfish efforts is continually strengthened. Doubtless many a ship is drowned on expeditions of discovery or rescue, and precious freights lie buried. But there was the good of manning and furnishing the ship with a great purpose before it set out.

We are going into Cambridgeshire this week, and are watching the weather with private views.

I have had some very interesting letters both from Jews and from Christians about Deronda. Part of the scene at the club is translated into Hebrew in a German-Jewish newspaper. On the other hand a Christian (highly accomplished) thanks me for embodying the principles by which Christ wrought and will conquer. This is better than the laudation of readers who cut the book into scraps and talk of nothing in it but Gwendolen.[4] I meant everything in the book to be related to everything else there.

I quite enter into Miss Jekyll's [5] view of negative beauty. Life tends to accumulate 'messes' about one, and it is hard to rid oneself of them because of the associations attached. I get impatient sometimes and long, as Andrew Fairservice would say, to "kaim off the fleas" [6] as one does in a cathedral spoiled by monuments out of keeping with the pillars and walls.

Your affectionate
Marian.

4. Most readers have persisted in doing this. Dr. F. R. Leavis, for example, says, "Henry James wouldn't have written *The Portrait of a Lady* if he hadn't read *Gwendolen Harleth* (as I shall call the good part of *Daniel Deronda*), and, of the pair of closely comparable works, George Eliot's has not only the distinction of having come first, it is decidedly the greater. . . . As for the bad part, there *is* nothing to do but cut it away." (*The Great Tradition,* [1948], 85, 122.)

5. Miss Gertrude Jekyll.

6. Discussing the removal of saints' statues from Glasgow cathedral during the Reformation, Andrew Fairservice says

## GE TO MRS. ELMA STUART, LONDON, 4 OCTOBER 1876

*MS:* British Museum. *Published:* Stuart, pp. 64–65.

The Priory | 21 N.B., | October 4. 76.

Dearest Elma

The blue slippers and the soft white kerchief, opened by my husband, lay against my plate when I came down this morning, and they made the best part of my breakfast. My own particular Providence in Brittany is wonderfully well-informed, for this cream-coloured silk kerchief is just what I wanted, and without my said little Providence I should never have got it. I shall make many 'actions de grâce' when I am wearing it.

We are going this morning into Cambridgeshire to pass three days with a friend of ours of whom I daresay you know something—the Mr. Hall who was once the Mr. Bullock gratefully remembered in the country round Sedan. He found an excellent second wife there, the sister of the Protestant pastor, and she plays her part admirably as the helpmate of an English country gentleman.[7]

Some of our continental bloom has left us in the London air and under the transitions from warm to cold and from cold back again. But we are not yet quite run down to the old level. Mr. Lewes has begun the printing of his third volume of Problems [8] and is very happy in revision of his written sheets.

Will you write us some news of you soon?—how far you have become learned in archæology and have been fascinated by archæologists etc. etc. Your letters cheer us. I wish we could do more for you—not because you need it, but because our hearts long for it.

Always your loving
Mother.

it "stood as crouse as a cat when the flaes are kaimed aff her." *Rob Roy,* ch. 19.

7. Berthe, youngest daughter of Auguste Goulden of Bischwiller, Alsace, whom he married 15 July 1875. (Burke, *Landed Gentry.*) They met in 1870 while he and Willie and Mary Cross were conducting a soup kitchen during the siege of Sedan.

8. The MS was sent off to the printer 23 September; the first proofs arrived 2 October. (GHL Diary.)

## GHL DIARY, SIX MILE BOTTOM, 4–7 OCTOBER 1876

*MS:* Yale. *Hitherto unpublished.*

**Wednesday 4 October 1876**

We went on a visit to the Halls at Six Mile Bottom. M. Scherer [9] was the only visitor today. He took a long walk with us—superb sunset.

**Thursday 5 October 1876**

Today our party was encreased by the Sidgwicks, a German, and Dr. Paget [1] (the latter only to dinner). After lunch we drove to Newmarket to visit the stables of a trainer. Saw *Kisber,* the winner of the Derby and Grand Prix—a beautiful creature. Other horses—dogs—and the trainer himself a refined Bambridge [2] who said the Baroness Rothschild,[3] whose picture he showed us, was a *beautiful skinned lady!* He treated Polly with great deference, always styling her My Lady and much struck by her having pointed out a defect in the build of Kisber.[4]

**Friday 6 October 1876**

Today Mrs. Higford Burr [5] joined the party and at dinner Dr. and Mrs. Humphry.[6] Very pleasant. I played Lawn Tennis with the Sidgwicks after lunch and read Heyse, Die Kinder der Welt. Dr. Paget told us of an auctioneer who was kicked down stairs and at the bottom shook his fist exclaiming "Another kick, sir, and you'll rouse the lion in me." He afterwards went insane and continued "knocking down" every object he saw to an imaginary buyer. He would sit in his garden and 'put up' the trees or cattle. One day at Church he 'knocked down' the preacher "tub and all" for 5/6.

**Saturday 7 October 1876**

Came home at 4 to find several letters and parcels. . . .

9. Edmond Schérer (1815–89).

1. George Edward Paget (1809–92), Regius Professor of Physic at Cambridge 1872–92.

2. The horse dealer in *Middlemarch.*

3. Emma Louisa, wife of Sir Nathan Meyer de Rothschild (1840–1915), 2d Baronet, Baron of the Austrian Empire.

4. Kisber, owned by Alexander Baltozzi, won the Derby in 1876. An obituary of GE in the *Daily News,* apparently by W. H. Hall, says: "On one occasion the writer took 'George Eliot' to view Kisber, a Derby winner, and to the utter astonishment and surprise of the trainer, she drew attention to the fine points of the horse."

5. Higford Daniel Burr of Hereford.

6. George Murray Humphry, Professor of Anatomy at Cambridge and like Paget on the staff of Addenbrooke's Hospital.

## JOHN BLACKWOOD TO WILLIAM BLACKWOOD ST. ANDREWS, 11 OCTOBER 1876

*MS:* National Library of Scotland. *Hitherto unpublished.*

**Strathtyrum | St. Andrews | N.B.**
October 11/76.

My dear Willie

I had two famous rounds of the Links yesterday and am thankful to say that I am now as fit as can be. When I came in from the Links if anything were wanted to complete my cure it was thoroughly done by the most charming letter from George Eliot. I must keep it beside me to answer before sending it to delight Simpson and you. The substance is that she had been looking over my old letters and cannot resist writing to say how much she owes me, in fact pretty much that she could not have gone on without me. You may conceive this in her language.[7] It is the greatest compliment a man in my position could possibly receive, and that and the context about herself brought warm tears to my eyes.

ever yours affectionately
John Blackwood.

## GHL TO ELMA STUART, LONDON, 12 OCTOBER 1876

*MS:* Amy Lowell Autograph Collection, Harvard. *Hitherto unpublished.*

**The Priory, | 21. North Bank, | Regents Park.**
12 October 1876.

Dear Elma

I shall someday find you a letter of Macaulay's but meanwhile I have come upon the only two very precious autographs that I have hitherto thought worth preserving for myself—a letter of Shelley to Keats and a letter of Sanson the executioner.[8] But the thought that they would give you pleasure is irresistible—so I part with them not with reluctance—be sure of that—but with joy. I also add one of Franz Liszt and one for the sake of the beautiful writing of Varnhagen von Ense.

7. Unfortunately this letter, dated 8 October 1876, has not been found.

8. Shelley's letter (Harvard), dated July 27, 1820, was published in Stuart, pp. 175–177. Charles Sanson (1740–93) and his son Henri (1767–1840) both served as executioner in Paris.

We have been paying a visit to a friend in Cambridgeshire, one whom we are very fond of you may be sure, as it is difficult to get Madonna away from her own home. It was extremely agreeable and now we are back again at work—I printing my new volume, she reading my m.s. and proofs when she is not absorbed in her Hebrew literature. By the way we have both been much gratified at the fervent admiration of the Chief Rabbi and other learned Jews, and their astonishment that a Christian should know so much about them and enter so completely into their feelings and aspirations. This is all the more welcome because the Christian public—at least a large part of it—is decidedly unsympathetic towards that part of D.D.

We heard from Edith yesterday. Her brother is about to be married (*not* Augustus but the clergyman) [9] so that her mother will come and live with her.

Send us word how you and dear Roly are getting on and give my love to Mrs. Menzies.

Ever your affectionate
G. H. L.

## JOHN BLACKWOOD TO GE, ST. ANDREWS, 12 OCTOBER 1876

*MS:* National Library of Scotland. *Hitherto unpublished.*

**Strathtyrum | St. Andrews | N.B.**
October 12/76.

My Dear Mrs. Lewes

The very kind expressions in your letter of the 8th move and gratify me deeply. Tears came into my eyes, and I read the passage at once to my wife who was sitting beside me when I received the letter. I look upon such expressions coming from you, as the very highest compliment that a man holding the position I do could receive, and I shall keep the letter for my children as a memorial that their father was good for something in his day. You are too good about my poor letters which I always felt to be too meagre and too few but I do look back upon our correspondence with pride and pleasure. Each letter from you is a treat and last summer being pressed for your autograph I turned over a number of your letters, but in each there was a feeling

9. William Henry Simcox, Rector of Weyhill since 1869, married 7 November 1876 Annie, daughter of the late Rev. Thomas Ludlam of Guildford. (*Pall Mall Budget,* 18 November 1876, p. 37.)

or something that I could not part with or deface by cutting off the signature so my friend went without an autograph.

That one who has risen so high as you have should be the subject of idle gossip is almost inevitable. It is a thing for which the public have a depraved appetite and I say "idle" not evil as I do not think it is intentionally mischievous but why are great authors not to enjoy the privacy of common life? I do not know whether living gossips or posthumous memoir writers make me most savage. It is but little of such idle trash that I hear as no one would venture to speak to me of you with ought but praise and of that I do hear ample store.

You will have heard how Deronda is going on and I think the sales are very satisfactory and equal. The discussion about the book still goes on, especially in private company and the great point is that the book is discussed and disputed over as a reality. We had a good scene the other night. My wife said to a young friend staying with us "Have you read 'Daniel'?" the familiar name of the book in this house. He stammered and said "No" and forthwith began to turn over his remembrances of the Book of Daniel. Then he turned out to have been a regular student of Deronda and forthwith an animated discussion of all the characters began. Mr. Simpson says that no one could write a review of the Book to please me unless I did it myself.

About Professor Dowden I fear that I am in fault. The strange thing is that I cannot recollect Lewes giving me the review containing the paper on your works. Did he hand it to me or send it to me? In spite of my carelessness I never almost lose anything and I am writing to Edinburgh to see if it is there. I wrote to Professor Dowden asking him to send me a specimen of what he proposed, but it was after many days that I wrote, and I was not surprised that he did not answer as he had probably gone on his holiday.[1] What you say interests me much in him and I shall now write again.

I have been suffering severely of late from irritation I suppose of the mucous membrane. There is an uncommonly good remark in Norman Macleod's Memoirs [2] about that membrane which he says he has been told "covers the whole of his interior and certainly covers all the rest of the world when there is anything the matter with it." I am now happily quite well and fit both for business and golf which had both been in abeyance for nearly a fortnight. I hope Lewes and you are well and settling down comfortably for the winter. Our season here will be

1. Edward Dowden's letters to Blackwood are dated 1 July and 14 August 1876. (NLS.)

2. Donald Macleod, *Norman Macleod: A Memoir,* 2 vols., 1876.

winding up soon and the horrible wet weather reconciles one to the thought of Town. Still we have occasional bright days in the midst of the deluge which is so fatal to the outlying crops.

My wife sends her best regards and hoping that there are many years of pleasant correspondence before us Believe me

always yours truly
John Blackwood.

## GE TO MRS. WILLIAM SMITH, LONDON, 14 OCTOBER 1876

*Text:* Cross, III, 291–293.

I had felt it long before you let me have some news of you. How could you repeat deliberately that bad dream of your having made yourself "objectionable"? I will answer for it that you were never objectionable to any creature, except perhaps to your own self—a too modest and shrinking self. I trusted in your understanding last spring that I was glad to hear from my friends without having to make the effort of answering, when answering was not demanded for practical purposes. My health was not good, and I was absorbed as to my working power, though not as to my interest and sympathy.

You have been in my mind of late, not only on your own account but in affectionate association with our dear Mrs Ruck,[3] whose acquaintance I owe to you. On my return from abroad I found among my heap of letters a delightful one from her, written, I think, at the end of June, as bright and cheering as the hills under the summer sky. And only a day or two after we saw that sad news in the 'Times.'[4] I think of her beautiful, open face, with the marks of grief upon it. Why did you write me such a brief letter, telling me nothing about your own life? I am a poor correspondent, and have to answer many letters from people less interesting to me than you are. Will you not indulge me by writing more to me than you expect me to write to you? That would be generous.

We both came back the better for our three months' journeying, though I was so ill after we had got to the south that we thought of returning, and went northward in that expectation. But Ragatz set me up, so far as I expect to be set up, and we greatly enjoyed our fresh glimpses of Swiss scenery.

3. Mary Ann Ruck, from whose house in London Mrs. Smith was married 5 March 1861.

4. I cannot identify this news.

Mr Lewes is now printing his third volume of 'Problems of Life and Mind,' and is, as usual, very happy over his work. He shares my interest in everything that relates to you; and be assured—will you not?—that such interest will always be warm in us. I shall not, while I live, cease to be yours affectionately.

## JOHN BLACKWOOD TO GE, EDINBURGH, 19 OCTOBER 1876

*MS:* National Library of Scotland. *Hitherto unpublished.*

**45, George Street, | Edinburgh.**
October 19/76.

My Dear Mrs. Lewes

Along with this I have written to Lewes with a proposal for renewed lease of your works which may I hope prove agreeable to your views.[5] At all events I am ready to meet any suggestions for alterations as I am bent upon continuing your publisher as well as friend through life.

We have a long career of successive triumphs to look back upon and I hope there is much yet before us.

It must be some 21 years since Amos Barton was published, and although during that long term of years we have had our share of sickness and sorrow, I dare venture to say we are as little decayed in thought and feeling as most people.

always yours truly
John Blackwood.

I have found the Contemporary Review all right.

5. John Blackwood writes to William Blackwood, 5 October 1876 that he feels the sale of GE's works will be much greater in the next decade, since it has increased so much during the last half of their lease. "We must risk a good deal and go in for the whole works." Three days later he discusses an idea of issuing them in three-penny numbers, "for which Adam Bede, Middlemarch, and at least three of the others are admirably adapted." (NLS.)

## JOHN BLACKWOOD TO GHL, EDINBURGH, 19 OCTOBER 1876

*MS:* National Library of Scotland. The memorandum is in Mrs. Carrington Ouvry's collection. *Hitherto unpublished.*

**45, George Street, | Edinburgh.**
October 19/76.

My Dear Lewes

Our ten years' lease of Mrs. Lewes' Works, Adam Bede, Mill on the Floss, Silas Marner, Scenes of Clerical Life and Felix Holt is now nearly run out, and both from personal and professional feeling my anxious wish is that we should always continue to be her publishers.

I have been thinking and talking over with my nephew and Mr. Simpson what we can offer for another lease of ten years, and I hope the following may meet her views and yours, or if not I shall be ready to consider any suggestions for alterations in terms that you may think of to meet contingencies.

I now beg to offer the sum of Four Thousand Pounds (£4000) payable over a term of three years for another lease of ten years of the above mentioned works with the addition of Middlemarch, Romola, and Daniel Deronda. I am not sure from my own letters when the present lease strictly terminates but it does not matter and I would propose to make the new arrangement date from the first of January next with the exception in your favour that the 21/- edition of Deronda should be paid to you by a lordship as in the case of Middlemarch.

From the outward aspect of opinion I do not think we can calculate upon such a sale of Deronda at 7/6 as for Middlemarch. The inclosed Memoranda will show you what the first named five books have done in the past nine years and we have made our estimate of sales on a sort of medium between the sales during the past three years and the whole nine. In the event of your accepting the above offer it is understood that the size and price of the works are to be as before at our discretion. Trusting that we may in some form or other at all events be able to meet each other's views I am ever

yours truly
John Blackwood.

G. H. Lewes Esq.

GEORGE ELIOT'S WORKS

| | |
|---|---|
| Paid Author | £1000. |
| Interest on Do until recouped by Sales | 268. |
| When Cheap Edition was commenced in May 1867 our right over Felix Holt was given to it and there was a loss on it at that date of £1168. | |
| The Profit on Sales of Cheap Editions to July 1876 amounts to exclusive of Author | £1772. |
| The First Part of Cheap Edition was published in May 1867. | |

## GE JOURNAL, LONDON, 20 OCTOBER 1876

*MS:* Yale. *Published:* Cross, III, 293.

October 20. Looking into accounts àpropos of an offer from Blackwood for another ten years of copyright I find that before last Christmas there had been distributed 24,577 copies of Middlemarch. Magnificat anima mea!

## GHL TO JOHN BLACKWOOD, LONDON, 23 OCTOBER 1876

*MS:* National Library of Scotland. *Hitherto unpublished.*

**The Priory, | 21. North Bank, | Regents Park.**
23 October 76.

My dear Blackwood

We have been duly pondering your liberal offer for another ten years lease of the novels, but the various considerations which present themselves keep us in a fluctuating state, and we must have another week before finally deciding. In any case be assured that we are as anxious as you can be that the books should continue to appear under the old flag. Mrs. Lewes begs me to add that she is quite sure there will be no difference in our views whatever the ultimate arrangement may be.

You are quite correct as to the termination of the old lease in December. Only one doubt remains which I wish to put before you, namely whether we are to have any of the contingent advantage notified in the old agreement? Your proposal was either 2 thirds of the profit—or 1000 £ with 500 £ contingent on success "should the edition prove a success i.e. sell at any time during the next five years within an average of 2000 sets." Well, during the first five years that success was not achieved, but was it not during the next five? Does not the sale of

46,765 copies in those five years—and of 73,398 in the whole ten years—pretty well accord with the notion you had of a success? Perhaps you have already considered this point; perhaps not; at any rate I bring it before you just as it lies in my mind.

Yours faithfully
G. H. Lewes.

John Blackwood Esq.

## JOHN BLACKWOOD TO GHL, ST. ANDREWS, 28 OCTOBER 1876

*Text:* Copy in Blackwood Letter Book. *Hitherto unpublished.*

Strathtyrum | St. Andrews October 28/76.

My dear Lewes

I had much pleasure in receiving your Letter which leaves me little doubt that we shall arrange about the work to the satisfaction of all concerned.

I am not surprised that you put the question about the contingency of an additional £500 on the sale of 2000 sets mentioned in my letter making the offer ten years ago.[6] Some time back I said to Willie who had copied it "Why you must have made a blunder in copying; I intended twenty thousand sets," and I never doubted that I had so written. Now it turns out that the blunder is my own, but how such a blunder could have escaped both myself and copyist I cannot understand. I meant not an average sale per year but an average sale of the volumes overhead in that number of years for which 2000 would have been an absurdly inadequate figure. Simpson and Willie both think now they must have taken it up as a yearly average and that seems to be your impression.

Anyway the mistake is clearly mine and I ought to suffer. I would not grudge it a bit especially on books with which we have been so successful but I see that this £500 will sweep up the whole publisher's profit on this long transaction and the idea running in my head that we could afford to pay £500 when we had sold 20000 sets was obviously a fair one. In regard to what you say of the success, admirable and recuperative as the sales have been since the publication of Middlemarch, you will see that the total number sold is still some 8000 volumes short of the numbers on which we based our estimate. You should have heard from me sooner but I was perplexed when I saw by your letter that

6. See 21 December 1866.

I must have made a stupid blunder and I had to communicate with Edinbr. to see whether they could clear it up there.

ever yours truly

(Signed) John Blackwood.

G. H. Lewes Esq.

## GE TO MRS. HARRIET BEECHER STOWE, LONDON, 29 OCTOBER 1876

*MS:* Mr. Lyman Beecher Stowe. *Published:* Cross, III, 293–296.

October 29. 76.

Dear Friend

'Evermore thanks' for your last letter, full of a generous sympathy that can afford to be frank. The lovely photograph of the grandson will be carefully preserved. It has the sort of beauty which seems to be peculiarly abundant in America—at once rounded and delicate in form.

I do hope you will be able to carry out your wish to visit your son [7] at Bonn, notwithstanding that heavy crown of years that your dear Rabbi has to carry. If the sea-voyage could be borne without much disturbance, the land-journey might be made easy by taking it in short stages—the plan we always pursue in travelling. You see, I have an interested motive in wishing you to come to Europe again, since I can't go to America. But I enter thoroughly into the disinclination to move when there are studies that make each day too short. If we were neighbours, I should be in danger of getting troublesome to the revered Orientalist, with all kinds of questions.

As to the Jewish element in 'Deronda,' I expected from first to last in writing it, that it would create much stronger resistance and even repulsion than it has actually met with. But precisely because I felt that the usual attitude of Christians towards Jews is—I hardly know whether to say more impious or more stupid when viewed in the light of their professed principles, I therefore felt urged to treat Jews with such sympathy and understanding as my nature and knowledge could attain to. Moreover, not only towards the Jews, but towards all oriental peoples with whom we English come in contact, a spirit of arrogance and contemptuous dictatorialness is observable which has become a national disgrace to us. There is nothing I should care more to do, if it were possible, than to rouse the imagination of men and women to a vision of human claims in those races of their fellow-men who most differ from them in customs and beliefs. But towards the Hebrews we

7. Charles Edward Stowe (1850–1934) was studying at Bonn.

western people who have been reared in Christianity, have a peculiar debt and, whether we acknowledge it or not, a peculiar thoroughness of fellowship in religious and moral sentiment. Can anything be more disgusting than to hear people called "educated" making small jokes about eating ham, and showing themselves empty of any real knowledge as to the relation of their own social and religious life to the history of the people they think themselves witty in insulting? They hardly know that Christ was a Jew. And I find men educated at Rugby supposing that Christ spoke Greek.[8] To my feeling, this deadness to the history which has prepared half our world for us, this inability to find interest in any form of life that is not clad in the same coat-tails and flounces as our own lies very close to the worst kind of irreligion. The best that can be said of it is, that it is a sign of the intellectual narrowness—in plain English, the stupidity, which is still the average mark of our culture.

Yes, I expected more aversion than I have found. But I was happily independent in material things and felt no temptation to accommodate my writing to any standard except that of trying to do my best in what seemed to me most needful to be done, and I sum up with the writer of the Book of Maccabees—'if I have done well, and as befits the subject, it is what I desired, but if I have done ill, it is what I could attain unto.'[9]

You are in the middle of a more glorious autumn than ours, but we too are having now and then a little sunshine on the changing woods. I hope that I am right in putting the address from which you wrote to me on the 25th September, so that my note may not linger away from you and leave you to imagine me indifferent or negligent.

Please offer my reverent regard to Mr. Stowe, and believe me, dear Friend

Always your gratefully affectionate
M. E. Lewes.

We spent three months in East Switzerland, and are the better for it.

8. A number of GE's friends, among them Congreve and John Cross, had been at Rugby.

9. II Maccabees 15:38.

## GHL TO JOHN BLACKWOOD, LONDON, [29 OCTOBER 1876]

*MS:* National Library of Scotland. *Hitherto unpublished.*

**The Priory, | 21. North Bank, | Regents Park.**
Sunday.

My dear Blackwood

The more we ponder your proposal the more we feel that a *royalty* is the most satisfactory arrangement for all parties. It is not that we are in any way dissatisfied with the sum you propose; but that we would rather be relieved from the sense that the arrangement might turn out disadvantageous to you; and also that we should like to have free command over editions and prices.

The Jews seem to be very grateful for Deronda—and will perhaps make up for the deadness of so many Christians to that part of the book which does not directly concern Gwendolen. When the cheap edition is issued we shall perhaps see the effect of this Jewish sympathy. The Jews ought to make a good public—as the doctors did for Middlemarch.

Ever yours
G. H. Lewes.

## GE TO JOHN BLACKWOOD, LONDON, 3 NOVEMBER 1876

*MS:* National Library of Scotland. *Extract published: John Blackwood,* pp. 397–398.

**The Priory, | 21. North Bank, | Regents Park.**
November 3. 76.

My dear Mr. Blackwood

A cloud of cold having rolled off my brain, it seems clear to me that I owe you a letter. I was much gratified by your handsome proposal about my books, but no one will understand better than you that I incline to keep up a sort of active parental relation to those grown-up children. Also I prefer sharing their vicissitudes and saving everybody from risk as far as anything in this changing world can be saved from that condition. I was uncomfortable about the former arrangement while I feared that it had not answered. We are not greedy, though we are far from being indifferent to money, having relatives to depend on us—a widowed daughter-in-law and two little grandchildren in Natal became entirely our charge last year. We told hardly anyone at the time (because Mr. Lewes dreaded letters of condolence) that his youngest son Herbert died after an illness which ended in severe bronchitis. The sad news came to us when we were at Rickmansworth, quite out of this world, and we did not have it put in the Times. A little boy had been born only a month before the father died. The marriage was a very satisfactory union of two affectionate industrious young creatures who seemed to have a happy life before them till the fatal illness came.

It will be rather interesting to see what is the sale of Deronda compared with Middlemarch. Miss Helps, who sees a great many people, and makes her one copy a sort of lending library, says that she never observed a case in which the 'opinions of the press' so totally differed from the impression produced on readers. And indeed from what Mr. Lewes tells me of such reviews as he has seen, I should imagine that no reader of the reviews would conceive from them that the book in question had caused the least excitement in the public or had been followed with any unusual interest. Certainly, if I had not very strong private proofs to the contrary I should conclude that my book was a failure and that nobody was grateful for it, though a certain tenderness was accorded to the production as that of an author who had done more tolerable things. But I am saved from concluding that I have exhibited my faculties in a state of decay by very delightful letters from unknown readers and reported judgments from considerable authorities. A statesman who shall be nameless has said that I first opened to him a vision of Italian life, then of Spanish, and now I have kindled in him a quite new understanding of the Jewish people. This is what I wanted to do—to widen the English vision a little in that direction and let in a little conscience and refinement. I expected to excite more resistance of feeling than I have seen the signs of, but I did what I chose to do —not as well as I should have liked to do it, but as well as I could.

This is an answer, and is not to be answered, so all the chat has at least the agreeableness of being cheap to you and drawing no further on your time than is required for the reading.

Yours always truly
M. E. Lewes.

## JOHN BLACKWOOD TO GE, ST. ANDREWS, 5 NOVEMBER 1876

*MS:* National Library of Scotland. *Hitherto unpublished.*

**Strathtyrum | St. Andrews | N.B.**
November 5/76.

My Dear Mrs. Lewes

It gives me much pleasure to receive your interesting letter and to hear that you have got quit of the cold which our damp wretched autumn had spread so freely.

I quite understand your feeling of wishing to keep up parental relations with your goodly progeny of good works, and I think we shall have no difficulty in arranging a system of lordship to your satisfaction.[1] This is to be our last week here for the season so tell Lewes I propose not to go into the matter until I go to Edinburgh where I intend to be on the 13th or 14th.

The loss of his promising son at Natal must have been a heavy blow to him. It is hard to see the useful and active taken away while bad shillings always keep cropping up from the uttermost ends of the earth.

You need not disturb yourself about reviews of Deronda, while people keep discussing the book like a great historical event about which there is a difference of opinion. The discussion would not exist if the book were not felt and doing its work even among those who most dissent. I always knew that the strong Jew element would be unpopular, but your picture of the Jew family at home did wonders in overcoming the public distaste to a kindly human view of the Jewish character.

This is a glorious day here and the woods are looking beautiful with as many colours as Joseph's Coat. The weather looks too as if it would last and give us a good wind up of the season here.

My wife and daughter are sorrowing that we are so soon to go, and to me the move to Edinburgh is always the mark that another year is gone. We are all well and so are the numerous animals, bar old Tickler the terrier, whose skin and temper show increasing marks of age and irritability. I shall have a good many golf matches this week and tomor-

1. Sending GE's letter to William Blackwood, John Blackwood wrote: "I think we are just as well with the lordship—it would have been a long time for £4000 to come back." (6 November 1876, NLS.)

row one of my antagonists is Mr. Whyte Melville now in his 80th year but looking as young as his son.[2]

always yours truly
John Blackwood.

## GHL TO MRS. ELMA STUART, LONDON, 19 NOVEMBER 1876

*MS:* British Museum. *Published:* Stuart, pp. 66–67.

**The Priory, | 21. North Bank, | Regents Park.**
Sunday | 19 November 76.

Dear Elma

We both exclaimed "What a handsome fellow!" as the photo met our eyes—he has indeed a sweet and noble expression, and I have placed him, beside his mother, in the small album reserved for Family Phizzes —away from the herd.

Madonna in bidding me send her love hopes that with each anniversary of our friendship-making there will be a renewal of love, and

Here a visitor [3] interrupted my sentence and what it was going to be I can't recover. Never mind, it was something loving you may be sure.

She has been ailing a good deal lately, toothache succeeded by tooth drawing [4]—biliousness and general depression. But she seems all right again now. I have had lumbago,[5] but have not been prevented doing my work, which is all I can expect. Charles and Gertrude have left their country cottage and come back into our fogs—they and the children flourishing.

At no distant time—when I have made use of them—I shall send you for your autograph collection several pages of notes by Charles Darwin written by him àpropos of my articles on his hypothesis which appeared some years ago in the Fortnightly Review.[6] They are very interesting as notes—and as autographs you may prize them; at any rate there is no one I would sooner give them to.

Ever your loving
G. H. L.

2. John Whyte-Melville (1796–1883), father of the novelist George John Whyte-Melville (1821–78).
3. Trübner. (GHL Diary.)
4. "Polly had a tooth out under laughing gas." (GHL Diary, 9 November 1876.)
5. His latest attack, 12–15 November. (GHL Diary.)
6. See 23 December 1876.

## JOHN BLACKWOOD TO GHL, EDINBURGH, 21 NOVEMBER 1876

*MS:* National Library of Scotland. *Hitherto unpublished.*

**45, George Street, | Edinburgh.**
November 21/76.

My Dear Lewes

Since I came into Edinburgh I have been looking again into the cost and produce of The Works, and I am disappointed to find as I feared, that the inclosed offer of lordship cannot be much varied.

The printing paper and binding are put in the accompanying statement as cheaply as they can be done and the advertising etc. at a less rate than we have estimated during these ten years. The discounts to the Trade are very large, but we do not see how to lessen them without checking the sale—as Dickens and other similar works are sold at the same rates of discount. For instance the 3/6 volumes of Dickens are sold by the agent here to the retailers at sale price 2/6 13 as 12 to 6 Mos. Acct. and 2½ per cent discount, so the Agent must have 10 per cent off sale to cover his transaction.

I am disappointed at the result as I was ten years ago when I calculated the whole matter, but I did not then or now see a better form, and we have all reason to be pleased with the steady increasing sale the books have met in their present shape.

While Middlemarch goes on as it is doing it will not be desirable to make any change there, and it is to be hoped Deronda will follow suit. We are going to bring out the Deronda at 21/- immediately and I hope we have not been rash in printing 2000.[7]

When Middlemarch and Deronda have run their course as separate books at 7/6, the plates will readily print on paper uniform with the other works, perhaps as two volumes each and they with Romola [8] may give the whole series a fresh start. By that time too I hope there may be a new book to be reckoned among the works of George Eliot.

ever yours truly
John Blackwood.

G. H. Lewes Esq.

7. In the Blackwood records it appears as 2100.

8. See 13 February 1877.

WORKS OF GEORGE ELIOT CABINET EDITION

| | Pages | |
|---|---|---|
| Romola | 918 | 2 Vols. |
| Silas, Lifted veil and Jacob | 416 | 1 Vol. |
| Scenes | 644 | 2 Vols. |
| Adam Bede | 800 | 2 Vols. |
| Mill on the Floss | 822 | 2 Vols. |
| Felix Holt | 780 | 2 Vols. |
| Middlemarch | 1276 | 3 Vols. |
| Deronda | 1230 | 3 Vols. |
| Gypsy | 320 | 1 Vol. |
| Jubal | 154 | 1 Vol. |
| | 7360 | 19 Vols. |

7360 pages make 230 Sheets

*Cost*

| | |
|---|---|
| Setting type 230 sheets | 460 |
| Stereotyping | 368 |
| | 828 |

*Production of Stock*

| | | |
|---|---|---|
| Sets | | |
| 1000 Copies 230 Sheets | | |
| Press-work | 290.10. | |
| Paper | 530. 8.9 | |
| Boarding | 475. . | |
| Advertising | 150. . | 1445.18.9 |
| Cost of 1st thousand | | 2273.18.9 |
| | | 1445.18.9 |
| Cost of first two Thousand | | 3719.17.6 |
| Selling at 4/6 per Vol. 1000 copies produce 25 as 24 less 5% | | 2743.12. |
| add Second Thousand | | 2743.12. |
| | | 5487. 4. |
| deduct cost of 2000 | | 3719.17.6 |
| Gain on 2000 Sets Selling @ 4/6 per Vol. | | 1767. 6.6 |
| Selling at 3/6 per Vol. | | |
| 1000 Copies produce 25 as 24 less 5% | | 2166. |
| add Second Thousand | | 2166. |
| | | 4332. |
| deduct cost of 2000 Sets | | 3719.17.6 |
| Gain on 2000 Sets Selling @ 3/6 per Vol | | 612. 2.6 |

That is to say On the third and following thousand Sets

| | |
|---|---|
| the gain would be at 4/6 per Vol | 1297.13.3 |
| " " at 3/6 per Vol | 720. 1.3 |

## WILLIAM BLACKWOOD AND SONS TO GHL, EDINBURGH, 21 NOVEMBER 1876

*Text:* Copy in Blackwood Letter Book. Mrs. Ouvry has the original table. *Endorsed* [*by GHL*]: Novr. 1876. Agreement for cheap edition of first 5 English Novels; [*by GE*] Proposal for Cheap Editions Nov. 1876; [*by Mrs. C. L. Lewes*] Important as still going in 1897 on that footing. *Hitherto unpublished.*

Edinburgh | 21st November 1876.

Dear Sir

By the accompanying Table you will see what Adam Bede The Mill Silas Scenes and Felix Holt will produce in their present form and we now beg to offer the following lordship to Author.

On Adam Bede £1.10/ on each hundred copies sold

| | | | |
|---|---|---|---|
| " | Mill on the Floss | 1. 7.6 | ditto |
| " | Silas Marner | 1.17.6 | ditto |
| " | Scenes of Cl. Life | 1.10.0 | ditto |
| " | Felix Holt | 1.17.6 | ditto |

This new arrangement to commence from the beginning of 1877 and accounts to be settled annually at that date.

Mr. Blackwood writes along with this in further explanation. We are, Dear Sir

Yours faithfully
Wm. Blackwood and Sons.

G. H. Lewes Esq.

| | *Bede* | *Mill* | *Silas* | *Scenes* | *Holt* |
|---|---|---|---|---|---|
| Printing Paper Boarding and Cuts 1050 Copies | 80.13.- | 82.13.- | 43.12.- | 64.13.- | 75.13.- |
| Advertising and incidents. | 5. 9.- | 5. 9.- | 3.16.- | 4.10.- | 5. 9.- |
| | 86. 2.- | 88. 2.- | 47. 8.- | 69. 3.- | 81. 2.- |
| Yield of 1050 Sold 13 as 12 less 10 per cent | 109. 2.6 | 109. 2.6 | 76. 7.9 | 90.11.9 | 109. 2.6 |
| Gain | 23. 0.6 | 21. 0.6 | 29. 0.0 | 21.15.9 | 28. 0.6 |
| Net profit per 100 copies | 2. 3.9 | 1.19.7 | 2.14.2 | 2. 1.6 | 2.12.1 |
| Proposed payment to Author per 100 | 1.10.0 | 1. 7.6 | 1.17.6 | 1.10.- | 1.17.6 |
| Gain per Vol. | 5d ¼ | 4d ¾ | 6d ½ | 5d | 6d ¼ |

## GE TO SARA SOPHIA HENNELL, LONDON, 22 NOVEMBER 1876

*MS:* Yale. *Extracts published:* Cross, III, 296–297.

**The Priory, | 21. North Bank, | Regents Park.**
November 22. 76.

My dear Sara

I am sadly disappointed to find that you have been, and are, suffering so much, Cara's last account having suggested a more cheerful picture of you. Any one who knows from experience what bodily infirmity is—how it spoils life even for those who have no other trouble—gets a little impatient of healthy complainants strong enough for extra work and ignorant of indigestion. I at least should be inclined to scold the discontented young people who tell me in one breath that they never have anything the matter with them and that life is not worth having—if I did not remember my own young discontent. What a pity that you did not get to Penmaenmaur before the bad weather set in! When I think of your cough and trouble of breathing, it makes my own ailments seem small—I imagine so vividly the distressing effect on your head. It is a comfort that Cara is comparatively strong. Please tell her that I want to be 'posted up' in her affairs by another little noteful of news.

We are perfectly happy, save and excepting the old headaches and other newer infirmities incident to our advancing years.[9] Mr. Lewes is getting his third volume through the press—it turns entirely on the physiology of the nervous system—though he can't work half so long as he used to do, he works with much enjoyment, reviving quickly after a crushing headache or an attack of lumbago. It is remarkable to me that I have entirely lost my *personal* melancholy. I often, of course, have melancholy thoughts about the destinies of my fellow-creatures, but I am never in that *mood* of sadness which used to be my frequent visitant even in the midst of external happiness. And this, notwithstanding a very vivid sense that life is declining and death close at hand.

Perhaps it will amuse you to know that our friend Mr. Spencer, who used to despise biography as the least profitable occupation of brain, is now busily collecting the materials of his own family and personal history! [1] The Spencer family is really interesting. H. S's father was a

9. This was written on GE's 57th birthday.

1. Herbert Spencer began to write his *Autobiography* in May 1875; by October 1889 both volumes were in print, though it was not published till after his

strong, peculiar character, and there seems to have been a strain of mental force through former generations.

We are waiting with some expectation for Miss Martineau's autobiography, which I fancy will be charming so far as her younger and less renowned life extends. All biography diminishes in interest when the subject has won celebrity—or some reputation that hardly comes up to celebrity. But autobiography at least saves a man or woman that the world is curious about from the publication of a string of mistakes called 'memoirs.'

Apropos—you will not think me blasphemous if I pass to the memoirs of Jesus Christ. I remember you used to possess a volume containing the apocryphal gospels. If you don't use it, will you lend it me for a few months? I shall be very grateful.

It would be nice if we could be a trio—I mean you, Cara and I—chatting together for an hour as we used to do when I had walked over the hill to see you. But that pleasure belongs to "the days that are no more." [2] Will you believe that an accomplished man some years ago said to me, that he saw no place for the exercise of *resignation* when there was no personal Divine Will contemplated as ordaining sorrow or privation? He is not yet aware that he is getting old, and needing that unembittered compliance of soul with the inevitable which seems to me a full enough meaning for the word 'resignation.'

I wish I had more news to tell you about people whom we know in common. Madame Bodichon is still, I think, at the coast with Miss Julia Smith, to whom she is a very loving, duteous niece. What a pretty delicate little old lady that aunt was the last time I saw her! With best love to Cara. Always, dear Sara,

Your faithfully affectionate
Pollian.

death, 8 December 1903. Six copies of it were circulated among his friends for criticism after they agreed to a formidable list of conditions such as keeping the volumes under lock and key, not lending them or allowing the servants to see them, etc. See his letter to J. W. Cross, 13 October 1889. (Yale.) Later Part XIII was added to bring it down to 1893. The work was published in 1904. Most of the private letters used in it were destroyed by Spencer himself; those he reserved for his biographer, David Duncan, were "scrapped by order of the Trustees soon after the book was written." (Information given me by Mr. T. W. Hill, later secretary to the Spencer Trustees, 9 November 1943.) So far as I know no letters that passed between GE and Spencer at the time of their closest intimacy are now accessible, though some have been preserved.

2. Tennyson, *The Princess*, IV, 43.

## GHL TO JOHN BLACKWOOD, LONDON, 22 NOVEMBER 1876

*MS:* National Library of Scotland. *Hitherto unpublished.*

**The Priory, | 21. North Bank, | Regents Park.**
November 22nd 76.

My dear Blackwood

We quite agree to your proposal.

Mrs. Lewes would have been glad to know that you were going to issue the 21/ edition of D.D. as she wished to correct three or four errors—however it is too late now, and we must wait for the 7/6. But *I* am a little surprised that you did not content yourself with risking 1,000—as the types were ready to reprint a second 1,000 if needed—for I have grim doubts of your getting through with the 2,000£. There seems to be so general a sense of disappointment—so much deadness to the Jewish element—that my only hope for a large sale until the public has learned to get over its first disappointment is in the Jewish public and they can only, I fear, be caught by the cheap edition. (Don't allude to the disappointment in any letters to me—she only knows that Judaism is unpopular not what is said otherwise about the book.) [3] I remember that 'Romola' was received with a universal howl of discontent—and now it is the book most commonly placed at the head of her works—or at any rate after 'Middlemarch.' If Deronda is the book I take it to be we shall see a revival or rather a reversal of opinion. Curiously enough in America it seems to have surpassed 'Middlemarch.'

Ever yours
G. H. Lewes.

## JOHN BLACKWOOD TO GHL, EDINBURGH, 25 NOVEMBER 1876

*MS:* National Library of Scotland. *Hitherto unpublished.*

**45, George Street, | Edinburgh.**
November 25/76.

My Dear Lewes

I have much pleasure in receiving your frank acceptance of our proposal for The Works and I sincerely hope the result will be a good steady sum to be settled yearly.

3. Writing to Sidney Colvin, who was reviewing the book in the *Fortnightly*, John Morley said: "Say what you like about George Sand. You will naturally spare George Eliot's feelings as much as critical honesty will permit." (E. V. Lucas, *The Colvins and Their Friends*, New York, 1928, p. 97.)

Like you I was rather startled when I found we had printed 2000 of Daniel in the 21/ form although I have no doubt I had settled or assented to the number. However even if it should hang on hand for a time it will always be good stock and I would not allow it to interfere with bringing out the 7/6 edition when the right time comes.

I am sorry to hear of the three or four errors. Are they worth mentioning in an Errata at the end or a cancel or two? Simpson says he wrote to inquire whether there were any corrections for the reprint and the answer was no. I too remember something of this when we printed for Australia.

The Jews should be the most interesting people in the world, but even *her* magic pen cannot *at once* make them a popular element in a Novel. The discussion however goes on and the power she has expended on the despised element will tell and force its way. The fact is that Mrs. Lewes stands on such a pinnacle that the Critics are (unconsciously perhaps) glad to fix upon anything they can possibly mention as a flaw. Great success always bears this penalty with it. Bulwer felt it keenly and so did Dickens and Thackeray in a lesser degree. I remember a very hearty laugh with dear old Aytoun. He was complaining humorously of his treatment by the Press in his maturer years and said "Confound the fellows. They used to make me blush at their praises but now they have found out I am a Sheriff and a Professor they won't leave a literary feather on my back." [4]

We have famous wintry weather here now and I hope it is agreeing with Mrs. Lewes and you. My wife and I are alone, our daughter having gone to visit her Aunts in England. It is a sad blank in the house but we have always a good deal to talk and think about.

ever yours truly
John Blackwood.

## GHL DIARY, WEYBRIDGE, 29–30 NOVEMBER 1876

*MS:* Yale. *Hitherto unpublished.*

**Wednesday 29 November 1876**

Liebmann Analysis der Wirklichkeit.[5] We went with Johnnie to Witley to see a house.[6] Met him at Waterloo at 11.30 and reached Witley

4. William Edmondstoune Aytoun became Professor of Rhetoric and Belles Lettres at Edinburgh in 1845 and was appointed Sheriff of Orkney in 1852. (*DNB.*)

5. Otto Liebmann (1840–1912), *Zur Analysis der Wirklichkeit,* Strasbourg, 1875.

6. The Heights. Cross describes the house and gives an engraving of it, III, facing p. 298.

at 12.40. Enchanted with the house and grounds. The day transcendently beautiful made everything look glorious. We then accompanied him to Weybridge where we passed the day and night, having a good walk before dinner.

**Thursday 30 November 1876**

Walk on St. George's Hill after breakfast and looked in on the Druces. Home by 4.30. Wrote to Cole about the house. 'Times.' Revue Scientifique. Frazer's Magazine.

## GE JOURNAL, LONDON, 1 DECEMBER 1876.

*MS:* Yale. *Published:* Cross, III, 297–298.

1 December 1876. Since we came home at the beginning of September I have been made aware of much repugnance or else indifference towards the Jewish part of Deronda, and of some hostile as well as adverse reviewing. On the other hand there have been the strongest expressions of interest—some persons adhering to the opinion, started during the early numbers, that the book is my best—delighted letters have here and there been sent to me, and the sale both in America and in England has been an unmistakeable guarantee that the public has been touched. Words of gratitude have come from Jews and Jewesses, and there are certain signs that I may have contributed my mite to a good result. The sale hitherto has exceeded that of Middlemarch as to the £2/2s four-volumed form, but we do not expect an equal success for the guinea edition which has lately been issued.

## GE JOURNAL, LONDON, 11 DECEMBER 1876

*MS:* Yale. *Published:* Cross, III, 298.

We have just bought a house in Surrey,[7] and think of it as making a serious change in our life, namely, that we shall finally settle there and give up town.

7. Having heard the surveyor's report, GHL commissioned Cross's solicitor Frederick Leigh Hutchins to bid as far as £5000 for the house. Two days later "News came that 'Witley Heights' was secured for £4950." (GHL Diary, 6–8 December 1876.)

## JOHN BLACKWOOD TO GE, EDINBURGH, 12 DECEMBER 1876

*MS:* National Library of Scotland. *Hitherto unpublished.*

**45, George Street, | Edinburgh.**
December 12/76.

My Dear Mrs. Lewes

It gives me the most sincere pleasure to learn by Lewes' letter today,[8] that you have bought a place in the country which seems likely to suit you both in every way.

Most heartily do I congratulate you and hope that this permanent anchorage in the country may be a long continued source of health and happiness to you such as I should ever wish your home to be. My nephew joins in congratulations and it will be a labour of love to Mr. Simpson to hasten the preparation of the statements of your books from knowing the happy end to which the results are to be applied.

The Magnate correcting you about Grandcourt and Gwendolen walking into a room arm and arm [1] amused me but after all I half think that at the date of the story you are right. The custom of the husband following the wife into a room resulted from the overflowing skirts etc. of the ladies. My wife has a favourite story of her uncle Canon Guthrie [2] who was also Vicar of Calne having been told jokingly by the Marquis of Lansdowne that it was no longer the custom for husbands to come in with their wives on their arm. This would be about 30 years ago and the change must have been new then, as the Canon was as punctilious a church dignitary as ever I saw and both he and his wife thoroughly members of the best stamp of society all their lives which made the joke against them in their nieces whom they told the story.

I am glad you like the appearance of the new edition of Deronda. Do you not wish copies to give away. As yet I fear it is not doing much but I shall let Lewes know. With all good wishes I am

always yours truly
John Blackwood.

8. The letter has not been found.
1. Ch. 35.
2. John Guthrie (1794–1865), B.A. Trinity College, Cambridge, 1817, was appointed Chaplain to the Marquis of Lansdowne in 1834, Vicar of Calne, 1835, and Canon of Bristol, 1858.

## GE JOURNAL, LONDON, 15 DECEMBER 1876

*MS:* Yale. *Published:* Cross, III, 299–300.

15 December 1876. At the beginning of this week I had deep satisfaction from reading in the Times the report of a lecture on Daniel Deronda delivered by Dr. Hermann Adler to the Jewish Working Men, a lecture showing much insight and implying an expectation of serious benefit. Since then, I have had a delightful letter from the Jewish Theolog[ical] Seminary at Breslau written by an American Jew named Isaacs,[3] who excuses himself for expressing his feeling of gratitude on reading Deronda, and assures me of his belief that it has even already had an elevating effect on the minds of some among his people—predicting that the effect will spread.

I have also had a request from Sigr. Bartolommeo Aquarone, of Siena, for leave to translate Romola,[4] and declaring that, as one who has given special study to the History of San Marco and has written a life of Fra Jeronimo Savonarola, he cares especially that 'Romola' should be known to his countrymen for their good. Magnificat anima mea!

And last night I had a letter from Dr. Benisch, editor of the Jewish Chronicle, announcing a copy of the paper containing an article written by himself on reading 'Deronda' (there have long ago been two articles in the same journal reviewing the book) and using strong words as to the effect the book is producing. I record these signs, that I may look back on them if they come to be confirmed.

## GE TO ABRAHAM BENISCH,[5] LONDON, 16 DECEMBER 1876

*MS:* Jewish Museum, London. *Published: Anglo-Jewish Letters,* ed. Cecil Roth, 1938, p. 312.

**The Priory, | 21. North Bank, | Regents Park.**
December 16. 76.

Dear Sir

Heartfelt thanks for your kind letter and the copy of the current 'Jewish Chronicle.'

3. Abram Samuel Isaacs (1851–1920), born in New York, was later Professor of Hebrew at New York University.

4. Bartolommeo Aquarone (b. 1815). His letter 10 December 1876, is in my possession. In addition to his *Vita di Frà Jeronimo Savonarola,* Alessandria, 1857–58, he refers to his translation of Giovanni Buffoni's *Doctor Antonio,* 2d ed., Milan, 1875. GE added later: "He afterwards found out that a previously existing translation was a hindrance, though out of print."

5. Abraham Benisch (1811–78), born

You are probably better aware than I am that the elements in 'Daniel Deronda' which have called forth your generously appreciative words have met in the ordinary public chiefly with an ignorant surprize and lack of sympathy. This was what I expected. But I did not expect the cordial encouragement [by] which you and other instructed men have given me to believe that my anxious effort at a true presentation is not a failure, and may even touch the feeling of your people to welcome issues.

I am not accustomed to write with much confidence in my effect, my choice of subjects being adjusted to my own taste and not to any prevalent mode, and I certainly could never have written 'Daniel Deronda' if a deep impersonal historic interest had not made me independent of minor considerations. Nothing could have caused me to regret my work except the evidence that Jews of high character and culture felt my presentation to be unreal and unjust.

I am indebted to you—and also to Dr. Hermann Adler—for the most authoritative assurance that I have no such cause for regret. And it may interest you to know that close upon your letter there came one from a gentleman now in the Jewish Theological Seminary at Breslau, apparently as a professor, whose words are in perfect agreement with your own. I remain, dear Sir,

Yours sincerely
M. E. Lewes.

## GE TO ELIZABETH STUART PHELPS, LONDON, 16 DECEMBER 1876

*MS:* The late Mr. Gabriel Wells. A copy found among the Cross papers is at Yale. *Published: Century Magazine,* 104 (September 1922), 644–645.

**The Priory, | 21. North Bank, | Regents Park.**
December 16. 76.

My dear Miss Phelps

I am very grateful to you for your generous words of sympathy and I am deeply touched by the image you suggest to me of yourself struggling under delicate health to fulfil worthily an office that may make a new precedent in social advance and which is at the very least an experiment that ought to be tried.[6] America is the seed-ground and nursery of

in Bohemia, came to England in 1841. His learning and devotion to Judaism won him a high reputation among English Jews. He edited the *Jewish Chronicle* 1854–69 and again 1875–78. (*DNB*.)

6. Miss Phelps's letter to GE, 1 De-

new ideals, where they can grow in a larger, freer air than ours.

Your lecture if you are good enough to send it will, I am sure, be read with interest by Mr. Lewes, but I hardly ever read anything that is written about myself—indeed, never unless my husband expressly wishes me to do so by way of exception.[7] I adopted this rule many years ago as a necessary preservative against influences that would have ended by nullifying my power of writing. Mr. Lewes reads anything written about me that comes in his way and occasionally gives me reports of what he reads if it happens to shew an unusual insight or an unusual ineptitude. In this way I get confirmed in my impression that the criticism of any new writing is shifting and untrustworthy. I hardly think that any critic can have so keen a sense of the short-comings in my works as that I groan under in the course of writing them, and I cannot imagine any edification coming to an author from a sort of reviewing which consists in attributing to him or her unexpressed opinions, and in imagining circumstances which may be alleged as petty private motives for the treatment of subjects which ought to be of general human interest.

But I am confident, dear Miss Phelps, that whatever you have spoken or written is free from any such characteristics as those I refer to—nay, is full of a spirit animated and guided by a wide-reaching fellowship. I have only been led into this rather superfluous sort of remark by the mention of a rule which seemed to require explanation. It is perhaps less irrelevant to say, àpropos of a distinction you seem to make between my earlier and later works,[8] that though I trust there is some growth in my appreciation of others and in my self-distrust, there has been no change in the point of view from which I regard our life since I wrote my first fiction—the 'Scenes of Clerical Life.' Any apparent change of spirit must be due to something of which I am unconscious. The principles which are at the root of my effort to paint Dinah Morris are equally at the root of my effort to paint Mordecai. Enough of me and my doings.

You and Mrs. Stowe might well beguile me by your loving invitations to cross the wide Atlantic,[9] if it were not that Mr. Lewes's health is

cember 1876, describes her four lectures "before the College of Boston University, the new, and so far successful co-educational experiment." (Yale.)

7. "If I ever publish my lectures, which is uncertain, for I'm hardly able to put them in shape for the press, I shall do myself the honor of sending them to you."

8. "Knowing me to be a believing Christian, you will foresee the points in which I should mourn over your later works."

9. "P.S. Will you not come and make me a visit this summer? . . . My Gloucester home is but a few miles from one of the most charming homes in America—that of my friend Mrs. James T. Fields of Boston, whom I think you have met. She spends her summer on the shore. Will not *that* tempt you if my little shell cannot?"

threatened in a peculiar way by any such perturbation of the heart's action as might come from a sea-voyage. It is this that hinders me from carrying out my longing to go to the East,[1] and that must forbid me equally from seeing your land of the Future. You speak of friends—Mr. and Mrs. Fields of Boston—to whom I should be glad to have my best remembrances offered when you see them.

Once more, dear Friend, believe in a gratitude which I will venture to call affectionate, from yours in sincerity

M. E. Lewes.

## GE TO MRS. CHARLES BRAY, LONDON, 21 DECEMBER 1876

*MS:* Yale. *Brief extract published:* Mathilde Blind, *George Eliot,* 1883, pp. 172–173.

**The Priory, | 21. North Bank, | Regents Park.**
December 21. 76.

Dear Cara

Your letter is quite precious to me, notwithstanding that there is much in it of a saddening kind—I mean, about the bodily suffering and the prospect of more. But one would rather grieve with one's friends than have them grieving without one's knowing anything of it.—I cannot quite agree that it is hard to see what has been the good of *your* life. It seems to me very clear that you have been a good of a kind that would have been sorely missed by those who have been nearest to you and also to some who are more distant. And it is this kind of good which must reconcile us to life—not any answer to the question, 'What would the universe have been without me?' The point one has to care for is, 'Are A B and C the better for me?' And there are several letters of the alphabet that could not have easily spared you in the past and that can still less spare you in the present.

These returns of bronchitis must shake dear Sara very painfully and cannot but have a depressing effect on her mind as well as on her average bodily state. I trust that Mrs. Cash and other neighbours help you to cheer her by sympathetic attentions, but we have to face the terrible fact that, even where everything kind is done, there are periods in the majority of lives when pain dips the scale so low that comfort seems nought.

I am so glad to think that poor Frank Hennell's lot is brightened by

1. A letter to GE from Lady Strangford, 30 May 1874, gives advice about travel in Egypt and the Near East so detailed as to suggest that GE was then contemplating it. (Yale.)

his marriage and that the new niece's visit can be looked forward to with pleasure. A great load must have been lifted off Mrs. Call's mind, and she will perhaps now be able to settle down finally in England with a prospect of satisfaction.—We too are thinking of a new settling down, for we have bought a house in Surrey about four miles from Godalming on a gravelly hill among the pine trees, but with neighbours to give us a sense of security. Our present idea is that we shall part with this house and give up London except for occasional visits. We shall be on the same line of railway with some good friends at Weybridge and Guildford.

George Dawson was strongly associated for me with Rosehill—not to speak of the general Baptist Chapel where we all heard him preach for the first time (to us). And do you remember Mr. R. R. R. Moore? [2] His son has come to the border of my scenery as a friend of Madame Bodichon's. I have not seen him, but she thinks most highly of his character and powers. He is an anatomist. I have a vivid recollection of an evening when Mr. and Mrs. Flower dined at your house with George Dawson when he was going to lecture at the Mechanics' Institute, and you felt compassionately towards him because you thought the rather riotous talk was a bad preface to his lecture. We have a Birmingham friend [3] whose acquaintance we made many years ago in Weimar, and from him I have occasionally had some news of Mr. Dawson. I feared—what you mention—that his life had been a little too strenuous in these latter years.

The 'Sir Charles Grandison' you are reading must be the series of little fat volumes you lent me to carry to the Isle of Wight,[4] where I read it at every interval when my father did not want me, and was sorry that the long novel was not longer. It is a solace to hear of any one's reading and enjoying Richardson. We have fallen on an evil generation who would not read 'Clarissa' even in an abridged form. The French have been its most enthusiastic admirers, but I don't know whether their present admiration is more than traditional, like their set phrases about their own classics.

I don't know what you refer to in the 'Jewish World.' Perhaps the report of Dr. Hermann Adler's Lecture on Deronda to the Jewish Work-

2. Robert Ross Rowan Moore (1811–64), who came to Coventry several times in behalf of the Anti-Corn-Law League. (Mrs. Bray's Diary, March 1842, 25 February 1845, 14 October 1847.) His only son Norman Moore (1847–1922), Warden of St. Bartholomew's Hospital Medical School, married in 1880 Amy Leigh Smith, a niece of Mme Bodichon. He wrote many lives for the *DNB,* including hers.

3. Samuel D. Williams, Jr., son of a lime merchant of Easy Row, Birmingham. GE mentions him in her Journal, 27 September 1854: "Mr. Williams, an agreeable, unaffected young man, took coffee with us."

4. See 13 October [1847].

ing Men, given in the Times. Probably the Dr. Adler whom you saw is Dr. Hermann's father, still living as Chief Rabbi. I have had some delightful communications from Jews and Jewesses both at home and abroad. Part of the club scene in D. D. is flying about in the Hebrew tongue through the various Hebrew newspapers which have been copying the 'Magid,' in which the translation was first sent to me three months ago. The Jews naturally are not indifferent to themselves.

The other night[5] we went to hear the Bach Choir, a society of Ladies and Gentlemen got together by Jenny Lind, who sings in the middle of them, her husband acting as conductor. It is pretty to see people who might be nothing but empty fashionables taking pains to sing fine music in tune and time with more or less success. One of the baritones we know is a Grosvenor[6] who used to be a swell guardsman, and has happily taken to good courses while still quite young. Another is a handsome young Gurney[7]—not of the unsatisfactory Co. but of the Russell Gurney kin. A soprano is Mrs. Ponsonby—wife of the Queen's Secretary, General P.—the granddaughter of Earl Grey and just like him in the face. And so on. These people of "high" birth are certainly reforming themselves a little.

Mr. Lewes has just come up to me after reading your letter and says, "For God's sake, tell her not to have the photograph reproduced!" —and I had nearly forgotten to say that the fading is what I desired. I should not like the image to be perpetuated. It needs the friendly eyes that regret to see it fade, and must not be recalled into emphatic black and white for indifferent gazers. Pray let it finally vanish.

Please give my best love to Mrs. Cash and dear Mrs. Pears, who often returns to my thought because of my fear that she has had some heart-troubles about her daughter. Do let me know the good news when the Sydenham house is let, and do not forget your promise that you will not suffer any lack which I could hinder—you know, I mean lack of comforts for that difficult breath, such as might come from a sense that expensiveness obliged renunciation. With much affection all round,

Yours always
Marian.

5. 19 December. (GHL's Diary.)

6. The Hon. Norman de l'Aigle Grosvenor (1845–98) had been a captain in the Grenadier Guards.

7. Edmund Gurney (1847–1888), a nephew and ward of Russell Gurney (1804–1878), Recorder of London.

## GHL TO MRS. ELMA STUART, LONDON, 23 DECEMBER 1876

*MS:* British Museum. *Published:* Stuart, pp. 67–69.

**The Priory, | 21. North Bank, | Regents Park.**
23 December 76.

A merry Christmas, dear Elma, to you and Roly! and if wishes will draw down blessings, you will be blessed.

Herewith I send you the precious autograph, which you alone among my friends I care to give it to—it is the batch of notes which Darwin wrote at my request on some articles of mine on his hypothesis, which appeared in the "Fortnightly Review," April, June, July and November 1868.

You will be glad to hear that at last we have secured a place in the country which promises to fulfil our expectations. There are 8 acres of beautiful grounds and wood, with a house not too large for us, five minutes from a station, 70 minutes from town, sandy soil, lovely country, and nice neighbours. It is called "The Heights"—Witley, near Godalming, Surrey. Next door on either side are Birket Foster and Sir Henry Holland [8]—the son of our old friend. It is *there* we intend to have you as a guest next summer. Owing to the dreadful state of the money market we have got this place for £3000 less than was asked! Isn't that luck?

Madonna is pretty well just now, greatly comforted by the testimonies she receives from Jews and Jewesses in Germany, France, America and England—especially the learned Rabbis who seem to think "Deronda" will instruct, elevate, and expand the minds of Jews no less than modify the feelings of 'Christians' towards the Jews.

We are to spend Christmas with our fervid Scotch friends at Weybridge—our own children having their family gathering with Gertrude's relatives.

When I asked Madonna if she had any special message for you she said that beyond her dear love there was nothing but to say how she wished to hear full particulars of your joys and sorrows, occupations and plans whenever you care to send them. "She knows I like receiving letters—it is the answering them I don't like!"

Ever your loving
G. H. L.

8. Sir Henry Thurstan Holland (1825–1914), 2d Baronet, son of Sir Henry Holland (1788–1873).

## GHL TO WILLIAM BLACKWOOD, LONDON, [29 DECEMBER 1876]

*MS:* National Library of Scotland. *Hitherto unpublished.*

**The Priory, | 21. North Bank, | Regents Park.**
Friday.

My dear Willie

Tell Von Moltke[9] that Mrs. Lewes and myself are grieved—and surprised—to hear of [so] great a strategist being unable to dodge the miserable rabble which calls itself 'the season' and allow it to steal a march upon him. Your uncle is more execrable—because more reckless!

Such is the height of virtue from which we unbronchial people can look down on weak brethren! But this weather is too bad—and has prevented our going down to look after our property which by the way we have only seen once!

As to the payment for the same, if your checque arrives on 18th that will be in good time.[1] If the accounts are not ready we can adjust when they are.

Except that every day almost some fresh indication crops up that there *are* people deeply interested in the Jewish part of Deronda I don't know anything to say in the way of news.

Our best wishes to all of you for the coming time.

Yours ever
G. H. L.

9. George Simpson. See 12 January 1877.

1. GHL's accounts show receipts from Blackwood in January 1877 of £2215.15.6 and £2050.15.-. In the same month there are two payments to Prater, one for £500, the other for £4450.

# The Cabinet Edition

| | |
|---|---|
| *1877 January 10* | GE and GHL call on W. B. Scott. |
| *1877 January 22* | GHL has rheumatic gout. |
| *1877 February 8* | Blackwood agrees to add *Romola* to his list. |
| *1877 February 19* | GE has a severe renal attack. |
| *1877 February 27* | GHL proposes the Cabinet edition to Blackwood. |
| *1877 March 30* | GE and GHL give party to hear Tennyson read. |
| *1877 May 3* | Liszt writes introducing the Richard Wagners. |
| *1877 May 15* | GE and GHL dine at the Goschens with the Princess Louise and the Marquis of Lorne. |
| *1877 May 19–21* | Visit Jowett at Balliol College, Oxford. |
| *1877 May 31* | Rabbi David Kaufmann sends *George Eliot und das Judenthum.* |
| *1877 May 31–June 4* | GE and GHL visit the Sidgwicks at Cambridge. |

## GE TO MRS. ELMA STUART, LONDON, 1 JANUARY 1877

*MS:* British Museum. *Published:* Stuart, pp. 70–73.

**The Priory, | 21. North Bank, | Regents Park.**
New Year's Day, 1877.

Dearest Elma

Your dear letter telling us how you have had the blessedness to be an angel of mercy to one in the last great need,[1] is the most precious thing the Christmas week brought me—better than winter roses which came with fresh white petals all the way from Wales.[2] The old, old poet says that the lingering years bring each something in their hand to every mortal [3]—having in his mind perhaps the something good rather than the many things evil. To me it seems that a year could never bring any one a more substantial good than the certitude of having helped another to bear some heavy burthen—of having lessened pain and given the sweetness of fellowship in sorrow. That is just the one good which seems the more worth having, the more our own life is encompassed with shadows.

Does this sentence sound like a moan—as if I were thinking *myself* an object for pity? I should deserve an extra whipping for such ingratitude. I have no sorrows of my own beyond a rickety body and the prospect of the great parting. But the ruinously rainy weather, and the threat that mortals may make fresh miseries for each other by rushing into war,[4] are a dark curtain round us all at this ending and beginning of times.

I have been pleasantly interrupted in my writing by a box—imagine what box!—the sacred bon-bons, which we will deliver, unviolated even by our eyes, to the little ones at Hampstead the next time that the weather lets us drive up the hill.

You know all the news about us from my 'corresponding partner.' We have only seen our new country house once, and that by the finest

1. Roland Stuart explains that this refers to the request of a dying Englishwoman that Mrs. Stuart take care of her little dog. "I need not add that my mother and cousin nursed the poor lady to the end, and that the little dog had the happiest life as long as it lived." (pp. 69–70.)

2. From Mrs. Ruck, who had a house at Machynlleth.

3. Cf. Emerson's poem "Days."

4. Lord Salisbury had sent the British ultimatum to the Sultan of Turkey, 26 December 1876.

weather, so that I rather tremble to take another view. And we both of us like to live undisturbedly in our ideal world, where furniture and tradespeople are an inexpensive comedy—rather than to see about our own wants and give orders. In fact, we don't like our own business, in the external sense. But these are the grievances of people who have more than their share in the world.

You, dear, are greatly blessed in having a friend [5] to *your* share, who is of one mind with you in your best wishes and deeds. Please ask her to accept my love and to think of me as one who would like to know her better. I hope also that Roland's memory will grow with his legs and that he will not get strange to the friends who knew him first when he was a small fellow.

I have several letters to answer this morning, so do not think me quite gratuitously shabby that, writing so seldom, I write so little. I am not in good condition just now, and seem to be keeping my head above a slough with some difficulty. But doubtless a crisp frost will do me good along with the country in general. Always, dearest Elma,

Your anxiously affectionate
Mother.

## JOHN BLACKWOOD TO GHL, EDINBURGH, 12 JANUARY 1877

*Text:* Copy in Blackwood Letter Book. MS of statements in Mrs. Ouvry's collection. *Hitherto unpublished.*

45 George Street | Edinburgh January 12/77.

My Dear Lewes

I have the pleasure of enclosing a cheque on the Royal Bank in London for £2215.15.6d due to Mrs. Lewes as per accompanying statement which will I hope be found satisfactory.

The only disappointing element is the sudden check in the sale of Deronda and there can be no doubt that we have made a mistake in printing 2000 of the 21/ edition, but where there is so much to congratulate ourselves upon such a mishap counts for little. There will be a rally in Deronda certainly at least when we come to 7/6 form.

The 88 Middlemarch at 21/ and the 3927 at 7/6 are most satisfactory entries. I am delighted also to see that Jubal and the Spanish Gypsy keep up in sale and this will I am sure please Mrs. Lewes.

At the foot of the statement is appended a note of the stock in hand of the edition of the other novels in five volumes, and on this stock the lordship will fall to be paid when sold. You never I think answered what

5. Mrs. Menzies. See [1 November 1874].

I said about the blunder in my letter arranging the terms for this edition ten years ago and I should like to settle that matter in any way you think most just.

I hope the year has begun well with Mrs. Lewes and you and that it may prove a happy one to you in your new abode. Mr. Simpson I am happy to say has got the better of his delicate throat sooner than we had ventured to hope and reappeared here today in full activity.

He joins my nephew and me in every good wish to Mrs. Lewes and you and believe me

always yours truly
(signed) John Blackwood.

G. H. Lewes Esq.

Observe that in the cheque they have written your name Lewis so in endorsing you had better spell it both ways.

STATEMENTS OF SALES DECEMBER 30TH 1876

DANIEL DERONDA

In Books

| On hand per last statement | I | II | III | IV | V | VI | VII | VIII |
|---|---|---|---|---|---|---|---|---|
| | 1214 | 302 | 162 | 204 | 202 | 1200 | | |
| | | 350 | 450 | 400 | 400 | 300 | 7913 | 7913 |
| | 1214 | 652 | 612 | 604 | 602 | 1500 | 7913 | 7913 |

| | *On hand June 1876 and Since printed* | *On hand Dec. 30 1876* | *Presentation copies to Reviews etc.* | *Withdrawn for Binding in Sets* | *25th Book given to Trade* | *Sold* |
|---|---|---|---|---|---|---|
| Book I | 1214 | 611 | 9 | 348 | 10 | 236 |
| II | 652 | 74 | 9 | 348 | 9 | 212 |
| III | 612 | 94 | 9 | 348 | 6 | 155 |
| IV | 604 | 91 | 9 | 348 | 6 | 150 |
| V | 602 | 67 | 13 | 348 | 7 | 167 |
| VI | 1500 | 267 | 16 | 348 | 35 | 834 |
| VII | 7913 | 228 | 121 | 348 | 289 | 6927 |
| VIII | 7913 | 285 | 122 | 348 | 286 | 6872 |
| | 21010 | 1717 | 308 | 2784 | 648 | 15553 |

In 4 Volumes at £2.2.0

| | | |
|---|---|---|
| 348 | Made up from Stock in Books | |
| | 4 | delivered Author |
| | 1 | " Contemporary Review |
| | 40 | Unsold |
| 348 | 303 | Sold. |

In 4 Volumes at £1.1.0

| | | |
|---|---|---|
| 2100 | Copies printed | |
| | 4 delivered Author | |
| | 1 " | Dr. Cox |
| | 1749 On hand | |
| 2100 | 346 Sold | |

MIDDLEMARCH

In 4 Volumes at £1.1.0

| | |
|---|---|
| On hand December 31st 1874 | 140 Copies |
| " " " " 1876 | 52 " |
| Sold | 88 |

In 1 Volume at 7/6

| | |
|---|---|
| On hand December 31st 1875 | 1721 Copies |
| Printed April 24th 1876 | 2100 |
| " November 29th " | 2100 |
| | 5921 |
| On hand December 30th 1876 | 1994 |
| Sold | 3927 |

JUBAL

2nd Edition

| | |
|---|---|
| On hand December 31st 1875 | 633 Copies |
| " " " " 1876 | 375 |
| Sold | 258 |

SPANISH GYPSY

| | | |
|---|---|---|
| On hand December 31st 1875 | 5th Edition | 158 Copies |
| Printed March 31st 1876 | 6th " | 525 " |
| | | 683 |
| On hand December 30th 1876 | | 381 |
| Sold | | 302 |

ROYALTY payable on

| | | | | | | | | | |
|---|---|---|---|---|---|---|---|---|---|
| 15,553 | Books | Daniel Deronda | | | @ | 2/ | 1555 | 6 | |
| 303 | Copies Less 25th Book | " " | 4 Vols. | price 42/ | @ | 16/ | 232 | 16 | |
| 346 | " " " " | " " | 4 " | 21/ | @ | 5/ | 83 | 5 | |
| 88 | " " " " | Middlemarch | 4 " | 21/ | @ | 5/ | 21 | 5 | |
| 3927 | " " " " | " | 1 " | 7/6 | @ | 1/6 | 282 | 15 | |
| 258 | " " " " | Jubal | | | @ | 1/6 | 18 | 12 | |
| 158 | " " " " | Spanish Gypsy 5th Ed. | | | @ | 1/6 | 11 | 8 | |
| 144 | " " " " | " " 6th " | | | @ | 1/6 | 10 | 8 | 6 |
| | | | | | | | 2215 | 15 | 6 |

GEORGE ELIOT'S WORKS CHEAP EDITION 5 VOLS.

Stock on hand December 30th 1876

| | | | |
|---|---|---|---|
| Vol. I | Adam Bede | 611 | Copies |
| II | Mill on the Floss | 1054 | " |
| III | Silas Marner | 803 | " |
| IV | Scenes of Clerical Life | 1472 | " |
| V | Felix Holt | 988 | " |

## GHL TO JOHN BLACKWOOD, LONDON, 13 JANUARY 1877

*MS:* National Library of Scotland. *Hitherto unpublished.*

**The Priory, | 21. North Bank, | Regents Park.**
13 January 77.

My dear Blackwood

With the unusual gleam of sunshine this morning came your gleam of a letter with its checque and statement. The sales—except D.D. at 21/- are indeed very satisfactory—those of the Poems the most gratifying to G.E. The 88 copies of the 4 volume Middlemarch leads one to hope that D.D. will also in time get run off. *Why* the Jews don't come in I don't understand.

There is only one omission I notice in the statement, and that is of the advertisements in D.D.

If I forgot to say anything respecting your blunder in arranging terms for the copyright it was because after your explanation the whole thing passed out of my mind. I had not only interpreted your letter but had *mis*interpreted the figures of the statement of sales.

Apropos of forgets I mean to convict you of forgetting to send me back the Contemporary Review, with Dowden's article as well as of clearing up that story—if it ever *was* cleared up.

We are both tolerably well but troubled in our minds with the prospect of furnishing and moving.

Ever yours
G. H. Lewes.

John Blackwood Esq.

## JOHN BLACKWOOD TO GHL, EDINBURGH, 16 JANUARY 1877

*MS:* National Library of Scotland. *Hitherto unpublished.*

**45, George Street, | Edinburgh.**
January 16/77.

My Dear Lewes

By a curious coincidence the inclosed from Mr. Dowden came by the same post as your pleasant letter. I wish he had sent the paper to me and I wonder he did not after my note.

I thought I had sent back The Contemporary to you but it goes by this post certainly. Simpson had not forgot the Advertiser in Deronda, but had to postpone settlement owing to difficulties with some of the advertisers.[6]

I feel for you both in the troubles of moving and furnishing but I trust the move will be to a pleasant anchorage for life, and I am sure her heart has always been in the country.

I have some experience of furnishing troubles, of late our house having been re-done up. I had staved off this operation for years telling my wife that "her auld *hoose* looked better than mony ane's new" but she stuck at it and trained her visitors to remark on the seediness of the fittings, as to which there was some truth after 20 years' service. We have one visitor at present a stern old Scotch country wife who used to take care of the house at Strathtyrum in winter. From the state of the house here there was nothing for it but to put her into the best spare bed room. She remonstrated vehemently against such grandeur saying "Oo I'll just creep in beside onybody." Worthy Mrs. Hunter is 5 feet 9 at least and fully built to match. The idea of her creeping in beside

6. See 19 March 1877.

any body utterly upset me and if you saw her would make you roar with laughing.

always yours truly
John Blackwood.

## EDWARD DOWDEN TO MESSRS. BLACKWOOD, DUBLIN, 13 JANUARY 1877

*MS:* National Library of Scotland. *Hitherto unpublished.*

Winstead, | Temple Road, Rathmines, | Dublin | January 13. 1877.
Gentlemen,

You may remember that last Autumn I wrote to you about a proposed extension of an article of mine on "George Eliot" in the *Contemporary Review* into a small volume. I wish to let you know that a press of work of various kinds made it impossible for me to carry out my intention, nor can I hope now to find time to do so. But I wrote what would have formed one long chapter of the book—on "Middlemarch and Daniel Deronda." This I disposed of by sending it to *The Contemporary Review* in which it will appear.[7] It was a great satisfaction to me to have an opportunity of saying my say about "Daniel Deronda," which seems to me to move in a higher plane of thought and feeling than any other work of its author. I am

Faithfully yours
Edward Dowden.

Messrs. Blackwood and Sons.

## GE TO JAMES SULLY,[1] LONDON, 19 JANUARY 1877

*Text:* Cross, III, 301.

I don't know that I ever heard anybody use the word "meliorist" [2] except myself. But I begin to think that there is no good invention or discovery that has not been made by more than one person.

7. 29 (February 1877), 348–369. Both essays were reprinted in Dowden's *Studies in Literature 1789–1877,* 1878, pp. 240–310.

1. James Sully (1842–1923), originally destined for the Nonconformist ministry, turned in 1871 to literature and philosophy. He published *Sensation and Intuition: Studies in Psychology and Æsthetics* in 1874, and he reviewed GHL's *Problems of Life and Mind* in the *Examiner,* 10 and 17 July 1875, pp. 773–774, 803–804. He was frequently at the Priory.

2. In *Pessimism; a History and a Criticism,* 1877, p. 399, he writes of the

The only good reason for referring to the "source" would be, that you found it useful for the doctrine of meliorism to cite one unfashionable confessor of it in the face of the fashionable extremes.

## GHL TO MRS. ELMA STUART, LONDON, 23 JANUARY 1877

*MS:* British Museum. *Published:* Stuart, pp. 73–74.

**The Priory, | 21. North Bank, | Regents Park.**
23 January 77.

Dear Elma

*Cook* sends her duty to Mr. Roland and cannot sufficiently thank him for his kind thought of her.

*Elizabeth* [3] ditto, and declares she "will never part with her needle-book."

*Madonna* ditto, with a kiss for her Eau de Cologne, which she *will* part with—to her, or *your,* handkerchief. The violettes are still full of perfume.

*G.H.L.* sends his love to Mrs. Menzies whose cake has her own rare combination of sweetnesses.

But why, dear Elma, when you had pen in hand, refrain from telling us more about yourself? For example what was the history of your *protégé* dog—and his former master? The story deeply interested us—with a sort of shadowy fear lest the man should turn out a bad lot after all.[4] This didn't make your and Mrs. Menzies' conduct a whit less loveable—only in our experience weak brethren are so often vicious brethren, and one gets to repent having spent so much sympathy on them.

The sun has come at last after these weeks of rain. We have got through the bad weather wonderfully. But now the bother of the house, its alterations, and new arrangements with servants etc. are depressing.

Ever your loving
G. H. L.

term Meliorism, "for which I am indebted to our first living woman-writer and thinker, George Eliot." By it he means not merely the power of lessening evil but also the ability to increase the amount of positive good. The first use of the word cited in the *OED* is in 1858 from John Brown, *Horae Subsecivae,* 3 vols., 1858–82, I, 19.

3. Mrs. Dowling was GE's cook and Elizabeth her parlor maid.

4. In his note about Mrs. W——, the English woman who left her dog to his mother, Roland Stuart says: "I may add that there was a husband—a poor weak creature—who was also very substantially helped by my mother and cousin." (p. 70.)

## GE TO JOHN BLACKWOOD, LONDON, 30 JANUARY 1877

*MS:* National Library of Scotland. *Mostly published:* Cross, III, 301–303.

**The Priory, | 21. North Bank, | Regents Park.**
January 30. 77.

My dear Mr. Blackwood

Now that you are untethered from next month's Maga, I am not too merciful to write to you on business.

What are we to do about 'Romola'? It ought to range with the cheap edition of my books—which, exceptis excipiendis, is a beautiful edition —as well as with any handsomer series which the world's affairs may encourage us to publish. And this edition is sufficiently distinguished from the 2/6 form which Smith and Elder have chosen. Also, I find that 'Romola' will make a volume about 50 pp. thicker than 'The Mill,' which is a sheet or so thicker than 'Adam'—and hence the volume ought to be priced rather higher. The only difficulty lies in the illustrations required for uniformity. The illustrations in the other volumes are, as Mr. Lewes says, not queerer than those which amuse us in Scott and Miss Austin [sic]—with one exception, namely, *that* where Adam is making love to Dinah, which really enrages me with its unctuousness. I would gladly pay something to be rid of it. The next worst is that of Adam in the wood with Arthur Donnithorne. The rest are endurable to a mind well accustomed to resignation. And the vignettes on the title-pages are charming. But if an illustrator is wanted, I know one whose work is exquisite—Mrs. Allingham.

This is not a moment for new ventures, but it will take some time to prepare 'Romola.' I should like to see proofs, feeling bound to take care of my text. And I have lately been glancing into a book on Italian things where almost every citation I alighted on was incorrectly printed. Mr. Simpson must, I think, have mistaken the intention for the act when he imagined that he had asked me for corrections of 'Daniel Deronda,' which it grieves me sorely to think of as uncorrected even in its melancholy repose.

I have just read through the cheap edition of 'Romola,' and though I have only made a few alterations of an unimportant kind—the printing being unusually correct—it would be well for me to send this copy to be printed from. I think it must be nearly ten years since I read the book before, but there is no book of mine about which I more thoroughly feel that I could swear by every sentence as having been written with my best blood, such as it is, and with the most ardent care for veracity of which my nature is capable. It has made me often sob with a sort of painful joy as I have read the sentences which had faded from my memory. This helps one to bear false representations with patience, for I really don't love any gentleman who undertakes to state my opinions, well enough to desire that I should find myself all wrong in order to justify his statement.

I wish, whenever it is expedient, to add "The Lifted Veil" and "Brother Jacob," and so fatten the volume containing "Silas Marner," which would thus become about 100 pp. thicker.

Will you kindly think and consult over these matters and let me know when you have come to any clear result?

Always yours truly
M. E. Lewes.

## GHL TO EDWARD DOWDEN, LONDON, [FEBRUARY 1877]

*Text:* Maggs Brothers Catalogue 328 (July–August 1914), item 1956.

She has been pained to find many dear friends and some of her most *devoted* readers, utterly dead to all the Jewish part. The phrase uttered to one lady which was reported to me, 'I never *did* like the Jews and I never shall,' expresses pretty plainly the general state of feeling. That Jews are human beings, and as such are of some interest, and that the race has played a great part in the world, have no avail against this prejudice. . . .

Had not learned Jews and impassioned Jewesses written to her from Germany, Poland, France, as well as England and America, assuring her that she had really touched and set vibrating a deep chord, Mrs. Lewes would have been very despondent; for it is in vain that she abstains from reading what is written about her; there is always enough reaching her by indirect routes to tell her how her purpose has been misunderstood or has met with indifference.

The deep insight, and that upon which all might is founded, the sympathy, expressed in your article has therefore been peculiarly grateful both to her and me. . . . Caring supremely as I do for the criticism which is culture, and detesting the knowingness and cuckoo iteration which passes for criticism, I rejoiced in your article as a type of the way in which alone great writers should be treated. . . . We only see what interests us, and we have only insight in proportion to our sympathy. Now both these fundamental principles are forgotten by critics who ask, 'Who can be expected to feel interest in the Jews?'—'Who can believe in such a prig as Deronda?'—'Mordecai is a Shadow,' etc. . . . Your defence of the stupidity about scientific pedantry was especially called for . . . because the reproach is singularly unjust as applied to George Eliot, whose sins certainly do not contain Parade among them. . . . Those who know the Greek poets recognize in a thousand subtle indications her familiarity with them,[5] but where—except in the 'Clerical Scenes'—in a passage intended as a blind[6]—are the Greeks? And so of the rest. . . .

When you were writing about Shakespeare so finely, you had the whole world to back you, and the sympathetic attitude was de rigueur.

## GE TO JOHN WALTER CROSS, LONDON, [3 FEBRUARY 1877]

*MS:* Yale. *Hitherto unpublished.*

Saturday.

Dearest Nephew

When I say that I am delighted with the delicate azalias and deep pansies (pensées) I am showing myself a very greedy person. Ought I to be glad that so much falls to my share? I fear the only excuse for my having these flower-feasts would be that I was lame with lumbago[7]—whereas I am nearly well today and have been enjoying a long drive and walk in the milder air.

Much love to all from

Your affectionate Aunt
M. E. Lewes.

5. For the best account of GE's knowledge of Greek and Latin see a valuable series of articles [by Vernon Rendall] "George Eliot and the Classics," in *Notes and Queries,* 142 (13 and 27 December 1947), 544–546, 564–565; 143 (3 April 1948), 148–149; and 143 (26 June 1948), 272–274. He finds GE "a capable classical scholar."

6. See 2 November 1860.

7. "Polly had lumbago and I went to Concert alone." (GHL Diary, 27 January 1877.)

## GE TO MRS. ELMA STUART, LONDON, 5 FEBRUARY 1877

*MS:* British Museum. *Published:* Stuart, pp. 75–77.

**The Priory, | 21. North Bank, | Regents Park.**
February 5. 77.

Dearest Elma

I think I should not tell you that Mr. Lewes is ill with a severe attack of rheumatism in the left leg, if it were not that we long for you to know how precious your *beautiful Highland stick* is to us now that his dear legs will not carry him along even for a few steps without its help.[8]

But what immediately urges me not to delay writing you just a few lines is your having told us that you have been troubled in mind by that article of W. H. Mallock's in the Contemp. Rev.[9]—an article which I must think unworthy of the respect implied in your perturbation. Only turn to the page (I think, 182) where he writes of virtue being rendered void and needless by perfect government, and your strong sense will surely guide you into further criticism of a writer who can vent such nonsense as the supposition that a perfect government can arise or be sustained through any other means than the growing virtues of mankind—and who moreover throughout his article rests on the conception that apart from two doctrines there is nothing in the constitution of things to produce, to favour, or to demand a course of action called right. What kind of God can he boast himself to believe in, on that basis?—I hope I do no injustice to his writing, which I have no time to give any particular attention to. And I wish

8. GHL Diary, 22 January 1877: "Violent attack of Rheumatism in left leg prevented my getting up till 12. Then after *very* hot bath managed to come down to read papers." He took another hot bath that evening and slept in a shawl. Next day the rheumatism was gone and he walked in the Park. 31 January: "Headache not gone, but nevertheless accompanied Polly and Mr. Hoole to Witley. On the way severe pains in the leg caused me to return home, leaving her to go with Mr. Hoole. Hot bath and bed. Rheumatic pain." Sunday, 4 February: "Rheumatic Gout all the week. Came down this morning and corrected proofs, but after lunch pains came on and continued all day." He bore up, playing host to 20 visitors; but the next four days were spent in bed.

9. "Modern Atheism: Its Attitude towards Morality," 29 (January 1877), 169–186. In Mill's Utopia "all the useful functions of virtue, which it shares in common with far-sighted vice, will be secured completely by a perfect government or by some other means. How then . . . could the Socrates in the Utopia make out that he was objectively better off than the pig?" (p. 182.)

I could say more to help you than my present troubled distraction of mind will let me. I can only suggest to you that you should put the words 'cleanliness' and 'uncleanliness' for 'virtue' and 'vice,' and consider fully how you have come not only to regard cleanliness as a duty, but to shudder at uncleanliness; and what are the doctrines which, if taken from you, would make you at once sink into uncleanly habits yourself, and think it indifferent to the health of mankind whether such a habit as that of cleanliness existed in the world or not.

This analogy is <very> imperfect, but its very imperfection will serve to throw the more light on the wide-spreading roots of social and personal good.

No more at present from your sadly troubled but always loving

Mother.

## JOHN BLACKWOOD TO GE, EDINBURGH, 8 FEBRUARY 1877

*MS:* National Library of Scotland. *Hitherto unpublished.*

**45, George Street, | Edinburgh.**
February 8/77.

My Dear Mrs. Lewes

I should have answered your very interesting letter sooner had I not been very busy and also rather unwell, two things which do not suit each other. The last few fine days however have made me much better and we have had a talk here over the Novels.

I most cordially agree with you as to including Romola in the uniform cheap edition of your Works. Smith and Elder's 2/6 edition, which I suppose they are entitled to go on with, will doubtless interfere with the sale, but we must hope the handsome uniform edition will hold its own.

Seeing that there is this cheaper edition and that it would be a little confusing to have Romola 4/ while Adam Bede and the Mill were 3/6 I doubt about going beyond latter price, and perhaps it will be better to meet the difference in thickness partially by putting a little more into the page of Romola which the public would hardly perceive. As to illustrations we are of one mind, and if Mrs. Allingham can satisfy you let us try her. Will you or Lewes speak to her on the subject? Bear in mind that the book will not bear much expense in that way, and I think we should not attempt more than two or three illustrations to Romola.

The two illustrations you justly denounce in Adam shall be burked in future <editions> reprints. Silas Marner is such a perfect thing that I incline to keep it a small volume by itself and rather to make the Lifted Veil and Brother Jacob another thin volume.[1] What you say of reading Romola after an interval of ten years is very striking and adds another proof to many I have seen that your books are the permanent work of your heart and will be permanent in the heart of the world. I had a remarkable instance of this in a letter this morning from my dear old friend Mr. Brown, who has so long been chief reader and corrector of press with us and whom I think I introduced to Lewes when he was in Edinburgh. He came into my father's house when he was a boy and has been with us all these <45> 47 years and is now about 60 or 61 years old. I am in great grief about him as for many months he has been confined to the house by a most painful illness which threatens to prove chronic in the stomach. It is most touching to see how the true gentle nature of the man comes out in his illness and I have seen him many a time much more impatient and complaining over a printer's blunder than he is in the midst of all his sufferings. It seems a relief to him to write a long letter to Mr. Simpson or some of us here every morning and the following is [an] extract from his letter today which will I am sure affect you. Speaking of a Novel he had been reading he says "George Eliot's I don't rank as Novels but as second Bibles. I think I never enjoyed anything so much. You never think or feel you are reading fiction, but biography told with the most exquisite simplicity, and biography of people into whose minds and hearts you can enter with the intensest sympathy. Such books are worth nine tenths of the Sermons ever preached or published and they must be dull both in mind and soul who can read them without feeling the better for them." I quite agree with him.

always yours truly  
John Blackwood.

1. GE's preference eventually prevailed; the Cabinet edition published the three stories together.

## GE TO WILLIAM ALLINGHAM, LONDON, 13 FEBRUARY 1877

*MS:* Yale. *Published: Letters to William Allingham,* ed. H. Allingham and E. Baumer Williams, 1911, pp. 177–178.

**The Priory, | 21. North Bank, | Regents Park.**
February 13. 77.

Dear Mr. Allingham

I don't know how far Mrs. Allingham may be able to think of business just now, so I address you on a subject which directly concerns her, that you may communicate or reserve it according to circumstances.

Mr. Blackwood is going to include 'Romola' in the cheap edition of my books (Smith and Elder having only the right to continue its publication in the one *format* which they have finally chosen), and as that edition has unhappily made for itself the precedent of 'illustrations' it is needful to get for 'Romola' two drawings from the story and a vignette for the title-page, in correspondence with the other volumes.

I mentioned to Mr. Blackwood my wish that, if it were possible, the desired drawings should be executed by Mrs. Allingham, and he has asked me to ascertain for him whether she can consent to undertake this minor work and also whether her professional charges would come within the publisher's economical calculations for a 3/6 book.

If Mrs. Allingham wished to avoid the subjects chosen by Mr. Leighton, I trust that it would not be impossible to find two additional scenes sufficiently pictorial. Miss Martineau [2] I believe made a pretty thing out of Romola finding little Lillo on the sunshiny pavement. But her picture was not memorable enough to make a reason against repeating the subject.

However, on all these points Mrs. Allingham is the only proper judge, if she chooses to trouble herself about the matter. There is no immediate hurry for the drawings, as the book has to be printed.

We are full of sympathy with you under that exasperating affair of the 'Echo.' [3] It is certainly worse to have letters forged for one than opinions. But this latter injury happens to people every week. The

2. Edith Martineau, A.R.W.S.

3. "A vulgar letter, purporting to be by Allingham, had appeared in the *Echo,* and proofs of it had been posted to many of Allingham's friends. Their acknowledgments to him were the first intimation he had of the stupid and annoying hoax." (p. 178.)

other, I should have thought, might be brought under the head of libel by a sufficiently ingenious judge.

Always yours sincerely
M. E. Lewes.

## GE TO MRS. MARK PATTISON, LONDON, 18–19 FEBRUARY 1877

*MS:* British Museum. *Extracts published:* Sir Charles W. Dilke, *The Book of the Spiritual Life,* 1905, pp. 51–52.

**The Priory, | 21. North Bank, | Regents Park.**
February 18. 77.

My dear Goddaughter

The last three weeks have been educating us into more complete sympathy with your sufferings, for Mr. Lewes has been under a sharp attack of rheumatic gout which has quite lamed him for walking. If you happen to remember how very quick and light his step was by nature, you will imagine something of my acute distress at seeing him unable to put his foot to the ground, and, when he rose from his bed, only able to walk by dint of using two sticks. He is not able yet to take walking exercise out of doors.[4] Oh, how many nights and days you have had of such acute and disabling pain as I have been witnessing for a little while in him! Ever since you came to see me with your white face and lips I have been haunted by the sense that the opportunity had been wanting to me of saying or doing anything that expressed how far I felt with you—felt at least as one who can only imperfectly imagine what she grieves for.

But now your account of yourself is as cheerful as can be in one respect. I mean in the proof it gives that you have kept your mental energy. The loss of that is often the most dreadful part of a bodily suffering which is intermittent. As long as severe pain lasts I don't suppose anybody can care about such loss, but to get up from the rack and find oneself half imbecile—the chief sign of any intellect left being the consciousness that one's intellect is almost gone, is a horrible lot which I have seen a little in quite young sufferers. Let us be thankful that your mind is as vivacious as ever.

What a paradise of country you paint where 'only man is vile.' It made me uncomfortable for a day or two after I read your account of

4. "Tried to walk out, but after about 100 yards cramps came on so had to hobble back again." (GHL Diary, 16 February 1877.)

your rural neighbors, to think that I could find no good reason why your bit of country should be exceptionally unfortunate in its inhabitants. But surely something may be set down to the fact that Grasse is under the same sort of influence from being a place of foreign resort as Switzerland and other regions where strangers get the aspect of lawful prey. Certainly what you tell me of your Southern peasants is sadly unlike what I have learned of the French country people in other parts. And one knows society could not hold together if it were all of such rottenness.

You know quite well how the world is going on here—the Grosvenor gallery built, for one thing, and everybody darkening counsel by words without knowledge [5] on the terrible Eastern question, and the rain only just beginning to cease raining every day. Without wanting to find fault, I cannot help being impressed with the bad figure the Opposition makes with its readiness to impeach and its barrenness of any definite recommendations as to a policy to be pursued. It is piteous to see men talking diffusely and to no purpose about what has been or what ought to have been when the only object of statesmanship should be to find the best course that *can be.*

But we small people have to go on minding our own small affairs, and so we have bought a house in Surrey—in a lovely position—and now are beginning to wish we had not bought it because of the trouble of thinking about it. Mr. Lewes is as disinclined as I am to think much about the outsides of our life. I like others to have pretty things, but I don't like having to procure them for myself, and would rather put up with imperfections of all sorts in my garments and house than go through transactions with tradespeople in the effort after more (or less) perfection. You who have a genius for getting all these things to your mind will hardly understand this contemptible cowardice and laziness.

Our Saturdays had been for three weeks blank of concerts until yesterday, when I saw some unknown face extremely unlike yours, looking frequently over the balcony at me from your wonted place. I wish you could entertain the prospect of being able in future years to take that place again in February. That would mean that you were strong and active again and could defy the climate of damp and gloom.

The Rector told me that your good Madame Morran———I had got so far in my letter yesterday before being called away, and this

5. Cf. Job 38:2.

morning I am kept in bed by the troublesome pain which the doctor declares to be renal.[6] I finish my letter and send it off lest I should get worse.

Farewell. Believe always that I care much to know of your having more ease either of body or of mind.

Your affectionate
M. E. Lewes.

## GHL TO JOHN WALTER CROSS, LONDON, [22 FEBRUARY 1877]

*MS:* Yale. *Hitherto unpublished.*

**The Priory, | 21. North Bank, | Regents Park.**
Thursday.

My dear Nephew

Your loving and suffering aunt—who begs me to say that she was not too subdued by pain to enjoy the sweet perfume of the flowers you sent, and the sweet feeling which moved the sender—is of the opinion that the 2000 £ [7] had better be invested without any risk—so we leave you to choose the most favorable Scotch and English Debentures.

Dr. Clark says there is no sort of doubt that all her late discomfort and present pain arise from the renal calculus. The dear man came up last night after his late dinner and long day's work to see her and this morning Mrs. Clark called and left some fine Scotch oatmeal for gruel. Clark hearing that she wished for Scotch oatmeal exclaimed to think of the hundreds of Scotchmen who if they heard George Eliot wanted oatmeal wouldn't hurry up with sacks of it to her door! And so his wife was the buglewoman of the Scotch corps!

My gout decidedly better and to-day the aunt is in less pain. Altogether it has been a much milder attack than the former ones.

Yours ever
G. H. L.

6. GE was in bed all day but got up to dinner and sat in her study. (GHL Diary, 19 February 1877.)

7. The second half of the payment for *Daniel Deronda*. See 12 July 1876.

## GHL TO JOHN BLACKWOOD, LONDON, [27 FEBRUARY 1877]

*MS:* National Library of Scotland. *Hitherto unpublished.*

**The Priory, | 21. North Bank, | Regents Park.**
Tuesday.

My dear Blackwood

For the last month I have been laid up by an attack of rheumatic gout, and as soon as I began to get about again—though feebly—Mrs. Lewes was laid low by a return of her old malady. She I am happy to say seems decidedly on the mend now, but has had a bad time of it.[8]

In my wearisome seclusion from work and friends I read Dowden's article on Middlemarch and Deronda with intense gratification—it made me regret the contretemps which had prevented his carrying out his idea of a book, and I dare say he might still be induced to resume that idea if you thought fit to nudge his elbow a little.

I also read Romola again with fresh delight. Mrs. Allingham is unable to undertake the illustrations, and we should both prefer the republication without anything more than a frontispiece.

I have been "dallying with the faint surmise" [9] of a new and uniform edition of the works of G.E. to begin with Romola—to continue with Silas Marner—with Brother Jacob and Lifted Veil. Each volume to be six shillings (except Silas—Middlemarch and Deronda)—the type of the present edition would do very well but a larger margin and a new cover, would disguise this. My belief is that the public is always attracted by a novelty—be it only that of the binding!—and that six shillings would be just as freely paid as 2/6 by a great many people. This need not interfere with the cheap edition. The main difficulty is about Deronda. When do you think we ought to issue the 7/6 edition? It would of course be made to range with the edition I speak of.

While Mrs. Henry Wood, Miss Braddon, Wilkie Collins [1] etc. sell their novels at 6/- surely G.E. may expect a public?

8. Friday, 23 February 1877 GE had a visit from Mrs. Burne Jones. "But after dinner while about to take my nap I was alarmed by her violent screams in the drawing room and rushing in found her hysterically screaming and sobbing—*not* from pain but strange and excessive irritation in the kidneys. She quieted and then felt as if she had taken chloroform. As the evening advanced she got better and before bed time became quite chatty." 27 February GHL reports "Polly very much better." The next day "the old pains in kidneys" had returned. (GHL Diary.)

9. *Lycidas,* line 153 reads "false surmise."

1. Ellen Price Wood (1814–1887), author of *East Lynne,* 1861; Mary Elizabeth Braddon (1837–1915), author of *Lady*

I send the corrected Romola by post. With our kindest regards to you and yours believe me

Yours ever
G. H. L.

## GE TO MRS. WILLIAM CROSS, LONDON, 27 FEBRUARY 1877

*MS:* Yale. *Envelope:* Mrs. Cross | Weybridge Heath | Weybridge | S.W. *Postmarks:* LONDON-N.W | C 4 | FE 27 | 77; WEYBRIDGE STATION | A | FE 28 | 77. *Hitherto unpublished.*

**The Priory, | 21. North Bank, | Regents Park.**
February 27. 77.

My dear Mrs. Cross

Oatmeal as the gift of friendship, and taken always mixed with thoughts of the giver, is doubly efficacious. I am really better this morning, and my mind, in performing its 'actions de grâce,' turns first to you—after the dear Doctor, who came on Sunday evening looking worn with work, to give us advice and comfort.

A heartful of thanks for your goodness, including Willie's who took the trouble to bring me the nutritive packet and added the more spiritual cheer of Spring flowers.

Poor Mr. Lewes's headache of Sunday did not get well all yesterday, but this morning he has brightened and been able to rewrite a Preface,[2] which is always a severe *crux* to an author.

You see by my straggling handwriting that I am in need of the tonic which the Doctor promises me as a reward for getting better. It is something of a tonic to hear of other, heavier sufferers getting well and enjoying gruel, as I do—dear Mrs. Hall for example, to whom pray give my affectionate congratulations. A general embrace to the young ones.

Your always loving
M. E. Lewes.

Do you, by chance, want a highly recommended Parlour Maid or Housemaid? I have just heard of one, but am no longer in need, Elizabeth's inauspicious engagement being broken off, and the *status quo* re-established in our domestic affairs.

*Audley's Secret,* 1862; William Wilkie Collins (1824–1889), author of *The Woman in White,* 1860. All three were prolific writers, publishing a new novel almost every year.

2. To *Problems of Life and Mind,* Vol. II, *The Physical Basis of Mind.*

Said servant is warmly recommended by her mistress, with whom she has lived 3½ years, and who only parts with her because she (the mistress) is giving up her establishment. The address of the recommending lady is Mrs. Webber Smith, <22 Berners> [3] 2 Keppel Street, Russell Square. The young woman is willing to take either a housemaid's or parlourmaid's place, but not a combination of the two.

Her mistress says, "I have found her *good* in every respect . . . and am most anxious to find her a comfortable home."

## GE TO WILLIAM ALLINGHAM, LONDON, 8 MARCH 1877

*MS:* Privately owned. *Published:* Cross, III, 303–305.

**The Priory, | 21. North Bank, | Regents Park.**
March 8. 77.

Dear Mr. Allingham

Mr. Lewes feels himself innocent of dialect in general and of Midland d[ialect] in especial. Hence I presume to take your reference on the subject [4] as if it had been addressed to me. I was born and bred in Warwickshire, and heard the Leicestershire, North Staffordshire and Derbyshire dialects during visits made in my childhood and youth.

These last are represented (mildly) in 'Adam Bede.' The Warwickshire talk is broader and has characteristics which it shares with other Mercian districts.

Moreover dialect, like other living things, tends to become mongrel, especially in a central fertile and manufacturing region attractive of migration: and hence the Midland talk presents less interesting relics of elder grammar than the more northerly dialects.

Perhaps unless a poet has a dialect ringing in his ears, so as to shape his metre and rhymes according to it at one jet, it is better to be content with a few suggestive touches, and I fear that the stupid public is not half grateful for studies in dialect beyond such suggestions. I have made a few notes, which may perhaps be not unacceptable to you, in the absence of more accomplished aid.

We hope soon to hear that Mrs. Allingham is as flourishing as Baby.

3. The deleted address is that of the Society for Promoting the Employment of Women.

4. A pencil note signed W.A. says that this refers "to a dialogue in verse 'Old Master Grunsey and Goodman Dodd, Stratford-on-Avon, AD 1597,'" found in Allingham's *Songs, Ballads and Stories*, 1877, pp. 186–190.

Mr. Lewes is pretty well again, and for the last fortnight I have been taking his place as the household invalid.

Yours sincerely
M. E. Lewes.

1. The vowel always a double sound—the y sometimes present, sometimes not: either *aäl* or *yaäl. Hither* not heard except in *C' moother* addressed to horses.

2. *Thou* never heard. In general the 2d pers. sing. not used in W. except occasionally to young members of a family and then always in the form of *thee* i.e. *'ee. Can't* pron. *Cawn't.* For the *emphatic* nominative *Yo,* like the Lancashire. For the accusative *Yer,* without any sound of the r.

3. Not year but 'ear. On the other hand with the usual 'compensation' *head* is pronounced yead.

4. "A gallows little chap as e'er yer see."

5. Heres *to* yer, Maäster. Saäme to yo.

6. Never *V.*

7. The demonstrative *those* never heard among the common people (unless when caught by infection from the parson etc.).

8. *Self* pron. *Sen.*

9. The *f* never heard in *of,* nor the *n* in *in.*

Perhaps, however, these imperfect indications may only determine you to reject all but the faintest signs of dialect in your well-to-do farmers who have been to London.

## GHL DIARY, LONDON, 16 MARCH 1877

*MS:* Yale. *Hitherto unpublished.*

Read over M.S. Walk in Park. We went to an afternoon music party at Leighton's. Joachim, Petre, Piatti, Agnes Zimmermann and Henschel. Very delightful. Many people we knew there. Lady Airlie told me Lady Herbert [5] wished to be introduced to me. Surprised at this inversion of etiquette, I of course expressed myself pleased, and sat beside her during great part of the concert talking of Spain among other things. Talked with Mrs. Erle, Mrs. Locke, Mrs. Benzon, Burne Jones, Lady Blanche Ogilvie,[6] Mrs. Ponsonby, etc. Home at 6.15 and at 8.30 we went to St. James Hall grand concert for the Blind. Orchestra,

5. Gwendolen Ondine Herbert, sister of the Earl of Carnarvon.

6. Henrietta Blanche (b. 1852), eldest daughter of the Earl of Airlie.

Joachim and Petre repeated the duet they played at Leighton's. Beethoven's Symphony in A. Came away after first part.

## JOHN BLACKWOOD TO GHL, EDINBURGH, 19 MARCH 1877

*MS:* National Library of Scotland. *Hitherto unpublished.*

**3 Randolph Crescent**
March 19/77.

My Dear Lewes

You will have been surprised at not hearing sooner from me in reply to your last interesting letter. The fact is that I have been out of sorts and languid and being very much puzzled what to advise about the Novels, I have put off writing from day to day.

I feel that there is too little being made out of those admirable books and we must try something to give a semblance of novelty to a complete edition of George Eliot's Works.

After many talks with Simpson and Willie I think we all point to something very like what you propose viz. a 6/- edition beginning with Romola in the same type as the present edition but printed on larger and finer paper which being adopted with the other volumes would make them like entirely new editions and fully worth 6/- except of course Silas Marner. As long as Middlemarch continues to sell as it is doing it will be advisable to keep it at 7/6 and Deronda the same. These two are so much larger than the other volumes that the difference in price could not reasonably be objected to. Deronda we may I think start at 7/6 in Spring some time. We would propose to cancel the illustrations to the present edition and give in each volume an engraved vignette frontispiece like what we have in Middlemarch. We would continue the 3/6 edition or at all events be guided by circumstances as we found how the two editions worked abreast. The Lifted Veil and Brother Jacob are wonderful Tales but both so desperately painful that I have a scruple in coupling them with Silas. Mrs. Lewes and you however are by far the best judges of this.

The Agent we employed for the Deronda advertiser did not do his work so efficiently as we expected [7] but inclosed I have the pleasure of sending cheque £128-17-3d being the balance to author as per inclosed statement.

7. Beginning with 16 pages, the advertising fell in Book III to 12, then 8, and 4, returning to 8 pages in Book VIII.

I hope Mrs. Lewes and you are both well and getting cheerily through your preparations for moving to the country. I quite look forward to coming to see you in May or June.

For the last day or two I have been keeping to the house owing to cold and general malaise but I hope to be about all right tomorrow.

ever yours truly
John Blackwood.

DANIEL DERONDA ADVERTISER

| | | | | |
|---|---|---|---|---|
| By Amount charged for Advertisements | | | | |
| 1876 Feb. 1 in Book | I | | | 53.14.0 |
| Mar. | " | II | | 56. 8.9 |
| Apl. | " | III | | 44. 3.9 |
| May | " | IV | | 44. 3.9 |
| June | " | V | | 33. 1.9 |
| July | " | VI | | 42.10.9 |
| Aug. | " | VII | | 32.10.6 |
| Sept. | " | VIII | | 37.11.9 |
| | | | | 344. 5.0 |
| Deduct cost of Printing and Paper | | | | 86.10.7 |
| | | | | 257.14.5 |
| To Author's Share one half | | | | 128.17.3 |
| " Commissions to Canvassers paid by Publishers | | | 51.12.10 | |
| " Publisher's Share | | | 77. 4. 4 | 128.17.2 |
| | | | | 257.14.5 |

## GE TO JOHN BLACKWOOD, LONDON, 20 MARCH 1877

*MS:* National Library of Scotland. *Hitherto unpublished.*

**The Priory, | 21. North Bank, | Regents Park.**
March 20. 77.

My dear Mr. Blackwood

We both thank you for your letter of yesterday, enclosing the cheque for the advertisements in Deronda. I am sorry to find that you have been a fellow-sufferer in the matter of health. I am only just clambering out of a Slough of Despond where I have been feebly struggling for the last three weeks and more, since Mr. Lewes recovered from his sharp touch of rheumatic gout and left me time to think that I was ailing. We are likely still to be in town when you come, for we shall hardly be able to leave till the beginning of June, and for this Summer we shall only make a sort of bivouac in our Surrey house, only putting absolutely necessary things in it, so that we may test its conveniences and inconveniences and have all the needful alterations and the more troublesome cleansings set about after we leave it for the winter. We have made up our minds not to give up our London shell till we have made more complete experiments as to the conditions of life at Witley.

About a more expensive edition of my books, I one day mentioned a plan which Mr. Lewes wants me to tell you of. I was enjoying the fine octavo page of an edition of Fielding which we possess, when it occurred to me that I should like my own books to be published in *eight* volumes of like size with fine type and paper: the six long novels making each a volume, a *seventh* being made by the Scenes of Cl[erical] Life, Silas Marner, the Lifted Veil and Brother Jacob, and the *eighth* by the Spanish Gypsy and the Poems. I don't know how this would do financially. There is a difficulty in adjusting prices. Mr. Lewes thinks that each volume should not cost more than 7/6 (I had been thinking of 10/), and the Sp[anish] Gypsy is already 7/6, the volume of Poems 6/. There would be the advantage of a wider difference between the two editions, the one for purchasers with little money, the other for people who are amateurs of handsome volumes and can afford to pay for them. The suggestion is only an item to be added in the further discussion between you and other experts. I speak as that crudest of judges, an author.

We cannot enter into your objection to coupling the cheerful story with sadder aspects of human experience, the cheerfulness in the one mitigating the impression of sadness from the other which might be too strongly felt in separate publication.

I hope that you will come up in May—that the sun will shine cheerily enough to tempt you away from Edinburgh and keep you here till we have flitted, so that we may see you both in town and country.

We have been reading Miss Martineau's autobiography,[8] which is pathetic and interesting throughout the childhood and early youth. But afterwards when she has to tell about her writings and what others said and did concerning them, the impression on me was one of shuddering vexation with myself that I had ever said a word to anybody about either compliments or injuries in relation to my own doings. But

8. *Harriet Martineau's Autobiography. With Memorials by Maria Weston Chapman,* 3 vols., published by Smith, Elder and Co. 1 March 1877.

assuredly I shall not write such things down to be published after my death.

Always yours truly
M. E. Lewes.

## GE TO MRS. CHARLES BRAY, LONDON, 20 MARCH 1877

*MS:* Yale. *Extracts published:* Cross, III, 305–306.

**The Priory, | 21. North Bank, | Regents Park.**
March 20. 77.

My dear Cara

Your letter on the breakfast table was just what I had long been wishing for, and I had not earned the good by writing to you only because I had rather dolorous news to tell of ourselves. At the beginning of February Mr. Lewes was seized with rheumatic gout, and for some time was either not able to leave his bed or else only able to move by the help of two sticks. Imagine my anguish in sight both of that present and the possible future—for him whose light quick step has always been unlike every other to my ear. But at the end of three weeks he could get along without a stick and now he walks as well as ever. I was not well before his attack came, but of course I forgot all about my back-ache in running and carrying, standing and lifting, as a nurse must do—and I suppose all this was the worst possible regimen for my body, so that as soon as my patient got well, I broke down with my old ailment which only began to mend greatly four or five days ago. However, I am able now to take a walk as well as a drive, and to sit through a long concert,[9] and unless I have a relapse into evil conditions I hope soon to be no weaker than usual.

Your good news really helps the cure. The relief to dear Mr. Bray's bodily suffering is the foremost good, but next to that I rejoice in your getting freedom from the greater part of the monetary anxieties which have worried you. I think Mr. Bray's mind will be much the easier, and this is so important when all one's energy is demanded to bear pain of body that I can't help longing for the sale of the Sydenham house too,

9. GHL's Diary shows that they attended Saturday Pop concerts at St. James's Hall 3, 10, 17, and 24 March, a concert for the blind 16 March, and a performance of Beethoven's posthumous quartets 21 March.

seeing that Mrs. Winnall[1] might be provided with another by the help of her parents.

Please give my tender love to Sarah [*sic*] and tell her that the years make the memory of her always dearer to me. I grieve to think of this liability to bronchitis which I feel sure is a greater trial than anything I have known—tearing chest and head at once. One can only long that the spring will be a gentle one and confirm her recovery.

You must read Harriet Martineau's Autobiography. While I was ill Mr. Lewes took my office of reader and for the most part read the first two volumes to me. The account of her childhood and early youth is most pathetic and interesting, but <like> as in all books of the kind the charm departs as the life advances, and the writer has to tell of her own triumphs. One regrets continually that she felt it necessary not only to tell of her intercourse with many more or less distinguished persons—which would have been quite pleasant to everybody—but also to pronounce upon their entire merits and demerits, especially when, if she had died as soon [as] she expected, these persons would nearly all have been living to read her gratuitous rudenesses. But I rejoiced profoundly in the conquest of right feeling which determined her to leave the great, sad breach with her once beloved brother in almost total silence, and as I did not read Mrs. Chapman's volume (Mr. Lewes having glanced through it and told me that it was worthless) I was feeling hardly anything about the book but satisfaction in the picture of a life which was on the whole thoroughly virtuous, beneficent and dignified, until I found (what Mr. Lewes had not observed) that this wretched Mrs. Chapman has been so forsaken of all the good as to enter into details and accusations connected with that very quarrelling which Harriet Martineau had willed to bury in silence. Really there is nothing but imbecility to be pleaded as a reason why Mrs. Chapman's conduct should not be called wicked. Then again, she has published H.M's private letters—at the end of the very book which begins with a solemn protest against any such publication!

Browning observed to me that Miss Martineau's procedure in demanding back her own letters, made it the more reprehensible for her to enter into statements about her relations with others, because her own letters being destroyed there remained no evidence to check her statements. And one cannot help being convinced that her representations are often false, not from any untruthfulness in her but from the extremely self-satisfied point of view with which she regarded her

1. Mrs. Bray's niece, who was occupying Charleston Villa at Sydenham.

transactions with business acquaintances and her intercourse with friends.

Still, in spite of Mrs. Chapman, I hope the book will do more good than harm. Many of the most interesting little stories in it about herself and others she had told me (and Mr. Atkinson) when I was staying with her, almost in the very same words. But they were all the better for being told in her silvery voice. She was a charming talker, and a perfect lady in her manners as a hostess. It is a comfort to think—looking back on the vile treatment she received from the Quarterly and Frazers, making people believe that she was a coarse-minded, repulsive woman [2]—that such blackguardism in print could not be tolerated now, and that it would hardly enter into anybody's mind to conceive such sentences for any form of outward utterance.

I do hope that Rufa is coming home to some years of settled domestic enjoyment, now that her chief anxiety about Frank is removed. If you write to her again will you ask her to remember that we always think of her and Mr. Call with affection and hope to see them before we go into the country. That will not be till June. And we are only going to bivouac in our Surrey home for a few months, to try what alterations are necessary. We shall come back to this corner in the Autumn. [*3 words deleted.*] We don't think of giving up London altogether at present—but we may have to give up life before we come to any decision on that minor point.

Your loving
Marian.

## GHL TO MRS. WILLIAM CROSS, LONDON, [20 MARCH 1877]

*MS:* Yale. *Hitherto unpublished.*

**The Priory, | 21. North Bank, | Regents Park.**
Tuesday.

Dear Friend

Knowing how you sympathize with me and rejoice in any pleasing tribute to Madonna I send you the North American Review which contains a review of D.D.[3] I consider it one of the very best that has appeared. When you have all done with it Johnnie or Emily may bring it back, as I shall keep it.

2. The most notorious attack appeared in the *Quarterly Review,* April 1833.

3. "Daniel Deronda," *North American Review,* 124 (January 1877), 31–52 was by E. P. Whipple.

She is slowly mending, but only slowly. Dr. Clark has kindly instructed me in his methods of examination[4] and every morning I set to work and keep him informed of any variation in her state.

Is Gwen[5] perfect? and are your grandmaternal joys sufficient by their warmth to keep out this cold? Kiss that small person for us—and the mother, too, who did *not* appear on Sunday as she was expected. And the other small person, how is she? and *her* mother?—Hall gives no sign of her or himself—but we don't attribute it to any *bad* motive!

We are going to the Beethoven quartetts tomorrow afternoon, to Millais's and the concert on Friday evening, and Saturday concert again[6]—so you see our stony troubles don't confine us to the house. Yesterday she took her first walk. Love to all

Ever your loving
G. H. L.

## GE TO MRS. ELMA STUART, LONDON, 23 MARCH 1877

*MS:* British Museum. *Published:* Stuart, pp. 77–79.

**The Priory, | 21. North Bank, | Regents Park.**
March 23. 77.

Dearest Elma

Your sweet filial letter came as dew on the withered herb last night. Before I tell you of sufferings, understand that they have nearly passed away. You see, I am able to write to you, instead of employing Elizabeth, whose pen would ill represent that power of 'fine language' which is displayed in her speech.

The dear Husband has been trotting about with his usual lightness for the last three weeks, and it is I who have been playing the part of invalid for that length of time. The fact was that I had taken cold and had already felt a troublesome weakness of back before Mr. Lewes's attack came on, and the excitement of attending to him, while it hindered me from taking account of my own ailments, also made me run about, lift, and carry perhaps more than was necessary. So when

4. See GHL Diary, 4 March 1877.

5. Gwendolen Otter, b. 1876. The "other small person" is probably Elizabeth Lucy Hall (b. 5 February 1877.)

6. "Beethoven's Posthumous quartetts. Henschel sang In questa tomba, the Busslied, and two other songs of Beethoven—grandly." (GHL Diary, 21 March 1877). The evening concert Friday at the Academy of Music offered quintets by Beethoven and Schubert and a sextet by Brahms. After noting the Saturday Pop GHL adds: "The last of the concerts."

he got better I found myself ill with what Dr. A. Clarke declares to be the old trouble of the renal sort. However, after being a dolorous object to look at and exceedingly unpleasant to myself for a long while, I am now able to walk, and to sit through long concerts, and, in general, to return nearly to my old use and wont.

I am ready to be angry with you for not writing us long letters about yourself. You keep us sadly starved of knowledge about you. Do you forget that we are greedy of letters from our loved ones, and only object to writing in return?

Make up for the past silence by sending us as much pretty gossip about your life as you can call to mind. Are you coming northward by and by? And how is your health? And are you contemplating any change for Roly in the way of further schooling?

Yesterday came the last proof of Mr. Lewes's new volume, which is thus off his mind, leaving him at leisure—to feel how nipping the spring is! These frosts which we should have welcomed at Christmas come now as a threat. All things else are happy with us. Elizabeth, who was going to be married, has given up her unworthy suitor, and we are not any longer expecting domestic disturbance.

Please ask Mrs. Menzies to accept my affectionate remembrances and believe in me always—with or without proofs—as

Your loving
Mother.

## GHL TO RICHARD LIEBREICH, LONDON, [26 MARCH 1877]

*MS:* Yale. *Hitherto unpublished.*

**The Priory, | 21. North Bank, | Regents Park.**
Monday.

My dear Liebreich

On Good Friday Evening Alfred Tennyson is coming to read some of his poems.[7] I don't know whether you and Mrs. Liebreich would enjoy such a reading, but if you would, we shall be so happy to have you among the half dozen chosen. Reading begins at 9.30.

Yours ever
G. H. Lewes.

7. GHL met Tennyson and his son Hallam in the Park and had a long walk with them 24 March. The next day, Sunday, Tennyson and both his sons called at the Priory, and Monday, 26 March GHL lunched with them. The reading was agreed upon for 30 March. (GHL Diary.)

## JOHN BLACKWOOD TO GE, EDINBURGH, 27 MARCH 1877

*MS:* National Library of Scotland. *Hitherto unpublished.*

**45, George Street, | Edinburgh.**
March 27/77.

My Dear Mrs. Lewes

Thanks for your pleasant letter and I hope the improved health which had begun when you wrote has gone on with you both in spite of the weather, which with us at least is bad as ever.

We all here incline for an edition of your works in goodly octavo. Can you refer us to the edition of Fielding you possess or send down a volume to guide us? It is difficult to get novels of length such as yours into one volume octavo at once portable and with an open readable page. I would be inclined to go in for 10/- volumes if we fix upon 8vo but uniformity in price would not be necessary.

Pretty early in May I certainly expect to be in London and I am very glad to hear that you are still to retain The Priory. You are quite right to feel your way before finally settling in the Country. I am going for a few days change to North Berwick and my wife and children go with me. The weather is most uninviting but as it has rained steadily for four days we are hopeful and as N. Berwick is only 20 miles off we can easily come back. It is a pretty country and there is a *Golfing Links.*

I am afraid you will think the Magazine review of Miss Martineau [8] too severe but in the main I think it is right. The paper on the French army [1] I have every reason to think as authentic and accurate as such things can be and you will be glad to see that France seems fit for self defence. It is a fearful comment upon all the talk about peace and goodwill among men to see France and Germany more than ever like two great armed camps watching each other.

We lost our good old Mr. Brown about ten days ago. At the last he only suffered from total prostration of strength. My nephew and Mr. Simpson are both well and join me in best regards to Lewes and you.

always yours truly
John Blackwood.

8. "Harriet Martineau," *Blackwood's,* 121 (April 1877), 472–496. It was by Mrs. Oliphant.

1. "The French Army in 1877," pp. 391–409, was written by F. Marshall assisted by M. Le Faure of the *Journal de France.* (Author's Book, NLS.)

## GHL TO MME EUGÈNE BODICHON, LONDON, [28 MARCH 1877]

*MS:* Mr. Philip Leigh-Smith. *Address:* Madame Bodichon | 5 Blandford Square | N.W. *Postmark:* ST. JOHNS WOOD N.W | A 2 | M 28. *Hitherto unpublished.*

The Priory.

Good Friday Evening is fixed for the reading—begins at 8.30. Il y aura salle pleine, aussi il faut se faire belle!

G. H. L.

## GE TO JOHN BLACKWOOD, LONDON, 29 MARCH 1877

*MS:* National Library of Scotland. *Hitherto unpublished.*

**The Priory, | 21. North Bank, | Regents Park.**
March 29. 77.

My dear Mr. Blackwood

Our edition of Fielding is dated 1871 and is fathered or godfathered by Bickers and Son and H. Sotheran and Co. It consists of eleven volumes, two of which are taken up by Tom Jones, and the eleventh is a very thin one.[2]

Before your letter arrived I was going to tell you of a small experience which had shaken my admiration for the 8vo in relation to imaginative works. We went the other day to choose a complete edition of Tennyson—rather in a hurry, because the poet was coming to read to us, and we did not possess quite everything he had written. So we turned into Bumpus's where we could have the various editions displayed to us. We asked first for the Library Edition, meaning to be rather grand, but when a volume of it was put into our hands we were disgusted with its weight and unmanageableness and turned with relief to the next size in five volumes, perhaps a trifle larger than your 'Port Royal Logic.' Since then I have been feeling the advantage of your former idea, that our new edition should have the existing type printed on finer, tinted paper, with more margin and with a nice bit of landscape to each volume. And if you think the volumes

2. In the sale of GE's books at Sotheby's, 27 June 1923, item 531 was an edition of "Fielding's Works, with Essay by A. Murphy, edited by J. P. Browne, with Supplement, 11 vol., *portrait, half morocco (rubbed), g.t.,* 1871–2."

need not be all of the same price, or approximately alike in thickness, might not the 2 volumes of poetry be issued in the series? Then there would be a handsome row. To this, however, there may be some obstacle of which I am not sufficiently aware—though, if it were desirable that the actual form of the poems should be continued, I suppose the varying editions might run on together. It would certainly be an advantage to have all the works range perfectly together.

There is no shame in being shilly-shally before any practical step has been taken, and being in committee we shall all do well to consider and reconsider. I don't know that I have any other idea to contribute, except that I think an olive green something like the 'Abode of Snow' would be a good colour to distinguish the new edition from the cheaper, and that to my fancy it does not answer to put the vignette of the title-page in gold on the outside. The little *tondi* on the covers of the 3/6 edition are charming.

The loss of Mr. Brown must make a sad breach for you in the long-valued associations of your life. We are grieving for the loss of a newer but also valued friend—Mrs. Nassau Senior,[3] that fair, bright useful woman whom, I remember, Mr. William Blackwood met at our house one day and accompanied or rather conducted helpfully to some destination, finding en route that she was the daughter of an old friend of your family.

I take an intense interest in foreign politics just now, and shall care much to read the article you mention on the French army. By the way I forgot to tell you of my gratitude to the writer of the article on the House of Commons a month or two ago.[4] It was thoroughly well done. I heard a lawyer who has mounted to the House of Lords say that he found it a dreadfully dull place after the Commons. But the Eastern Question, with Lord Beaconsfield's new presence,[5] made a flash of vivacity a little while ago.

We are very glad that you are coming to town before very long. My health is improving at last, and I am beginning to feel myself more alive. Best regards to Mr. William and to Mr. Simpson, to whose judgment I commend my imperfect notions in relation to saleableness. I hope you will enjoy your Easter holiday at N. Berwick.

Yours always truly
M. E. Lewes.

3. Mrs. Nassau John Senior died 24 March 1877. (*DNB*.)

4. "Inside the House of Commons," *Blackwood's*, 121 (January 1877), 25–46 was by William Forsythe, M.P.

5. Disraeli was created Earl of Beaconsfield 21 August 1876, and became the leader of the House of Lords.

## GHL DIARY, LONDON, 30 MARCH 1877

*MS:* Yale. *Hitherto unpublished.*

Revue Positive. Notes. Walk in Park and drove to Willesden. Had a party to hear *Tennyson read:* Barbara, Charles and Gertrude, Johnnie Mary and Florence Cross, Hall, Burton, Myers, Gurney, Rich[ard] and Norman Grosvenor, Mrs. Benzon and Lilly, Mr. and Mrs. F. Lehmann, Mr. and Mrs. Liebreich, Lewis Morris, Tennyson and Hallam Tennyson, Beesly. It was a great success. Tennyson read 'Maud' and the two 'Northern Farmers.' Broke up at 12.

## GE TO MRS. FREDERICK LEHMANN, LONDON, 2 APRIL 1877

*Text:* R. C. Lehmann, ed., *Memories of Half a Century,* 1908, pp. 145–146.

The Priory, | April 2, 1877.

Dear Friend,

Nina's [6] little paper is full of the best promise. It has the double strength of simple, direct expression, and of observant lovingness.

You remember what old Ben Jonson wished for his perfect woman. Besides 'each softest virtue' she was to have 'a manly soul.' [6a] And I hope we shall see that grander feminine type—at once sweet, strong, large-thoughted—in your Nina. But don't let us tell her all the good we think of her.

I suppose the word 'abrupt' is meant as an admonition by the teacher. But to me, the beginning to say at once what she has to say without the artificiality of an introduction is one of the good signs.

Yours affectionately,
M. E. Lewes.

## JOHN BLACKWOOD TO GHL, EDINBURGH, 4 APRIL 1877

*Text:* Copy in Blackwood Letter Book. *Hitherto unpublished.*

45 George Street | Edinburgh April 4/77.

My Dear Lewes

I am greatly troubled to see by your letter to Simpson that Mrs. Lewes is so unwell and suffering. The weather has changed at last

6. The Frederick Lehmanns' second child, born 1861.

6a. Epigrams, 76, "On Lucy, Countess of Bedford."

today and become quite mild. I sincerely hope that this will help to put her all right and that you will be able to reply to this with good accounts of her. Her pleasant letter last week followed me to North Berwick and came in most agreeably to help the change of air in cheering and doing me good.

My wife, son, and daughter went with me and we had a capital expedition from which I am thankful to say I have come back with health quite restored. North Berwick is a very pretty place with breezes blowing fresh from *Noroway* but I golfed doggedly on and came in daily hungry as a hunter, a sensation I had not experienced for some months. Fresh air and a change are the best of all restoratives.

My room is furnished now with every conceivable form of book for another edition of the Works of George Eliot and we intended to have a sitting on the subject today but Simpson was feeling poorly and had to go home. My thoughts turn very much to a handy handsome edition in 5/ volumes something like the two volume edition of Felix Holt.

Hoping in your next to hear that Mrs. Lewes is better I am

always yours truly

(signed) John Blackwood.

## GE TO MRS. JOHN CASH, LONDON, 10 APRIL 1877

*MS:* Miss Mary Kirby. *Hitherto unpublished.*

**The Priory, | 21. North Bank, | Regents Park.**
April 10. 77.

My dear Mrs. Cash

I thank you sincerely for associating me with an event which is full of the tenderest memories for you and your Brother. Not of grief. For your Father's [7] long and well-filled life seems to me to have been thoroughly cheerful and cheering, and your account of his death shows that the long bright day had such an ending as one would have wished for.

I trust that your silence about the family round your own hearth is a sign of untroubled health and peace. Please thank your Brother for me that he remembers me with friendly interest.

I cannot just now improve upon the news he heard of us from our friends at Barr's Hill, for I am still in a troublesome and fluctuating state of health, and Mr. Lewes, though his activity has returned, is a

7. John Sibree (1795–1877), Minister of the Vicar Lane Chapel in Coventry. See Introduction.

good deal tormented with headache. But we are enjoying our lives nevertheless—which shows that we have less than our share of mortal ills. He remembers you with much pleasure, and is glad to be borne in mind by you in return.

Always, dear Mrs. Cash,

Yours affectionately
M. E. Lewes.

## GHL TO ALEXANDER MAIN, LONDON, 17 APRIL 1877

*Text:* Main's copy owned by Mr. John R. Sprunt. *Hitherto unpublished.*

**The Priory, | 21. North Bank, | Regents Park.**
17 April 77.

My dear Main

The article is very interesting but I have queried one place where there is a défaut de la cuirasse. I hope you will find assimilable food in the volume. The printing has been very tedious.

We have been both invalids. For three weeks I was laid up with rheumatic gout, and no sooner did I get about again than Madonna had another attack of her old enemy—and that is eight weeks ago yet she is not free. We shan't get down into the country before June—if then—the workmen will not have left the house. But I look forward to five months quiet and country air as a restorative for both. I am impatient to begin "Feeling and thought."

If Madonna is well enough we are going at the end of May to Cambridge for a visit. These visits to the universities are always interesting though very fatiguing. When I see Knowles [8]—if I see him—I will mention your paper. We are plotting a symposium for the XIX Cent[ury] "on the dread and dislike of science." [9] Mrs. Lewes sends her kind regards.

Ever yours
G. H. L.

8. James Thomas Knowles (1831–1908), editor of the *Contemporary Review* 1870–77, founded the *Nineteenth Century* in March 1877. He called at the Priory 22 April.

9. GHL's article appeared in the *Fortnightly,* 29 (1 June 1878), 805–815.

## GE TO [MRS. C. T. SIMPSON], LONDON, [APRIL 1876]

*Text: Letters and Recollections of Julius and Mary Mohl,* ed. M. C. M. Simpson, 1887, p. 359.

The Priory, 1877.

But please tell our dear Madame Mohl that I retain a happy memory of her pleasant visit here during her last stay in London, and that I am glad to have some news of her through you. The last I had was from M. Scherer, to whom his wife had sent word that she had found the dear old lady sobbing bitterly in her solitude.[10] That left a sad impression on my mind, and I like to know now that you are added to the other friends of many years who can give her their cheering presence.

M. E. Lewes.

## GHL DIARY, LONDON, 20–25 APRIL 1877

*MS:* Mrs. Carrington Ouvry. *Hitherto unpublished.*

**Friday 20 April 1877**

Cabanis.[1] Notes. Morning concert at F. Lehmann's: Paul Viardot, Hausmann and Henschel played a trio of Schumann. Fraülein Löwe sang and Henschel sang superbly. Sat next to Mrs. Goschen and her daughter and had pleasant chat. Polly's cold got much worse as the day advanced and she went to bed instead of accompanying me to the dinner at Lord Charlemont's.[2] There were present the Marquis of Sligo,[3] Lord Houghton, Lady Barron,[4] Mad. DuQuairo,[5] Mr. and Mrs. Fellows and two other gentlemen. A quiet but very pleasant dinner. Good stories and I had a good innings.

**Saturday 21 April 1877**

Headache from the dinner! Polly's cold very bad. Unable to do anything. Charles called to ask if he might come here for a week while his house was being set in order.

10. Julius Mohl died 4 January 1876.

1. Pierre Jean Georges Cabanis (1757–1808), a follower of Condillac, is often regarded as the founder of modern physiological psychology.

2. Sir James Molyneux Caulfeild, 3rd Earl of Charlemont (1820–92).

3. George John Browne, 3rd Marquis of Sligo (1820–96).

4. Augusta Anne, daughter of Lord Charles Somerset, was the widow of Sir Henry Winston Barron, Bart. (1795–1872), M.P. for Waterford.

5. Mme. Du Quairo lived at 14 Wilton St., Grosvenor Place.

**Sunday 22 April 1877**

Headache contd. Polly worse—sick and headachy. She did not come down. Cabanis.

Johnnie and Eleanor, Charles, Barbara, Miss Greatorex,[6] Miss Rintoul, Alice Helps, Leslie Stephen, Du Maurier, Knowles, Mrs. Orr. Balzac 'Correspondence.' [7]

**Monday 23 April 1877**

Cabanis. Notes. Polly better. Lunched with Tennyson. His sister [8] present who exasperated me by her nonsense and ignorance on Vivisection. Mr. Hoole [9] called about 'The Heights.' Balzac Correspondence. Lubbock 'Origin of Civilization.' [10]

**Tuesday 24 April 1877**

Cabanis. Polly up to breakfast. Notes. Johnnie called to say Mrs. Stewart [1] would buy the Heights if we were disposed to sell. Balzac 'Correspondence.' Lubbock Origin of Civilization. Charles came.

**Wednesday 25 April 1877**

Charles, who is staying with us for a week, breakfasted with me. Cabanis. Notes. Park. Went to the Conversatione at the Royal Society. Talked with Darwin, Tyndall, Harrison, Burden-Sanderson. Home by 11.

## GE TO MRS. EDWARD BURNE-JONES, LONDON, 28 APRIL 1877

*MS:* Yale. *Hitherto unpublished.*

**The Priory, | 21. North Bank, | Regents Park.**
April 28. 77.

Dearest Mignon

To have a loving note from you is the next best thing to seeing you. We both felt it good to have you here [2] in that distant past before I had an attack of Influenza which has stretched out the ten days into a purgatorial period. However, I am better now, and disposed to think

6. Emily Greatorex, a friend of Mme Bodichon.

7. *Correspondence de Honoré de Balzac, 1819–1850,* 2 vols., Paris, 1876.

8. Miss Matilda Tennyson.

9. Elijah Hoole, architect, 30 Russell Square.

10. John Lubbock, *The Origin of Civilisation and the Primitive Condition of Man,* 1870.

1. Perhaps Mrs. Duncan Stewart, whom GHL had met 2 April 1877.

2. "Mr. and Mrs. Burne Jones to dinner." (GHL Diary, 18 April 1877.)

that your troubles with your maidens are the stronger appeal to sympathy.

If the Lindsays [3] had not happened to send us tickets for the private view, we should have been most grateful for those you offer us, but now we are supplied.

I wonder what I ought to have for a morning dress to wear at breakfasts and walk out in on visits at Oxford and Cambridge. I have just had a black silk, of the robe species, such as I humbly trust you would approve, for my dinner dress. But I want something less heavy and dust-showing for the day-time. I like plain silk better than anything, but it is hard to get the right colour. These remarks are to give you a faint idea of my heavy private anxieties—not to urge you into taking the trouble to write me advice.

Our best love to both.

[*Signature cut away.*]

## GHL TO MRS. ELMA STUART, LONDON, 28 APRIL 1877

*MS:* British Museum. *Published:* Stuart, pp. 79–81.

**The Priory, | 21. North Bank, | Regents Park.**
28 April 77.

Dear Elma

How came you to know that the 18th was my birthday? my 60th! I begin to see my 'peau de chagrin' shrivelling at a rapid pace!

Madonna has been getting somewhat the better of her renal trouble, though not yet free from it; but en revanche has had her share of headache, biliousness, and influenza, which prevented her fulfilling one engagement—a dinner with the grandeurs (the dismay of the aristos assembled when no George Eliot was forthcoming!) but has not prevented her hearing a good deal of fine music. On the 15th we dine with the Princess Louise, on the 19th go to Oxford on an annual visit to Jowett, at the end of the month to Cambridge on a visit to the Sidgwicks—and these with 'private views' of Grosvenor Gallery and Royal Academy, and our Sunday receptions will be the final blaze of dissipation before escaping to the peace of Surrey. We shall get there by the beginning of June I hope.

We have Charles staying with us just now. The drains of his house

3. By invitation of Sir Coutts Lindsay Burne-Jones exhibited eight of his pictures at the opening of the Grosvenor Gallery, 30 April 1877.

are being attended to, and Gertrude has carried off the children to the seaside. From Natal we have cheerful accounts.

Lord Lytton knowing my love of good stories has sent me this one. A Bengalee Baboo under examination has this question put: "Who was Mary Stuart? Mention some remarkable incident in her life." *Answer:* "Mary Stuart was a most unfortunate queen of Scotch; who in the seventh year of her pregnancy blew up her husband very severely"!

Àpropos of Mary Stuart, Maddox Brown [4] the painter, notorious for malaprops, said "I don't understand these attempts to whitewash her. I know nothing good of her. She never showed any affection for any one—except for *Boswell* for a few months!"

Madonna sends love and kisses.

Ever yours affectionately
G. H. L.

Give the sweet Mrs. Menzies a kiss for me in answer to her message.

## JOHN BLACKWOOD TO GE, EDINBURGH, 30 APRIL 1877

*MS:* National Library of Scotland. *Hitherto unpublished.*

**45, George Street, | Edinburgh.**
April 30/77.

My Dear Mrs. Lewes

After much puzzling and consideration we have pretty well come to the old conclusion that the handiest and most handsome form for your works will be an edition in 19 or 20 volumes somewhat similar to the 2 volume edition of Adam and Felix. We have been further assisted to this conclusion by looking at a set of your novels which had been bound and cut to as near as might be a uniform size to catch the eye of some of your worshippers here. This set I send to you by rail and I think it will look well in the library or drawing room in Town or country.

This continual North East wind has again made Simpson's throat a little rough and he is keeping to the house for a day or two but the inclosed note and calculations will show you that he is busy as usual. The calculations will assist Lewes and you in coming to a decision. The only other form would be the novels in one volume octavo but it is impossible to make that a handy volume to read by the fireside. You

4. Ford Madox Brown (1821–1893).

will see that Simpson shrinks from making the vols. 5/- but I incline for the five and so does Willie. I expect to reach London by the 10th or so when we can talk over all these matters.

So there is War at last [5] and where it will end none can tell. On coming into the breakfast room the other morning I exclaimed to my daughter "The Russians have crossed the Pruth and entered Jassy. It seems but as yesterday (although 24 years since) that I read these same words in this room, and papa would have gone to the Crimea but he had met Mama and was going to visit some of her friends in Derbyshire." History is repeating itself with a vengeance. It is impossible to say how long we may be able to keep out of the mischief.

This is the Golf Spring meeting week and I am going to St. Andrews for a few days to brace myself for the London campaign. I go en garcon to join some other golfing maniacs in lodgings. I hope this will find Lewes and you well and believe me

always yours truly
John Blackwood.

## GHL TO MME EUGÈNE BODICHON, LONDON, [4 MAY 1877]

*MS:* Mr. Philip Leigh-Smith. *Hitherto unpublished.*

**The Priory, | 21. North Bank, | Regents Park.**
Friday.

Dear Barbara

Fearing that in my medical ignorance I might have spoken too absolutely about Mad. Mario I yesterday went to consult Hughlings Jackson who has made the subject his speciality,[6] and he confirms everything I said and more, for he insists that galvanism or any other local application is quite useless: "There is but one prescription—absolute rest."

In case Mad. Mario MUST write and can't dictate, let her by all means use the left and not the right hand; but rest for the brain is the main point. Urge upon her the fact that a short interval of rest now may save her from a very long forced rest in a little while.

You will have seen what a poor affair the Vivisection discussion ap-

5. Russia declared war on Turkey 24 April 1877.

6. John Hughlings Jackson (1835–1911), a specialist in diseases of the central nervous system, was on the staff of the National Hospital for the Paralysed and Epileptic 1862–1906.

peared in the reports and especially in the "Times" leader of today.[7]

We are preparing for the Private View,[8] and on Monday we go to Guildford to look after furniture. On the 15th we dine with the Princess Louise and on the 18th [9] go to Oxford—so you see our work of dissipation is getting serious, and the peace of Witley will be all the more welcome.

Ever yours affectionately,
G. H. L.

Wagner [1] has arrived and last night his wife sent me a letter of introduction from her father (Liszt) so I go to see her after the Private View and I suppose we shall have them both on Sunday.

## GE TO EDWARD BURNE-JONES, LONDON, 8 MAY 1877

*MS:* Yale. *Hitherto unpublished.*

**The Priory, | 21. North Bank, | Regents Park.**
May 8. 77.

Dear Friend

Is the request I am going to make too great? It is, that I may be allowed to bring to you Madame Wagner at a time when you will be personally at liberty.

She is, I think, a rare person, worthy to see the best things, having her father's (Liszt's) quickness and breadth of comprehension. Monday is the day we have conditionally proposed to ourselves. Can you confirm our plan by your permission? Madame Wagner will lunch with us, and we could drive to you afterwards so as to be with you about three—or later, if this were more convenient to you.

Yours always truly
M. E. Lewes.

7. The *Times,* 4 May 1877, p. 9c–d upheld the existing regulation, regarding Holt's bill to suppress vivisection as fanatical.

8. At the Royal Academy, 4 May 1877. "Many friends and acquaintances." (GHL Diary.)

9. i.e. the 19th.

1. Wilhelm Richard Wagner (1813–83), married in 1870 his 2nd wife Cosima (1837–1930), daughter of Franz Liszt and the Comtesse d'Agoult. She had been divorced by Hans von Bülow in 1869. Liszt's letter arrived 3 May; GHL called on the Wagners the next day, "found her very agreeable; reminds me both of her father and mother. Wagner I only saw for a few minutes." She came to the Priory the following Sunday, and they met almost daily during Wagner's season in London.

## GE TO MRS. PETER ALFRED TAYLOR, LONDON, 10 MAY 1877

*MS:* Parrish Collection, Princeton. *Hitherto unpublished.*

**The Priory, | 21. North Bank, | Regents Park.**
May 10. 77.

Dear Friend

I have to thank you for two kind attentions. First, for the magnificent volume of the 'Memoirs,' [2] a loan which made me feel so responsible that I was anxious to return it as soon as I had looked through it. We left it in the hands of your Concierge last Saturday, and I trust that it is unblemished.

Next, for the Pen and Pencil volume [3] which came yesterday when I had just returned from Guildford and gone to bed ailing from a chill [4] —the frequent result to me of outgoings in our May weather.

How little the views of your Aubrey House give one the idea of the London 'residence' which House agents recommend! I don't wonder at your regrets in parting with it. And the members of your 'Club' must be glad to have a visible memorial of their meetings in that unique home with one of the gentlest of presidents.

Always yours affectionately
M. E. Lewes.

## GE TO MME EUGÈNE BODICHON, LONDON, 15 MAY 1877

*MS:* Mr. Philip Leigh-Smith. *Hitherto unpublished.*

**The Priory, | 21. North Bank, | Regents Park.**
May 15. 77.

Dear Barbara

We will ourselves certainly give £10 towards paying Miss Grüner's [5]

2. Peter Alfred Taylor, *Some Account of the Taylor Family,* 1875.

3. *Auld Lang Syne. Selections from the Papers of the "Pen and Pencil Club,"* printed for private circulation, [London], 1877. The frontispiece shows the Taylors' residence, Aubrey House, Notting Hill, W.

4. GE and GHL went to Guildford to spend the night and look after some furniture for the Heights. During the night "Polly had a return of her renal pain, so we gave up going to Witley and came home; gave her hot bath and got her to bed. Wrote letters and chatted with her." (GHL Diary, 9 May 1877.)

5. Joan Frances Ottilie Grüner (1848–1936) had been at Girton College since 1874. In 1877 she attained the standard of the Ordinary Degree.

expenses, but we have not yet been able to think of anyone else who would do the same.

Pray bring Madame Mario to see us again. But bear in mind that on Sunday the 27th—which probably will be our last Sunday in London—Holmes [6] the violinist is coming to play, with Mrs. Vernon Lushington [7] to accompany him. They are to be here about 4 o'clock, and I beseech you to come in early—between 3 and 4—so as not to disturb any music that may have been begun. For Mr. Holmes is nervous. And don't mention to anyone else that he and Mrs. L. are coming, lest the audience should be larger than he wishes.

Please tell Madame Mario that I have received an interesting parcel of books from Italy, with pretty words of her husband's on his card. I am much pleased to have such a present from her and him.

We are working a little too hard at 'pleasure' just now. This morning we are going for the third time to a Wagner rehearsal, at 10 o'clock.[8]

I could scribble a great deal of gossip to you, but I have another letter to write before we start.

Always your loving
Marian.

## GE TO SARA SOPHIA HENNELL, LONDON, 15 MAY 1877

*MS:* Yale. *Extracts published:* Cross, III, 306–308.

**The Priory, | 21. North Bank, | Regents Park.**
May 15. 77.

Dear Sara

Delightful to have a letter from you once more, and to feel that there is anything you care to say to me!

I have not read, and do not mean to read, Mrs. Chapman's volume,

6. Henry Holmes (1839–1905), brother of the more famous violinist Alfred Holmes (1837–76), who had recently died.

7. Jane, daughter of Francis Mowatt, M.P., was married in 1865 to Vernon Lushington, Q.C. (1832–1912). Neither Mrs. Lushington nor Holmes came 27 May, when the list of 27 visitors is headed by the noted violinist Wilma Maria Norman-Neruda, wife of Charles Hallé. (GHL Diary.) Three letters from GE to Mrs. Lushington, 5, 10, and 23 May 1877, were offered by E. M. Lawson and Co., Sutton Coldfield, Birmingham, Catalogue 117 (January 1938), item 286.

8. At the 1st rehearsal, 11 May 1877 they heard *Walküre* and *Tannhäuser;* GHL sat next to Mme Wagner, and was introduced to Amalie Materna, the soprano, and Carl Haag, the German-born British painter. At the concert the next day GHL again sat next to Mme Wagner, but did not enjoy the music so much: "Effect not so great on us as at rehearsal. The monotony of the recitative seemed greater." *Siegfried* and *Lohengrin* were played at the 2nd rehearsal, 14 May: "Mad. Wagner came back with us to

so that I can judge of it only from report. You seem to me to make a very good case for removing the weight of blame from her shoulders and transferring it to the already burthened back of Harriet Martineau.

But I confess, that the more I think of the book and all connected with it, the more it deepens my repugnance—or rather creates a new repugnance in me—to autobiography, unless it can be so written as to involve neither self-glorification nor impeachment of others. I like that the "He, being dead, yet speaketh," [9] should have quite another meaning than that.

I agree with you in feeling that James Martineau was deplorably in the wrong in writing that article on his Sister.[10] That was a public affair, and I imagine that so far as it has been remembered it has been generally condemned. Probably J.M. himself has condemned it, but one must hesitate to say that 'retraction' was quite practicable and incumbent on him. What his sister thought of his motives was no public concern. [*3 words deleted.*] You must be quite right in your conclusion that she was the causer of her imputation being made public, for the statement that he was from the very beginning of her success continually moved by jealousy and envy towards her must have come readily to her lips, since she made it to a person so far from intimate with her as I was.

But however the blame may be distributed, it remains a grievously pitiable thing to me that man or woman who has cared about a future life in the minds of a coming generation or generations should have deliberately, persistently mingled with that prospect the ignoble desire to perpetuate personal animosities, which can never be rightly judged by those immediately engaged in them. And Harriet Martineau, according to the witness of those well acquainted with facts which she represents in her autobiography, was quite remarkably apt to have a false view of her relations with others. In some cases she gives a ridiculously inaccurate account of the tenor or bearing of correspondence held with her. One would not for a moment want to dwell on the weaknesses of a character on the whole valuable and beneficent, if it were not made needful by the ready harshness with which she has inflicted pain on others.

No! I did not agree with you about Mrs. Stowe and the Byron case

lunch and then accompanied us to Burne Jones's studio. Delightful day." (GHL Diary.)

9. Hebrews 11:4.

10. "Mesmeric Atheism," a review of her *Letters on the Laws of Man's Nature and Development,* written in collaboration with H. G. Atkinson, *Prospective Review,* 7 (1851), 224–262, was easily recognized as the work of her brother James Martineau. For his defence of it see James Drummond, *The Life and Letters of James Martineau,* 2 vols., New York, 1902, I, 222–225.

(though I have good reason to love Mrs. Stowe and think highly of her motives). In my judgment the course she took was socially injurious. I understand by the teaching of my own egoism—and therefore I can sympathize with—any act of self-vindicating or vindictive rage under the immediate infliction of what is felt to be a wrong or injustice. But I have no sympathy with self-vindication or the becoming a proxy in vindication deliberately bought at such a price as that of vitiating revelations—which may even *possibly* be false. To write a cruel letter in a rage is very pardonable—even a letter full of gall and bitterness, meant as a sort of poisoned dagger. We poor mortals can hardly escape these sins of passion. But I have no pity to spare for the rancour that corrects its proofs and revises and lays it by, chuckling with the sense of its future publicity.

Neither have you, I am sure. And I have written those sentences rather superfluously, gliding on from Mrs. Stowe to Harriet Martineau.

Be sure that I never connected any wish of yours with the least bit of such mean egoism as I have been referring to. I think that I have not at all misunderstood any serious communication that you have ever made to me.

We are in a crowd of engagements just now. Best love to all from

Your ever lovingly faithful
Pollian.

## GHL DIARY, LONDON, 15–17 MAY 1877

*MS:* Yale. *Hitherto unpublished.*

**Tuesday 15 May 1877**

Caird.[1] Wagner Rehearsal. Talked with Mad. Wagner, Frau Materna, and Norman Grosvenor, who walked through the Garden with us. After lunch called on Chapman and George Smith. Revue Positive. Brehm, 'Thierleben.' [2]

Dined at the Goschens' [3] to meet the Princess Louise [4] and Marquis of Lorne (at her special request). She was very attentive to Polly who was taken down by John Bright.[5] Instead of asking that Polly should

1. Edward Caird, *A Critical Account of the Philosophy of Kant,* 1877.

2. Alfred Edmund Brehm, *Das Thierleben,* 6 vols., 1864–69.

3. George Joachim Goschen (1831–1907), Liberal statesman, was First Lord of the Admiralty 1871–74.

4. Princess Louise Caroline Alberta, Marchioness of Lorne (1848–1939), Queen Victoria's 4th daughter, the 1st member of the royal family to marry a subject of the sovereign, was interested in higher education for women.

5. John Bright (1811–89).

be presented to her, she asked to be introduced to Polly, and was taken up to her! Admiral Seymour, Capt. Barnaby (just arrived from Khiva) Huxley, Mr. and Mrs. H. Goschen, and Mrs. Hayter formed the rest of the party. I took down Mrs. Hayter. At 11 we left and drove to Mrs. Benzon's Music Party. Henschel sang divinely. Home at 1.

**Wednesday 16 May 1877**

Letter from Eliza. Wrote to her. Walk in Park. The Blackwoods called. Brehm, Das Thierleben. Music.

**Thursday 17 May 1877**

Caird. Philosophy of Kant. Unable to work we went out for a walk. Dined at the Dannreuters [6] with the Wagners—no one else present, until the evening when a small party assembled to hear Wagner read his 'Parzival' which he did with great spirit and like a fine actor. Home at 11.30.

## GE TO MME EUGÈNE BODICHON, LONDON, 16 MAY [1877]

*MS:* Mr. Philip Leigh-Smith. *Address:* Madame Bodichon | Poor House, Zennor | St. Ives | Cornwall. *Postmark:* LONDON-N.W | C I | MY 16 | 77. *Hitherto unpublished.*

P. N.B. May 16.

Several names for the Water-Wagtail current in Italian: Cotremola, Codéta, Ballerina, Monachina, Cutréttola. Probably the commonest are Ballerina and Cutréttola, since they are specified in the ordinary dictionaries. The last, perhaps, would be the one to choose.

M. E. L.

## GHL TO MME EUGÈNE BODICHON, LONDON, [18 MAY 1877]

*MS:* Mr. Philip Leigh-Smith. *Hitherto unpublished.*

Friday.

Dear Barbara

Helas! we shall be at Cambridge on the 31st unless Madonna has a relapse. She is bearing the dissipation very well but the dissipation is great for her. Yesterday [i.e. Tuesday] the dinner at the Goschens'

6. Edward Dannreuther (1844–1905), pianist and writer on Wagner.

was a great success. The Princess Louise had told Mrs. Ponsonby with great glee that she was going to meet us; and showed her pleasure in a very unusual way, for instead of Madonna being presented to her she asked, immediately on arriving, to be presented to Madonna, and at once sat down beside her and entered into friendly chat. After dinner they had a long talk—very agreeable. We went from the Goschens' to a music party and didn't get home till 1. Bright took her down to dinner and charmed her.

Yesterday Wagner read aloud to us his poem of 'Parzival' and this morning we were at the Rehearsal for tomorrow.[7]

We are both in love with Mad. Wagner! We have seen a great deal of her. You remember Nanny said she liked her very much. No such woman has appeared on our horizon for a long time.

Ever your
G. H. L.

## GE TO MME EUGÈNE BODICHON, LONDON, 19 MAY 1877

*MS:* Mr. Philip Leigh-Smith. *Hitherto unpublished.*

**The Priory, | 21. North Bank, | Regents Park.**
May 19. 77.

My dear Barbara

I have been rather annoyed by Mr. Lewes having told me only yesterday that some unpleasantness had arisen between Miss Bernard and the students at Girton about the invitation sent to me.[8] This puts me in rather an unpleasant position, for in accepting the invitation (conditionally), I promised to write to Miss Müller[9] whenever I went to

7. *Tristan und Isolde* was played. "To the Albert Hall at 10:30 for rehearsal. . . . Wagner in an awful rage at one moment. Watched George Eliot's repulsively ugly face." (*Mary Gladstone's Diaries,* ed. Lucy Masterman, 2d ed., [1930], p. 124.)

8. Miss Marianne Frances Bernard (1839?–1906), Mistress of Girton College (1875–84), when she resigned to marry Dr. Peter Wallwork Latham. "With much personal distinction and charm, Miss Bernard had a cool judgment and a manner of austere dignity, which was something of a bar to intimacy with the students, though beneath it there lay a real interest in their welfare." (Barbara Stephen, *Emily Davies and Girton College,* 1927, p. 298.)

9. Frances Henrietta Müller, born in Chile, came to Girton in 1873, "when past girlhood," according to an obituary in the *Times,* 17 January 1906, p. 6d–e. While there she was interested in efforts to establish Women's Trade Unions, and after leaving Girton in 1878 became an active feminist, travelling alone in Eu-

Cambridge, and propose a day and hour for my visit. What am I to do now? We are engaged to go to Mr. Sidgwick's on the 31st. If I don't keep my word to Miss Müller, will she understand that you have communicated the state of the case to me? Or will you write to her and tell her why I remain silent?

Mr. Lewes says that you suggested my calling simply to see the college in the ordinary way, but this affair with Miss Bernard makes me disinclined to appear there at all. All I desire is to be set right with Miss Müller, towards whom I feel in danger of seeming to act very unscrupulously. I am sorry to trouble you, but I can see no way out of the disagreeable position I am in without learning more from you.

We are going to start for Oxford but shall be at home again on Tuesday evening.

Your loving
Marian.

## GHL DIARY, OXFORD, 19–21 MAY 1877

*MS:* Mrs. Carrington Ouvry. *Hitherto unpublished.*

**Saturday 19 May 1877**

Caird. Went on our visit to Jowett at Oxford. Spottiswoode,[1] his wife and her sister, the other guests. Dinner party of 16: Sir C. and Lady Trevelyan,[2] Dean Liddell, Green [3] etc.

**Sunday 20 May 1877**

Sunday called on Henry Smith and Rolleston, at whose house met Prof. Turner,[4] and Lady Richardson.[5] 16 again at dinner—Stubbs,[6] Bradley,[7] Sir C. Trevelyan, Butcher [8] etc.

rope, America, and Asia, living in China and for many years as a native in India, studying the position of women.

1. William Spottiswoode (1825–83), physicist. His wife was the eldest daughter of William Urquhart Arbuthnot.

2. Sir Charles Edward Trevelyan (1807–86). Lady Trevelyan was his 2nd wife Eleanora Anne Campbell, whom he married in 1875.

3. Thomas Hill Green (1836–82), philosopher, said to be the original of Mr. Gray in Mrs. Humphry Ward's *Robert Elsmere.*

4. William Turner (1832–1916), Professor of Anatomy at Edinburgh.

5. Widow of Sir John Richardson (1787–1865), who conducted the expedition in search of Sir John Franklin.

6. William Stubbs (1825–1901), Regius Professor of History at Oxford, 1866–84.

7. George Granville Bradley (1821–1903), Master of University College.

8. Samuel Henry Butcher (1850–1910) migrated to Oxford in 1876 to accept a tutorship at University College.

**Monday 21 May 1877**

After breakfast smoked a cigar and chatted with Mark Pattison. Home by 3. Walk. Read Wilson Fox on Dyspepsia.[9] Henry Taylor's Autobiography.[1] Paget's Hunterian Oration.[2]

Stout elderly lady in a crowded room is accosted with "I fear you can find nothing to sit on?" "It isn't *that*, but I can't find a place for it."

## GE TO WILLIAM ALLINGHAM, LONDON, 21 MAY 1877

*MS:* Yale. *Envelope:* William Allingham Esq | 12 Trafalgar Square | Chelsea | S.W. *Postmark:* ST. JOHN'S-WOOD | MY 22 | 77. *Hitherto unpublished.*

21 North Bank | May 21. 77.

Dear Mr. Allingham

Sincere thanks for your kind remembrance. I shall take the book[3] into the country, where we hope to be in a fortnight.

Before then I trust that I shall hear, perhaps through Barbara, a better account of your dear wife. Always with high regard for her and you,

Yours very sincerely
M. E. Lewes.

## GE TO ALEXANDER MACMILLAN, LONDON, 22 MAY 1877

*MS:* University of Texas. *Hitherto unpublished.*

21 North Bank | May 22. 77.

Dear Mr. Macmillan

May I trouble you to address the enclosed letter to the author of "Betsy Lee"?[4] A letter from him does not make me quite sure of his title or of his locality.

Yours always sincerely
M. E. Lewes.

9. Wilson Fox (1831–87), *On the Diagnosis and Treatment of the Varieties of Dyspepsia,* 1867.

1. Sir Henry Taylor (1800–86), dramatist, whose *Autobiography,* 2 vols., 1885 was privately printed in 1877.

2. Sir James Paget, *The Hunterian Oration Delivered . . . on the 13th of February, 1877,* 1877.

3. *Songs, Ballads and Stories,* 1877. See 8 March 1877.

4. *Betsy Lee: a Fo'c'sle Yarn* by [Thomas Edward Brown] was published by Macmillan in 1873.

## GE TO MRS. MARK PATTISON, LONDON, 25 MAY [1877]

*MS:* British Museum. *Hitherto unpublished.*

**The Priory, | 21. North Bank, | Regents Park.**
May 25.

I too was sorry, dear Figliuolina, because that was my only chance of seeing you this summer.

We leave town on the 31st—for Cambridge in the first instance, but from thence to our country refuge in Surrey.

I was a little comforted about you by hearing from Miss E. Smith that you were really in better bodily condition. But I should have valued the opportunity of a leisurely tête-à-tête.

Yours always affectionately
M. E. Lewes.

## GE TO MRS. ELMA STUART, LONDON, 27 MAY 1877

*MS:* British Museum. *Published:* Stuart, pp. 81–83.

**The Priory, | 21. North Bank, | Regents Park.**
May 27. 77.

Dearest Elma

What other fingers than yours could have put in those myriad stitches slowly growing into apple and cherry blossoms for my sake? I must have known who was the sender of the little packet that came last night even if it had not had your writing on it.

I hope that the lovely flowers on the pale blue were created in spare moments when you were either chatting happily or meditating peacefully, and that you never looked at the petals through gathering tears, unless the tears were of that sort which come from a sense of good too deep for smiles to express. I can imagine various ornamental uses to which the precious square—fair enough for an altar—might be put. But I should like to know what use you had in your mind, and how you have been conceiving its place, so that I may carry out your idea as completely as possible.

On Thursday the 31st we go to Cambridge while our servants will be busy in removing furniture, and from Cambridge we shall pass straight to our Witley home, where we hope to rest in quiet for four or five months. I think we have told you the address, but I repeat it for security—'The Heights, Witley, Surrey.' We are going to camp there experimentally, merely sending down necessaries. For if we like the house and decide to keep it, there is still a great deal of work to be done to it, so that it must in any case have been emptied again. I wish we never had to think of these outside things. The small remainder of our lives seems all too little for the emotions and ideas which are aloof from our own chairs and tables, dinner-service and paper-hangings.

Let us know what you mean to do this summer and whether you think of coming to England. It is too long since we had precise news of you. How is Roland? Our love to him, and wishes that he may be growing in grace and favour with the best judges. Mrs. Menzies' gentle face has doubtless looked benignantly at my apple blossoms, if her fingers have not here and there put in a stitch. Commend us to her kind remembrance. Always, dearest Elma

Your loving Mother (in the spirit)
M. E. Lewes.

## GE TO DAVID KAUFMANN,[5]
## LONDON, 31 MAY 1877

*Text: Athenaeum,* 26 November 1881, p. 703.

The Priory, 21, North Bank, May 31, '77.

My dear Sir,

Hardly, since I became an author, have I had a deeper satisfaction, I may say a more heartfelt joy, than you have given me in your estimate of 'Daniel Deronda.'[6]

I must tell you that it is my rule, very strictly observed, not to read the criticisms on my writings. For years I have found this abstinence necessary to preserve me from that discouragement as an artist which ill-judged praise, no less than ill-judged blame, tends to produce in me. For far worse than any verdict as to the proportion of good and

5. David Kaufmann (1852–99) was educated at the Rabbinerseminar at Breslau, where he also studied at the University. He took his degree at Leipzig in 1874. In 1877 he became a professor at the newly established Jewish Theological Seminary in Budapest. (*Encyclopaedia Judaica.)*

6. "George Eliot und das Judenthum," *Monatschrift für Geschichte der Wissenschaft des Judenthums,* 26 (1877), 172 ff., 214 ff., 255 ff. GHL notes it in his Diary, 28 May 1877.

evil in our work, is the painful impression that we write for a public which has no discernment of good and evil. My husband reads any notices of me that come before him, and reports to me (or else refrains from reporting) the general character of the notice or something in particular which strikes him as showing either an exceptional insight or an obtuseness that is gross enough to be amusing. Very rarely, when he has read a critique of me, he has handed it to me, saying, "*You* must read this." And your estimate of 'Daniel Deronda' made one of these rare instances.

Certainly, if I had been asked to choose *what* should be written about my book and *who* should write it, I should have sketched—well, not anything so good as what you have written, but an article which must be written by a Jew who showed not merely sympathy with the best aspirations of his race, but a remarkable insight into the nature of art and the processes of the artistic mind. Believe me, I should not have cared to devour even ardent praise if it had not come from one who showed the discriminating sensibility, the perfect response to the artist's intention, which must make the fullest, rarest joy to one who works from inward conviction and not in compliance with current fashions. Such a response holds for an author not only what is best in "the life that now is," but the promise of "that which is to come." I mean that the usual approximative, narrow perception of what one has been intending and professedly feeling in one's work, impresses one with the sense that it must be poor perishable stuff without roots to take any lasting hold in the minds of men; while any instance of complete comprehension encourages one to hope that the creative prompting has foreshadowed, and will continue to satisfy, a need in other minds.

Excuse me that I write but imperfectly, and perhaps dimly, what I have felt in reading your article. It has affected me deeply, and though the prejudice and ignorant obtuseness which has met my effort to contribute something to the ennobling of Judaism in the conception of the Christian community and in the consciousness of the Jewish community, has never for a moment made me repent my choice, but rather has been added proof to me that the effort was needed—yet I confess that I had an unsatisfied hunger for certain signs of sympathetic discernment, which you only have given. I may mention as one instance your clear perception of the relation between the presentation of the Jewish element and those of English Social life.

I work under the pressure of small hurries; for we are just moving into the country for the summer, and all things are in a vagrant condition around me. But I wished not to defer answering your letter to an uncertain opportunity. . . .

My husband has said more than once that he feels grateful to you. For he is more sensitive on my behalf than on his own. Hence he unites with me in the assurance of the high regard with which I remain

Always yours faithfully,
M. E. Lewes.

## GHL DIARY, CAMBRIDGE, 31 May–4 June 1877

*MS:* Mrs. Carrington Ouvry. *Hitherto unpublished.*

Finished packing of books. After lunch we started for Cambridge on a visit to the Sidgwicks. Gurney and his bride [7] went down with us. Our stay at Cambridge one uninterrupted excitement—guests at breakfast, lunch and dinner. Very delightful. We visited Girton and Newnham Hall. Went to Trinity Chapel on Sunday afternoon.[8] Eustace [9] and Arthur Balfour, Prof. Stewart,[1] Jebb, Foster,[2] Stanford,[3] Lord Edmund Fitzmaurice,[4] Trotter,[5] Dr. Kennedy,[6] Jackson, Myers, Colvin, and several others.[7] Went over the Fitzwilliam Museum.

7. Edmund Gurney (1847–88), Fellow of Trinity College, Cambridge, married at St. Peter's, Eaton Square, Miss Kate Sibley, daughter of the late Henry J. Sibley. See 2 [August] 1877.

8. This was probably the occasion F. W. H. Myers describes in his much-quoted account in the *Century Magazine,* 23 (November 1881), 62: "I remember how, at Cambridge, I walked with her once in the Fellow's Garden of Trinity, on an evening of rainy May; and she . . . taking as her text the three words . . . *God, Immortality, Duty,*—pronounced, with terrible earnestness, how inconceivable was the *first,* how unbelievable the *second,* and yet how peremptory and absolute the *third.* . . . I listened, and night fell; her grave, majestic countenance turned toward me like a sibyl's in the gloom. . . ."

9. Eustace James Anthony Balfour (1854–1911).

1. James Stuart (1843–1913), Fellow of Trinity College and 1st Professor of Mechanism and Applied Mechanics in Cambridge.

2. Michael Foster (1836–1907).

3. Charles Villiers Stanford (1852–1924), organist at Trinity College.

4. Lord Edmond George FitzMaurice (1846–1935), son of the 4th Marquis of Lansdowne.

5. Coutts Trotter (1837–87), Fellow of Trinity, and University administrator, lectured in physical science.

6. Benjamin Hall Kennedy (1804–89), Headmaster of Shrewsbury 1836–66 and Professor of Greek at Cambridge, 1867–89.

7. Reginald Baliol Brett, later Viscount Esher (1852–1930), another Trinity man, wrote in his Journal, 1 June: "I spent four hours this afternoon in the society of George Eliot. She talks like the best part of her books, the parts where she analyses without dissecting, the parts out of which compilers get her 'wise, witty, and tender' sayings. She is wonderfully thoughtful, even in trifles. She shut

**Monday 4 June 1877**

Left Cambridge at 1 and reached Witley at 5.15 to find only a portion of the furniture arrived.

up George Lewes when he tried to talk about her. She does not seem vain. She adores Charles Darwin because of his humility. I suppose it is an event to have spent a day in her company." (*Journals and Letters of Reginald, Viscount Esher*, ed. M. V. Brett, 4 vols., London, Nicholson and Watson, 1934–38, I, 40.)

# The Heights, Witley

| | |
|---|---|
| *1877 June 4–October 25* | At Witley; see much of Sir Henry and Lady Holland. |
| *1877 June 24* | Elinor Southwood Lewes born. |
| *1877 August 28* | Cross introduces GE to lawn tennis. |
| *1877 September 17* | GE and GHL at Tennyson's. |
| *1877 October 25–29* | Visit Halls at Six Mile Bottom. |
| *1877 October 29* | Return to London. |
| *1877 November 5* | Cross introduces GE to badminton. |
| *1877 November 10* | GE refuses to do Shakespeare for English Men of Letters series. |
| *1877 November 22* | GHL a candidate for rectorship of St. Andrews. |
| *1877 December* | Main edits *The George Eliot Birthday Book.* |

## GE TO CHARLES RITTER, WITLEY, [5 JUNE 1877]

*MS:* Bibliothèque Publique et Universitaire, Geneva. *Hitherto unpublished.*

The Heights | Witley | Godalming.

Dear M. Ritter

I am sure you will excuse my delay in acknowledging your kind letter of the 25th with the accompanying translations,[1] when I tell you that in the interim we have been paying a visit to Cambridge where the days were filled with the excitement of constant society, among new friends as well as old, and that we only yesterday arrived at this country home, where we are still in some hurry and incompleteness as to our arrangements.

Mr. Lewes and I both feel that we can congratulate you on the neatness and felicity of your rendering in the little collection of extracts which you have sent me as a specimen of your labours. It is a real joy to me that a mind like yours can care to dwell on what I have written so as to find expression for me in a foreign tongue requiring so much delicate precision as the French. And I must again assure you, as I have probably done several times already, that your sympathy with my work will always be to me an unforgotten source of encouragement.

Thanks, too, for your kind present of your photograph—though I have so keen a memory of faces that the sun-picture is less complete than the remembered image. I must beg you, however, in relation to your photograph, to be Christianly content with giving, asking for nothing again. The process of being photographed is one that I have promised and vowed to myself never to undergo.

It was a sincere pleasure to me to shake hands with you [2] and behold you in all the strength of your best age, correcting my conception of you as an elderly personage with white or iron-grey locks.

We shall always be delighted to renew our conversation with you on any future visit you may make to England. And surely a residence in London of some months would be a valuable experience to you. We English are more lovable when seen at home than foreigners who

1. At Yale. The translations were some "Fragments" from *Daniel Deronda* that he was preparing for a French review, *La libre Recherche.*

2. Ritter called at the Priory Sunday, 29 April 1877. (GHL Diary.)

observe us wandering only are likely to believe. I remain, dear M. Ritter,

Very truly yours
M. E. Lewes.

Mr. Lewes, if he were not busy with the builders, would desire to have his best remembrances offered to you. But this is a moment of varied demands such as we both of us dislike fulfilling—demands about the externals of our life, chairs, tables, water-pipes that will not act properly, and workmen who misunderstand orders.

## GHL TO JOHN WALTER CROSS, WITLEY, [10 JUNE 1877]

*MS:* Yale. *Hitherto unpublished.*

The Heights, Witley | Godalming | Sunday.

My dear Johnnie

"Witley Cross" is more ravishing than we fancied it—especially in this splendid weather—and the walks and drives are so much better than Society! (with a big S). Indeed although we are not yet settled, and have still the workmen in the house, and although there have been botherations with pipes, and mattings—tomorrow all the matting will have to be relaid—we don't grumble at anything but stroll about our property and say "how lovely!"

Your aunt has borne the Cambridge excitement and moving remarkably well and is much stronger than she was. Our visit to Cambridge was a continual success. We came here on Monday evening, but not till the next evening did all the furniture arrive from London—promised faithfully for Saturday!

We find the commissariat a difficulty—grocer only calls once a fortnight—and our fishmonger. By the way would you kindly look in as you pass on the fishmonger at the Waterloo Station and ask him on what terms he will supply us regularly with whatever may be the *fish of the day*—on Wednesdays and Saturdays. Tell him we are but two, and therefore want ordinarily but a small dish; and we will let him know the day before when we want something extra for visitors. If he can send them to the station by the first train our coachman will bring them up.

And what news of the mother of Gracchi? and the Gracchi? and the Doves? and the Six Milers? [3] Love, Love, Love, to them all

Ever yours
Uncle.

Gurney's bride is charming!

## GE TO FREDERIC HARRISON, WITLEY, 14 JUNE 1877

*MS:* Tinker Collection, Yale. *Envelope:* Frederic Harrison Esq | 1 Southwick Place | London | W. *Postmarks:* GODALMING | D | JU 14 | 77; LONDON. W | Y7 | JU 15. *Published:* Cross, III, 311–312.

The Heights | Witley | Godalming | June 14. 1877.

Dear Mr. Harrison

I am greatly indebted to you for your letter.[4] It has done something towards rousing me from what I will not call self-despair but resignation to being of no use.

I wonder whether you at all imagine the terrible pressure of disbelief in my own {duty / right} to speak to the public, which is apt with me to make all beginnings of work like a rowing against tide. Not that I am without more than my fair ounce of self-conceit and confidence that I know better than the critics, whom I don't take the trouble to read but who seem to fill the air as with the smoke of bad tobacco.

But I will not dwell on my antithetic experiences. I only mention them to show why your letter has done me a service, and also to help in the explanation of my mental attitude towards your requests or suggestions.

I do not quite understand whether you have in your mind any plan of straightway constructing a liturgy to which you wish me to contribute in a direct way. That form of contribution would hardly lie within my powers. But your words of trust in me as possibly an

3. Mrs. Otter, the Otter children, the Cross girls, and the Halls.

4. Harrison's letter has not been found. In his "Reminiscences of George Eliot" (1901) Harrison explains that, while nothing like a "service" was attempted in the Positivist chapel during the first years, "as our children grew up from infancy, their mother was called upon to supply some equivalent for family prayer. We consulted George Eliot, who, with her deep sympathy with the inmost emotions of humanity, had so great a gift of poetic expression. The letter of June 14, 1877, was the outcome of this appeal." (*Memories and Thoughts,* Macmillan, 1906, p. 155.)

organ of feelings which have not yet found their due expression is as likely as any external call could be to prompt such perfectly unfettered productions as that which you say has been found acceptable.

I wasted some time three years ago in writing (what I do not mean to print) a poetic dialogue embodying or rather shadowing very imperfectly the actual contest of ideas.[5] Perhaps what you have written to me may promote and influence a different kind of presentation. At any rate, all the words of your letter will be borne in mind and will enter into my motives.

We are tolerably settled now in our camping, experimental fashion. Perhaps before the summer is far advanced you may be in our neighbourhood, and come to look at us. I trust that Mrs. Harrison is by this time in her usual health. Please give my love to her and believe me always, with many grateful memories,

Yours sincerely
M. E. Lewes.

Mr. and Mrs. H. Crompton are coming to lunch with us today.

## GHL TO JOHN BLACKWOOD, WITLEY, [20 JUNE 1877]

*MS:* National Library of Scotland. *Hitherto unpublished.*

The Heights, Witley, Godalming | (Telegrams to be addressed: *Witley Station*) | Wednesday.

My dear Blackwood

I write instead of telegraphing, because there is more to say than can be conveniently put into a telegram.

*Any* day will suit us, that is most convenient to yourself; only Wednesdays and Saturdays are in *this* respect the best that on those days we get our Fish from London! Barring that, one day is the same as another.

Then as to trains, which may not be very convenient for you. If you can spare us a *long* day—which however with your press of London friends and engagements may not be easy—there is a train which leaves Waterloo at 11.30 and reaches this 12.43. We dine at 1.30 and you could then lunch or dine with us, rest during the heat of the day,

5. In her Journal, 19 May 1874 GE says "I have lately written A Symposium." I take this to be the dialogue in blank verse published in *Macmillan's Magazine,* 38 (July 1878), 161–179 as "A College Breakfast-Party" and thereafter reprinted with the *Jubal* volume. The MS is dated April 1874. (BM.)

have a delicious drive in the cool, back at 7.30 or so to supper, and home by the 8.25 train. But if you can't spare all this time, there is a train from Waterloo at 2.35 reaching this at 3.54. We could then dine at 6.30 and you return by the 8.25; or if you came by the 11.20 and lunched with us you could return by the 4.13, or 7.5.

These are the alternatives—choose the one which best suits your engagements and be sure of a hearty welcome whichever it is!

This place is Paradise. Or it would be if Madonna were only free from pain, and the bloom only return to her cheek.

Let us know when to expect you—and with kindest regards to Mrs. Blackwood and the fair Ebonina.[6] Believe me

Yours ever
G. H. L.

You might bring down the *Pilot and his Wife*[7] if it is to hand and portable; or Reade's novel;[8] literature is not abundant in these diggings.

## GHL DIARY, WITLEY, 22–24 JUNE 1877

*MS:* Mrs. Carrington Ouvry. *Hitherto unpublished.*

**Friday 22 June 1877**

Since the last entry[9] life has moved on its regular routine, the weather transcendent, the *work* successful. Polly has been better and has read aloud Keats's Life.[1] The clergyman[2] has called; and I have written many letters. Yesterday we were overtaken by a tremendous storm which the Victoria only partially protected us from.

**Saturday 23 June 1877**

Work and walk. Blackwood spent the day with us. Drove him to Hinde Head; weather fine and not hot. When he left at 8.25 read papers.

**Sunday 24 June 1877**

Lotze, Medizinische Psychologie.[3] Worked at vol. IV. Wrote to

6. Miss Mary Blackwood, the diminutive of a black wood.

7. Jonas Lie (1833–1909) published this best known of his novels, *Lodsen og hans Hustru* in 1874. In 1877 Blackwood published a translation of it by G. W. Tottenham.

8. Charles Reade's novel was *A Woman Hater,* just reprinted in 3 vols.

9. 17 June 1877.

1. *Life, Letters, and Literary Remains of John Keats,* ed. R. M. Milnes, was in GE's library.

2. Leonard Francis Burrows, late Fellow of Wadham College, Oxford, B.A. 1843, became Vicar of Witley in 1876.

3. Rudolf Hermann Lotze (1817–81), Leipzig, 1852.

Kaufmann about the translation of his "George Eliot und das Judenthum." Drove to Hambledon and Godalming. Charles Reade's 'Woman Hater.' Charles wrote announcing birth of his third daughter.[4]

## JOHN BLACKWOOD TO WILLIAM BLACKWOOD, LONDON, 25 JUNE 1877

*MS:* National Library of Scotland. *Hitherto unpublished.*

Fishers Hotel. | June 25/77.

My Dear Willie

I had a most delightful day with the Leweses. She is looking well and full of happiness in the lovely spot where they are settled. Nothing could be more suitable and it gave me real pleasure to see her settled in such a home. The view is perhaps finer than that from Richmond Hill. I said something should be born here, and the answer was in the nature of assent.

We dined about ½ p. one and drove about among the most lovely woodland and gorse for some three hours afterwards. I have often heard of the country—indeed it is not far from the scene of the Battle of Dorking, but I did not think it had been so very fine. Chesney[5] with whom I was yesterday says it beats them hollow at Coopers Hill and that is not easily done. . . .

We propose to come down by the night express upon Wednesday and Julia has written to your mother.

ever yours affectionately
John Blackwood.

## GE TO JOSEPH M. LANGFORD, WITLEY, 29 JUNE [1877]

*MS:* Mrs. Dorothy Hicks. *Hitherto unpublished.*

The Heights | Witley | Godalming | June 29.

Dear Mr. Langford

I am quite willing that the extract should be made from 'Silas Marner' for the Sixth National Reading Book.

4. Elinor Southwood Lewes, now Mrs. Carrington Ouvry.

5. General George Tomkyns Chesney (1830–95), President of the Royal Indian Civil Engineering College at Cooper's Hill, published a fictitious account of "The Battle of Dorking," in *Blackwood's,* 109 (May 1871), 539–572.

Will you oblige me by sending a copy of *'Middlemarch,'* with a copy of *Smith and Elder's 'Romola'* to

Madame Mario | Poor House | Zennor | St. Ives | Cornwall? [6]

Thanks for your friendly wishes which greeted us on our arrival at this country home. We enjoy our quiet blessings greatly and want nothing but health.

I was glad to hear from Mr. Blackwood that you are now in excellent condition.

Always yours sincerely
M. E. Lewes.

## GHL TO JOHN BLACKWOOD, WITLEY, 9 JULY 1877

*MS:* National Library of Scotland. *Hitherto unpublished.*

The Heights, Witley, | Godalming | 9 July 77.

My dear Blackwood

By this post I send you the German pamphlet on George Eliot and Judaism. On a second reading I find it—as two friends also do—a very remarkable production, eloquent and highly interesting even to outsiders. It is so finely written that you will do well to be careful in selecting a competent translator and then I think the public will welcome it. At all events it will do the books good.

Since you left we have had cold winds which have not increased our happiness—the more so as Madonna's renal troubles are incessant; she has never two days of consecutive quiet; not often great pain, but constant uneasiness with headache, sickness and inability to work.

We continue exploring the beauties of this country and enjoy our solitude, and our books. By the way tell Lockhart that his opening number [1] kept me in one gurgle of delight—so very different from the constant grating of "A Woman Hater"! Jonas Lie also was pleasant. Now we are reading Mad. D'Agoult's Mémoires [2]—not for her sake but for the sake of her daughter Mad. Wagner.

Lytton sends me this story taken from the official report of ex[amination] of Native Students.

"Describe the Horse."

6. Mme Mario was staying with Mme Bodichon, who had suffered a stroke of paralysis about the beginning of June.

1. "Mine is Thine," *Blackwood's,* 122 (July 1877), 1–26. It ran until June 1878.

2. Daniel Stern (Mme D'Agoult), *Mes Souvenirs,* 1806–33, Paris, 1877.

"The horse is a noble animal; but if irritated *he will not do so.*"

Mrs. Lewes sends kindest regards to you and yours.

Ever yours
G. H. L.

## GE TO MME LOUIS BELLOC, WITLEY, 10 JULY [1877]

*MS:* The Countess of Iddesleigh. *Envelope:* Madame Belloc | 17 Wimpole Street | London | W. *Postmarks:* GODALMING | D | JY 11 | 77; LONDON.W | C7 | JY 12 | 77. *Hitherto unpublished.*

The Heights | Witley | Godalming | July 10.

Dearest Bessie

Your letter this morning was a blessing, for the last account had thrown me into a state almost of despondency—we thought the signs of nervous irritability so alarming. But now I can think of our dear Barbara with less of a pang, indeed with the comforting hope that since she has recovered thus far, she will at last be set entirely free from the fetters on her speech. You say nothing about the Doctor,[3] so I am wondering whether he is coming to England or not, and cannot tell myself what to wish on the subject.

I wonder too how you are feeling about French affairs. However, your two little ones and your two venerable ladies [4] connect themselves with interests and feelings happily more stable than forms of political life. I hope you will all prosper in the sunshine.

We delight in this region. It is more beautiful than I had imagined, having both wildness and culture in delightful alternation. I have been *souffrante,* but am content to bear my share of such trouble, or rather an amount which is much less than my share if there were equal division.

Mr. Lewes brought me in your letter which he had ventured to open seeing where it came from, and he said, "Famous news of Barbara!" with a radiant face. He had almost feared from the last account that some permanent injury had set in.

He sends his best regards and thanks with mine.

Yours ever lovingly
M. E. Lewes.

3. Eugène Bodichon.
4. Her children Hilary and Marie, her mother-in-law Mme Belloc, and Mlle Adelaide Montgolfier.

GHL TO MRS. ELMA STUART,

WITLEY, 12 JULY 1877

*MS:* British Museum. *Published:* Stuart, pp. 84–87.

The Heights, Witley, | Godalming | 12 July 77.

Dear Elma

I should have written to you soon after our arrival here, 5 weeks since, had I not suspected that you would have moved towards England or Scotland, and expected to hear from you of your whereabouts.

First as to Madonna—she is, and has been, ever since February, in constant uneasiness, varied by pain, and occasionally a day or two's interval of relief. This is the only cloud in our heaven—and by dint of persistence it ceases to have a *very* black aspect; but till she is at something like her normal condition I can't help being anxious.

Next as to the new home—it is a small paradise. With many objectionable points in the arrangement and structure of the rooms, there is so much beauty, healthiness, and peace in the grounds and surrounding country that we are in perpetual delight. I turn into my wood to meditate, and the squirrels contemplate me with astonished contempt: "What, little sir! are *you* there, straddling among the fir cones and unable to run up among these branches—pondering problems and unable to enjoy nuts—a two fisted, two legged, troublous and troubled animal!"—The thrushes and blackbirds have their musical remarks to make—and the cuckoo occasionally throws in a distant observation—the pigeons coo and the moles dart into their burrows. The sweet sunshine irradiates the scene—and the blessed sunshine of affection irradiates my interior.

We have seen none of our neighbours yet—except Tennyson [5]—having adroitly called when they were out, and ourselves been out, or 'engaged,' when they called—so that our solitude à deux has not been spoiled.

It is very pretty of Mrs. Menzies (to whom my love) and like herself to give her mind to your domesticities; and I know you will enjoy making Mrs. Chesney happy during her stay—for that is your function in life. Her evasion of Mrs. Senior's question reminds me of the young Cantab who in his examination on being asked whether the earth turned round the sun or the sun round the earth? answered "Some-

5. During their drive 6 July they met Tennyson and Hallam, who lived about three miles south of Witley at Aldworth on Black Down.

times one and sometimes the other." And this leads me to tell you a delicious bit which Lord Lytton sent me the other day from the official report of the examination of native students. Question: "Describe the Horse." Answer: "The Horse is a noble animal; but if you irritate him, *he will not do so.*" Some weeks ago Lytton sent me this also: A native pleader in the High Court of Calcutta defending a native lady is interrupted by the Judge: "I beg pardon Mr. T— is your client an adult?"—"No, my lud; an adultress."

Charles and Gertrude have got another daughter—we wanted a grandson, but the superior powers thought otherwise. Perhaps they thought with Huxley, in this sense. The other day at dinner Madonna was talking with Bright about woman's suffrage, and the Princess Louise interposed with, "But you don't go in for the superiority of women, Mrs. Lewes?" "No."—"I think," said Huxley, "Mrs. Lewes rather teaches *the inferiority of men.*"

We are looking forward to September and having you here, so I need not describe the Heights, and as I have no more anecdotes to send I will cease this scribble—scribbled under oppressive headache.

Madonna calls to me that I am to be sure and give her tender love and assurance that you are not likely to be forgotten by her or

Yours affectionately
G. H. Lewes.

## GE TO CHARLES RITTER, WITLEY, 23 JULY 1877

*MS:* Bibliothèque Publique et Universitaire, Geneva. *Extracts published:* Cross, New Edition, p. 565.

The Heights | Witley | Godalming | July 23. 77.

My dear Sir

I have to thank you doubly. First, for your charming letter of the 15th and next for the present of your Translations from my books,[6] which have reached us in all safety. Mr. Lewes at once forwarded Mr. Main's copy as you desired.

Pray count yourself among the helpful influences of my life, and believe that when I am recalling the reasons I have had for being of good courage, the possession of such a reader as yourself is, and will always be, one of my most precious remembrances. I feel quite sure, from having had an interview with you, that you are nervously sensitive enough to enter into all the difficulties of a too susceptible nature, easily repressed and even paralyzed by signs of misunderstanding. And

6. *Fragments et pensées,* Geneva, 1877; 2d ed., 1879.

because of this ready sympathy, you can choose just the right means of cheering a rather morbidly diffident person like myself. The extract you have sent me from your correspondent's letter shows her to be a reader whom one can rejoice in. There is a kind of praise, a kind of interest expressed in one's books which can be more distasteful than neglect. But your friend has a delicate selectness of phrase which marks her as an uncommon person.[7]

Our son has been with us for a couple of days, and he read your translations admiringly, thinking that you had wonderfully overcome the difficulties of a task with which he is not unacquainted, having made translations from Platt-deutsch as well as High German.[8] And it is only those who have tried to render one language into another with scrupulosity that can estimate what is meritorious in such work.

You kindly ask about my health. It has been troublesome ever since we came into the pure air of this lovely country—a most uncomfortable paradox. But I have been better for the last week, and at present I think that Mr. Lewes's frequent headaches are a worse grievance to me than my own ailments.

He sends his best regards with mine and adds his thanks for his share in the benefit of your work and of your invaluable sympathy. Believe me

Sincerely yours
M. E. Lewes.

## GHL TO THE MISSES CROSS, WITLEY, 31 JULY [1877]

*MS:* Yale. *Hitherto unpublished.*

There dwelt beside the Weybridge ways [9]
(And often called 'the Doves')
Maidens who seeking no man's praise
Gained everybody's loves.

7. Mme Marie Koeckert wrote Ritter: "J'ai un besoin toujours plus ardent de cette divine pitié que Christ et Deronda ont voulu nous apporter comme suprême consolation; mais, à de rares exceptions près, ils n'ont pas donné leur secret à cette pauvre humanité. George Eliot possède ce génie religieux devant les réalités de la vie, et c'est pour cela que nous ne pouvons pas assez la bénir de nous faire part de son trésor sous les formes les plus diverses et les plus charmantes."

8. Charles Lee Lewes translated *In the Year '13. A Tale of Mecklenburg Life,* from the Platt-Deutsch of Fritz Reuter, 1867; Lessing's *Emilia Galotti,* 1868; and Ludwig Bamberger's *Count Bismark,* 1869.

9. Cf. Wordsworth's "She Dwelt among the Untrodden Ways."

Their Uncle dwelt on Witley Heights,
Who loved these maidens well
Though why they ne'er shared his delight
Of home--no man can tell.
Was it because he lived retired
With brain too much o'ertasked?
Or that they ne'er to come desired?
Or—were they never asked?

Dryden confessed that many a rhyme helped him to a thought,[1] and like Dryden I see the rhyme has helped me to the thoughts that perhaps the said maidens never *were* asked! Oh! Oh! Oh!—Well now they *are*. Madonna has been decidedly better these last ten days and we have had Gurneys and Harrisons two days to lunch [2]—so you see it is high time that the Doves

Thus far had I written when Madonna came into the room and told me Mrs. Harrison said *"Mrs. Cross* has returned to Weybridge" and might perhaps brave the heat and accompany the Doves! Well, that would be an additional delight. We leave it entirely to her and you girls to fix your day and hours next week (not Monday, though, because of Bank Holiday) and don't care if it is not reasonably fine.[3]

Your loving
Uncle.

July 31.

## GE TO WILLIAM BLACKWOOD, WITLEY, [JULY 1877]

*MS:* National Library of Scotland. *Extract published: John Blackwood,* p. 398.

The Heights, | Witley | Godalming.

My dear Mr. William

It was a very harmless breach you committed in opening my American letter, which happens to be one that I should have liked you to read. A young lady of New York [4] expresses much gratitude for being

1. See his Dedication of the *Aeneis, The Poetical Works of John Dryden,* ed. G. R. Noyes, Cambridge and New York, [1909], p. 513.

2. The Edmund Gurneys 30 July and the Frederic Harrisons 31 July. (GHL Diary.)

3. "Mrs. Cross, Johnnie and Eleanor spent the day with us." (GHL Diary, 9 August 1877.)

4. Miss Margaret Hollingsworth. Her letter, dated from 33 West 130th Street, New York, 13 June 1877, is now in the Berg Collection, NYPL.

saved, by reading Daniel Deronda, from marrying a man whom she could not love, but whom she was disposed to accept for the sake of his wealth, but she is so far from being absorbed by this momentous personal matter that she goes on to be still more effusive about the 'enjoyment and instruction' she has had from the Jewish elements in the book, and thinks the scene on the Bridge the best in the book—'flashing through one with a sort of electric sympathy' etc. Tell your uncle that America is the quarter of the world for "appreciative butter."

We were not very expansive on business when he was with us, but I think we settled what was needful in two questions and answers. First, we agreed that the 7/6 ed. of Deronda had better be deferred till Autumn, and secondly, that it would be well to carry out the last-approved conception of a complete edition of the works (7/6 per vol., novels 2 vols. each).

But it would also be well, before anything irrevocable is done, that Mr. Simpson should just write me word of the general plan. For in looking over the list of volumes designed, with Mr. Blackwood in London, we made a supposition as to the division of the shorter works, which may have been forgotten, and unfortunately I have not brought down the paper of statements about which we were consulting.

I also agreed with Mr. Blackwood that Romola should be included in the 3/6 edition, as well as in the 7/6.

I fear we tired your uncle with too long a drive over our hills, which are like a bit of Scotland dropped into the midst of Southern pastures and hedgerows. I am glad to hear that he enjoyed the day nevertheless—as we did. Perhaps if we keep this spot, you too will run the risk of being tired in the same way. Mr. Lewes unites with me in best regards.

Yours always sincerely
M. E. Lewes.

I have corrected copies of 'The Lifted Veil' and 'Brother Jacob' which I will send when they are needed.

## GE TO MME EUGÈNE BODICHON, WITLEY, 2 [AUGUST] 1877

*MS:* Mr. Philip Leigh-Smith. *Envelope:* Madame Bodichon | Poor House | Zennor | St. Ives | Cornwall. *Postmark:* GODALMING | D | AU 2 | 77. *Mostly published:* Cross, III, 312–313.

The Heights | Witley | Godalming | July [5] 2. 77

Dearest Barbara

It was a draught of real comfort and pleasure to have a letter written by your own hand, and one so altogether cheerful. I trust that the warmer weather is salutary to you and that you will by and by be able to write me word of continued progress. Hardly any bit of the Kingdom, I fancy, would suit your taste better than your neighbourhood of the Land's End. You are not fond of bushy midland-fashioned scenery.

We are enjoying the mixture of wildness and culture extremely, and so far as landscape and air go, we would not choose a different home from this. But we have not yet made up our minds whether we shall keep our house or sell it.

Some London friends are also occasional dwellers in these parts. The day before yesterday we had Mr. and Mrs. Frederic Harrison, whose parents have a fine old Tudor house—Sutton Place—about 3 miles beyond Guildford. Mrs. Harrison asked with much interest about you, and was glad to hear of Madame Mario also, of whom Dr. Bridges had spoken very prettily to her. And do you remember Edmund Gurney? He and his graceful bride lunched with us the other day. She was very poor before her marriage and had worked in an exemplary way both to help her mother and educate herself—her father having lost his property and left his family destitute.

And Miss Thackeray's married today to young Ritchie.[6] I saw him at Cambridge and felt that the nearly 20 years' difference between them was bridged hopefully by his solidarity and gravity. This is one of several instances that I have known of lately, showing that young men with even brilliant advantages will often choose as their life's companion a woman whose attractions are wholly of the spiritual order.

Do you care about this gossip? I am wondering how long Madame Mario will be able to remain with you. Please ask her to send me a

5. An obvious slip for *August*.

6. Anne Isabella Thackeray (1837–1919) was married 2 August 1877 to Richmond Thackeray Willoughby Ritchie (1854–1912)

line in case of her leaving you. But August is an inauspicious month for returning to Italy.

We are poor creatures—headachy and feeble but not the less affectionate in our memories of our too far-off friend. I often see you enjoying your sunsets and the wayside flowers.

Always your loving
Marian.

## GE TO MRS. ELMA STUART, [WITLEY], 4 AUGUST 1877

*MS:* British Museum. *Published:* Stuart, pp. 87–91.

**The Priory, | 21. North Bank, | Regents Park.**
August 4. 77.

Dearest Elma

A letter from your dear Roland this morning tells me that you are only just beginning to recover from a very painful attack. I am most thankful to the dear fellow for writing me word of this. For it is one of the qualities of Love to desire that the loved one should not go through suffering and that suffering remain all the while unknown and unfelt for. I should like to make you promise that you will never hide your pain or sorrow from me. I rather suspect that you follow Shakespeare in that tender desire not to be thought of—

"For I love you so
That I in your sweet thoughts would be forgot,
If thinking on me e'er should cause you woe." [7]

Give up that doctrine or habit with regard to me. Because I would rather be sorry that you were sorry than be ignorantly merry when you were in anguish.—We are fearing that your illness may be made the more trying to you because you have a visitor—Mrs. Chesney, is it not? —and we know something, or have well imagined something, of your ardent hospitality, which would make you regret your illness as an elderly friend of mine once regretted that she was obliged to have a tooth out—it must be so disagreeable to the dentist to attend to an old woman's mouth!

To gratify this excessive altruism of yours I will tell you that I am much better and able to take a good walk. Mr. Lewes too is full of enjoyment, though under the drawback of frequent headache. He is enraptured with this part of the country, and we are hoping that you

7. Shakespeare, *Sonnets*, 71.

will come and see it in September, when it will be magnificent with the first touches of autumn's golden finger. Tennyson, you perhaps know, is within a drive of us, and he too lives (for a few summer months) on a hill where he commands the double, contrasted beauties of this wonderful county—the wide high heath and the fertile plain. But perhaps you know all about these parts better than I do, and we shall not be able to show you any novelty in a drive to Hind Head.

We have brought your tables down with us for the summer, and a lady who came here the other day was struck with admiration, setting down the table as an expensive bit of Japanese work! We value it much more than if it had been made by unknown Mongolian fingers.

The exquisite blue table-cloth is not brought down, being reserved for a time when our surroundings will be less make-shift and camp-like. We have no spare-bed, and our own bed-room looks rather as if we had been distrained for rent. But happily we are within 3 minutes of the railway station, so that when you come we can have a good long day together.—You must please let Roly write again and let me know how you are going on. I imagine what tender care you are having from him and from your guardian angel Mrs. Menzies. That is a great comfort to me in thinking of you.

And when you are once more able to write with your own hand, tell me all about Roly—whether any inclination to a special career has declared itself, or whether you have come to any definite arrangement concerning his future. He writes very prettily—I mean, that his hand-writing is very clear and well-shapen, as it was bound to be according to any satisfactory results of *hérédité*.

You see, I am scribbling hastily, in order that my letter may go off this morning at 10 o'clock—our only post on Sunday. Always, dear one,

Your loving
Mother.

## GHL TO MRS. ELMA STUART, WITLEY, 11 AUGUST 1877

*MS:* British Museum. *Published:* Stuart, pp. 91–93.

The Heights, Witley, Godalming | 11 August 77.

Dear, good Elma!
Reprehensible Idiot!

Your conduct with regard to the Chesneys is inexcusable. But to make you feel it properly I must put it before you as I often have to put her conduct before Madonna—that is to point out how injurious to *others* the neglect of self may be. Not only do you give pain to those who love you, by such wilful disregard of your health, but you hamper your own powers of doing good. There!

Again, do you suppose for an instant that your friends would have been pained or any way inconvenienced by your simple statement of the fact that your tooth was loose and that your eating must be slow? It is an insult to them!—But the notion is so characteristic of you and of Madonna that I can't be as indignant as I ought.

Now you are getting better of course Madonna and I shall be only too pleased to hear all you can tell us of your plans for Roly (to whom our love) and yourself. When we have the delight of seeing you here you will go into detail, but meanwhile we shall be glad of a sketch.

Kiss that dear Mrs. Menzies for us—not in payment of her constant goodness to you because she gets ample payment for that in the indulgence of her own generous nature—but in acknowledgment on our part that there is a debt to pay.

When you write next to Mad. Jaubert [8] tell her how very much we have been interested in her account of Heine, which we have lent to friends who were also interested, and how we admired the part she herself played in that pathetic story.

If you want a delightful book get 'Mes Souvenirs' by Daniel Stern —Mad. D'Agoult—the mother of Mad. Wagner. It is a remarkable picture of the ancien régime. Love from Madonna and

Yours ever,
G. H. L.

## GE TO WILLIAM ALLINGHAM, WITLEY, 26 AUGUST [1877]

*MS:* Parrish Collection, Princeton. *Published:* Cross, III, 313–314.

The Heights, | Witley, | Godalming | August 26.

Dear Mr. Allingham

I hope that this letter will not find you at the old address but that it may be sent on to you in some delicious nook where your dear wife

8. Mme Caroline Jaubert (1802–82), according to Roland Stuart, "was a most delightful little French lady who came to reside next door to us at Dinan. She was like a little fairy, and was always called by Heine his 'Marraine.'" (p. 92.) In her *Heinrich Heine. Erinnerungen aus den letzten 20 Jahren seines Lebens,* Paris and Leipzig, 1884, his letters to her begin "Kleine Fée."

is by your side preparing to make us all richer with store of new sketches.

I almost fear that I am implying unbecoming claims in asking you to send me a word or two of news about your twofold—nay fourfold self. But you must excuse in me a presumption which is simply a feeling of spiritual kinship bred by reading in the volume you gave me before we left town.[1] That tremendous tramp—"Life, Death; Life, Death," makes me care the more, as age makes it the more audible to me, for those younger ones who are keeping step behind me.

It is a burthen to write notes, but let us bear it in turn. With affectionate remembrances to your wife,

Always yours truly
M. E. Lewes.

## GE TO MRS. RICHMOND T. W. RITCHIE, WITLEY, 29 AUGUST [1877]

*MS:* Mr. Gordon N. Ray. *Hitherto unpublished.*

The Heights | Witley | Godalming | August 29.

Dear Mrs. Ritchie

Your letter came on to me this morning. I am so glad to have it, for I have been long wishing that some sign of remembrance from you would fall to my share. No one has thought of your twofold self with more sympathy than 'meine Kleinigkeit,' with more earnest desire that you may have the best sort of happiness.

Do come and see me. By the beginning of November we shall be in town again. Either there or here we should heartily welcome a visit from you and Mr. Ritchie. At lunch time—half-past one—we are sure to be at home.

Knowing this glorious country you can imagine how we delight in it. It is to the honour of the house that you assisted at its foundation, but the superstructure is not worthy of that beginning. Still we like the place on the whole—which is the utmost that can be said of nearly all such likings. Ask Mr. Ritchie to remember me kindly.

Always sincerely yours
M. E. Lewes.

1. The line GE quotes is found in Allingham's poem "The General Chorus," *Songs, Ballads and Stories,* 1877, pp. 113–114.

## GE TO MRS. ELMA STUART, WITLEY, 14 SEPTEMBER [1877]

*MS:* British Museum. *Published:* Stuart, pp. 94–95.

The Heights | Witley | Godalming | September 14.

Dearest Elma

The beautiful clasp arrived this morning—a day after your dear letter. I half want to scold you for devoting too much of your time, strength and substance to creating pleasures for me. But I cannot find in my heart to say "Do otherwise than your lovingness prompts you." And I am fond of my silver clasp, which is just what I wanted. Bless you, dear, for all your tender thoughts and faithful affection, and believe that every sign you make is precious.

About Roly's destination I rejoice, taking for granted that after his training at the Military College he will be free to choose another vocation than the military, supposing his bent lay away from it.

But two points in your letter are less cheerful to us. First, that you say nothing of your coming to England (though we encourage the expectation that you must come to plant Roly at Oxford), and secondly, that you confess to being still in a poor state of health. Please remove our uneasiness on these points whenever you can. We expect to remain here until the end or nearly the end of October, and it would be a delight to Mr. Lewes to step down to the railway station and meet a triple group—Elma, Mrs. Menzies (otherwise known as the guardian angel) and Roly, grown perhaps almost out of recognition. Let this vision of mine be a case of second sight.

All is well with us. We are better in health, perhaps from getting acclimatized. And when the weather permits we play at lawn tennis, yielding to the persuasions of an athletic friend who calls me 'aunt' and has insisted on fixing up the necessary apparatus on our lawn.[2] Should you not be amazed to see your mother using the bat and running after the vagrant balls? It has done me good, however.

We are very glad to have a kiss from Mrs. Menzies, and always find our thoughts about you the happier for their inclusion of her. We look to her as the remedy and restraint of a certain "idiocy"—a not-knowing-how-to-take-care-of-herself which belongs to one filled with the inspira-

2. Johnnie Cross "brought an apparatus for *Lawn Tennis* and fixed it. Then initiated Polly at the game and we played till we perspired freely." (GHL Diary, 28 August 1877.) Thereafter they played almost every day.

tion to take care of others. Mr. Lewes, though shut up in his study, is one with me as I write.

Your ever loving
Mother.

On turning over this page I was shocked to see how dirty a sheet of paper I had taken. Pray excuse it, and don't attribute the smears to my fingers.

## GE TO DAVID KAUFMANN, [WITLEY], 12 OCTOBER 1877

*Text: Athenaeum,* 26 November 1881, pp. 703–704.

The Priory, 21, North Bank, Regent's Park, | October 12, '77.
My dear Sir,

I trust it will not be otherwise than gratifying to you to know that your stirring article on 'Daniel Deronda' is now translated into English by a son of Prof. Ferrier, who was a philosophical writer of considerable mark.[3] It will be issued in a handsomer form than that of the pamphlet, and will appear within this autumnal publishing season, Messrs. Blackwood having already advertised it. Whenever a copy is ready we shall have the pleasure of sending it to you. There is often something to be borne with in reading one's own writing in a translation, but I hope that in this case you will not be made to wince severely.

In waiting to send you this news I seem to have deferred too long the expression of my warm thanks for your kindness in sending me the Hebrew translations of Lessing and the collection of Hebrew poems, a kindness which I felt myself rather presumptuous in asking for, since your time must be well filled with more important demands. Yet I must further beg you, when you have an opportunity, to assure Herr Bacher [4] that I was most gratefully touched by the sympathetic verses with which he enriched the gift of his work.

I see by your last letter to my husband [5] that your Theological Seminary was to open on the 4th of this month, so that this too retrospective letter of mine will reach you in the midst of your new duties. I trust that this new Institution will be a great good to professor and

3. *George Eliot and Judaism: An Attempt to Appreciate* Daniel Deronda, translated from the German by John Ferrier, son of James Frederick Ferrier (1808–64).

4. Simon Bacher, *Nathan der Weise* [in Hebrew], Vienna, 1866 and *"Jom Malkénu,"* Budapest, 1873.

5. Dated Budapest, 6 July 1877. Enclosed is a translation of Bacher's Hebrew inscription in the volume he sent GE. (G. S. Haight.)

students, and that your position is of a kind that you contemplate as permanent. To teach the young personally has always seemed to me the most satisfactory supplement to teaching the world through books, and I have often wished that I had such a means of having fresh, living, spiritual children within sight.

One can hardly turn one's thought toward Eastern Europe just now without a mingling of pain and dread; but we mass together distant scenes and events in an unreal way, and one would like to believe that the present troubles will not at any time press on you in Hungary with more external misfortune than on us in England.

Mr. Lewes is happily occupied in his psychological studies. We both look forward to the reception of the work you kindly promised us, and he begs me to offer you his best regards. Believe me, my dear Sir,

Yours with much esteem,
M. E. Lewes.

## JOHN BLACKWOOD TO WILLIAM BLACKWOOD, ST. ANDREWS, 15 OCTOBER 1877

*MS:* National Library of Scotland. *Hitherto unpublished.*

**Strathtyrum | St. Andrews | N.B.**
October 15/77.

My Dear Willie

I have been considering the calculations for the works of George Eliot. I have long felt that we could make but very little of this edition and the author not much but it will be a steady on-going thing, a capital leading franchise in the business and we must do the best we possibly can for the author. I feel that in not beginning to pay a lordship until we have sold 750 copies we are making ourselves too much dormie. If Simpson can reconcile himself to it I incline to offer 1/2 per volume for the Novels and to begin the lordship after the sale of 500 copies.

This edition must be the permanent one of these works and the publisher of it the natural successor to all the people's editions which surely will come. The Lewes's have I think our calculations of the printing and will feel that we are doing what we can for them as well as presenting her works in the handsomest possible shape. Write what Simpson and you think of this. . . .

ever yours affectionately
John Blackwood.

## GE TO THE HON. MRS. HENRY FREDERICK PONSONBY, WITLEY, 17 OCTOBER 1877

*Text:* Magdalen Ponsonby, *Mary Ponsonby,* 1927, pp. 102–124. *Published:* Cross, III, 316–318.

The Heights, Witley, | *October* 17*th,* 1877.

Dear Mrs. Ponsonby,

I like to know that you have been thinking of me and that you care to write to me, and though I will not disobey your considerate prohibition so far as to try and answer your letter fully, I must content my soul by telling you that we shall be settled in the old place by the end of the first week in November, and that I shall be delighted to see you there. I long to know how far that purpose for which you made your residence in London months ago has been fulfilled. And there are many other subjects, more common to all of us, that I shall have a special pleasure in talking of with you.

Let me say now, that the passage quoted from your legal friend's letter is one that I am most glad to find falling in with your own attitude of mind. The view is what I have endeavoured to represent in a little poem called "Stradivarius," which you may not have happened to read:

"I say, not God Himself can make man's best
Without best men to help Him." [6]

And next—it will perhaps surprise you to know that, having read the *New Republic* [7] I think it one of the most condemnable books of the day; not simply because the Master of Balliol is a friend for whom I have a high regard. If I had known nothing of Mr. Jowett personally, I should equally have felt disapprobation of a work in which a young man who has no solid contribution of his own to make, sets about attempting to turn into ridicule the men who are most prominent in serious effort to make such contribution. With that impression from the *New Republic* I was not inclined to read anything by the same writer until I heard that he had repented and been converted to the emotions of gratitude and reverence. I think that kind of direct personal portraiture (or caricature, for except of Mr. Jowett and one other, the drawing is mere distortion) is a bastard kind of satire that I am not disposed

6. *The Legend of Jubal and Other Poems,* 1874, p. 229.

7. Jowett appears as Dr. Jenkinson, the chief target of satire; Mrs. Pattison as Lady Grace; Matthew Arnold as Mr. Luke; Pater as Mr. Rose; Huxley as Mr. Storks, etc. See W. H. Malloch, *The New Republic,* ed. J. M. Patrick, Gainesville, 1950, pp. xv–xxiv.

to think the better of because Aristophanes used it in relation to Socrates. Do you know that pretty story about Bishop Thirlwall [8]—that when somebody wanted to bring to him Forchhammer as a distinguished German writer, he replied, "No! I will never receive into my house the man who justified the death of Socrates."

But I am running on with a gossip not particularly warranted by the occasion. "O that we were all of one mind, and that mind good!" is an impossible-to-be-realised wish, and I don't wish it at all in its full extent. But I think it would be possible that men should differ speculatively as much as they do now, and yet be "of one mind" in the desire to avoid giving unnecessary pain, in the desire to do an honest part towards the general well-being which has made a comfortable *nidus* for themselves, in the resolve not to sacrifice another to their own egoistic promptings. Pity and fairness—two little words which, carried out, would embrace the utmost delicacies of the moral life—seem to me not to rest on an unverifiable hypothesis but on facts quite as irreversible as the perception that a pyramid will not stand on its apex.

I am so glad you have been enjoying Ireland in quiet. We love our bit of country and are bent on keeping it as a summer refuge always.[9] Dear Mrs. Ponsonby,

Yours affectionately,
M. E. Lewes.

## GE TO WILLIAM BLACKWOOD, WITLEY, 18 OCTOBER 1877

*MS:* National Library of Scotland. *Hitherto unpublished.*

The Heights | Witley | October 18. 77.

My dear Mr. William

It was pleasant to see your nice handwriting again. Thanks for the copy of the subscription list, which seems encouraging.

The parcel of (4) copies [1] is come, and I am well satisfied with the sobriety and clear lettering of the volume. The compact form is very welcome to me for my own behoof. Naturally, we did not bring copies

8. Connop Thirlwall (1797–1875). I have not found this story about Peter Wilhelm Forchhammer (1801–94), whose *Die Athener und Sokrates: die Gesetzlichen und der Revolutionär,* Berlin, 1837, offended him.

9. Cross omits "always."

1. *Daniel Deronda,* 1 vol., 7/6. "A Cheap Edition in One Volume. . . . Uniform with the one-volume edition of 'Middlemarch.' With Vignette engraved by Jeens." (*Athenaeum,* 27 October 1877, p. 546.)

of my own books in our small cargo, and I have often been wanting a "Deronda".

We are rather sorry to think that we shall be in the murky air of town again on the 30th., the air here entering into one's consciousness as some mysterious source of good spirits. I hope you will happen to be on a visit to England next year during the time of our 'villeggiatura,' so that you may come and see our beautiful bit of country.

On the 25th we move from this house to leave the servants time for emptying it of our 'bits o' things' and getting them in order in their old places at the Priory. So that after the 25th proofs or anything else should be addressed to me in London.

Yes, we are having delicious autumnal skies—a sharp air, though, and our share of the storms blowing off our tiles with a thunderous sound that made us imagine the chimney was falling.

I hope that, in spite of the unkind season in the North, you have been having some pleasant holidays. But I imagine that the sort of holiday you care most for begins in November.

[*The rest of this letter has been cut away.*]

## GE TO MME EUGÈNE BODICHON, WITLEY, 18 OCTOBER 1877

*MS:* Mr. Philip Leigh-Smith. *Hitherto unpublished.*

The Heights | Witley | October 18. 77.

Dearest Barbara

We shall get to the Priory on Monday the 29th., and the next day, if I may, I shall call to see you—a much longed-for comfort to my heart.

We are both very well, and have liked our new summer house. Till the 29th.,

Your ever loving, old
Marian.

## GE TO CHARLES RITTER, WITLEY, 20 OCTOBER 1877

*MS:* Bibliothèque Publique et Universitaire, Geneva. *Extracts published:* Cross, New Edition, pp. 567–568.

The Heights | Witley | October 20. 77.

Dear M. Ritter

I am quite willing that you should translate any passages from those articles of mine mentioned in your letter,[2] if you think them worthy of that trouble. The only other article which occurs to me just now as easy to be found by you is one on Mr. Lecky's 'Modern Rationalism' in the first number of the Fortnightly Review, published, I think, in 1866.[3]

For many years I have renounced all anonymous writing, and with regard to the republication of small productions no longer current, I am anxious not to add to that calamity of our age, superfluous literature. A passage here and there may be worth selecting, but I should hardly overcome the scruples which hinder me from making up a volume out of occasional writings which at best would not be so fruitful to the reader as some neglected work by one of our elder writers. Do you not mourn with me over the dissipation of men's time on ever-multiplying periodicals, and new books that say badly what was well said in our own language by some dead author whose contribution ought to live in our grateful consciousness?

We are about to return to London, so that any communication you may wish to make to me, must be sent to the old address. I am grieved to hear of M. Scherer's heavy domestic loss.[4] But all France is a subject of grief now, is it not? One reads the 'Times' with more anxiety about the French question than about the Russo-Turkish War. The prospects of our Western civilization seem more critically involved in the maintenance of the French Republic than in the result of the Bulgarian struggle—momentous as that too is felt to be by prophetic souls.

Thanks for your friendly wishes about our health. We have both highly enjoyed our country home, and are in much better health than when we had the pleasure of seeing you.

2. In his letter to GE, dated Morges, 10 October 1877 Ritter asks permission to translate passages from GE's articles on Heine, Riehl, and Young, which GHL had shown him in the *Westminster Review,* and to give the author's name. (Yale.)

3. "The Influence of Rationalism," *Fortnightly Review,* 1 (15 May 1865), 43–55.

4. Edmond Schérer's son died 6 August 1877.

Mr. Lewes unites with me in kind regards, and I am always

Yours most sincerely

M. E. Lewes.

## JOHN AND WILLIAM BLACKWOOD TO GHL, ST. ANDREWS, 25 OCTOBER 1877

*MS:* National Library of Scotland. *Hitherto unpublished.*

**Strathtyrum | St. Andrews | N.B.**

October 25/77.

My Dear Lewes

The calculations of cost and produce of new edition of The Works of George Eliot have been sent over to me and I now beg to inclose formal offer for this edition.

I knew that the profits on it must be small unless the sale went beyond what we could reasonably hope for, but it was necessary to have such a standard edition round which I hope to see the more popular editions cluster and flourish.

You will see that we do not propose the lordship on each volume to commence until it has reached a sale of 500 copies and the reason for this is that it will take a sale of some 750 copies to pay the preliminary expences stereotyping etc.

With a somewhat similar edition of Lytton's works we had a painful warning to be cautious but in this case although a large sale cannot be looked for at first, my hope is that there will be a quiet but steady sale which will gradually bring in a steady little income. The book will I think be as handsome as well could be and form I hope a permanent and creditable presentment of George Eliot's Works.

Willie sent me Mrs. Lewes' charming letter to him and I rejoice to think that her stay in your country home has done you both so much good. For her sake I shall always think of that lovely place with pleasure and gratitude. The constant temptation to wander out of doors is the great thing in the Country but the dear old Priory has its pleasantnesses too and I hope this will find you comfortably established there for the winter. The Books, Friends, and other comforts not exactly such as The Bailie sighed for in "the Saut Market" will make some amends for the woods and walks of Witley. Our weather has been so sadly broken that I should have been frightened to press Mrs. Lewes to come here at this season. We had nearly continuous rain for a month at what should have been our midsummer. In the midst of it my daughter gazing gloomily out of the window exclaimed "We might as well be in Edinburgh." This disparaging allusion to the Town which contains 45 George St. and 3 Randolph Cres[cen]t rather riled me, but in the circumstances I let it pass. Since that deluge we have had broken weather but some very fine days and I hope your last days in the country have been as bright as it has been with us today.

I am very pleased that you like the translation of the Jewish Rabbi's tribute to Deronda so much. To me it reads as a very striking and original pamphlet and I hope the press will take it up.

I have been very remiss in correspondence of late but I have been constantly thinking of writing to Mrs. Lewes or you. The fact is I knew that this edition would not afford such a sum as I should like to give the author for any edition of her works and that worried and made me put off writing. You however know as much about paper and print as I do and have also I think our calculations for printing etc. and will not I hope be disappointed.

ever yours truly
John Blackwood.

G. H. Lewes Esq.

P.S. My Uncle has sent me this to forward to you and told me to add anything that he had omitted to allude to in his letter. The only point that occurs to me is as to the edition of Romola published by Smith and Elder at 2/6. I think my Uncle's understanding was that their edition was or is to be withdrawn as it would not be pleasant to have it run in opposition to our editions at 10/- and at 3/6. Their stereotype plates of it would not I suppose serve for our reissue but should they not be transferred to us? Please give my best thanks to Mrs. Lewes for writing me so charming an answer to my letter, and I hope to send her a further memo of Deronda sales beginning of next month. Mrs. Lewes is quite right in supposing that the kind of holiday I like is commencing now and I have already had two or three cheering gallops.

W. B.

## JOHN BLACKWOOD TO GHL, ST. ANDREWS, 25 OCTOBER 1877

*MS:* National Library of Scotland. *Endorsed:* Proposal for Cabinet Edition 1877. *Hitherto unpublished.*

**Strathtyrum | St. Andrews | N.B.**
October 25/77.

My Dear Lewes

We now beg to make the following offer for the library edition of the Works of George Eliot now in preparation in nineteen volumes to sell nominally at 5/- per volume. On the 17 prose volumes we propose to pay a lordship of 1/1½ on each copy of every volume sold after the first 500, and on the two volumes of Poetry, The Spanish Gipsy and Jubal, a lordship of 1/6 and 1/8 respectively on the same condition of a first free sale of 500 copies.

In the letter accompanying this I have further explained the principle on which this offer is made and we hope it may meet Mrs. Lewes' views and yours.

It is about what can be afforded on this edition of the books but we are ready to do anything we possibly can to meet your ideas in the matter.

yours most sincerely
John Blackwood
Wm Blackwood and Sons.

G. H. Lewes Esq.

## GHL DIARY, SIX MILE BOTTOM, 25–27 OCTOBER 1877

*MS:* Mrs. Ouvry. *Hitherto unpublished.*

**Thursday 25 October 1877**

Horrible weather all day. Reached Six Mile Bottom at 5. Party to dinner—music in the evening.

The difference between Universalists and Unitarians. The one think God too good to d--n people, the other think themselves too good to be d----d.

Three men on a raft being swept down Niagara. "Can no one sing a hymn?" "No." "Nor a prayer?" "No." "We must do something religious—let's make a *collection.*"

An old man left his property to his nephew but with a life rent of it to an old woman of 80, bedridden. When the will was read the Nephew rose and said "I take ye all to witness that I'll bide the Lord's time."

A Frenchman entered the hotel salon at Chamouny declaring he had just made an expedition up Mont Blanc. "Vous avez fait l'ascension?" "Je crois bien!" "Jusqu'au sommet?" "Pas précisément jusqu'au sommet—mais jusqu'au Montanvert."

A very merry party on board a Cunard Steamer. Plenty of stories told; one man never smiled nor made a remark. The capt. asked him why this was. "Why you see, sir, I'm a liar myself."

**Friday 26 October 1877**

Sedley Taylor [5] came to Halls, and played and read at the *Penny Reading* which Hall got up for the farm servants etc. I recited 'Chesnut Horse', 'Garrick and the Cock' and the Frenchman at the station. Lawn Tennis. Read *Deronda.*

**Saturday 27 October 1877**

Johnnie, Sedley Taylor, Prof. Stewart [6] etc. guests. great fun and interesting talks. Lawn Tennis. Deronda.

## GE TO MRS. EDWARD ATKINSON,[7] LONDON, 29 OCTOBER 1877

*Text:* Chicago Book and Art Auctions, Inc., Catalogue 32 (11–12 April 1933), item 129.

The Priory.

Many kind letters come to me from your side of the Atlantic which want of time and strength for unnecessary correspondence obliges me to leave unanswered.[8] But I cannot allow you to imagine me discour-

5. Sedley Taylor (1834–1920), Fellow of Trinity, and President of the University Music Club. Most of the stories GHL notes were his.

6. James Stuart describes the visit in his *Reminiscences,* 1912, p. 123. He was disillusioned at meeting GHL in the flesh, having thought of him with Homer and Virgil. He found GE's conversation "rather stately," and her features like Savonarola's. "I think she must have had a Jewish ancestry."

7. Mary Caroline Heath, wife of Edward Atkinson (1827–1905) of Brookline, Massachusetts.

8. Not all the letters were transatlantic. From Leonard A. Montefiore, 18 Portman Square, GHL received word 17 October [1877] that "having dreamt Mrs. Lewes was desperately ill, and being haunted by the dream continually, I have at last ventured to write to you to ask you to dispel it," and requesting that GHL merely put "Dream wrong" on the enclosed card and post it. (Yale.)

teously indifferent to your friendly recollections of our interviews in old days. That you are the mother of grown up children is one of the many reminders I am constantly receiving that the larger part of life's journey lies behind me. . . .

M. E. Lewes.

## GE TO JOHN BLACKWOOD, LONDON, 5 NOVEMBER 1877

*MS:* National Library of Scotland. *Hitherto unpublished.*

**The Priory, | 21. North Bank, | Regents Park.**
November 5. 77.

My dear Mr. Blackwood

I send by post the manuscript of a poem written early in 1874,[9] about which I have only the request to make that you will allow it to be printed for me to the extent of two proofs—simply that I may keep it by me for a gradual estimate in the more flaw-revealing form of type. And will you, please, ask that it may be printed in the same *format* as Jubal?

I should like you to read it when you have an hour's quiet leisure and tell me whether it makes itself easily intelligible and impressive for you. It is not a milky meal.

I am very glad to think that we have settled together on a satisfactory standing form for the series of books. And though I have little confidence in a great sale for such an edition in this un-book-buying world, I trust that there will be enough to hinder any regret.

If you think it not inconsistent with prudence or any wise consideration to print a 3/6 edition of 'Romola' under the existing right of Smith and Elder to continue their 2/6 edition, I shall like much to see it ranging with our handsome 3/6 volumes. But of course I should not wish anything in opposition to etiquette.

I imagine you will remain at Strathtyrum till the end of November and am hoping that you share our fine days. The summer was such as to make us resigned to giving up that journey to Scotland which was made tempting by your kind wish to see us there. I hope you are nevertheless the better for the month of country life. Town does not greatly commend itself to us as an exchange for our Heights.

9. "A College Breakfast-Party." One of the proofs with GE's corrections is in the Parrish Collection, Princeton.

A post card to say you have received the M.S. is the only needful response to this, until you have something that you care to say.

Always yours truly
M. E. Lewes.

## GE TO JOHN WALTER CROSS, LONDON, 6 NOVEMBER 1877

*MS:* Yale. *Envelope:* J. W. Cross Esq. | Weybridge Heath | Weybridge | S.W. *Postmarks:* ST. JOHNS-WOOD | C 5 | NO 6 | 77 | N.W; WEYBRIDGE-STATION | A | NO 7 | 77. *Extract published:* Cross, III, 318.

**The Priory, | 21. North Bank, | Regents Park.**
November 6. 77.

My dearest Nephew

If I could find it in my heart I should scold you for not observing a precept of the Seven Sages.[10] Two battledores and a shuttle cock would have been apparatus enough for my skill, or want of skill. And we find that with these we can play a modest game in our little entrance hall. I cannot bear to have that magnificent rainbow of a net and its polished poles exposed to the alternate smoke and rain of this avenue to Tartarus. But with all this grumbling at your too lavish generosity under these morose skies, I am deeply touched by your thoughtful kindness.

Still—which would you choose? An aunt who lost headaches and gained flesh by spending her time on tennis and Badminton,[1] or an aunt who remained sickly and beckoned death by writing more books? Behold yourself in a dilemma! If you choose the plump and idle aunt, she will declare that you don't mind about her writing. If you choose the pallid and productive aunt she will declare that you have no real affection for her. It is impossible to satisfy an author.

Apropos of authorship I was a little uneasy on Sunday [2] because I had seemed in the unmanageable current of talk to echo a too slight way of speaking about a great poet. I did not mean to say Amen when

10. Cleobulos, one of the Seven Wise Men of Greece, had for his maxim "Avoid extremes"—the golden mean. (E. C. Brewer, *The Reader's Handbook,* 1923, p. 987.)

1. "Johnnie sent up a Badminton. We tried it in the garden but the wind was too strong." (GHL Diary, 4 November 1877.) "Battledore and shuttlecock in the drawing room." (6 November.) The first reference to badminton in the *OED* is in 1874.

2. The callers listed in GHL's Diary for Sunday, 4 November 1877 are Edith [Simcox], Johnnie [Cross], Mr. and Mrs. George Howard, Herbert Spencer, Dr. Youmans, Norman and Richard Grosvenor, Sanderson, Leslie Stephen, and Burne-Jones.

'The Idyls of the King' seemed to be judged rather 'de haût en bas.' I only meant that I should value for my own mind 'In Memoriam' as the chief of the larger works, and that while I feel exquisite beauty in passages scattered through the Idyls, I must judge some smaller wholes among the lyrics as the works most decisive of Tennyson's high place among the immortals.

Not that my deliverance on this matter is of any moment, but that I cannot bear to fall in with the sickening fashion of people who talk much about writers whom they read little, and pronounce on a great man's powers with only half his work in their mind, while if they remembered the other half they would find their judgments as to his limits flatly contradicted. Then again, I think Tennyson's dramas such as the world should be glad of—and would be if there had been no pre-judgment that he could not write a drama.

Perhaps you will reflect that all this scribbling is my Badminton for a wet morning.

Your affectionate Aunt
M. E. Lewes.

## GE TO ALEXANDER MACMILLAN, LONDON, 10 NOVEMBER 1877

*Text:* C. L. Graves, *Life and Letters of Alexander Macmillan,* Macmillan and Co., 1910, pp. 343–344.

The Priory, | North Bank, | Regent's Park. | November 10, 1877.

The quotation from Sainte-Beuve which I mentioned to you[3] is on page 11 of his 'Cahiers': "La critique pour moi (comme pour M. Joubert) c'est le plaisir de connaître les esprits, non de les régenter."

As to the work in which you have done me the honour to ask for my co-operation,[4] I feel obliged to decline your proposal, though your

3. John Morley had projected the series of short biographies later known as the English Men of Letters. Matthew Arnold and Seeley having refused to undertake the volume on Shakespeare, Morley asked Macmillan to propose it to GE. GE did not refuse at once, promising to consider the matter. When he lunched with her at the Priory 9 November, she quoted this passage from Ste. Beuve, which she thought might be the motto for the series. The next day she wrote this letter. For an account of the negotiations see also Charles Morgan, *The House of Macmillan,* 1943, p. 117, which adds a passage from Macmillan's letter to Morley omitted by Graves: "It is clear that our *Prima Donna* must be paid on a different scale from the others —whether 3 or 5 times we must consider and consult."

4. John Morley wrote GE 12 November 1877 expressing his regret that she would not write the volume: "I feel as

kindness has given me many reasons for wishing to meet your views. I like to think that you will not be at a loss to find a writer who will treat that supreme subject in literature at once reverently and with independence.

## GE TO MRS. PETER ALFRED TAYLOR, LONDON, 10 NOVEMBER 1877

*Text:* Cross, III, 319.

Never augur ill because you do not hear from me. It is, you know, my profession *not* to write letters. Happily I can meet your kind anxiety by contraries. I have for two months and more been in better health than I have known for several years. This pleasant effect is due to the delicious air of the breezy Surrey hills; and further, to a friend's insistence on my practising lawn-tennis as a daily exercise.

We are in love with our Surrey house, and only regret that it hardly promises to be snug enough for us chilly people through the winter, so that we dare not think of doing without the warmer nest in town.

## GE TO ELIZABETH STUART PHELPS, LONDON, 13 NOVEMBER 1877

*MS:* The late Mr. Gabriel Wells. A copy misdated 13 March 1877 is at Yale. *Published: Century Magazine,* 104 (September 1922), pp. 646–647.

**The Priory, | 21. North Bank, | Regents Park.**
November 13. 77.

My dear Miss Phelps

Sincere thanks for your kind letter and for the copy of Avis [5] which has been duly sent to me. I have read several chapters, and shall continue to read the work with interest, but as I shall read it slowly, taking it up at odd moments, I cannot defer all sign of my sympathy till I reach the end. What you say of broken health as a hindrance and a severe demand for submission to doing the smaller thing where you had hoped to do the greater, goes straight to my heart. This sort of

if the sun had gone out of the sky, editorially speaking, since yesterday. It would have made such a difference in the spirits and good heart of us all, if you had consented to lead us." (Alderman Library, University of Virginia.)

5. *The Story of Avis,* Miss Phelps's partly autobiographical novel of a strong-minded woman, published at Boston in the autumn of 1877.

renunciation or resignation enters more or less into the life of every ardent soul, for its vision and longing must always be larger than its achievement, but when the limit is fixed by bodily weakness or malaise the trial is incomparably hard. I know something of this.

I find the writing of these early chapters filled with indications of that keen sensibility and observation which are only to be attained through much inward experience, which always means a large proportion of pain as well as enjoyment. But do not expect 'criticism' from me. I hate 'sitting in the seat of judgment,' and I would rather try to impress the public generally with the sense that they may get the best result from a book without necessarily forming an 'opinion' about it, than I would rush into stating opinions of my own. The floods of nonsense printed in the form of critical opinions seem to me a chief curse of our time, a chief obstacle to true culture.

In general—perhaps I may have told you—it is my rule not to read contemporary fiction, and I have had to say so in many cases to country-women of yours. But you are an exceptional woman to my feeling, and I read your 'Avis.' Only let this be *entre nous.* I am usually studying some particular subject, and the reading I take outside that line is done aloud to Mr. Lewes. I daresay you will understand that for my own spiritual food I need all other sorts of reading more than I need fiction. I know nothing of our contemporary English novelists with the exception of Miss Thackeray's and (a few of) Anthony Trollope's works. My constant groan is, that I must leave so much of the greatest writing which the centuries have sifted for us, unread for want of time.

I can answer your kind inquiries about my health more cheerfully than usual. A summer spent on the breezy hills of Surrey and in untravelling quietude has sent me back to town with a sense of strength which I had not known for the last two or three years.

O that difficult question—how to make men temperate.[6] One moves despairingly in a circle: they can't leave off drinking till they have something else to cheer them, and they can't get a taste for that something else till they leave off drinking. At least, this is the form of fact in the case of our own day-labourers. But of course, we as well as you, have the drinking mania which is part of the idle-wealthy craving for excitement.

Always yours sincerely,
M. E. Lewes.

6. A bar-room murder at Gloucester, Massachusetts, where Miss Phelps spent her summers, impelled her to work actively for temperance among the fishermen of the town. See Mary Angela Bennett, *Elizabeth Stuart Phelps,* Philadelphia, 1939, pp. 67–69.

## GE TO SARA SOPHIA HENNELL, LONDON, 16 NOVEMBER 1877

*MS:* Yale. *Extracts published:* Cross, III, 320–322.

**The Priory, | 21. North Bank, | Regents Park.**
November 16. 77.

My dear Sara

Having a more secure freedom than I may have next week, I satisfy my eagerness to tell you that I am longing for the news of you which you have accustomed me to trust in as sure to come at this time of the year. You will give me, will you not?—something more than an affectionate greeting. You will tell me how and where you have been and what is the actual state of your health and spirits—whether you can still interest yourself in writing on great subjects without too much fatigue, and what companionship is now the most precious to you.

Jot me down a few particulars at a time, so that the letter may not be too great a bore to you, and be assured that the most trivial jotting will have interest for me.

We returned from our country home (with which we are much in love) at the beginning of this month, leaving it earlier than we wished because of the need to get workmen into it. Our bit of Surrey has the beauties of Scotland wedded to those of Warwickshire, and in front of our hill we have a valley which would be equal to what one sees from Richmond Hill—if the river were not wanting. Water is the one deficiency.

During the last two months of our stay there I was conscious of more health and strength than I have known for several years. Imagine me playing at lawn tennis by the hour together!

The other day [7] we went to see Mr. and Mrs. Call for the first time since their return to England. We were sorry to find the husband ailing, but Mrs. Call seems to me brighter and freer from any check of suffering than she was years ago. It is a most hopeful fact that when she was at Rome, she had a long span of entire freedom from rheumatic pain. But our visit was spoiled by the entrance of two ladies, who sent us away before we had heard enough. I hope that Frank is now a source of comfort rather than of anxiety.

Last night a little packet sent by Mr. Bray seemed a cheerful sign that his health allows of much interest and activity. Perhaps dear Cara will be moved to send me a line or two about herself and him.

Do you know that our dear Madame Bodichon, whose life was so

7. 8 November 1877. (GHL Diary.)

full of active benevolence, was some months ago stricken with an attack of aphasia and other symptoms of nervous weakness? She had gone to a cottage she has in Cornwall for the sake of taking there Madame Mario, whose overtasked frame was much in need of change and rest, and lo, Barbara herself was stricken and Madame Mario became her energetic nurse. The attack has long passed its worst, and she is completely like herself in everything except strength. Just now she is at Hastings.

Madame Belloc (Bessie Parkes) has lately lost her aged mother,[8] but is bent on settling in London with her little boy and girl, that their education may be thoroughly English. Every year she takes them to France to meet two old, old little ladies, her mother-in-law and her (the mother's) inseparable companion Mademoiselle Montgolfier, daughter of the aëronaut.[9]

Another common acquaintance, Herbert Spencer, is coming to lunch with us today. He is very flourishing and, as usual, cheerful. His old objection to biography is so far dropped that he is preparing materials for his own. I think I never see any one else whom you know. But some weeks ago I had a note from Miss Julia Smith, written in almost as pretty a hand as ever, telling me about Barbara.

The Saturday before last we went to the christening of a new little Eleanor,[1] Charles and Gertrude's third baby, born in June last. The christening took place in Dr. Sadler's chapel[2] where Miss Marshall, eleven years ago, came to look on at their marriage. Dr. Sadler is a benignant-faced refined man whose voice and manner make the occasion such as affects one without any moral jar. Our two little ones at Natal are delicate, and so is their mother, but we are assured that the climate there gives the best hope of their being reared. The widowed mother writes with a loving unselfishness which has given us an affection for her all across the ocean.

I can't think of any other news that would be likely to interest you, for the world I live in is chiefly one that has grown around me in these later years, since we have seen so little of each other. Doubtless, we are both greatly changed in spiritual as well as bodily matters, but I think we are unchanged in the friendship founded on early memories. I, for

8. Elizabeth Rayner Priestley Parkes died 10 October 1877 at 17 Wimpole St., aged 80. (*Pall Mall Budget,* 19 October 1877.)

9. Mme Louis Belloc and Mlle Adelaide Montgolfier. For a charming account of these ladies see Mrs. Belloc Lowndes, *"I, Too, Have Lived in Arcadia,"* New York, 1942.

1. Elinor Southwood Lewes, now Mrs. Carrington Ouvry.

2. Thomas Sadler (1822–91), minister of the Rosslyn Hill Unitarian Chapel, 1861–91, conducted GE's funeral.

my part, feel increasing gratitude for the cheering and stimulus your companionship gave me, and only think with pain that I might have profited more by it, if my mind had been more open to good influences.

Your loving
Pollian.

## JOHN BLACKWOOD TO GE, EDINBURGH, 21 NOVEMBER 1877

*MS:* National Library of Scotland. *Hitherto unpublished.*

**45, George Street, | Edinburgh.**
November 21/77.

My Dear Mrs. Lewes

I inclose proof of The "College Breakfast Party" which I should have written with before, but the subject of this striking dialogue is not one on which I feel well qualified to write or speak although I daresay I have thought as much as most people about it.

Were I to attempt to criticise the conversation of Hamlet and his friends [3] I fear I should be as much puzzled as any of the interlocutors, but one does not require to be a philosopher or theologian to appreciate the poetical beauty of the thoughts and language. There are lines without end for quotation and the whole picture is characteristic of the Youth of the present day who are given to beating out their brains upon what it is not granted to them to understand.

What a comment upon most sermons is your concluding line. They do indeed "leave the soul in wider emptiness." Confident divines do not allow their lips to be sealed as Hamlet does. What form of publication do you think of?

Simpson is writing to you about the omission of the Motto [4] in the 7/6 edition of Deronda for which he has visited the printing office justly and severely. The edition I am happy to say is going off well and we have only some 400 left of the 5250 printed.

The Cabinet edition of the novels is going to be a beautiful book and we shall be happy to meet Lewes' suggestion of increasing the

3. The speakers in "A College Breakfast Party" are "Young Hamlet, not the hesitating Dane, | But one named after him, who lately strove | For honours at our English Wittenberg," and his friends Horatio, Osric, Rosencranz, Guildenstern, Laertes, and the Priest. The tone of the conversation and many of the opinions reflect those of the group of men GE met at Trinity College, Cambridge in May 1873.

4. Ch. 29, the motto from Whitman. See 18 April 1876. It was restored in the Cabinet edition.

lordship after the sale of 2000 copies by making it after that number are sold 1/3 on each of the 17 volumes and 1/7 and 1/10 on each of the other two volumes.

Smith and Elder's cheap edition will be a formidable competitor to our 3/6 edition of Romola, but we shall print it in that form like the others.

How have you been since you came back to Town? The weather has been very trying but I hope you have not suffered from it and have been able to take advantage of the occasional fine days for walking.

We left Strathtyrum about a fortnight ago, and as usual there was weeping and wail at leaving the country. "It's awfu' dull when ye're away" was the pathetic farewell of the gardner's wife to my wife and daughter, and her words found an echo in their hearts. However we are pretty cheery in Town and I hear of various ongoings contemplated. The weather makes one think more of the unfortunate wretches on both sides in Bulgaria and Asia Minor. It is too horrible.

With best regards to Lewes and hoping to get good accounts of you I am

always yours truly

John Blackwood.

P.S. I had nearly forgot to send the inclosed from friend Main. What do you think? We are willing to undertake the book if you approve.[5]

## GE TO JOHN BLACKWOOD, LONDON, 22 NOVEMBER 1877

*MS:* National Library of Scotland. *Hitherto unpublished.*

**The Priory, | 21. North Bank, | Regents Park.**

November 22. 77.

My dear Mr. Blackwood

Thanks for your kind letter with its agreeable news. I am much comforted by the speedy sale of the 7/6 edition. Beforehand, I should have thought 5000 a rash number to print.

On the specimen title-page for the Cabinet Edition, which Mr. Simpson has sent, Mr. Lewes has written a suggestion which I think will be found an improvement. The design for the cover we like very much. I had thought of a rich olive green for the colour—a hue which

5. Main proposed *The George Eliot Birthday Book,* a kind of diary with short extracts from the works of GE at the headings and opposite the space for the names of friends to be written.

sets off well both the gold and the black.[6] But Mr. Simpson promises to let us see specimens. Is it not desirable to omit any numbering of the volumes *according to the series?*—for two reasons: first, because the order of publication is not the chronological, in which they should ultimately be ranged, and secondly, because it would be a disadvantage for the independent sale of the several works. Is it not usual to omit such serial numbering?—for example the volumes of De Quincey's works are not numbered except furtively, by stars, and Thackeray's not at all.

As to Mr. Main's proposition, we have never seen or heard anything of the said 'Birthday Books'—have you? They may be the vulgarest things in the book stalls for what we know. *Entre nous,* I am a little shocked by the tone of Mr. M's letter. How could he be so ignorant as to suppose that any other publishing house than yours could issue such a book?

I can give no opinion about a 'George Eliot Birthday Book' unless I saw the 'Tennyson do.' [7] with which it is to follow suit. But in general such suits are not what—I should be fond of following or having followed on my behalf. Nor can I see that the book of 'Sayings' is insufficient for the purpose which Mr. Lewes mentions as the only motive for sanctioning a new issue of extracts, namely, that it is always a way of spreading acquaintance with one's writing. It is true that the book of 'Sayings' is bulky. But I must refer the matter to your judgment. Burns and Shakspeare books are no criterion for a living writer. The Tennyson book would be such, and I confess I should like to see its aspect before consenting. I believe that you, as much as I, hate puffing, gaudy, claptrappy forms of publication, superfluous for all *good* ends. But anything graceful which you consider an advantage to the circulation of my works we are not averse to.

Please tell Mr. Simpson that I agree with him as to the moderating the 'heels' of the design for the cover—and also that I am [*The rest of this letter is lacking.*]

6. The 1st ed. was bound in green cloth.

7. *The Tennyson Birthday Book,* ed. by E[mily] Shakespear, was published by H. S. King, 1877.

## GE TO MME EUGÈNE BODICHON, LONDON, 22 NOVEMBER 1877

*MS:* Mr. Philip Leigh-Smith. *Hitherto unpublished.*

**The Priory, | 21. North Bank, | Regents Park.**
November 22. 77.

Dearest Barbara

I was very glad to have your nephew's letter giving me some news of you, and I trust that if he were to write again now he could tell me of your more rapid progress in strength. Here the weather alternates daily from dismal raininess and mugginess to clear, sharp cheeriness. At Hastings I hope you are spared the dark days.

The day before yesterday we drove to Mrs. Allingham's to see her pictures—a charming little collection.[8] We were heartily glad to see her looking healthy again, and there were also the children to admire, the boy a striking beauty from his rare tone of colour.

Everything is well with us according to the town standard, except that you are away and not yet robust. We have seen many pleasant friends on our Sundays, and now our Saturday concerts have begun to give us our weekly musical food. The sadder part of one's life is reading the Times reports about France,[9] and imagining the sufferings of the poor unglorified fellows in the ranks both Russian and Turkish.

By the way, have you read Tourguéneff's *Terre Neuve?* [1] It is worth reading. But of course you take care—or Miss Scott [2] takes care for you—not to let your head get tired. And I too must take care not to tire you with too many suggestions.

God bless you, dear. Offer my best regards to Miss Scott.

Your ever loving
Marian.

8. "Went to see Mrs. Allingham's drawings for the Water Colour." (GHL Diary, 20 November 1877.)

9. The struggle for control of France following President MacMahon's resignation in October 1877.

1. *Terres Vierges,* Paris, 1877. GE's copy is now in Dr. Williams's Library.

2. Charlotte Angus Scott (1858–1931), at Girton from 1876 to 1880. See 5 February 1880.

## GE TO MRS. CHARLES BRAY, LONDON, 23 NOVEMBER 1877

*MS:* Yale. *Hitherto unpublished.*

**The Priory, | 21. North Bank, | Regents Park.**
November 23. 77.

My dear Cara

About Nelson's intention to 'burke' your 'Morals,' Mr. Lewes is incredulous. He thinks it does not lie in the sane publisher's nature to waste material in that way, after he has paid for it. But who shall say what does or does not lie in human stupidity, whether well or ill-intentioned?

Thank you very much for the accounts you have sent me of Mr. Bray's state of health and our friends Mrs. Pears and Mrs. Cash. I long that we may have a mild winter to save Mr. Bray and you from an increase of his bronchial trouble. But the prospect for poor Mrs. Pears seems to me more dismal than it can ever be for your husband with his mental activity and cheerfulness.[3]

Please give my love to dear Mrs. Cash. I think one may reasonably hope that her constitution will surmount the present symptoms about the heart. Our landlady (for three years at Richmond) had a severe attack of angina pectoris and her physician said to me in a solemn tone —"Ah, poor Mrs. Croft will not last long—she has organic disease". But she *did* last long and in very comfortable health.

When I had read your letter to Mr. Lewes, he said, "What a pretty picture that is of Cara playing the Messiah every Sunday for forty years!" I see the picture as it *used* to be, in the dear old drawing-room at Rosehill.

Tell Mr. Bray he has not seized the drift of Mr. Lewes's chapter on Motion.[4] But we get along mainly by a pathway of misunderstandings —proving good cases against somebody who has never questioned them.

Mrs. Merridew I think must be a very beautiful sight in her old age —there was a nobleness of type in her face that years would not spoil. Yours always lovingly

M. E. L.

I enclose a note to Sara.

3. Mrs. Bray wrote GE: "Poor Mrs. Pears is sadly out of health from sheer want of nourishment, her throat growing too narrow and too sore to swallow without severe pain and effort." (9 September 1876. NYPL.)

4. *Problems of Life and Mind,* II, 202–210, ch. 5.

## GE TO SARA SOPHIA HENNELL, LONDON, 23 NOVEMBER [1877]

*MS:* Yale. *Hitherto unpublished.*

November 23.

My dear Sara

I enjoyed your letter greatly. Thank you for the exertion you undertook for my sake. I thoroughly appreciate the effort it requires to give oneself forth in a letter, and I hardly know how I should get through my life with decent regard to gratuitous correspondents' feelings if Mr. Lewes did not come to my rescue and do most of my 'answering' for me.

But I want to tell you that you must not interpret H. S's indifference to your ideas and authorship as any special negation towards you because you are a woman. He has, whenever it was possible, shown just the same blank towards Mr. Lewes, who certainly has more claims on him as an older friend <who was> very generous to him in the days of his obscurity. With regard to not reading books or listening to ideas, I must again plead for him, as I have done before, that he is not a reader, and that his mind both "spontanément and systématiquement" rejects everything that cannot be wrought into the web of his own production.[5] He has this in common with many productive minds. And you must not regard him in the light of a person who will be moved by sympathies. We have long given up vain expectations from him and can therefore enjoy our regard for him without disturbance by his negations. He comes and consults us about his own affairs, and that is his way of showing friendship. We never dream of telling him *our* affairs, which would certainly not interest him. I write this only to prevent you from retaining the belief that he has any specially ignoring or contemning disposition towards you either as to your personality or your womanhood.

Your description of your astronomical pleasures at Llandudno makes us envy you. We have never seen Saturn's ring, nor Jupiter's moons—'nor nuffin'—except the wondrous eclipse of the moon which exhibited itself to perfection in front of our drawing-room window.[6]

I am rather amazed at your enjoyment of 'the New Republic.' To

5. Cf. Huxley's remark that Spencer's definition of a tragedy was the spectacle of a deduction killed by a fact. See also [29 June 1852].

6. The eclipse 23 August 1877 was total from 10:19 to 12:03 in a cloudless sky. See *Times,* 24 August, p. 9f.

me it was a hateful book. But the Master of Balliol who is chiefly insulted is my particular friend.

Your loving
Pollian.

## GE JOURNAL, LONDON, 26 NOVEMBER 1877

*MS:* Yale. *Extracts published:* Cross, III, 322.

The other day we saw in the Times that G's name had been proposed for the Rectorship of St. Andrews.[7] Blackwood writes me that in less than a month they have sold off all but 400 of the 5250 printed. And in October were sold 495 of the 3/6 Adam Bede. Magnificat anima mea!

Our friend Dr. Allbut came to see us last week, after we had missed each other for 3 or 4 years.

## GE TO FRANÇOIS D'ALBERT-DURADE, LONDON, 27 NOVEMBER 1877

*Text:* Copy by D'Albert-Durade in Tinker Collection, Yale. *Hitherto unpublished.*

The Priory | 21 North Bank | Regent's Park | November 27. 77.
My dear Friend

I have just received and read aloud to my husband your kind letter and answer it at once that I may not again seem [un]mindful of my tenderly remembered and remembering friends.

Your account of Madame D'Albert comforts me. That she retains her soundness of mind and can enjoy this change of visiting you daily at your post [8] gives me a delighted sense that life is not a burthen to her. Assure her of my constant love and lively memory of her goodness. It seems rather astonishing that Mr. Alphonse has a grown up daughter! We realize our own age chiefly in the growth of the young ones who date from our latter time. Our now only son Charles, has a third little daughter who was christened Eleanor about three weeks ago. In these children and in all other conditions of our life we are thoroughly happy, and my health has of late been much improved. I hardly know

7. Browning, Arnold and Tyndall had all declined the offer. At a mass meeting 21 November Lord Selborne, Gathorne-Hardy, GHL, and George Macdonald were proposed. The first two were nominated; Lord Selborne was elected. (*Times,* 22 November 1877, p. 10e; 23 November, p. 6e.)

8. Conservateur de l'exposition permanente de l'Athénée.

whether I told you that we have bought a house in the loveliest part of Surrey for a summer residence, no longer liking so well to travel abroad as we used to do. Long railway journeys and crowded hotels are a heavy price to pay for that sight of out[-of-door] nature which we can get with more undisturbed benefit at home.

Yes! the state of affairs in France is a grief for all Europe, and many of us here are more deeply concerned about it than about the Eastern question. The arrest of trade, already in a depressed condition before the 16th May [9] is a deplorable, widely dispersed calamity. People here have greatly reduced their establishments and general expenditure, and here as with you artists find poor sale for their pictures.

We are settled in our London home for the winter and shall hardly be able to get into the country again before the end of May. That change is one which we both greatly enjoy. London, in spite of our utmost efforts to ward off visits and other engagements, is a place of continued unrest and interruption. Letters and other small claims eat away much time and leave no corresponding benefit.

You are quite right not to accede to the stupid suggestion of the publishers to reduce Romola.[1] You only have the means of judging whether "Brother Jacob" would find a welcome in any of your periodicals. I have no objection to your using it, now that you have taken the trouble to translate it, and am glad you so appreciate it. I have given the authorisation to translate "Daniel Deronda" to a Jewish writer, the brother-in-law of Calman Levy, and the translation is finished but has not yet appeared.[2]

I have had so many letters at different times from French men and women asking leave to translate first one book and then another of mine! They seem ignorant that any of them has been translated. And I really am not anxious that those which are not yet put into French should ever receive that introduction. My French public must be small. It gratifies me that your Rabbi is gratified with my work, and I thank you for putting it within his reach.

Mr. Lewes is as usual very bright and happy, working industri[ous]ly at his favourite studies, though much checked by dyspeptic headache. He begs to be remembered in my messages and heartily reciprocates

9. On this date President MacMahon replaced the Simon ministry with conservatives and caused the Senate to dissolve the Chamber of Deputies. In the October elections the Union of the Left won control.

1. D'Albert-Durade's translation of *Romola* was published by Sandoz at Neuchâtel and Geneva, by Sandoz and Fischbacher at Paris, 1878.

2. The French translation by Ernest David was published by Levy, Paris, 2 vols., 1881.

yours and Madame D'Albert's friendly regards. With earnest wishes for her and your sustainment in strength and courage as the years become more and more taxing, I remain always, dear friend

Yours affectionately
M. E. Lewes.

## GHL TO MME EUGÈNE BODICHON, LONDON [27 NOVEMBER 1877]

*MS:* Mr. Philip Leigh-Smith. *Hitherto unpublished.*

**The Priory, | 21. North Bank, | Regents Park.**
Tuesday.

Dear Barbara

Madonna begs you will give Miss Scott her kind regards and thanks for her welcome letter with its good news of your slow but sure progress. I don't know of any wicked plays to send you but the following books I do commend:

Mad. D'Agoult: *Mes Souvenirs* (very interesting picture of the Ancien Régime. She was Mad. Wagner's mother.)
Bryce: *Transcaucasia and Ararat* [3]
Huc: Voyage à Thibet [4] (*Very* good—old.)
Kaufmann: *George Eliot and Judaism* (eloquent and interesting)
Victor Hugo: *Histoire d'un Crime* [5] (I haven't read it.)

London fogs and society have rubbed the bloom off Madonna's cheeks and given us more headache than is desirable. But we plod on, with summer and the Heights in the distance.

Here's a charming story Lord Lytton sent me a day or two ago. He offered to give a little girl at Simla a new doll as hers was very dilapidated. "No thank you, Sir," she said. "I could never love a new doll as I do my dear old one. For see, she has only one leg, and only one eye, and who would love her if I didn't? New dolls know how to get on in the world—this one can't get on without me." Sweet womanhood!

Ever yours affectionately
G. H. L.

3. By James Bryce, 1877.
4. Évariste Régis Huc, *Souvenirs d'un voyage dans la Tartarie, le Thibet, et la Chine,* 1850.
5. 1877–1878.

## GE TO MRS. EDWARD BURNE-JONES, LONDON, 3 DECEMBER 1877

*MS:* Yale. *Mostly published:* Cross, III, 322–323.

**The Priory, | 21. North Bank, | Regents Park.**
December 3. 77.

Dearest Mignon

I have been made rather unhappy by my husband's impulsive proposal about Christmas. We are dull old persons, and your two sweet young ones ought to find each Christmas a new bright bead to string on their memory, whereas to spend the time with us would be to string on a dark shrivelled berry. They ought to have a group of young creatures to be joyful with. Our own children always spend their Christmas with Gertrude's family, and we have usually taken our sober merrymaking with friends out of town. Illness among these will break our custom this year,[6] and thus 'mein Mann' feeling that our Christmas was free, considered how very much he liked being with you, omitting the other side of the question—namely, our total lack of means to make a suitably joyous meeting, a real festival, for Phil and Margaret. I was conscious of this lack in the very moment of the proposal, and the consciousness has been pressing on me more and more painfully ever since. Even my husband's affectionate hopefulness cannot withstand my melancholy demonstration.

So pray consider the kill-joy proposition as entirely retracted, and give us something of yourselves only on simple black letter days when the Herald Angels have not been raising expectations early in the morning. I have been putting off too long the writing of this true deliverance, and I feel that to defer what I have to say till Friday for the chance of seeing you then might leave your mind inconveniently hampered with considerations about an arrangement with us.

I am not afraid of your misunderstanding one word. You know that it is not a little love with which I am

Yours ever
M. E. Lewes.

6. Mrs. William Cross had been confined for some time with what proved tc be her last illness. (Cross.)

## JOHN BLACKWOOD TO GE, EDINBURGH, 5 DECEMBER 1877

*Text:* Blackwood Letter Book. *Hitherto unpublished.*

45 George Street | Edinburgh December 5/77.

My Dear Mrs. Lewes

It was a great pleasure to receive your charming and most interesting letter and had I not been going off to Golf I would have sat down and written to thank you at the moment.

The inclosed is the last we have from Mr. Main and I like his choice of extracts. They at all events are undeniable good things for man whatever may be thought of the scheme of such books. To me it will be like another collection of Sayings by you.

Mr. Simpson has attended to the details you wrote about and is thinking over the best form for the Birthday Book. When we get back this specimen from you we shall try it in type.

Tell Lewes I shall be glad to hear from him how you are bearing this gloomy depressing weather. It seems to be worse in London than here where it is bad enough.

My daughter paid a visit to some friends at St. Andrews last week. Her first walk was of course to Strathtyrum where she was rapturously received by the section of dogs left there. In the midst of his gambols the collie jumped clean over her head when she turned to caress another favourite. Otherwise the place looked terribly desolate and wintry.

always yours truly
(signed) John Blackwood.

## GE TO JOHN WALTER CROSS, LONDON, 13 DECEMBER 1877

*MS:* Yale. *Envelope:* J. W. Cross Esq. | Weybridge Heath | Weybridge | S.W. *Postmarks:* ST. JOHNS-WOOD | A 3 | DE 13 | 77 | N.W; WEYBRIDGE-STATION | C | DE 13 | 77. *Published:* Cross, III, 323.

**The Priory, | 21. North Bank, | Regents Park.**
December 13. 77.

Dearest Nephew

Your note yesterday gave me much comfort, and I thank you for sparing the time to write it.

The world cannot seem quite the same to me as long as you are all in anxiety about her who is most precious to you—in immediate urgent anxiety, that is. For love is never without its shadow of anxiety. We have this treasure in earthen vessels. With best love to her and all

Your affectionate Aunt
M. E. Lewes.

## GE TO ALEXANDER MAIN, LONDON, 17 DECEMBER 1877

*Text:* Main's copy owned by Mr. John R. Sprunt. *Hitherto unpublished.*

**The Priory, | 21. North Bank, | Regents Park.**
December 17. 77.

My dear Mr. Main

Messrs. Blackwood have sent to me (and I have returned) your collection of extracts for the Birthday Book, of course with the desire that I should make any observations which occurred to me. I will only trouble you with such as appear to be quite practical.

On running through the pages I was impressed with the fact that certain small passages broken from their widely spaced dramatic connection in the complete novel where they have a value as characteristic dialogue over and above their general bearing, produce within the narrow compass of this selection a disadvantageous effect of recurrence to the same, or a similar, idea. There seem to be too many small epigrams from Mrs. Poyser and Bartle Massey on feminine perversity or stupidity, and of the former on that troublesome personage "Old Harry." I ventured rashly to mark one quotation as having been made twice. I beg pardon if I am wrong, but the quotation is one that might very well be altogether omitted.

The only other observation I have to make is, that the selections from "Daniel Deronda" seem to be noticeably scant and uncharacteristic of the work. Probably you were under pressure to get your pages ready, and writing out passages costs time. But I cannot understand why Messrs. Blackwood did not furnish sheets of the one volume edition for your use. If some of the less important quotations from the other works had been omitted in favour of more pregnant things from Deronda, this Birthday Book would have seemed less like a mere redistribution of the "Sayings."

The mottoes for the months seem very felicitously chosen.

I rather thoughtlessly, under the impulse of the first moment, put my pen across two passages and wrote "something else"—a freedom with your "copy" which would have been less unsuitable if I had thought in time of forwarding the parcel to you instead of to Edinburgh. Pray do not understand me as being disposed to find fault rather than to congratulate. I have only thought it a pity not to mention two points which may possibly serve as guidance in some small alterations or substitutions. I have put the pages to the severe test of reading them seriatim without pause, which no one else is likely to do, and besides, an author is by nature prone to think tenderly of his unquoted sentences.

Yours very sincerely
M. E. Lewes.

## JOHN BLACKWOOD TO GHL, EDINBURGH, 21 DECEMBER 1877

*Text:* Copy in Blackwood Letter Book. *Hitherto unpublished.*

45 George Street | Edinburgh December 21/77.

My Dear Lewes

I was delighted to get your note the other day with such pleasant accounts of Mrs. Lewes and I hope the approaching holiday time will find you both well and able to enjoy the congratulations of your friends.

I had a call today from Mrs. Wm. Smith who inquired for and sent most warm remembrances to you both. She is living with a niece and her husband, Mr. Constable, and I am happy to say looks well. I almost hesitated to send the enclosed for Mrs. Lewes as it may be from some "curious impertinent" but from the terms in which it is enclosed have deemed it best to forward it to you.

Thanks for your hint about Souvenirs of Madm. D'Agoult which I have sent for.

The Wars and possibilities of Wars fill one with uneasiness. I hope devoutly that we may be able to steer safely through it all. That France should be so helpless is a great embarrassment to all arrangements. What a strange turn *that* is when we think of past wars and their History.

Mr. Gathorne Hardy [8] was in Edinburgh for a banquet last week and stayed with us for a couple of days. I am happy to say that our Minister of War is I think a man who may be trusted at the helm. He

8. Gathorne Gathorne-Hardy (1814–1906) was Secretary of State for War under Disraeli, 1874–78, when he was raised to the peerage as Viscount Cranbrook.

is a very vigorous able man and also full of life and fun. We were all greatly taken with him.

Willie joins me in all good wishes and believe me

ever yours truly

(signed) John Blackwood.

Our weather is singularly mild and my wife and daughter are rejoicing in their rides.

## GE TO JOSEPH MUNT LANGFORD, LONDON, 22 DECEMBER 1877

*MS:* Mrs. Dorothy Hicks. *Hitherto unpublished.*

**The Priory, | 21. North Bank, | Regents Park.**
December 22. 77.

Dear Mr. Langford

Many years ago you mentioned, I think, that a friend of yours was acquainted with the daughter of the Rev. J. Gwyther—the very 'Emma' in whom the writer of the enclosed letter (just forwarded to me by Mr. Blackwood) has evidently a touching interest.

As I am absolutely ignorant about the present condition of the Gwyther family, I trust in your kind-heartedness so far as to trouble you with my correspondent's queries. Will you be so good as to look in the Clerical Directory for the Rev. Henry Gwyther, and note whether he is still at Yardley? [9] Or, it will be still more satisfactory if you can tell me what the inquirer asks about Miss (Emma) Gwyther. It would be very pretty if there were some blessing in store for her in the disguise of a 'Mr. Harris.' Let us help to make good romances of the practical kind if we can.

Don't you think the new edition of 'Romola' looks handsome—and handy?

I hope you are in good condition for enjoying the reputed pleasures of the season.

Yours very sincerely

M. E. Lewes.

9. Henry Gwyther (1795?–1872), a brother of John, was Vicar of Yardley, Worcestershire 1821–1872. Dr. J. A. Venn adds the interesting fact that during his incumbency "the church pew-opener, at his bidding, 'burnt three barrow-loads of parchments.'" (*Alumni Cantabrigienses,* III [1947], p. 182.)

## GHL TO MRS. WILLIAM CROSS, LONDON, 24 DECEMBER 1877

*MS:* Yale. *Hitherto unpublished.*

**The Priory, | 21. North Bank, | Regents Park.**
Christmas eve 1877.

My dear Friend,

It is too bad that you, of all people, should be on a sick couch at this time—cela te ressemble si peu!—and not even the thrice welcome news of your improvement, prevents our feeling that Christmas is gloomy because you are suffering. Why has not Dr. Lavardin arranged things better? [1]

Àpropos of the Dr.—Madonna and I were charmed with the way in which his story is related; but I made a secret note on one passage, and it is this: in a subtle psychological remark touching the difference between the graceful acting of a feigning love and the unbecoming benumbing diffidence of a real love, the authoress has betrayed to the keensighted Matchless that she has not a real love for *him*—for assuredly she never showed anything ungraceful in her acting towards him—none of the paralyzed awkwardness she *ought* to have displayed!

Madonna is in bed with a cold, and I have twinges of rheumatism, —that is our preparation for Christmas festivities. The said festivities will consist of being alone on Christmas day; having children and grandchildren on Boxing day; and dining with Mrs. Benzon that evening.[2] Not a very dissipated programme! How different from former Weybridgian 'masses!

The nephew is requested to take care of his sciatica—a gentleman whose attentions should be received with great suspicion.

To nieces and nephews, and their dear Mother, this Religious House sends fervent blessings and hopes (faint hopes) for their moral improvement. (NB: a course of Problems recommended.)

Ever yours affectionately
G. H. Lewes.

1. Mary Finlay Cross, "Docteur Lavardin: A Sketch," can be found in her *Railway Sketches,* 1899, pp. 112–127. These stories appeared originally in *Macmillan's,* the *Gentleman's Magazine, Vanity Fair, Black and White,* and *Hearth and Home.*

2. "Dinner at Mrs. Benzon's—18 people. Browning, the Lehmanns, Schlesingers, Mrs. Orr, Mr. Leighton, Eustace Smith." (GHL Diary, 26 December 1877.)

## GHL TO MRS. ELMA STUART, LONDON, 24 DECEMBER 1877

*MS:* British Museum. *Published:* Stuart, pp. 95–97.

**The Priory, | 21. North Bank, | Regents Park.**
Christmas Eve 1877.

Dear Elma

It would not be a perfect Christmas if our hearts did not specially go forth to you; and although Madonna, who was to have written to you, is in bed with a cold, and therefore is forced to write by her secretary, you know that what one says both feel.

Don't suppose it is more than a cold which keeps her in bed. She has been wonderfully well for a long time—every one remarks how well she looks—and she has not had a hint of pain.

Our Christmas is to be very quiet. We shall be alone tomorrow; and on Wednesday the children and grandchildren come to us. Beyond that our festal program does not extend.

Rowley will have brought you a full budget of Oxford experiences—we hope they are pleasant and promising. Tell us about him when next you write. Also about Mrs. Menzies, to whom give our Christmas offering—a kiss.

Did you see—and if so were you not amused at the idea—that they put me up as Rector of St. Andrews University, in company with Browning, Tyndall, Gathorne Hardy and Lord Selborne: pretty assemblage of names! Of course I should have declined, but I was pleased at the idea that there was a sufficient following among the students for the proposal to have been entertained.

Have you seen the translation of the Rabbi's pamphlet 'George Eliot and Judaism'? It is very interesting, I think; apart from the personal question. God bless you!

Ever your loving
G. H. Lewes.

## GE TO PHOEBE SARAH MARKS, LONDON, 25 DECEMBER 1877

*Text:* Evelyn Sharp, *Hertha Ayrton,* 1926, London, E. Arnold, p. 66.

December 25, 1877.

Dear Miss Marks,—

Your good news about our dear Madame Bodichon was the best of Christmas gifts to me this morning. . . . I shall be delighted to see you when you come to London, but do not call before half-past four, as I am always out between lunch and that time. I long to have more minute details about Mme. Bodichon than a note can give me. But that she has a drive and walk every day is at least a starting-point for pleasant fancies about her.

The *Voyage of the 'Challenger'* [3] is a splendid book, is it not? Your own studies and health have been going on well, I hope. But you will tell me everything when I see you.

Affectionately yours,
M. E. Lewes.

## GE TO MISS CHARLOTTE CARMICHAEL,[4] LONDON, 26 DECEMBER 1877

*Text:* Cross, New Edition, p. 571.

I thank you most gratefully for your kind greeting and pretty Christmas gifts, and am sympathetically touched by your care for your poor Islanders and Coastmen. The analogy you find between the Celt and the Hebrew seems to me also not fanciful but real. Both have a literature which has been a fount of religious feeling and imagination to other races. But I hardly see how I can do anything, as an author, to further that appreciation of the Celts which is now interesting many highly instructed writers. A sincere author, before he undertakes to handle any subject, must have not only the outward appeal, but the inward vocation which consists in special fitness.

3. Sir Charles Wyville Thomson, *The Voyage of the Challenger in the Atlantic,* 2 vols., 1877.

4. Charlotte Carmichael (d. 1929) was the daughter of a landscape painter in Edinburgh, where she was educated in classes conducted by friendly professors before the University was opened to women. In 1879 she married Henry Stopes, engineer and anthropologist, and settled at Upper Norwood. She wrote voluminously on Shakespeare, the Baconian controversy, etc. Her daughter Marie Stopes was the advocate of birth control. (*Times,* 9 February 1929, p. 10d; *Who's Who,* 1928.)

I am delighted to see from your little paper, which gives an affecting picture of the men that must "win the bairnies' bread" by going forth into deep waters, how we are agreed in loving our incomparable Wordsworth.

## GE TO FREDERIC HARRISON, LONDON, 26 DECEMBER 1877

*MS:* Tinker Collection, Yale. *Envelope:* Frederic Harrison Esq | 1 Southwick Place | W. *Postmarks:* ST. JOHNS-WOOD | XX | DE 26 | 77 | N.W; LONDON-W | P | DE 26 | 77. *Extract published:* F. Harrison, *Memories and Thoughts,* 1906, pp. 155–156.

**The Priory, | 21. North Bank, | Regents Park.**
December 26. 77.

Dear Mr. Harrison

I have now re-read more than once the Prayers we spoke of and withdraw my remarks (made under reserve) as not at all applicable. The prayers keep, I think, within the due limit of aspiration and do not pass into beseeching.

Certainly if just the right words could be found—what Vauvenargues [5] calls "cette splendeur d'expression qui emporte avec elle la preuve des grandes pensées"—a ritual might bring more illumination than sermons and lectures.

Mr. Lewes and I—please tell Mrs. Harrison—find the dictionaries on the side of prim'-er, not pri'-mer.

Always yours sincerely
M. E. Lewes.

## GE JOURNAL, LONDON, 31 DECEMBER 1877

*MS:* Yale. *Published:* Cross, III, 323–324.

Today I say a final farewell to this little book which is the only record I have made of my personal life for sixteen years and more. I have often been helped by looking back in it to compare former with actual states of despondency from bad health or other apparent causes. In this way a past despondency has turned to present hopefulness. But of course as the years advance there is a new rational ground for the expectation that my life may become less fruitful. The difficulty

5. Luc de Clapiers, Marquis de Vauvenargues (1715–1747), "Reflexions et maximes," No. 280 in *Oeuvres Complètes,* 3 vols., Paris, 1821, II, 64.

is, to decide how far resolution should set in the direction of activity rather than in the acceptance of a more negative state. Many conceptions of works to be carried out present themselves, but confidence in my own fitness to complete them worthily is all the more wanting because it is reasonable to argue that I must have already done my best. In fact, my mind is embarrassed by the number and wide variety of subjects that attract me, and the enlarging vista that each brings with it.

I shall record no more in this book, because I am going to keep a more business-like diary.[6] Here ends 1877.

6. The Diary for 1878 has not been found.